First Edition April 2016   © **Copyright Nicholas ˙**

Who is this book for?
- Anyone who wants to learn the fundamentals of com

Does it cover all GCSE exam boards?
- It is primarily written for **Edexcel GCSE Computer Scie**.
    - This specification is comprehensively covered   ..ding the practical computing project.
    - Extension work is clearly marked and is not, strictly, part of the syllabus.
- It is an excellent textbook for Edexcel 2015, OCR 2018 and AQA 2018.
    - By careful selection of the extension work and with close attention to the specification almost all topics are covered.

Programming Language – Do I have to learn Python?   Yes and No
- All of the coding examples are in pseudocode and / flow charts.
- The principles are the same for most "procedural languages" like Java and Pascal.
- This book was written with Python in mind and Python is an excellent language.

Students
- This is your textbook for Computer Science. You should also complete a course on practical programming with a language like Python.

Teachers - Scheme of Work and Planning
- It is expected that the theory is taught in "parallel" with a practical programming course: 2 practical & 1 theory lesson / week, plus homework exercises.
- It is not expected that you work through the book "sequentially".
- First Year:
    - Section 3 Programming, coupled with practical programming classes
    - Section 4 Data, Section 2a Algorithms, Section 5 Computers and -Section 6 Databases
- Second Year:
    - Section 2 Sorting & Searching Algorithms; Programming Project
    - Section 7 Networks and Section 8 Impacts

About the author: I have a BSc in Biological Science from Exeter University and an MSc in Computer Studies from the University of Essex. I have been teaching science and computer science for over 20 years. (Feedback to the author at: nandharman@gmail.com)

Disclaimers:
I have made every effort to ensure that the contents of this book are accurate and true, though I will not be held liable either directly or indirectly for any omissions or mistakes. I welcome and encourage comments and suggestions for future editions.
The few images I have used have been clearly "marked for reuse, in the public domain and no attribution required" or are part of the "creative commons", in which case I have attempted to attribute the source. I apologise for any omissions on this score.

Contents

- **Section 1: What is Computer Science** 6
  - A brief history and introduction
- **Section 2: Computational Thinking: Algorithms & Abstraction**
  - **2a Algorithms and Abstraction** 15
    - Computational Thinking
    - Algorithms:
      - Flow charts, Pseudo code, implementation
      - Dry running and Trace tables
    - Abstraction:
      - Encapsulation, Generalisation and Modularisation
  - **2b Sorting Algorithms:** 26
    - Bubble and Merge Sort
    - Extension: Select and Quick Sort
  - **2c Searching Algorithms:** 40
    - Linear & Binary Search
- **Section 3: Programming**
  - **3a: High Level & Low Level Languages** 47
    - Assemblers & Machine code
    - Compilers & Interpreters
  - **3b: Operators** 54
    - Arithmetic (+,-,*,/)
    - Relational (<, >)
    - Logical (AND, OR, NOT) - Truth tables & gates
  - **3c: Data Types & Variables** 68
    - Data Types
    - Variables - declaring & assigning values
    - Constants
  - **3d: Selection, Decisions & IF THEN** 75
    - Selection IF THEN END IF
    - IF THEN ELSE IF
    - Extension: Case or Switch
  - **3e: Loops & Repetition (Iteration)** 81
    - WHILE loops
    - REPEAT loops
    - FOR loops
  - **3f: Data Structures** 91
    - Strings
    - Arrays & Lists
    - Python: Lists & Tuples
    - 1D and 2D arrays
    - Records and Python Dictionaries

- ○ **3g: Subprograms - Implementation of Abstraction** 112
    - Subprograms as Procedures & Functions
        - Parameters - passing data into subprograms
        - Return Values - getting data out of subprograms
    - Global and Local Variables - scope
    - Modularisation - Subprograms to tackle larger problems
- ○ **3h Input & Output** 128
    - Validation & Exception Handling
    - File Handling - Reading & Writing
    - Extension - CSV files
- ○ **3i Errors & Testing** 144
    - Errors: Syntax, logic & runtime
    - Test Plans & Test Data
    - Debugging & IDE
- **Section 4: Data Representation**
    - ○ **4a Numbers - Analogue & Digital - Binary and Hex** 155
        - Bits & Bytes,
        - Binary & Denary
        - Binary arithmetic
        - Binary negative numbers - Sign & Magnitude, Two's Complement
        - Binary bitwise operations - shifts (logical and arithmetic)
        - Extension: Floating point binary numbers
        - Hexadecimal
    - ○ **4b Characters & ASCII** 176
        - Representation of characters
        - Standard codes - ASCII
    - ○ **4c Images & Pixels** 181
        - Representation of Images with pixels
        - Resolution, Colour depth and memory calculations
        - Data Structures - arrays and images
        - Metadata
        - Extension: Vector Graphics
    - ○ **4d Sounds & Sampling** 189
        - Sampling and digitising sound waves
        - Sampling rate - quality and file size
        - Sample resolution - quality and file size
        - File size - memory calculations
    - ○ **4e Compression - Lossy & Lossless** 194
        - Need for data compression
        - Calculating transmission times and memory
        - Lossless compression - Run Length Encoding
        - Lossy Compression
        - Different file types
    - ○ **4f Encryption** 204
        - The need for data encryption
        - The Caesar cipher algorithm
        - Extension: Alan Turing and the Enigma machine

- **Section 5: Computers - Hardware & Software**
  - ○ **5a Digital Computer Systems** **212**
    - ▪ Input Process Output Model (Von Neumann)
    - ▪ Input & Output Devices
    - ▪ <u>Extension</u>: Control Actuators & Sensors
    - ▪ Embedded Systems
    - ▪ Backing Storage (Magnetic, Optical and Solid State)
    - ▪ "The cloud"
  - ○ **5b Central Processing Unit** **225**
    - ▪ Main Memory - RAM, ROM, cache
    - ▪ CPU - ALU, Registers, Clock, Buses
    - ▪ CPU - Fetch Decode Execute cycle
  - ○ **5c Software** **235**
    - ▪ Applications and Systems Software
    - ▪ Operating Systems and Human Computer Interface
    - ▪ Utility Software
    - ▪ Models & Simulations
- **Section 6: Databases**
  - ○ **6a Structured Data, Records and Databases** **248**
    - ▪ Structured & Unstructured Data
    - ▪ Records, Fields & Keys
    - ▪ Computer Databases
  - ○ **6b Relational Databases** **254**
    - ▪ Entity Attribute Relationship
    - ▪ Relational Database & Foreign Key Fields
    - ▪ <u>Extension</u> - Queries and SQL
- **Section 7: Networks & Internet**
  - ○ **7a Networks - Introduction** **267**
    - ▪ Standalone, LAN & WAN, Servers & Peer-to-Peer
    - ▪ <u>Extension</u>: PAN and VPN
    - ▪ Topology: Bus, Ring, Star & Mesh
    - ▪ Media: Wired & Wireless
    - ▪ <u>Extension</u>: Addressing (MAC addresses)
  - ○ **7b Networks - Data Transmission** **281**
    - ▪ Network Data Speeds (Mbps)
    - ▪ Network Protocols (Ethernet, HTTP etc.)
    - ▪ Packets - Layered Protocol (TCP / IP)
    - ▪ <u>Extension</u>: Error Detection (check sums)
  - ○ **7c The Internet** **290**
    - ▪ Architecture IP addressing & Routers
    - ▪ World Wide Web (WWW) - servers, URLs & ISP
    - ▪ HTML - Importance & introduction

- **7d Net Security** **300**
  - Cyber Attack
    - Social Engineering (Phishing, Pharming, Shouldering)
    - Data Transmission (USB devices and Eavesdropping)
  - Cyber Defence
    - Identify Vulnerabilities (Penetration Testing)
    - Access Control (Physical, Authentication and Firewalls)
    - Protecting Software (Best Practices, Patches, Audit Trail)
- **Section 8: Impacts of Technology on Society**
  - **8a Environmental Impact of Technology** **314**
    - Health
    - Energy Use
    - Resources
  - **8b Ethical Impact of Technology** **322**
    - Privacy
    - Inclusion
    - Professionalism
  - **8c Legal Impact of Technology** **332**
    - Intellectual Property
    - Copyright, Patents and Licensing
    - Software - Open Source & Propriety
    - Cyber-Security
- **Appendices:**
  - **Solving Large Problems: Controlled Assessments (NEA)** **346**
  - **Flowchart symbols** **377**
  - **Pseudocode syntax** **378**
  - **Recommended Reading** **381**

Section 1

What is Computer Science?

- **A Brief History and Introduction**

"Computer Science is not about computers, in the same sense that physics is not really about particle accelerators, and biology is not about microscopes and Petri dishes." (Hal Abelson)

0001

Jmi21qn2t q0 jm11mz 1piv 2ot6. M5xtqkq1 q0 jm11mz 1piv quxtqkq1.

Chapter 1: Computer Science – The Study of the Principles and Use of Computers.

This book could be your first step into a new world and maybe a new career. Either way programming will change the way that you think and the way you see the world.

A computer is a programmable machine to solve a wide-range of problems following step-by-step instructions (**algorithms**) written out as **programs**. A computer follows the sequence of operations in the program such that it can automatically receive **input** data, **process** that data and **output** the results.

In the 19th century Charles Babbage and Ada Lovelace designed and built a mechanical computer – A "Difference Engine" that was probably the world's first computer. Unfortunately it never worked.

In the early 20th century Alan Turing in his seminal work, "Computational Numbers", described a theoretical "Universal Machine" that could solve any problem. During the 2nd World War, Turing designed and built a mechanical machine with electrical relays used as fast switches. This "Bombe" was used to decode secret Nazi radio messages **encrypted** with the famous "Enigma Machine". Nonetheless a "Bombe" could not really be programmed and could only solve the kind of problems it had been designed to solve – "cracking" secret codes.

Both Turing and another computer pioneer, Von Neumann, quickly realised that trying to model the real world of continuously variable – "**analogue**" – data with continuously moving cogs and wheels simply would not work. A Computer would work best with electrical signals that were either "on" or "off".   These signals can be represented by **binary digits** (1 and 0). The "switches" would then process the data using simple binary arithmetic (base 2). Such a "**digital**" device could also use "**Boolean Logic**" to make "decisions" such as:

> **IF** (Result is True (1)) **THEN**
> > jump to this instruction,
>
> **ELSE** (Result is False (0))**THEN**
> > jump to another instruction.
>
> **END IF**

They also realised that in a computer program both the instructions (operations) and the data could be represented by binary numbers and stored together. Clearly the computer would need some way of storing the numbers and instructions that it was processing and a way of permanently storing the programs and data for later use - **main memory** (RAM) and secondary memory or backing storage. The smallest unit of memory would be one **B**inary dig**IT** (a **BIT**) while a single character could be represented as 8 bits (a **BYTE**) All of these ideas came together as the basic **INPUT → PROCESS → OUTPUT** model.

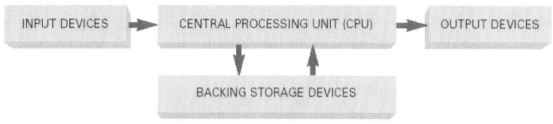

Just after the 2nd world war some progress was made using **electronic** valves as the switches and the first working electronic computer was built at Manchester University in 1949. These early computers were, nonetheless, very slow, unreliable and only had a very small memory.

> Example: Automatic Computing Engine (ACE) ran its first program in 1950:
> Storage: 32 instructions or data each of 32 bits - 1024 bits or 128 bytes
> Clock speed: 1 MHz

By the end of the 1940s the new technology of semi-conductor transistors and complex electronic circuits ("chips") would completely replace the electronic valves making the dream of a fast reliable Central Processing Unit (**CPU**) possible.

Intel 4004 - the first commercial microprocessor

So a modern definition of a computer would have to start with: "A computer is an **electronic**, **digital** machine ..."

At first these new computers were still large, slow and expensive. There was progress but even the best of these early computer scientists did not predict just how fast computer technology would actually develop:

"I think there is a world market for as many as 5 computers." - Thomas Watson, head of IBM, 1943.

"Computers in the future may weigh no more than 1.5 tons." - Popular Mechanics, 1949.

In fact computers would rapidly develop, becoming at once smaller, faster and cheaper.

More's "Law":

"The number of transistors in a dense integrated circuit doubles approximately every two years."

More of an observation than a law, it nonetheless held good from the 1970s up into the 21st century. So a chip in 1970 had around 2,000 transistors while by 2010 a chip would have more than 2,000,000,000.

By 1965 Olivetti were marketing their "Programma 101" Personal Computer – It cost about $3000, used a magnetic card storage system and was, perhaps, the first "desktop Personal Computer" (PC).

In 1981 IBM released one of the first, mass-selling PCs – The IBM PC 5150

     Memory: RAM 256 Kbytes   ROM 40 Kbytes

     Backing Storage (Floppy disks): 160 Kbytes

     Speed: about 3 MHz

The modern **computer system** consisting of the **hardware** (physical devices) and the **software** (programs) using the **INPUT → PROCESS → OUTPUT** model was now clear:

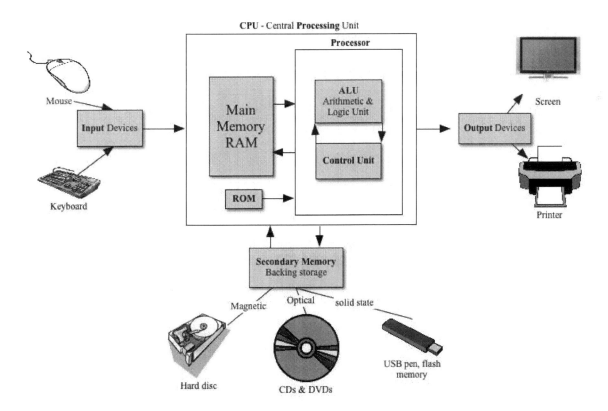

A bread-making machine analogy:

I recently bought a bread-making machine – appropriately enough via the Internet. It arrived with the two most important components – a book of recipes and the machine itself. All I needed now was some "**input**" (ingredients - flour, water, yeast, sugar, raisins etc.) and then the machine would "**process**" these ingredients to produce some "**output**" (a nice fresh-baked loaf of bread). The kind of bread that the machine produces is clearly dependant on the recipe I choose and the ingredients I put in. During the cooking process the machine follows a simple, built-in sequence of instructions. All the time it **controls** the cooking using **input sensors** such as temperature and a timer and sends control signals to **output devices** such as the mixing motor, the heater or the alarm signals. It is important to note that:

- What the machine can do is actually quite limited and simple.
- Without it's instructions and recipes the machine can't make anything.
- A recipe to make, for example, Italian Olive Bread, is not the same as a loaf of Italian Olive Bread – You can't eat a recipe!
- A recipe is a step-by-step list of instructions (an "**algorithm**") of how to make a particular loaf of bread.
- The recipes and instructions then form the system's programs or **software** while the physical machine itself forms the **hardware**.

In theory the bread-making machine can make hundreds of different kinds of bread – limited only by the number of recipes, availability of ingredients and some common-sense idea of what is possible. (A multi-layered wedding cake with a bride and groom on top may not be "bakeable"!)

INPUT - ingredients　　　PROCESS - follow instructions　　　OUTPUT - Bread

Hardware - Breadmaker

Software - Recipe
Mix yeast, sugar & water
Wait 5 mins
Add flour, water, Butter
Mix
Bake 1 hour at 200 °C

Data Representation: The "Universality" of these computer systems meant that computers could be programmed to deal with almost any kind of data that could be represented or "coded" by binary digits.

Numbers - Binary Digits (Bits)
Text – 1 Byte per character - ASCII
Images – Sampled as tiny individual dots or "Picture Elements" (Pixels)
Sound – Analogue waves sampled millions of time per second

Computers became easier to use. The software that interacts with the user and the computer – **the operating system** – became more and more "user friendly". The first commercially successful PC with a **G**raphical **U**ser **I**nterface (**GUI**) using a **W**indows, **I**cons, **M**enus and **P**ointer (**WIMP**) design – the **Apple** Macintosh– was released in 1984:

The world was introduced to the computer mouse and the concept of "clicking" on little pictures (icons) or selecting from a list of choices (menu) with an arrow on the screen (pointer) that could open and close views (windows) of what was on the hard disc. Microsoft soon followed with the hugely popular "Windows 95" operating system.

The 1960's saw the development of the idea of connecting "stand alone" PCs together to make a computer **network**. By the 1980's networks were connected to networks first nationally and then across the globe - the **Internet** was here. The development of mobile "smart" phones and global **communication technology** led to the 21st century idea of social media and the "Internet of things". Computers could be programmed to **control** everything from your social calendar to the temperature of your house. Human Computer Interaction (**HCI**) is now achieved just by touching the screen of tiny hand-held devices or simply talking to the computer.

Society has moved on from the "industrial revolution" to the "information age". This new industry requires new professional experts including electronic engineers and software engineers (programmers). A new way of studying how to solve problems – **computational thinking** – is needed.

The future, more so than ever, is impossible to predict but new and emerging technologies show the direction and potential of computer science in the next few decades: Artificial Intelligence (AI); Quantum Computing; Nano Computing and even DNA computing are all serious research areas.

There are problems associated with this "Brave New World":

Social & Ethical issues: Social exclusion of the "haves" and "have-nots"; Addiction, isolation and "cyber bullying" on social media; Invasion of Privacy and abuse of personal data by individuals, companies and even the state.

Legal Problems: Copyright of digital data and illegal copying ("piracy") and "stealing" of patents and original ideas.

Security: computer viruses and computer systems being "hacked".

All of these issues, and many others, will need to be confronted by society to ensure that the 21st century is an epoch of new development and not an "Orwellian" nightmare controlled by malevolent robots.

Questions on Chapter 1:

1. Which of the following devices could fit the modern definition of a computer? Whether you say "yes" or "no" you should consider if the device is: digital and electronic; follows the pattern of Input → Process → Output and can be programmed.
(a) A standard "4-function" (+, -, /, X) calculator.
(b) A modern microwave oven
(c) A string of lights for a Christmas tree.
(d) A "smart" phone like an iPhone.
(e) An automatic air-force drone bomber.
(f) A car that has a display telling you how many more kilometres you can travel with the amount of fuel you have left.

2. The word "computer" implicitly tells us that computers can calculate. The Spanish for computer is "ordenador". What other functions of a computer do you think this word suggests?

3. Moore's Law states that the number of transistors in computer "chips" doubles every two years.
    (a) Use Moore's Law to estimate the number of transistors that will be in computer chips in the 2030. Start at 2010 when chips had about 2,000,000,000.
    (b) In 2015 Gordon Moore foresaw that the rate of progress would reach saturation: "I see Moore's law dying here in the next decade or so." Use your estimate from (a) to suggest why Moore's Law may soon no longer apply and has "reached saturation".

4. Following the analogy of bread making in the text – describe a modern clothes washing machine in terms of input, process, output and hardware and software.

5. Ada Lovelace is sometimes credited as the first computer programmer. Find out a few points about her life and the name of the computer language that was named after her.

6. Find 3 other quotes from the past where commentators have made predictions about the future that turned out to be wildly wrong!

Section 2
Computational Thinking

- **2a Algorithms and Abstraction**
- **2b Sorting Algorithms**
- **2c Searching Algorithms**

"Intelligence, then, is the ability to attain goals in the face of obstacles by means of decisions based on rational (truth-obeying) rules." (Steven Pinker)

0010

Zptwsl pz il00ly 0ohu jvtwsl4. Jvtwsl4 pz il00ly 0ohu jvtwspjh0lk.

Chapter 2a Algorithms: Algorithms and Abstraction

Computational Thinking (CT):
CT is "a way of solving problems, designing systems, and understanding human behaviour by drawing on the concepts fundamental to computer science." (Jeanette Wing 2006). Computational Thinking is a fundamental skill for everyone, not just for computer scientists.

Points Covered:
- **Computational Thinking:** The problem solving process in computational thinking includes:
- **Algorithms**: step-by-step solutions to problems
    - Flow charts, pseudocode, implementation
    - Dry Running and Trace Tables
- **Abstraction**: The ability to ignore details to focus on the bigger picture.
    - Encapsulation: Hiding details from the user
    - Generalisation: Recognising that one solution can solve many similar problems
    - Decomposition & Modularisation: Divide the problem into sub-problems & sub-sub-problems, until the individual problems are easy.

Computational thinking is a **problem solving** process. Here's a traditional "river crossing" puzzle that dates back to the 9th century: A farmer has to cross a river with his purchases from the market: a fox, a goose and a cabbage. To cross the river by boat the farmer can only carry himself and one of his purchases. Constraints: If he leaves the fox with the goose, the fox will eat the goose. If he leaves the goose with the cabbage the goose will eat the cabbage. How can the farmer get himself and all his purchases safely across the river? If you don't know the answer, you may want to stop reading and try and work it out. The "**insight**" needed is that the farmer can take an item back across the river. An **algorithmic** solution (a series of steps) is shown below:
1. Take goose over
2. Return
3. Take fox over
4. Return with goose
5. Take cabbage over
6. Return
7. Take goose over

Algorithms are a way of automating solutions by writing down a sequential series of steps. Just like a recipe tells you how to make a cake, an algorithm tells you how to solve a problem.

Recipe Name: Aunt Monica's Vanilla Sponge Cake Recipe

Ingredients: 250g of butter; 500g of flour; 4 eggs; 200g of sugar; 10g of vanilla

Start Recipe:

1. Cream the butter
2. Add the flour and continue mixing until well blended.
3. Beat eggs until "fluffy"
4. Add sugar gradually to beaten eggs
5. Combine together the two mixtures
6. Add vanilla
7. Bake in a cake tin in the oven at 160ºC for 30 minutes

End Recipe

In other words, an algorithm is a sequence of steps specifying how to complete a task.

First you have to know exactly what the problem is. Then you can try to draw a solution as a **flow chart** and / or formally write down the problem in a structured way (**pseudocode**). Only then can you actually try and "code" the solution in a programming language.

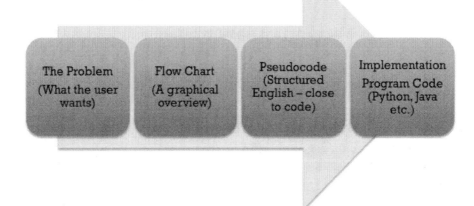

Note: The theory that follows will make more sense after reading the chapters devoted to programming. Nonetheless, even at a first glance, you should be able to basically see what is going on.

An Example: A maximum number problem:

1. The Problem: Taking in five numbers and outputting the largest value.

2. Flow Chart:

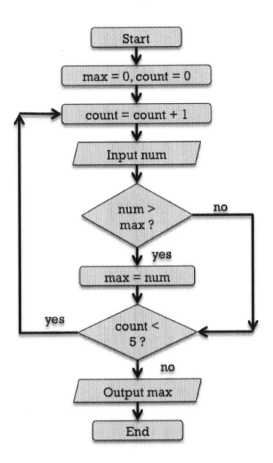

3. Pseudocode:
    BEGIN
        Declare & Initialise variables
           max, count, num : **INTEGER**
           max = 0, count = 0

        FOR count **FROM** 1 **TO** 5 **DO**
           INPUT num
           IF num > max **THEN**
               max = num
           END IF
        END FOR
        OUTPUT max, min
    END

4. Coded in Python:

```
#Problem:  Input five numbers and output the maximum
maxNum = 0                                    #set max to lowest possible
num = 0
for count in range(5):      #For loop we know how many times in advance
    num = int(input("Enter a small positive integer please: "))
    if (num > maxNum):
        maxNum = num
#End of for loop -----------------------------------------
print("Max number is: ", maxNum)          #Output the max
```

Here is a typical "run" of the above algorithm coded in Python:

```
Enter a small positive integer please: 6
Enter a small positive integer please: 7
Enter a small positive integer please: 4
Enter a small positive integer please: 3
Enter a small positive integer please: 2
Max number is:   7
```

Dry Running and Trace Tables

A dry run is a mental run of a computer program. It just means that you, the programmer, look at the code or pseudocode, and step-by-step or line-by-line determine what the program will do without actually running it on a computer. In particular you will want to know the **values of variables at any point** and what the final output should be. As your problems get more complex it becomes increasingly difficult to "run" the whole program in your head! Sometimes programmers print out code extracts on large sheets of paper and draw on them with felt pens trying to work out what is going on. There are programs, including the excellent online "Visualize from the Python Tutor website", which can help you:

Trace Table: Sometimes you just have to do it manually by filling in a table, which shows you the values of the variables at each line:

Max problem code and trace table

```
maxNum = 0
num = 0
for count in range(5):
    num = int(input("Enter number"))
    if (num > maxNum):
        maxNum = num
##End of for loop
----------------------------------------
print("Max number is: ", maxNum)
```

count	num	maxNum
0	0	0
0	6	6
1	7	7
2	4	7
3	3	7
4	2	7

Abstraction:

As a problem grows larger, it becomes difficult to keep track of all details at the same time. Abstraction is the ability to:

- **Encapsulate**: Ignore details to focus on the bigger picture
- **Generalise**: Have solutions that can solve a range of similar problems
- **Modularise**: Break down large problems into smaller and smaller easy problems

Abstraction is a way of thinking. A car consists of so many parts that it is impossible for a single person to know every detail. One way of looking at abstraction is as a process of removing unnecessary detail from a problem. Programming gives concrete form to the act of abstraction, & repeatedly shows how useful it is.

Abstraction

Think about the big picture without worrying about the detail.
I want a car that works!

Encapsulation:
One part of abstraction is then to look at parts of the problem as independent units that do one job. So in the above diagram the spark plug receives an electric current and generates a spark. The mechanic working on the engine does not need to know **how** it does this. He is only interested in **what** it does.

Procedures or Functions: A programmer writes short blocks of code that do one job. Once that code works other people can use that code to do that job. They do not need to know **how** it works. They are only interested in **what** it does.

Encapsulation

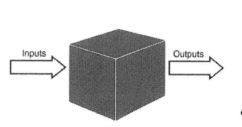

- Each Module
  (Procedure or Function)
  - Is independant
  - Does one job only
  - can be (re) used by other modules or progams
- Details are hidden or "encapsulated"
  - parameters pass data in
  - return values pass data out

Example: A programmer is asked to work out the maximum grades for exams in different classes of biology, physics and chemistry. Python has a built-in function "max(any list)" which **inputs** any list as a parameter and **outputs** (returns) the maximum number in that list.

```
>>> biolGrades = [8, 6, 6, 7, 5, 9, 4 ,8, 9, 3]
>>> maxBiol = max(biolGrades)
>>> print(maxBiol)
9
```

How does the function "max" work? Probably it uses a FOR loop to iterate over the list just like the algorithm above (shown as pseudocode, a flow chart and Python). But, at this level, the programmer does not need to know how the max function was implemented. The details are "hidden" from him. This is a good thing. He needs to focus on his problem of finding out the maximum grades in different science classes. If he had to worry about every detail of the problem he would never finish!

Generalisation:
Finding the maximum grade for the biology class is really no different to finding the maximum grade of any list of grades. So a good function can be used to solve a range of similar problems.

```
>>> physGrades = [6, 6, 5, 8, 7, 7, 4]
>>> maxPhys = max(physGrades)
>>> print(maxPhys)
8
```

Modularisation & Encapsulation:
Once you have grasped the idea of encapsulation it is now easy to imagine a large problem split into lots of little, connected, "capsules" or modules. For example the problem of designing a car could be broken down:

I.   Moving the Car
    a. Engine & Power
    b. Wheels & Tyres
    c. Steering & Braking
II. Carrying Passengers
    and so on ...

The process is:
- Divide the problem into sub-problems & sub-sub-problems, until the individual problems are easy: "**Divide & Conquer**".
- Each sub-problem, or module, is completely self-contained and does one job only.

One method to breakdown the problem into smaller and smaller sub-problems starts at the top and works down until the problem is trivial:

Top Down Problem Solving
Simpler & Simpler
Logo - The Wall problem

- To draw a wall –
  - A **wall** is made up of **layers**
  - **Layers** are made up of **bricks**
  - A **brick** is easy

```
TO BRICK
  REPEAT 2 [FD 10 RT 90 FD 20 RT 90]
END

TO LAYER
  REPEAT 10 [BRICK RT 90 FD 20 LT 90]
  LT 90  FD 10 * 20 RT 90
END

TO WALL
  REPEAT 5 [LAYER FD 10]
  BK 5 * 10
END
```

Each sub-problem is, in programming terms, a **procedure** or **function** or even a **sub program** (a short block of code that does one job). The code above is written in "Logo" – using its famous "turtle graphics". The Wall procedure "calls" Layer – "Draw me five layers please". The Layer procedure "calls" Brick – "Draw me 10 bricks please". The Brick procedure just draws a brick!   Refer to the programming chapter on functions & procedures for more work on using "**procedural abstraction**" to breakdown large complex problems into small, modularised, trivial problems.

Questions on Chapter 2a Algorithms and Abstraction

1. You can find hundreds of "logic puzzles" on the Internet, which can have algorithmic solutions. Here's one: Four Moroccan camels traveling on a very narrow ridge come across four Moroccan camels coming the other way.

Moroccan camels never go backwards. The camels can climb over each other, but only if there is a camel sized space on the other side.

The camels didn't see each other until there was only exactly one camel's width between the two groups.

How can all camels pass, allowing both groups to go on their way? Remember no camels can reverse.

You may want to try this with counters or beans but then show your solution as a step-by-step answer, using diagrams if you like.

2. The problem: The user inputs (enters) 5 numbers, one after the other, and the program has to output the **minimum** number. Follow the same procedure in the text for the "maximum number problem" to show a solution to this problem.
- Draw a flow chart
- Write down the solution as pseudocode
- Implement the solution in a programming language that you know.

3. Maria has a thermometer on her terrace. Every morning for one month (31 days) she records the temperature. She stores these results in a simple list (or array) of numbers. She wants a program to input this list of numbers and output the average temperature for that month. Show a solution to this problem by:
- Drawing a flow chart
- Writing down the solution as pseudocode
- Implementing the solution in a programming language that you know.

4. Here's a rather garbled version of a recipe for the Greek dish moussaka:
Slice, salt & clean 3 aubergines - leave to one side; fry minced lamb, onions, garlic and pepper, add tomatoes, tomato purée and red wine - cook for 30 minutes; fry aubergines in oil, dry; turn the oven on to 180ºC; make the white sauce with milk, butter and flour, beat in an egg and some cheese; place 1/3 of the meat in an ovenproof dish and cover with a layer of aubergines, repeat this 3 times making a total of 6 layers; pour over the white sauce and then bake in the oven for 45 minutes.
Use the ideas of **decomposition**, **modularisation** and **encapsulation** to:
- "Condense" the recipe into 3 named "sub-tasks" - include brief details of each task.
- Write an overall, or "main", named task that "calls" or uses the named sub-tasks to make and cook the whole dish.

5. "Dry-run" the code on the left and complete the "run table" on the right:

INTEGER i = 0
INTEGER x = 0
   WHILE (i < 4) **DO**
      x = x + i
      i = i + 1
   END WHILE

	i	x
Initial values	0	0
While loop		

What is the value of x when the while loop is complete?

6. Study the following flowchart very carefully:
   (a) Copy out & complete the trace table, shown below, for the following data set:
      15, -2, 0, 8, 0, -8, -12, 1, -7

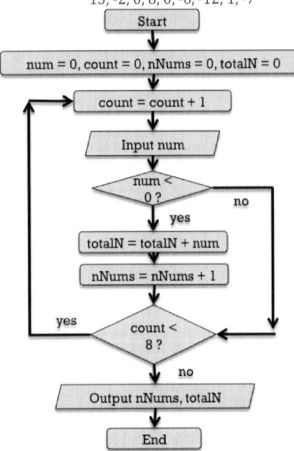

count	num	totalN	nNums
0	0	0	0

(b) What is the purpose of this algorithm? (That is: What does it do?)
(c) Extension: Write out the flow chart as pseudocode.

7. Customers can withdraw cash from an Automatic Teller Machine (ATM).
- Withdrawal is refused if amount entered > current balance
- Withdrawal is refused if amount entered > daily limit

Write an algorithm, as a **flow chart**, which:
- Inputs the current balance (the amount of money the person has in their account) and the daily limit for that customer.
- Inputs the amount of money the person has already taken out on that day.
- Inputs the amount of money they want to take out.
- And then "decides" if a withdrawal can be made.

If a withdrawal is refused then the algorithm should output the reason why.
If a withdrawal is accepted then the algorithm should take the amount withdrawn away from the current balance and add that amount to the amount taken out that day.

8. Write an algorithm, using a **flow chart** and **pseudocode**, which:
- Inputs the population and land area for 10 capital cities in Europe
- Calculates the population density of each city (population / area)
- Outputs the largest and smallest population density
- Outputs the average population for all 10 cities

Chapter 2b Algorithms: Sorting Algorithms

Standard Algorithms:
Every completely new problem needs a new algorithm. However some problems are so common that standard ways to solve them have been developed. Once again all of the algorithms that follow use standard programming constructs, which will make much more sense once you have covered the chapters on programming and, of course, done some practical, programming.

Points Covered: Sorting Algorithms:
Putting data in order is fundamental to many everyday tasks: Sort the names of the class alphabetically from A to Z; Sort the teams from top (highest number of points) to bottom ... and so on.
   1. Bubble Sort
   2. <u>Extension</u>: Select Sort
   3. <u>Extension</u>: Quick Sort
   4. Merge Sort

Don't panic: You only need to understand how some basic algorithms work. I have included full implementations in pseudocode and Python so that you can run the code yourself. It is not expected that you would be able to write code like this yourself.

1. Bubble Sort:
This is a "**comparison sort**" in which smaller elements "bubble" to the top of the list.

- **Repeatedly** step through list
  - Compare each pair of adjacent items
    - Swap them if wrong order.
- **Until** no swaps are needed
- The list is sorted.
- Smaller elements "bubble" to top of the list.
- It is a comparison sort.

A worked example:

Pass1: [5, 1, 4, 2, 8] --> [1, 4, 2, 5, 8]

     □ (5 1 4 2 8) → (1 5 4 2 8)   □ Swaps since 5 > 1.

     □ (1 5 4 2 8) → (1 4 5 2 8)   □ Swap since 5 > 4

     □ (1 4 5 2 8) → (1 4 2 5 8)   □ Swap since 5 > 2

     □ (1 4 2 5 8) → (1 4 2 5 8)   □ In order since (5 < 8)

Pass2: [1, 4, 2, 5, 8] --> [1, 2, 4, 5, 8]

     □ (1 4 2 5 8) → (1 4 2 5 8)

     □ (1 4 2 5 8) → (1 2 4 5 8)   □ Swap since 4 > 2

     □ (1 2 4 5 8) → (1 2 4 5 8)

     □ (1 2 4 5 8) → (1 2 4 5 8)

Pass3: Now, the array is already sorted, but our algorithm does not "know" if it is completed! The algorithm needs **one whole pass without any swap** to "know" it is sorted. Given a list or an array indexed from 0, such as: myList = [2, 4, 1, 9, 3, 7, 8, 5, 6, 10]

Implementation Pseudocode:

```
swap_done = True
  WHILE swap_done DO
    swap_done = False
    #Must not go up to index 9 ... last check is index 8
    FOR index FROM 0 TO LENGTH(myList) – 2 DO
      IF (myList[index]) > (myList[index+1]) THEN #swap
        temp = myList[index]
        myList[index] = myList[index+1]
        myList[index+1] = temp
        swap_done = True
      END IF
    END FOR
  END WHILE
```

Implementation Python:

```
swap_done = True
    while swap_done:
        swap_done = False
        #say list is 10 elements then index is 0, 1, ... 9
        #range is up to but not including so penultimate position is 8
        for index in range(len(myList)-1):
            if myList[index] > myList[index+1]: #swap
                temp = myList[index]
                myList[index] = myList[index+1]
                myList[index+1] = temp
                swap_done = True
```

Bubble Sort Algorithm - Efficiency:
- Large elements at the beginning are quickly swapped
- Small elements at the end move to the beginning very, very slowly
- It slows right down with large lists

Bubble sort is not a practical sorting algorithm with long ("normal") lists.

2. Selection Sort:

Imagine, in a card game, that you have just been dealt a random hand of cards. Probably you immediately start to sort your hand by:
- Finding the smallest card and putting it in "its place" at the left.
- Then find the next smallest, <u>from the rest of your hand</u>, and put it to the left.
- And so on.

This is selection sort: an intuitive ("common sense") approach that is easy to understand and implement. The algorithm divides the list into two parts: The sub list of items already sorted, which is built up from left to right at the front (left) of the list, and the sub list of items remaining to be sorted.

1. **Find the smallest element**

2. **Exchange (swap) 1st and smallest**

3. **Repeat step 1 and 2 with one less element (rest of the list)**

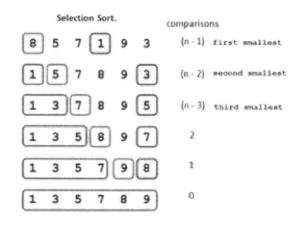

Example: myList = [8,5,7,1,9,3] so length is 6 and indexed as 0,1,2,3,4,5

Implementation - Pseudocode:

```
FOR index FROM 0 TO LENGTH(myList)-1 DO    #up to not including
    minIndex = index                          #set minimum place to beginning
    minValue = myList[index]                   #set minimum value to first element
    FOR place FROM index + 1 TO length(myList)-1 DO   #+1 so rest of list
        IF myList[place] < minValue THEN
            minIndex = place                    #store where min value is
            minValue = myList[place]            # store min value
        END IF
    END FOR
    myList[minIndex] = myList[index]         # put begin value to min place
    myList[index] = minValue                 #put min value at beginning
END FOR
```

Implementation - Python:

```python
    # Iterates along list moving smallest to front"""
    for index in range(len(myList)):
        minIndex = index                        #set minimum place to beginning
        minValue = myList[index]                 #set minimum to first element
        for place in range(index+1,len(myList)):    #+1 so rest of list
            if myList[place] < minValue:
                minIndex = place                 #store where min value is
                minValue = myList[place]          #store min value
            #end if ...........
        #end for ..................
        myList[minIndex] = myList[index]#put begin value to min place
        myList[index] = minValue #put min value at beginning
    #end outer for loop ..........................
```

Extension: Here is an implementation using an "advanced" technique called **recursion**. Recursion is when a procedure or function "calls itself". The code is here for completeness and for interest. Do not worry if you cannot understand it fully!

```
def selectSort(inList):
    """takes off minimum & recursively sorts what's left"""
    if len(inList) <= 1:            # 1 element or none so do nothing
        return inList
    else:
        minNum = min(inList)
        #find the index of where minNum is in list
        minIndex = inList.index(minNum)
        if minIndex > 0:            #minNum not in 1st or 0 index position
            #swap first with found minNum
            temp = inList[0]
            inList[0] = inList[minIndex]
            inList[minIndex] = temp
        #end if .........................
        #return concatenated list first + rest(sorted)
        del inList[0]              #remove 1st ie minNum sort the rest
        return [minNum] + selectSort(inList)
```

Select Sort Algorithm - Efficiency:

- Easy to understand and implement
- Usually faster than bubble sort
- Fast for small arrays (20 or less elements)
  - It slows right down with large lists where "divide and conquer" algorithms such as quick sort are much better.

Overall then, the select sort algorithm is not used much on "real" lists of data.

3. Quick Sort:

Quicksort is a **divide and conquer** algorithm developed by Tony Hoare in 1959. Quicksort first divides a large array into two smaller sub-arrays: the low elements and the high elements. Quicksort can then **recursively** sort the sub-arrays.

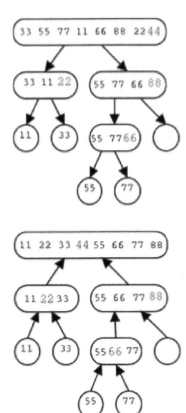

- Pick any element as a **pivot**
- Reorder the array
  - all elements with values less than pivot come before the pivot
  - all elements with values greater than pivot come after pivot
- pivot is now in its final position
- **Recursively** apply the above steps to the sub-array of elements with smaller values and separately to the sub-array of elements with greater values.
- The base case of the recursion is arrays of size zero or one, which never need to be sorted.

Implementation - Pseudocode:

```
FUNCTION quicksort(myArray)
    Variable ARRAY: less, greater
    IF LENGTH(myArray) ≤ 1 THEN
        RETURN myArray      #0 or 1 element so it is sorted
    END IF
    select and remove a pivot value from array
    FOR EACH num FROM myArray DO
        IF num ≤ pivot THEN
            append num to less
        ELSE
            append num to greater
        END IF
    END FOR EACH
    RETURN concatenate(quicksort(less), pivot, quicksort(greater))
END FUNCTION
```

Implementation - Python:

```
def quickSort(inList):
    """splits inList in two around a pivot & recursively calls each subList"""
    if len(inList) <= 1:              #only one or zero elements so do nothing
        return inList
    else:
        #randomly choose an index 0 length of list -1 and "pop" element off the list
        #eg [10, 3, 5, 7, 4, 6, 2, 9, 8, 1] --> 8
        pivot = inList.pop(random.randint(0, len(inList)-1))
        leftList = [ ]              #list to hold numbers less than pivot
        rightList = [ ]             #list to hold numbers greater than pivot
        #iterate over remaining elements adding them to left or right lists
        for num in inList:
            if num <= pivot:
                #less than pivot so add to left list
                leftList.append(num)
            else:
                #must be greater than pivot so add to right list
                rightList.append(num)
        #end for loop ................................
        #eg leftList [3, 5, 7, 4, 6, 2, 1] pivot 8 and rightList [10, 9]
        #now return the concatenated lists: left-quickSorted, pivot and right-quickSorted
        return quickSort(leftList) + [pivot] + quickSort(rightList)
```

Quick Sort Algorithm - Efficiency:

- Divide & Conquer, so is fairly good (fast)
    - When well implemented it can be 2 or 3 times faster than merge sort.
- It slows right down with:
    - "Very unsorted" lists & long lists
- But with an average-case (not too long & fairly sorted) it is pretty fast.

4. Merge Sort:

Merge sort is another **divide and conquer** algorithm that was invented by **John von Neumann** (A computer pioneer – see the section on hardware) in 1945.

The basic algorithm looks like this:

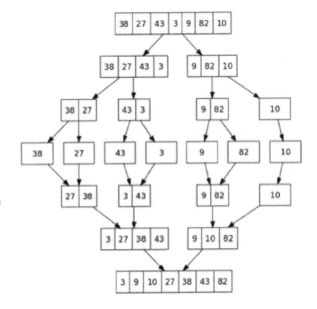

1. Divide: Split the list into two sub lists each of roughly equal size.

Repeatedly Split the list into lists of 1 element.

2. Conquer: Compare each element with the adjacent element to sort.

Merge: Compare and merge the two adjacent lists.

3. Repeatedly merge sub lists to produce new sorted sublists

Until there is only 1 sub list remaining. This will be the sorted list.

As you can see it is very similar to **quick sort**. The main differences are:

- In quicksort the sorting is done as the list is split (putting smaller elements on the left and larger elements on the right)
- In merge sort the "hard work" is done when the lists are merged.

Implementations of merge sort are, perhaps, a little advanced for this level. The most "elegant" versions again include "recursion" where a function calls itself. The main principles on a list **A** of **n** elements are:

- **Divide:** Split A down the middle into two sub lists, each of size roughly n/2.
- **Conquer:** Sort each sub list (by calling MergeSort **recursively** on each).
- **Merge** the two sorted sub lists into a single sorted list.

The implementations are provided for completeness. It is not expected that you will understand everything. You will certainly not be called upon to write code like this! Nonetheless the implementations do illustrate, very clearly, how to change a good plan for an algorithm into actual code.

Implementation - Pseudocode:

Top-down implementation which recursively divides the input list into smaller sub lists until the sub lists are trivially sorted, and then merges the sub lists while returning up the call chain.

```
FUNCTION mergeSort(myList)
  IF LENGTH(myList) <= 1 THEN  # Base case. A list of 0 or 1 is storted.
    RETURN myList
  END IF
  # Recursive case. First, divide the list into equal-sized sub arrays
  midPoint = LENGTH(myList) DIV 2
  left = myList[: midPoint] #slice up to not including mid point
  right = myList[midPoint : ] #slide from mid point to end

  # Recursively sort both sublists.
  left = mergeSort(left)
  right = mergeSort(right)

  # Then merge the now-sorted sublists by calling the merge function
  RETURN merge(left, right)
#In this example, the merge function merges the left and right sublists.
END FUNCTION


FUNCTION merge(left, right)
  result = [ ]  #empty list

  WHILE (left is NOT empty) AND (right is NOT empty) DO
    IF first(left) ≤ first(right) THEN
      append first(left) to result
      left = rest(left)
    ELSE
      append first(right) to result
      right = rest(right)
    END IF
  END WHILE

  # Either left or right may have elements left; consume them.
  # (Only one of the following loops will actually be entered.)
  WHILE left is NOT empty DO
    append first(left) to result
    left = rest(left)
  END WHILE

  WHILE right is NOT empty DO
    append first(right) to result
    right = rest(right)
  END WHILE
  RETURN result
END FUNCTION
```

Implementation - Python:

```
def mergeSort(myList):
    if len(myList)<= 1:              #base case, empty list is sorted
        return myList
    #end if ..........
    #recursive case. First divide list into 2 equal sublists
    midPoint = len(myList) // 2      #integer division
    left = myList[: midPoint]        #slice up to not including midPoint
    right = myList[midPoint :]       #slice from midPoint to end
    #recursively sort both sublists
    left = mergeSort(left)
    right = mergeSort(right)
    #Then merge the now-sorted sublists by calling the merge function
    return merge(left, right)
#end Function mergeSort ...........................................................................

def merge(left, right):
    result = [] #empty list to hold result
    while (left != []) and (right != []):
        if left[0] <= right[0]:
            result.append(left[0])
            left = left[1: ] # slice rest of list
        else:
            result.append(right[0])
            right = right[1: ] # slice rest of list
        #end if ..........
    #end while ...............
    #left or right may have elements left so consume them
    #only one of the following while loops will be entered
    while (left != []):
        result.append(left[0])
        left = left[1: ]
    #end while ...........
    while (right != []):
        result.append(right[0])
        right = right[1: ]
    #end while
    return result
#end Function merge ...........................................................................
#Main program starts here ...........................
sortedList = mergeSort(unsortedList)
```

Merge Sort Algorithm - Efficiency - Similar to quick sort
- Divide & Conquer, so is fairly good (fast)
    - Slower than quick sort but faster if the data can only be accessed sequentially
- It slows right down with:
    - "Very unsorted" lists & Long lists
- But with an average-case (not too long & fairly sorted) it is pretty fast.

Final Note: Maintaining lists of sorted data also makes it much quicker to find data in a list. This leads us on to the next chapter - Searching Algorithms.

Questions on Chapter 2b Sorting Algorithms

1. Bubble Sort
(a) Below is a simple Bubble Sort algorithm but the steps are in the wrong order.
Write down the steps in the correct order:
Until no swaps are needed
Repeatedly step through list
Swap them if wrong order
Compare each pair of adjacent items

(b) Copy and complete the table to show Pass 1 and Pass 2 of the bubble sort on a list of 4 numbers: [108, 100, 107, 102]

Unsorted	Pass 1	Pass 2	Pass 3
108			100
100			102
107			107
102			108

(c) Here is a full implementation of the Bubble Sort in Pseudocode:
```
swap_done = True
   WHILE swap_done DO
     swap_done = False
     FOR index FROM 0 TO LENGTH(myList)- 2 DO
       IF (myList[index]) > (myList[index+1] )THEN  #swap
         temp = myList[index]
         myList[index] = myList[index+1]
         myList[index+1] = temp
         swap_done = True
       END IF
     END FOR
   END WHILE
```
 Answer the following questions about the pseudocode:
    i. What is the data type of the variable "swap_done"?
    ii. This variable is assigned "True" to start off the while loop. State another circumstance that leads to the "swap_done" being assigned "True":
    iii. Assuming "myList" is set to [4, 7, 9, 5 , 8, 6] and index is set to 2, state the contents of the variables, shown on the right, after each line has been executed: (remember lists start with index 0)

                                                      Variables

	Variables
IF (myList[index]) > (myList[index+1]) **THEN**	
temp = myList[index]	temp
myList[index] = myList[index+1]	myList
myList[index+1] = temp	myList

2. Selection Sort

(a) Here's a simple overview the Selection Sort Algorithm:
- Find the smallest element
- Exchange (swap) 1st and smallest
- Repeat step 1 and 2 with one less element (rest of the list)

Here's a diagram showing the algorithm. Copy the diagram and next to each line state what is happening:

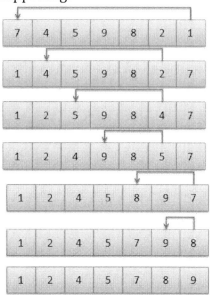

(b) Copy and complete the table to show each pass of a selection sort to arrange the numbers [29, 67, 11, 42] into ascending order:

Pass / Numbers	29	67	11	42
Pass 1				
Pass 2				
Pass 3				
Pass 4				

3. Quick Sort

(a) The diagram below shows the Quick Sort Algorithm on the list [33, 55, 77, 11, 66 , 88 , 22, 44]. Copy the diagram and annotate (add notes to both sides) the diagram to explain what is happening. Show clearly which number is the "pivot" and how this is used to split the list (or sub-list) into two:

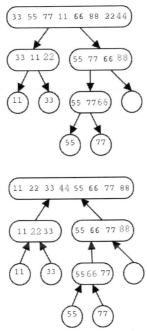

(b) Explain why this algorithm could be called a "**divide and conquer**" algorithm.

4 Merge Sort

(a) Copy out the following grid showing a merge sort and fill in the blank spaces.

Line

| 1 | | | | | | | | | | 56 | 29 | 35 | 42 | 15 | 41 | 75 | 21 |

Line 2: 56 | 35 | ; 15 | 75

Line 3: 56 | ; | 42 ; 15 | 41 ; | 21

Line 4: 56 | ; 35 | 42 ; | 41 ; 75 |

Line 5: 29 | ; 35 | 42 ; | ; 21 |

Line 6: | 42 | ; | 21 |

| 7 | | | | | | | | | | 15 | 21 | 29 | 35 | 41 | 42 | 56 | 75 |

(b) State the range of line numbers where:

    i. The list is progressively split into smaller and smaller sub lists.

    ii. The sub lists are progressively merged into longer sorted lists.

Chapter 2c Algorithms: Searching Algorithms

Storing huge amounts of data is one thing, finding what you are looking for is another. This problem is closely linked to sorting: Data that is sorted is much easier to search.

Points Covered: We will look at two main methods of searching data in lists or arrays:
1. Linear Search - On an unordered list;
2. Binary Search - On an ordered list.

Searching Algorithms:

1. Linear Search – just look along the list.

When your data is not sorted, you really have no choice except to start at the beginning and work your way along until you have found what are looking for or it is the end of the list.

- A linear search starts at the beginning of a list and goes through every item until it
  - finds the one you are looking for
  - or you come to the end of the list without finding the item.
- A real-life example of this might be: looking for a picture of your cousin's wedding in a pile of unordered printed photographs.
- You keep flicking through until
  - you find the photograph,
  - or until you've looked at all the photographs and conclude that the picture isn't there.

The list is not in any order (not sorted). Example: Search for 13 in a list with 9 elements
- Iterate over ("loop through") the list starting at the beginning
- As you go along check if the value found is 13
  - If it is return the index of where you are
- If you get to the end of the list and you have not found 13 then it is not in the list so return an "impossible" index like -1

```
locate(list, 9, 13);
```

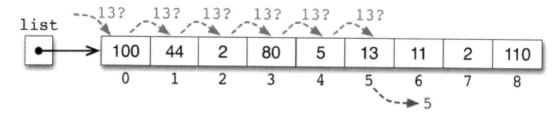

We know how many elements there are so this looks like a **for loop**:

Implementation – Pseudocode:

```
FUNCTION linearSearch(key, Array[ ])
 BEGIN FUNCTION
    FOR index FROM 0 TO LENGTH(Array) DO
       IF (Array[index] = key) THEN
          RETURN index        # this will exit the function
       END IF
    END FOR
    RETURN -1                 # end of loop not found return "dummy value"
 END FUNCTION
```

Implementation – Python:

```
def linearSearch(key, inList):
    """searchs inList for key returns index or -1 if not found"""
    for index in range(len(inList)):      #iterate over list with a for loop
        if inList[index] == key:          #found so
            return index                  #return & exit
        #end if ..........
    #end for loop ...............
    return -99                            #not found so return "dummy value"
```

Linear Search Algorithm - Efficiency:

Advantages
- Very simple to implement
- Will work on any list – sorted or not
- Will always find the item – if it is there!

Disadvantages
- If the number is at the end of the list you have to search nearly the whole list to find it!
- With long lists this is very slow

2. Binary Search – Divide & Conquer:
Maintaining lists of **sorted data** also makes it much quicker to find data in a list. The Binary Search algorithm takes advantage of this.

As an introduction imagine a "guess the number" game. Pretend I was thinking of a number between 1 and 100 (for example 22). Every guess you make and I'll say "higher" or "lower".
The most efficient way is to first guess 50.
- Lower so, guess 25.
- Lower so, guess 15.
- Higher so, guess 20.
- 22 Yes!

In other words by constantly cutting the "search area" in two you can guess the right number in only a few steps. This is how a binary search works:
It only works if you have a list of items that have **already been sorted** in order.
- You start with the middle item. If you find it first time, well done!
- Otherwise, the item you are looking for will either be in the top or bottom half of the list.
- Go to the middle of that half and eliminate the other half of the list.
- Continue chopping the list in half until
  - You have found the item
  - Or worked out that the item you're looking for is not in the list.

Example: Looking for the number 11 (the "key") in a sorted list using binary search:

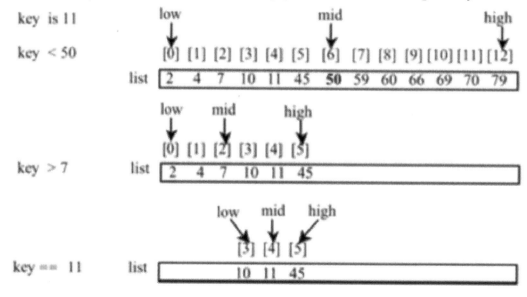

Implementation – Pseudocode:

```
FUNCTION binarySearch(key, Array[ ], min, max)
 BEGIN FUNCTION
    IF (min > max) THEN            #not in list return "dummy" index
        RETURN -1                  #return means exit function
    END IF
    midpoint = (min + max)//2      #integer division
    IF (key = Array[midpoint] ) THEN
        RETURN midpoint            #found key so return index & exit
    END IF
    IF ( key < Array[midpoint]) THEN      #key smaller, go left, new value max
        RETURN binarySearch(key, Array, min, midpoint-1)
    ELSE  # key must be bigger, go right, new value lower
        RETURN binarySearch(key, Array, midpoint + 1, max)
    END IF
END FUNCTION
```

Implementation – Python:

```
def binSearch(sList,key,lower, upper):
    """scan sList returns index if found else -1"""
    #lower starts at 0, beginning of list   #upper starts at last index, len(sList)-1
    if lower > upper:                # Base case: empty
        return -1
    mid = (lower + upper)//2         #recursive case
    if key == sList[mid]:
        return mid
    if key < sList[mid]:             # Go left - new value upper
        return binSearch(sList, key, lower, mid-1)
    else:                           # Go right - new value lower
        return binSearch(sList, key, mid+1, upper)
#end function binSearch ----------------------------
```

Binary Search Algorithm - Efficiency:

Advantages
- Every iteration eliminates half of the remaining possibilities.
- This makes binary searches very efficient - even for large collections.
- Finding an element in a list with a million elements needs only 20 comparisons!

Disadvantages
- Binary search requires a sorted collection.
- This means the collection must either be sorted before searching or elements added such that the list is always sorted

Questions on Chapter 2c Searching Algorithms

Linear Search:
1. A linear search starts at the beginning of an unordered list and goes through every item until it finds the one you are looking for or you come to the end of the list without finding the item.

(a) Why is it only sensible to use a linear search on an unordered list? (Hint: think about searching an ordered list!)

(b) A real-life example of this might be: looking for a picture of your cousin's wedding in a pile of unordered printed photographs. You keep flicking through until you find the photograph or until you've looked at all the photographs and conclude that the picture isn't there.
Describe another real-life example of a linear search:

2. In the following example:

```
locate(list, 9, 13);
```

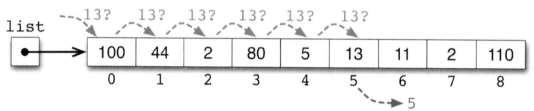

(a) What does the number 9 tell you about the list?
(b) How many steps did it take to find the number 13?
(c) What is the **index position** of the found value 13?

3. The following pseudocode for a linear search is incomplete.

FUNCTION linearSearch(key, Array[ ])
BEGIN FUNCTION
    FOR .... **FROM** .... **TO** .... **DO**
       IF (Array[index] = ...) **THEN**
          RETURN index # this will exit the function
       END IF
    END FOR
    RETURN .... # end of loop not found return "dummy value"
END FUNCTION
    (a) Copy and complete the pseudocode.
    (b)Explain why a FOR LOOP is more appropriate than a WHILE LOOP:
    (c) State two conditions when a linear search would become very, very **slow**:

Binary Search Questions

1. Binary search can be a very quick search algorithm.

(a) What is the condition of the list before a binary search can take place?

(b) Copy and rearrange the following steps in a binary search in the correct order
- Continue chopping the list in half until you have found the item –
- You start with the middle item. If you find it first time, well done!
- or worked out that the item you're looking for is not in the list.
- Otherwise, the item you are looking for will either be in the top or bottom half of the list.
- Go to the middle of that half and eliminate the other half of the list.

2. The following pseudocode is an incomplete implementation of a binary search.
FUNCTION binarySearch(key, Array[ ], min, max)
BEGIN FUNCTION
    IF (.............................) **THEN** #not in list return "dummy" index
       RETURN -1 #return means exit function
    END IF
    midpoint = (min + max)//2 #integer division
    IF (.......................... = Array[midpoint]) **THEN**
       RETURN midpoint #found key so return index & exit
    END IF
    IF (key < .... **THEN** #key smaller, go left, new max
       binarySearch(key, Array, ..., midpoint-1)
    ELSE # key must be bigger, go right, new value lower
       binarySearch(key, Array, ..., max)
    END IF
END FUNCTION

(a) Copy and complete the following pseudocode for binary search

(b) Explain why binary searches can be very fast and efficient:

(c) Explain what the main disadvantage is of a binary search:

(d) **Extension**: The function shown is a **recursive** algorithm. What does "recursive" mean in this context?

Section 3
Programming

- **3a: High Level & Low Level Languages**
- **3b: Operators**
- **3c: Data Types & Variables**
- **3d: Selection, Decisions & IF THEN**
- **3e: Loops & Repetition (Iteration)**
- **3f: Data Structures**
- **3g: Subprograms - Implementation of Abstraction**
- **3h Input & Output**
- **3i Errors & Testing**

"Everybody in this country should learn to program a computer, because it teaches you how to think" (Steve Jobs)

0011

Lrgz oy hkzzkx zngt tkyzkj. Yvgxyk oy hkzzkx zngt jktyk. Xkgjghoroz4 iu0tzy.

Chapter 3a Programming: High-Level & Low-Level Languages

Points Covered:
- Explain the difference between high-level code and machine code.
- Explain the need for translators to convert high-level code to machine code.
- Describe the characteristics of an assembler, a compiler and an interpreter.

As you will see in the chapters on data-representation, computers only "work" with electric signals and switches that are either ON or OFF. Humans represent these signals as binary (1-ON, 0-OFF).

- ● **Computers only "understand" 0s and 1s,**
  - Their native machine language.
- ● **All of the executable programs on your computer are a collection of these 0s and 1s**
  - That tell your computer exactly what to execute.

High-Level & Low-Level Languages:

As we saw in the section on computational thinking and algorithms, programming is all about solving problems. Here's a short piece of Python code showing a programmer working at the problem of coding a "guess my number" game:

```python
answer = 4
guess = 0
count = 0
while guess != answer:
    guess = int(input("Number 1 - 10 please: "))
    count = count + 1
#end while
print("Correct! number was: ", answer)
print("Number of guesses: ", count)
```

You can probably see how it works, after all Python is very close to a kind of "structured English". Of course the programmer wants his code to run on a real computer but right now he is solving a problem. He is not concerned with how that program will be **translated** to a stream of 0s & 1s, which is **machine code**. He is certainly not concerned about the complex electronics of a particular Central Processing Unit (**CPU** or "chip").

He is working at a "**high-level**" - that is a "long way" from the hardware. So computer-programming languages that are "close" to natural languages are considered to be **problem-orientated** or **high-level** languages. For example: Python, Java, C++ and Visual Basic.

Electronic Engineers who design and build computer chips do need to be concerned about how a particular **CPU** works. They work at a "**low-level**" - that is "close" to the hardware. However working directly with binary or machine code is very tedious and prone to errors. So engineers use a simple programming language called "**assembly language**". Here's the guess my number game in assembly language for an "ARM" CPU:

```
                LDR R0, [13]
                LDR R1, [14]
                LDR R2, [15]
askAgain        LDR R1, input
                ADD R2, R2, #1
                CMP R1, R0
                BNE askAgain
                STR R2, [15]
```

You don't need to understand this kind of code, yet. At this point it is only important to note that the code is very specific to one kind of CPU. This low-level language still needs to be translated to 0s & 1s. A translator called an "**Assembler**" does this.

Machine Code is a binary representation (encoding) of instructions for a specific microprocessor. Here's a fragment of what machine code could look like:

```
10100001 10111100 10010011 00000100
00001000 00000011 00000101 11000000
10010011 00000100 00001000 10100011
11000000 10010100 00000100 00001000
```

It means z = x + y.

Instructions & Data are just bit patterns – 001011011001111 - so a fair question would be: How does the CPU "know" which is which? In short, it can't! Nonetheless in the "fetch-decode-execute" cycle (see the chapters on hardware) the CPU "expects" the first bit pattern to be an instruction.

Here are the key points:
- Instructions & data are stored **sequentially** in RAM
- A program has a start address
- The first item must be an instruction
- Each instruction has 2 parts
    - Operator (instruction) for example: 1001 - ADD
    - Operand (data) for example: 1101 – memory location

Assembly Language: The idea behind assembly language is to make it easier for humans to write machine code. A program, called an assembler, **translates** assembly language to machine code:

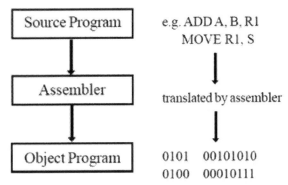

e.g. ADD A, B, R1
MOVE R1, S

translated by assembler

0101   00101010
0100   00010111

High Level to Machine code:

As we saw at the beginning of the chapter, even if you do program with a high-level language like Python that program still needs to be **translated** to machine code so that it can actually run on a computer.

Compilers and Interpreters:

There are two fundamentally different approaches to translating high-level languages.

Compilers are translators that read in the entire high-level code (**source code**) at once. If there are no syntax errors, all of this source code is translated at once to machine code (**object code**). On the other hand, if there was even one syntax error then the error is reported and no code is translated and nothing is run. This is a little bit like translating say a French film into English: You take the entire script, translate all of it into English and add the English sub-titles to the whole film.

Here's some Java code (written in the "Greenfoot" environment) being **compiled**:

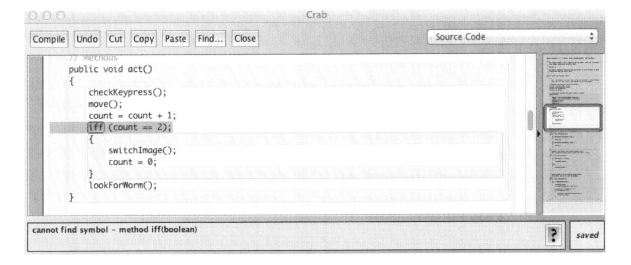

There is only one mistake in all of the source code (if is spelt incorrectly). The error is reported, no translation takes place and no object code is produced.

Interpreters read, translate and execute the high-level code line by line. If, perhaps halfway through the process, a syntax error is discovered then the error is reported and the translation process stops. This is a bit like a simultaneous interpreter working at the United Nations. The speaker says a sentence in Russian and the interpreter immediately translates that sentence into English and speaks that sentence. He then waits for the next sentence in Russian and so on to the end of the speech. The process could stop in the middle if the speaker says something grammatically incorrect in Russian, which the interpreter cannot translate.

Here's some Python code being **interpreted**:

The code	Output when run
print("Welcome to Password")	Welcome to Password
password = **input**("Enter your password: ")	Enter your password: Nick
if password == "secret":	Error!!
print("Access Granted")	
else:	
prrint("Wrong password")	NameError: name 'prrint' is not defined

Notice that there is a syntax error at line 6 (print is spelt incorrectly!). When the code is run each correct line is read, translated and executed. It is only when an attempt to translate the line with the error that the process is stopped and the error reported.

Here's a comparison of both types of translators:

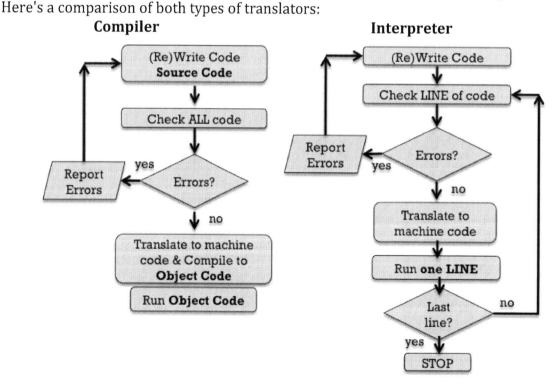

With a compiler, once you have the object code (machine code) you have an "executable" program. You don't need the compiler anymore. With interpreted code you always need the source code and the interpreter.

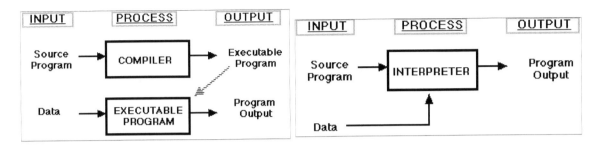

So which is "better" a compiled or an interpreted high-level language?

Compiler for Professionals?

Advantages

- During the compilation process the source can be "optimised" by carefully looking at the code as a whole.
- Object code runs fast with no compiler and can be run again & again & again ....
- Object code is "secret" (it does not reveal the high level code) and so can be sold to clients who cannot modify the code.
- Encourages careful development with blocks of structured code (procedures or functions)

Disadvantages

- If there is one syntax mistake in all of the code none of it will run
- This can be very frustrating for beginners when you know that most of the code is correct.
- The "bug" has to be found and the entire program has to be re-compiled.
- It is hard to quickly try some code, run it, see if it works & then correct it.

Interpreters for Beginners?

Disadvantages

- The interpreter is always needed so code can therefore run slowly
- Encourages "lazy", unplanned programming with a "try it and see" approach.

Advantages

- The code that is correct will run.
- When a syntax error is found the code stops at that point. This makes it easy to debug and find the problem
- Excellent for quick project development
- "Easier" for beginners. At least they can see some code working when there is an error.

Perhaps there is no "right" answer. Some languages can be interpreted during development but finally compiled at the end of a project. Other languages compile source code to "byte code" which is then interpreted by "virtual machines" which are specific to different operating systems. At the level of the CPU it could be argued that all languages are interpreted - that is executed line by line!

In summary:
High Level Languages
- Close to "natural" languages so easier to understand
- Problem orientated - focus on the algorithm not the code
- A long way from Binary & CPU so are "cross-platform" or not specific to one kind of CPU
- Compilers & Interpreters translates code to binary machine code

Low Level Languages
- Machine orientated so specific to a particular CPU
  - Can be very efficient, occupy small memory and and run very fast.
- Hard for humans to understand
- Close to Binary & CPU
- Assembly translates, line by line, to binary machine code

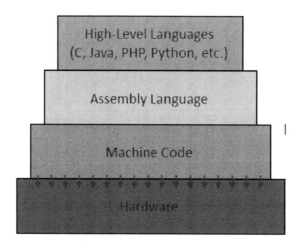

Questions on Chapter 3a High Level & Low Level Languages

1. Look at these two pieces of code:

```
A:      CLC                 B:  FOR Loop = 1 TO 4
        LDX #0                      INPUT Number1, Number2
 loop: LDA A,X                      Sum = Number1 + Number2
        ADC B,X                     PRINT Sum
        STA C,X                 NEXT
        INX
        CPX #16
        BNE loop
```

(a) Which of these pieces of code (A or B) is written in a high-level language?
(b) Give one benefit of writing code in a high-level language.
(c) Give one benefit of writing code in a low-level language.

Translators:
2. Look at the following code. There is a syntax error at line 3.
    1. age = 15
    2. print("The mind is a computer.")
    3. IFF age < 18:
    4.   print("You are very young.")

Write down what would be **output** to the screen when the code is run (translated) by a:
(a) Compiler   (b) Interpreter

3. A games developer is developing a computer game, which simulates tank battles in the 2nd World War. At work he does his programming on a Windows computer, while at home he works on a Mac computer.

     (a) The program is written in high-level code and then translated to machine code. State an example of **a high-level computer language**.
     (b) High-level languages are often referred to as "**problem orientated**". Explain this in the context of the programmer trying to develop this computer game.
     (c) While he is developing his program the translator he uses is an **interpreter**. Explain the advantages of using an interpreter while developing a program.
     (d) When he has finished the program he uses a compiler to compile the **source code** to **object code**.
Explain the terms: Source code & Object code.
     (e) The computer language he chose to code in is "**cross-platform**". What does "cross-platform" mean and why is it important in the context of how this particular programmer works?
     (f) The developer is now ready to distribute his game by burning copies onto DVDs. Explain why he chooses to put object code onto the disk rather than the complete interpreted version of the game.

Chapter 3b Programming: Operators - Arithmetic, Relational & Logical

Points Covered:
Understand the purpose of, and how to use the following **operators**:
- **Arithmetic** (add, subtract, divide, multiply, modulus, integer division)
- **Relational** (equal to, less than, greater than, not equal to, less than or equal to, greater than or equal to)
- **Logical** (AND, OR, NOT)

Computers do, after all compute. A good PC runs at over 3 teraflops. (A teraflop is one million million "calculations" per second.) Electronically it all takes place inside the Arithmetic and Logic Unit (**ALU**), which is part of the Central Processing Unit (CPU) – refer to the chapter on hardware.

Arithmetic Operators:
Real numbers ("continuously variable numbers") often referred to in computing as "floating point" numbers or just "floats":

$$1.2345 = \underbrace{12345}_{\text{significand}} \times \underbrace{10}_{\text{base}}\overbrace{^{-4}}^{\text{exponent}}$$

Don't worry too much about precise mathematical definitions. We just mean all "normal" numbers: positive and negative and including "decimal" or fractional numbers such as ¾, 8.75, - 89.768 and so on.
These behave exactly how we would expect, with just a couple of changes to the symbols that are used:

Sign	Meaning	Python
+	Plus or add	2.5 + 3.75 --> 6.25
-	Minus or subtract	2.5 - 3.75 --> -1.25
*	Multiply (never "X")	2.5 * 3.75 --> 9.375
/	Divide (never "÷")	2.5 / 3.75 --> 0.6666666666666666
^	Exponent ($2^3 = 2^3 = 8$)	2 ** 3 -- > 8

Notice how the simple exponent symbol (**) in Python enables simple square roots:
$\sqrt{81}$ --> 9   81 ** (0.5) --> 9.0

If you want to do even more complex arithmetic, most languages (including Python) have "libraries" or "modules" full of maths functions that you can import and use.
```
import math
math.sqrt(81)
9.0
```

Worried about how many decimal places? In Python just use the round function:
```
>>> 45 / 89
0.5056179775280899
>>> round(45/89 , 2)        #Round the calculation to 2 decimal places
0.51
```

Integers are "whole" numbers that can be written without a fractional component. For example, 21, -4, 0, 89 and –2048 are integers, while 9.75, 5½, and √2 are not.

+, - and * work just the same as for real numbers but care is needed with division:

Sign	Meaning	Python
DIV	integer division	
	10 **DIV** 3 --> 3	10 // 3 --> 3
	26 **DIV** 5 --> 5	26 // 5 --> 5

Note: This is **not** "rounding". The integer part is just "removed" so that:
    8 / 5 --> 1.6 but 8 // 5 --> 1 (not "rounded up" to 2)

MOD (modulo)	**remainder** of division	
	10 **MOD** 3 --> 1	10 % 3 --> 1
	57 **MOD** 5 --> 2	57 % 5 --> 2

Integer & Modulo division is a bit like when you were first taught how to divide in primary school and you would say something like:
    "57 divided by 5 is 11 with 2 left over (remainder 2)"
They are both used a lot in programming. For example converting seconds to minutes:
```
>>> mins = 125 // 60
>>> secs = 125 % 60
>>> print(mins," minutes and ", secs, " seconds")
2  minutes and  5  seconds
```

Brackets & Ordering
Most programming languages follow "normal" maths rules, so **BODMAS** applies: **B**rackets, **O**rders (powers), **D**ivision, **M**ultiplication, **A**ddition and **S**ubtraction.
    4 * (3 + 2)   --> 4 * 6   --> 24
    4 * 3 + 2   --> 12 +2   --> 14

Type coercion
In pseudocode (and Python for that matter) you can "mix" real and floating-point numbers and the final type will be ("forced" or "coerced" to) a floating point.
    For example: myNum = 3 + 8.25 --> 11.25 (integer + real = real)

There is a little bit more on this kind of issue in the section on data types but just bear in mind that not all languages are this "flexible" or "forgiving". For example in Java:
>   myNum = 3 + 8.25 will generate a "lack of precision" error message.

(How computers actually represent "real" numbers or "integers" in binary is covered in the section on data representation.)

Relational (Comparison) operators
These are all fairly obvious and work as expected.

Sign	Meaning	Python
=	equal to	= =
<>	not equal to	!=
>	greater than	>
>=	greater than or equal to	>=
<	less than	<
<=	less than or equal to	<=

Note that these operators are used to **compare** values. When you write "4 > 10" it is really a question " is 4 bigger than 10?" and the answer is "no it is not" or "false". In other words expressions with these operators "evaluate to" or return a **Boolean** (True or False). There is some more on this in the chapter on data types (and indeed in the section on logic!)

Meanwhile here's part of an interactive session with Python:

```
>>> 8 > 5
True
>>> 8 > 16
False
>>> 8 > 8
False
>>> 8 >= 8
True
>>> 8 = = 8
SyntaxError: invalid syntax        #Don't put a space between the equals
>>> 8 == 8
True
>>> 8 <> 8
SyntaxError: invalid syntax        # <> does not mean "not equals" in Python
>>> 8 != 8
False
```

You can compare other data types apart from numbers. Strings, for example, are compared "alphabetically" (based on their ASCII values):

>>> "a" > "b"

False

>>> "a" < "b"

True

>>> "a" == "a"

True

>>> "a" == "A"   #Lower case is not the same as Upper case!

False

But you can't compare types, which are not "compatible":

    "nick" > 10

TypeError: unorderable types: str() > int()

Finally be a little bit careful with what you really mean with "equals":

"2 + 3 = 5" is fine as a statement in maths or even: "x + 3 = 5" in an equation, but in most programming languages (including Python) a single " = " really means an "**assignment**", so that:

>>> 2 + 3 = 5

SyntaxError: can't assign to operator

While:

a = 5 means "assign" the integer 5 to the variable "a".

a = a + 1 means increment (or add 1) to variable "a". That is: add 1 to the present value or "contents" of variable "a" and assign this "new" value to the variable a.

>>> a = 5

>>> a = a + 1

>>> a

6

(See the section on variables for more about variables!)

Logical Operators:

Logic in programming depends on YES / NO or TRUE / FALSE responses. This is called **Boolean** (or even **Binary**) Logic as these states are represented by ON / OFF or binary 1 / 0 in a computer system. To solve logical problems we use the logical operators: NOT, AND, OR.

Binary Logic will help you to think clearly and help your programming. You use complex Boolean expressions to control loops and make selections:

Searching for an item in a file:

WHILE NOT (EndOfFile) **AND NOT** (ItemFound) .....

Checking if a discount applies or not:

IF (age < 16) **OR** (status == "student") **THEN** .....

For each of the operators (AND, OR, NOT) we will look at English, Logic gates, Truth tables and programming.

Logic Gates: Are the electronic components inside the computer (ALU) that represent Boolean logic. The gates are made of tiny components called transistors. As modern computer chips have millions of transistors, they can do a lot of logic! Logic gates typically have one or more wires running into them, called the **inputs**, and a single connection out the other end, called the **output**. The output from a logic gate can be thought of as the answer to a question, and so the output depends on what kind of logic gate it is and what the inputs are.

AND

Consider the following statement in English:

"Nick will only go to the theatre if a good play is on **AND** he has enough money."

Inputs		Output
Good Play?	Enough money?	Go to Theatre?
No	No	No
Yes	No	No
No	Yes	No
Yes	Yes	Yes

If only one factor or neither of them is true then Nick will not go to the theatre.

Logic Gate   **Truth table**

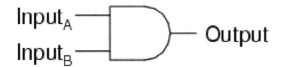

2-input AND gate

A	B	Output
0	0	0
0	1	0
1	0	0
1	1	1

Pseudocode:

         IF (goodPlay = True) **AND** (money >= price) **THEN** go to theatre

OR

In this case Nick is deciding to go to a party or not:

"Nick will only go to the birthday party if Maria **OR** Dave is going too."

Inputs		Outputs
Maria goes?	Dave goes?	Nick goes?
No	No	No
Yes	No	Yes
No	Yes	Yes
Yes	Yes	Yes

Nick doesn't need both inputs to be true because he will go to the party if one or the other of his friends will be there (and he'll still go if both Maria and Dave go).

Logic Gate   **Truth table**

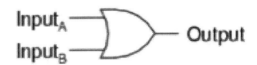

2-input OR gate

A	B	Output
0	0	0
0	1	1
1	0	1
1	1	1

Pseudocode:
>   **IF** (MariaGo = True) **OR** (DaveGo = True) **THEN** go to party

NOT

Here Nick is catching a bus to school: "Nick will catch the bus if he is **NOT** late".

Input	Output
Late?	Catch the bus?
NO	YES
YES	NO

For some reason the NOT operator can cause some confusion.
>   **IF** (Nick is **NOT** Late) **THEN** he must be on time so he can catch the bus.

Logic Gate   **Truth table**

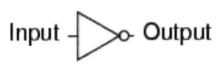

Input	Output
0	1
1	0

Pseudocode:
>   **IF NOT** (late = True) **THEN** catch the bus

Combining Logic Operators and Simple Boolean Algebra:

Once you have the basic operators (AND, OR, NOT) clear, it is easy to combine them together for more complex ideas. Consider this:

"Nick will only go to the party if both Maria AND Dave are going AND NOT Peter."

Logic Gate Circuit:

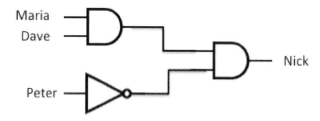

Boolean Algebra

N = (M **AND** D) **AND** (**NOT** P)

Truth Table:

Inputs			working out		Output
Maria going?	Dave going?	Peter going?	M AND D	NOT P	Nick going? (M AND D) AND (NOT P)
0	0	0	0	1	0
0	0	1	0	0	0
0	1	0	0	1	0
0	1	1	0	0	0
1	0	0	0	1	0
1	0	1	0	0	0
1	1	0	1	1	1
1	1	1	1	0	0

Applying Boolean Logic to Programming:

Problem: Search through a file to see if "Nick" is found at least once. So keep searching as long as Nick is **not** found **and** you have **not** got to the end of the file.
Logic Gate Circuit:

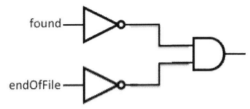

Pseudocode:
>   found = False
>   endOfFile = False
>   **WHILE** (**NOT** found) **AND** (**NOT** endOfFile) **DO**
>   **IF** item = "Nick" **THEN** found = True **END IF**
>   **NEXT** item
>   **IF** no more items **THEN** endOfFile = True **END IF**
>   **END WHILE**

Boolean Algebra:
>   Keep Searching = (**NOT** F) **AND** (**NOT** E)

Note that this can be simplified by "rephrasing" the statement to: So keep searching until either "Nick is found" **OR** "It is the end of the file":
Boolean Algebra:
>   Keep Searching = **NOT** (F **OR** E)

Which would give this circuit:

And this Pseudocode:
>   found = False
>   endOfFile = False
>   **WHILE** (**NOT** (found **OR** endOfFile))**DO**
>   **IF** item = "Nick" **THEN** found = True **END IF**
>   **NEXT** item
>   **IF** no more items **THEN** endOfFile = True **END IF**
>   **END WHILE**

Problem: There are two monkeys called "Nick" and "Andy". We are in trouble if they are both smiling or if neither of them are smiling. Let's apply the same logic as before and then look for a simpler solution afterwards!

Assume that nSmile, aSmile are Boolean variables, which are true when smiling!

Logic Gate Circuit:

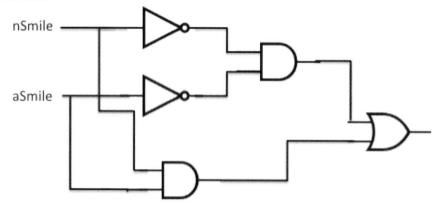

Pseudocode:

    IF nSmile **AND** aSmile **THEN** trouble = True **END IF**
    IF (NOT nSmile) **AND** (NOT aSmile) **THEN** trouble = True **END IF**

Boolean Algebra:

    trouble = (nSmile **AND** aSmile) **OR** ((**NOT** (nSmile) **AND** ((**NOT** aSmile))

There is, however, a simpler solution:

    trouble = (nSmile = aSmile)

You see what we are really saying is we are in trouble if nSmile and aSmile are the same.
(**Extension**: In this case we "want" the inputs to be the same. There is even a special logic gate for this called XNOR, which is beyond the scope of this book.)

Here's a similar problem:

Dave and Peter will not be seen together if they look the same. They have an agreement to only wear a hat if the other is not wearing a hat. Then they are happy, otherwise they are angry.

I will leave you to draw the circuit diagram and do the code.

Boolean Logic:

    happy = (dHat AND (NOT pHat)) OR ((NOT dHat) AND pHat)

Again there is a simpler programming version:

    happy = (dHat <> pHat)   (where "<>" means not equal to)

(**Extension**: Note in this case we "want" the inputs to be different and yes there is a special logic gate for this called: XOR "Exclusive OR")

Note using brackets:

      AND is like arithmetic X

      OR is like arithmetic +

Example problem: You have a loud talking parrot. You are in trouble if the parrot is talking and the hour is before 7 or after 20.

Here's the Boolean algebra solution:

      talking AND (hour < 7 OR hour > 20)

Let's simplify by saying early means hour < 7 and late means hour > 20

      talking AND (early OR late)

The brackets **are** needed: Perhaps it is clearer with letters and "maths" symbols?

      T X (E + L)

Can you see that the following is not the same?

      talking AND early OR late   (like: T X E + L)

AND "binds" more tightly than OR so this is really the same as:

      (talking AND early) OR late

Now you will be in trouble when it is late even if your parrot is a dead parrot!

Of course you can (and should) use brackets to make your expressions and code clearer even if you technically do not need them:

Example: My dad is dangerous when he is hungry and thirsty or just plain tired.

      (hungry AND thirsty) OR tired

The above is the same as:

      hungry AND thirsty OR tired

So the brackets are not necessary but they do make the statement clearer!

Boolean logic and control technology:

Problem: A bread-making machine has a built in alarm. The alarm sounds if:

      Either the temperature > 120 ºC and the mixer is off;

      Or the temperature is < = 120 ºC and acidity < ph 5

Use the following Boolean variables:

      temp > 120 ºC = True

      mixer is ON = True

      acid < 5 = True

Here's one solution as Boolean algebra:

      alarm = (temp **AND NOT**(mixer)) **OR** (**NOT**(temp) **AND** acid)

I will leave you to draw a logic circuit diagram!

Don't Panic! You will only be expected to solve very simple problems and to use your knowledge in your programming. You will **not** be expected to simplify complex Boolean expressions or circuit diagrams. Just bear in mind that real electronic engineers need to make their circuits as simple, efficient, fast and as cheap as possible. This very often means using as few logic gates as possible. Programmers meanwhile do want their code to run efficiently but they also want their code to be as clear as possible.

Python:
All of the above "logic" can be used in any programming language, including Python!
AND

      if uName == "Nick" **and** pWord == "openSesame123":

OR

      if mark > 77 **or** status == "King":

NOT

      if not finished:

Python can interpret almost any value as True or False.
A zero (0) evaluates to false.
Example: money is a variable referring to an integer, which can be 0. So the following two code extracts do the same thing:

```
if money :                              if money != 0 :
    print("You have paid!")                 print("You have paid!")
else                                    else
    print("You have no money!")             print("You have no money!")
#End if ------------------              #End if ------------------
```

An empty string ("") evaluates to false.
Example: By "testing" a string to see if it is empty, loop until a user does input something

```
while not username:                     while not username = = "":
    username = input("Username: ")          username = input("Username: ")
#End while ------------------            #End while ------------------
```

An empty list ([ ]) evaluates to false.
Example: myList = ["Nick", "Sally", "Maria", "Dave"]. I want to loop through printing and deleting elements until the list is empty.

```
while myList:               #Very "Pythonic" - empty list evaluates to False
    print(myList[0])
    del myList[0]

while len(myList) != 0:     #Very clear - keep going until length of list is 0.
    print(myList[0])
    del myList[0]

while myList != []:         #Fairly clear - when list is [ ] it is empty.
    print(myList[0])
    del myList[0]
```

In all these cases the explicit code that actually shows if something is equal to nothing, is perhaps preferable. Clarity is a good thing!

Questions on Chapter 3b Operators:

1. Evaluate the following mathematical expressions in pseudocode:

      10 + 1 * 3

      (10 + 1) * 3

      22 / 4

      22 DIV 3

      22 MOD 3

2. Integer Division (DIV) and Modulo (MOD):

Write a program (in pseudocode or a language or your choice) that:

- Inputs - a number of seconds
- Process - calculates how many minutes and seconds that is
- Outputs - The number of minutes & seconds in the following format:
  - num mins : num : secs

Example:

- Input: 128
- Output: 2 mins : 8 secs

Your code should be fully commented and use clear variable names

Extension:

- Extend the program to cater for hours, minutes and seconds.

Example:

- Input: 10930
- Output: 3 hours : 2 mins : 10 secs

3. What will the following pseudocode extract output?

```
IF "SALLY" > "sally" THEN
        OUTPUT "Upper Case is Bigger!"
ELSE
        OUTPUT "Lower Case comes first!"
END IF
```

Logic Questions:
1. (a) Draw the logic circuit: **P = (A AND B) OR C**

Copy and complete the truth table for this circuit:

Inputs				Output
A	B	C	A AND B	P = (A AND B) OR C
0	0	0		
0	0	1		
0	1	0		
0	1	1		
1	0	0		
1	0	1		
1	1	0		
1	1	1		

(b) Draw the logic circuit: **P = (A OR B) AND C**

Copy and complete the truth table for this circuit:

Inputs				Output
A	B	C	A OR B	P = (A OR B) AND C
0	0	0		
0	0	1		
0	1	0		
0	1	1		
1	0	0		
1	0	1		
1	1	0		
1	1	1		

(c) "AND" is like "X" while "OR" is like "+". Use this knowledge to decide which one of the Boolean algebra expressions, in questions 1(a) and 1(b), does not need brackets.

(d). A school is closed after 18:00 hrs or all day during the weekend.
When the school is closed an alarm sounds if the main door is open.
  i. Use the following symbols to write this situation in Boolean algebra:
Output: **P** – alarm,
Input: **C** – door open,   **A** – Time > 18:00 hrs,   **B** – weekend
  ii. Which of the circuits above (a or b) would be used for the alarm circuit?
  iii. Explain your answer by showing an example where the "wrong circuit" would not work:

2. Copy and complete the truth table for the following logic circuit:

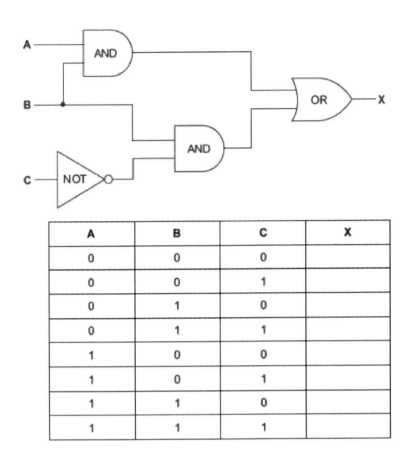

A	B	C	X
0	0	0	
0	0	1	
0	1	0	
0	1	1	
1	0	0	
1	0	1	
1	1	0	
1	1	1	

3. We can sleep in if it is not a weekday or we are on holiday.
Given the Boolean variables:
wDay (= True if the day is a weekday) and holDay (= True if the day is a holiday):
Write down an expression that decides if you should sleep in or not.
You should show your solution as a logic circuit diagram and as Boolean expression.

4. A plastic moulding machine has a built in alarm. The alarm sounds if:
     Either the pressure < 10 bars and the revolutions > 1000 revs / min;
     Or revolutions <= 1000 revs / min and temperature > 200 ºC
Use the following Boolean variables:
    Press >= 10 bars is True
    Revs > 1000 (revs / min) is True
    Temp <= 200 ºC is True
(a) Write down a solution in Boolean algebra that shows when the alarm will ring.
(b) Draw a logic circuit using AND, OR, NOT gates as appropriate.

Chapter 3c Programming: Data Types & Variables

Information and Data:
Following the basic **Input --> Process --> Output** model, the main purpose of a computer program is to input data, process that data and output an "answer" as data.

Information = Data + Meaning (context)

Data is the quantities, characters, or symbols on which operations are performed by a computer. Data then, can be any character, string of characters (text), numbers and so on that can be represented by electrical signals that a computer can process. (See the section on data representation.)

Information is the data put into a context so that it has some meaning and so is useful to humans.

Data 02061958 ... a stream of meaningless digits.

Information 02/06/1978 which is Nick's birthday. Now it means something.

Points Covered:
- Data Types
- Variables - declaring & assigning values
- Constants

Data Types:
Here is a table of the most commonly used data types in programming:

Data Type	Python	Example	Memory Size
Integer (whole number)	int	66, -7	1 to 8 bytes
Real (floating point) "decimal" numbers	float	3.6, -67.59	4 to 8 bytes
Character	string	"A", "3", "n"	1 byte
String	string	"Nick", "Wow!"	As big as main memory!
Boolean	True or False	True or False	1 bit

Note: All of the above are considered "**primitive data types**" in the sense that they are predefined by the programming language. Strings, while "primitive", are made up of sequences of characters (chars) - See the section on data structures.

Variables:
Ultimately all data that a computer program is using is stored in the main or RAM memory. Now 4GB of memory amounts to 4,000,0000,000 bytes or "locations" in memory. **Basically a variable is a named location in memory that can hold a value that can change**.

A simple analogy: Named shelves. All of the "storage locations" above have names and can store different things and their contents can change. Most of the time this analogy is fine. However in many programming languages (like Python) the label or "identifier" is more like a tag attached to an object. In effect the tag "points" to where the value or object is stored in memory. (More on this in assignment below.)

Naming Variables:

Syntax Rules: Most programming languages have strict rules about what you can, and cannot name variables. The most common 2 rules can be summarised as:
- A variable name can **only** contain letters, numbers and underscores (_)
- A variable name cannot start with a number and cannot have empty spaces.

So "my_age", "myage", "age", and "x" are all legal names while "2Class", "my age" and "why?" are not.

Good names: Apart from being legally correct variables names should be short but meaningful. Here are some guidelines.
- **Descriptive** - Clearly show what they represent. Here are some obvious, well named variables:
  - fName, eMailAd, errorMessage ... for strings
  - count, numTimesDone, ageYears, avMass ... for numbers
  - done, finished, carryOn ... for Booleans (remember "done?" is not allowed)
  - Names like "f" or "a" should be avoided as it is not clear what they represent. There are exceptions: x or y may be reasonable names for coordinates; i or j are often used as "index variables" in FOR loops.
- **Consistent** - Use the same system throughout:
  - You are not allowed spaces so "age of dog" is out and dogage is hard to read, so either choose:
    - dogAge or dog_age (with underscore)
  - Whichever you choose try and be consistent - use the same naming system throughout your code.
- **Reasonable length** - not too short & not too long:
  - While "n" is too short, "firstOrGivenNameOfStudent" is too long.
  - Long names lead to mistakes and may make code difficult to read.
  - Keep names to 15 characters or less. So "studFname" is fine.

Declaring Variables:

Declaring a variable is like a kind of statement of intent: "I am going to use a variable called 'counter' and it can hold only integer values." Once you have declared a variable, it is good practice to immediately **initialise** it with a "starting value".

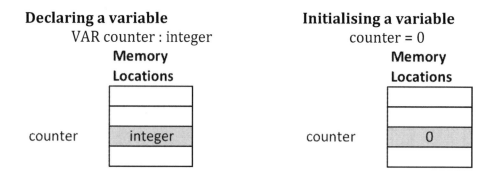

Java Example:

        int counter;   counter = 0;

Declaring a variable then sets up the named location in memory and states what kind of data type the variable can "store". Technically at this point the variable has no value. Some languages will probably automatically assign a value (0 in this case) but this should not be assumed. It is best to initialise the variable manually as shown.

Assigning Values to variables:

Once a variable has been declared its value can be changed - that's why it's a variable! This is done with the **assignment** statement:

        counter = 55

Note that the "=" does NOT mean "equals" - it is an assignment. It means: Overwrite what ever value "counter" used to have with the value on the right side of the "=".

To make clear this difference some languages use alternative symbols like:

        ":=" so the assignment becomes: counter := 55

Some versions of pseudocode try other ways of not using the "=" for assignment:

        "counter <-- 55" or even "**SET** counter **TO** 55"

Of course languages, like Python, that do use the "=" for assignment then use "= =" to mean "is equal to."

Incrementing a variable:

        counter = counter + 1

The meaning of this should be fairly clear: Access the value that counter has at the moment (say 55); Add 1 to that value (so 56) and that is the new value that counter has.

Note again that if the "=" did mean "equals" then the statement is mathematically nonsense: How can, say, x = x + 1 !!!?

Choosing the Correct data type is important:
Here are 3, alternative, blocks of pseudocode that all seem to do the same thing: assign whatever the user inputs to a variable called "age" and "add" 20 to that variable. Let's assume that in each case the user types in 15.

    age = (**STRING**) **INPUT** ("age please")
    age = age + 20   **OUTPUT** age

Firstly this line may "crash" as age "15" is a string and 20 is an integer so the types are "incompatible". Even if it did not crash or you "coerced" (cast) the integer to be a string:

    age = age + (**STRING**) 20

The output would not 35 (15 + 20). What you would have done is to "**concatenate**" (or join) two strings. So the result would be another string: "1520". Perhaps, if you only wanted to print a list of ages and never wanted to actually do any calculations, a string data type would be appropriate - otherwise not.

    age = (**FLOAT**) **INPUT** ("age please")
    age = age + 20.0   **OUTPUT** age

Now this would indeed output 35, or rather, 35.0, so that seems fine. But "floating point" numbers are complex for a computer to represent in binary. (See Data Representation) So it could slow your program down or you may end up with results like 34.9999999999999, which isn't really what you want.

    age = (**INTEGER**) **INPUT** ("age please")
    age = age + 20   **OUTPUT** age

This is the "right" answer. The output is 35. If your variable is never going to have values like 35.67 or 0.435 then why put the computer to the trouble of having to deal with "floats"? Integers occupy less memory and the computer can work with them quickly. All you want to do is to increment a small "whole" number, so an integer is the best choice. All in all - **choose your data types carefully!**

Python:
There is no need to declare a variable in Python - assigning a value is all that is needed.
    counter = 55
The above statement would create or declare the variable and assign it the value of 55, which is an integer. In Python (and other languages) the variable (counter) **refers** to the value 55 and doesn't really "store" the value like a box stores some biscuits. Think of it like this: My name is "Nick" so you refer to me using my name. But "Nick" does not, in any sense, "store" me.

The lack of a formal declaration in Python means that it can "dynamically" change what a variable is referring or pointing to. The following lines are perfectly legal in Python:
    counter = 55
    counter = "Nick"
The variable counter used to "point to" a location in memory holding 55 (an integer). Now it "points to" a location holding "Nick" (a string).

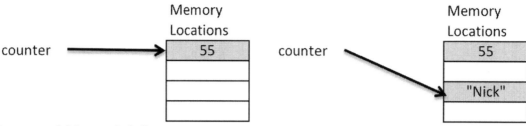

Java would "complain":
        int counter;
        counter = 55;
        counter = "Nicholas" ----------- Error: Incompatible types!
Java has a point! The variable counter should really only refer to integers. So it is best to avoid such confusion in your code and apply the maxim: "Just because you can do something does not mean you should!"

Constants:
Sometimes it makes sense for a value to never change in a program. For example if you are working with circles and have decided to use the value of 3.142 for "Pi" it would make sense to declare and initialise "PI" as a **constant** at the outset:
        CONSTANT float PI = 3.142
Note that it is a standard naming convention that constants are all in uppercase (capitals).
Java uses the key word "final" for constants so:
        final float PI = 3.142

This means that anywhere in your code you can now write clear statements like:
        circumference = PI*diameter
It also means that if later on you decide that it is necessary to use a more precise value for "Pi" you can simply change the constant declaration at the top of your code:
        CONSTANT float PI = 3.1416
and all references to PI will automatically change.
What you CANNOT do is to change the value of a constant in the middle of your code.
        PI = 36 .... ERROR: cannot assign a value to a constant.
This makes good sense - constants cannot and should not change their value!

Python:
You can use constants so the following line is perfectly good Python:
        SALESTAX = 0.22
In reality Python has no "true" constants so you could change a constant:
        SALESTAX = SALESTAX / 2
But you should NOT do this. By using uppercase you are reminding yourself, and other programmers, that you are using a constant, which does not change. Once again: "Just because you can do something doesn't mean you should!"

Questions on Chapter 3c Data Types and Variables:

1. You are working as a programmer for a company that sells cars.   Here is some data of a typical car:

Registration Number Plate:	KAC 738F
Type of Fuel:	Petrol
Number of doors:	4
Air conditioning:	Yes
Average consumption (litres / 100 Km):	6.72

In your programs you will need to refer to data like this as variables in your code.
For each data item suggest a suitable **variable name** and the correct **data type**.

2. Explain exactly what a variable is in computer programming. You must use a clear example and refer to computer memory in your answer.

3. Look at this simple line of Python code:
        student = "Nicholas"
(a) What is the **name** of the variable?
(b) What is the **data type** of the variable?
(c) The line of code is referred to as an "**assignment statement**". Explain what this means.

4. What is the result (output) of the following lines of Python?
        student = "Nicholas"
        print(student)
        name = student
        print(name)

5. For the following assignment statements you must decide if the variable name is illegal, "good" or "bad" and give a reason - Copy and complete the table:

Assignment	Illegal, good or bad	Reason
my cat = "spots"		
a = 12		
highScore = 55		
2name = "Harman"		
the_user_input_answer = "Y"		
big!Num = 555		
maxNum = "Madrid"		

6. Python will allow the following statements but other languages, such as Java, will not:
        cat = "lucky"
        cat = 10
Suggest why these lines would be illegal in Java.

7. You are working as a programmer for the European Space Agency (ESA). The physicists ask you to write a program to calculate the orbital speed of satellites in orbit around the earth. The equation they have given you is:

orbital speed = (2 X π X radius of orbit) / time period

radius of orbit = radius of Earth (6400 km) + height of satellite above earth.

(a) Most of the data will be represented as variables, such as "heightSat". **Two** items are **constants**. Identify these items and suggest **appropriate names** and **data types** for these constants.

(b) Use this example to explain **two** advantages of using constants in computer code.

8. A program includes the following code:

```
IF K > N THEN
        K = N
        N = K
END IF
```

(a) The code uses the variables K and N, which are of data type integer. Describe what the **data type** of a variable means.

(b) State the **final values** of the variables K and N if the values at the beginning of the code are:

i) K = 6 N = 12

ii) K = 8 N = 3

(c) The intention of lines 2 and 3 (inside the IF statement) is to swap the contents of the variables K and N. This does not work.

Rewrite the code so that the contents of the variables are swapped correctly.

(Hint: You should use another variable to hold a temporary value.)

Chapter 3d Programming: Selections, Decisions and IF statements

Selection - Decisions and Branching:
Most of the time computer code is run **sequentially** that is line-after-line. But sooner or later you will want to **control the flow** of a program and **branch** off in one direction or another depending on some **condition** being true or false. Your code has to "**decide**" which way to go.

Points Covered:
- IF THEN END IF
- IF THEN ELSE END IF
- IF THEN ELSE IF .... END IF
- Extension: Case or Switch

The basic structure of a "branch condition" is:

> **IF** (condition True) **THEN**
> > Do something
>
> **ELSE** (condition False)
> > Do something else.
>
> **END IF**

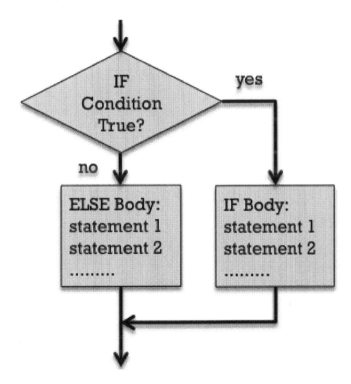

Imagine you are working on a problem where the user inputs a number from 1 to 12 representing the months of the year and your code needs to output the number of days that month has. Whatever the input there will be lots of decisions to be made:

FLOW CHART   **PSEUDOCODE & PYTHON**

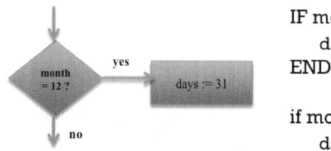

IF month = 12 THEN
    days = 31
END IF

if month == 12:
    days = 31

At first it looks like lots of **repeated IF** statements are required:

FLOW CHART   **PSEUDOCODE & PYTHON**

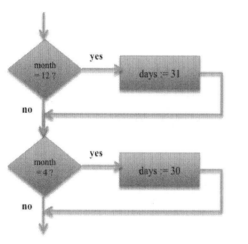

IF month = 12 THEN
    days = 31
END IF
IF month = 4 THEN
    days = 30
END IF

if month == 12:
    days = 31
if month == 4:
    days = 30

While this code works, it is inefficient. After all if I already know that the month is 12 then why do I need to ask at the next decision "is month = 4"?

This is where the **IF ... THEN ... ELSE IF** construct comes in:

| **FLOW CHART** | **PSEUDOCODE & PYTHON** |

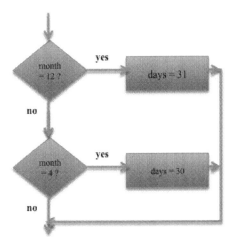

IF month = 12 THEN
    days = 31
ELSE
    IF month = 4 THEN
      days = 30
    END IF
END IF

```
if month == 12:
    days = 31
elif month == 4:
    days = 30
```

Extension: Case or Switch Statements:

Some languages can deal with multiple choices and **IF .. THEN ... ELSE IF** ... statements by considering what to do in each "case".

```
CASE month OF
        4,6,9, 11:              days = 30
        1,3,5,7,8,10,12:        days = 31
        2:                      days = 28
ELSE
        days = -99
END CASE
```

This code is fairly self-explanatory and is a neat solution. Java has a "**switch**" construct that works in a similar way. However Python does has not have either.

Mind you, although you will have to use IF .. THEN .. ELSE IF in Python, you could use structured types such as tuples or lists to make your code neater and more readable:

```
if month in (4, 6, 9, 11):
        days = 30
elif month in (1,3,5,7,8,10,12):
        days = 31
elif month == 2
        days = 28
else
        days = -99
```

(See the section on structured data)

A worked example of solving a problem with algorithms and if statements:

The Problem:

Customers can withdraw cash from an Automatic Teller Machine (ATM).

- Withdrawal refused if amount entered > current balance
- Withdrawal refused if amount entered > daily limit
- Otherwise allow withdrawal and take entered amount from the current balance

Write an algorithm, in pseudocode, which inputs a request for a sum of money and decides if a withdrawal can be made. Appropriate output messages should be included.

The beginning of a solution:

```
INPUT moneyEntered
INPUT currentBalance
INPUT dailyLimit
IF moneyEntered > currentBalance THEN
messsage
ELSE
now check daily limit
END IF
```

A complete solution soon follows:

```
INPUT moneyEntered
INPUT currentBalance
INPUT dailyLimit
IF moneyEntered > currentBalance THEN
        OUTPUT "Sorry not enough money in account"
ELSE
        IF moneyEntered > dailyLimit THEN
                OUTPUT "Sorry this will exceed your daily limit"
        ELSE
                currentBalance = currentBalance – moneyEntered
                OUTPUT "Your new balance is: ", currentBalance
        END IF
END IF
```

Logic

Conditions such as "moneyEntered > dailyLimit" evaluate to **true** or **false**. Obviously they can become more complicated using the logic operators **AND**, **OR** and **NOT**. Consider the following decisions:

Does the person get a 20% discount for the museum?
> **IF** (age < 18) **OR** (status = "student") **THEN** (discountRate = 0.20) **END IF**

What do I wear today?
> **IF** (raining) **AND** (windy) **THEN** use a raincoat
> **ELSE IF** (raining)**AND** (**NOT** windy) **THEN** use an umbrella
> **ELSE IF** (**NOT** raining) **AND** (windy) **THEN** use a jersey
> **ELSE** use a shirt only

(See the chapter on Logic Operators for more on these issues.)

Questions on Chapter 3d Selection, decisions and logic

In the following problems (1 to 4) use pseudocode, simple "IF THEN ELSE IF" statements and sensible variables names.

1. Write an algorithm for the following problem: Input a simple integer and output a "+" if it is positive a "-" if it is negative, otherwise output a "0".

2. There are 3 numbers p, q and r.
Write an algorithm that will output the smallest of the three numbers.
(Hint: Using a logical "AND" will help.)

3. To convert cat age to an equivalent human age, an accepted method is to add 15 years for the first year of life. Then add 10 years for the second year of life. After that, add 4 years for every cat year.
For example: A 4 year-old cat: 15 + 10 + (2 X 4) = 33 human years.
Write an algorithm that inputs the age of a cat (as an integer) and outputs the equivalent age in "human years" (also an integer)

4. Input a character and output if the character is lowercase, uppercase, a digit (0 -9) or none of these.
For example: Input "F" --> output "uppercase"; Input "?" --> output "none".
(Hint: You can compare characters using simple relational operators.
So "f" <= "z" is true. You will also need a logical "AND")

5. A shop has a special sale. Any books have a 10% discount while clothes have a 20% discount. Both of the following code extracts do the same job.

<table>
<tr><th>A</th><th>B</th></tr>
</table>

```
A                                          B
IF   itemType = "Books"  THEN              IF   itemType = "Books"  THEN
     itemCost = pCost * 0.9                     itemCost = pCost * 0.9
END IF                                     ELSE IF  itemType = "Clothes"  THEN
IF   itemType = "Clothes"  THEN                 itemCost = pCost * 0.80
     itemCost = pCost * 0.80               END IF
END IF
```

Explain which is the most efficient.

6. A student wants to change his password for his phone. A program in his phone does the following checks to see if the password is suitable:
 - Length must be between 8 and 15 characters
 - There must be at least one uppercase character
 - There must be at least one digit (0-9)

If any of these checks fails the program outputs a suitable error and stops.
Only if all of the checks pass is the new password accepted.
Draw a **flowchart** using "decision boxes" to show how this program works.

Chapter 3e Programming: Loops and Repetitions (Iterations)

Loops: **IF THEN ELSE** statements are one way that the **sequential flow** of a program is changed. Another fundamental way is to repeat an action many times. **A loop is a sequence of instructions that is continually repeated** until a certain condition is satisfied. **Iteration** is the formal name for repeating a process. Each repetition is called an iteration. You can say "iterating over" or "looping over" a list, for example.

Points Covered:
- **WHILE** loops - "condition controlled"
- **REPEAT .... UNTIL** loops
- **FOR** loops - "count controlled"

WHILE loops: A while loop is a control flow statement that allows a block of code to be executed repeatedly based on a given Boolean condition. Note that:
- The condition (which must evaluate to True or False) is tested **before** the block is executed.
  - So if the condition is not true at the beginning then the block of code is not executed at all.
- Once in the block of code there must be something that changes the condition.
  - Otherwise the loop will go on forever - an **infinite loop**.

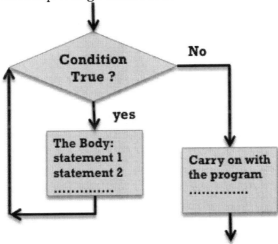

Example: A teacher wants to enter the grades of her students to find the maximum mark. But she doesn't know beforehand how many students there are in each class. Her solution is to repeat the code that enters a mark and checks that mark against the maximum mark so far, until the mark is -99. No one can actually score -99. It is a "dummy" or **"terminator"** value. Of course if the first mark she enters is -99 then the block of code inside the while loop is never run.

Pseudocode:

```
INPUT num
WHILE NOT num = -99 DO
        IF num > max THEN
                max = num
        END IF
        INPUT num
END WHILE
OUTPUT max
```

Flowchart:

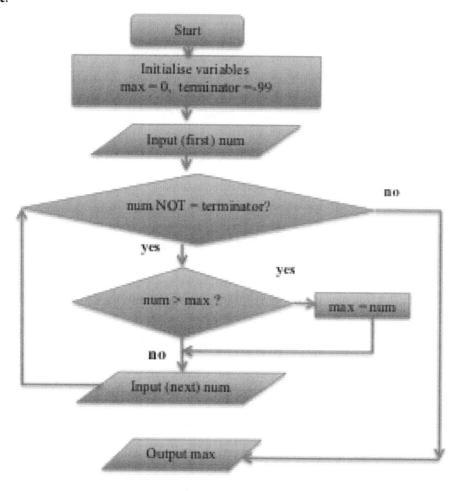

In summary: A while loop is run 0, 1 or many times - "while a condition is true" - and the condition is tested at the start of the loop.

Infinite loops: If the "entry condition" is always true - you can enter but never leave!

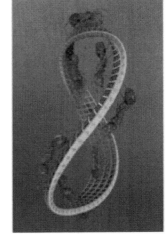

```
x = 1
WHILE x < 10 DO
    print(x)
    x = x – 1
END WHILE
```

What's wrong?

Usually infinite loops should be avoided! Make sure the code inside the loop can correctly change the condition so that it will be false and so leave the loop.

Repeat (Until): Some programming languages (not Python) have what is sometimes called a "post-conditional" loop. This kind of loop is very similar to a while loop but:

- The block of code inside the loop is executed then the "exit condition" is tested.
- As a result the loop must be done at least one time.

Pseudocode:

```
REPEAT
        INPUT num
        IF num > max THEN
                max = num
        END IF
UNTIL num = -99
```

Flowchart:

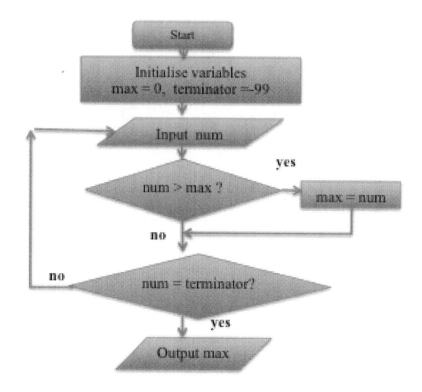

Python:

Although there is no direct equivalent of a repeat until loop in Python, it is easy enough to use a while loop where the "entry condition" is guaranteed to be true:

```python
maxNum = 0
finished = False
while not(finished):
    num = int(input("Number please. "))
    if num > maxNum:
        maxNum = num
    finished = (num == -99)
#end while ................
print("Max num was: ", maxNum)
```

Which, of course, means the loop must be done one time and the loop does indeed "repeat until finished".

FOR loops:

A for loop is used to repeat a section of code a **known** number of times. How many times a while loop is done is not "known" before the code is run. For loops are for when you do know how many times to do the loop before you enter the loop. As a simple introduction: Imagine you want to print out 0, 1, 2, 3, 4 ... Compare:

While loop	**For loop**
count = 0	FOR count FROM 0 to 4 DO
WHILE count < 5 DO	print (count)
print (count)	END FOR
count = count + 1	
END WHILE	

Note how much easier the for loop is. The variable, count, increments (goes up by one) each time automatically.

Example: That same teacher wants to enter the grades of her students to find the maximum mark. But this time she **knows** there are 4 students in the class:

Pseudocode:

```
FOR count FROM 1 TO 4 DO
        INPUT num
        IF num > max THEN
                max = num
        END IF
END FOR
OUTPUT max
```

This loop will execute exactly 4 times. The variable count (which could be any name) is incremented (count = count + 1) automatically at each iteration (loop).

Flowchart:

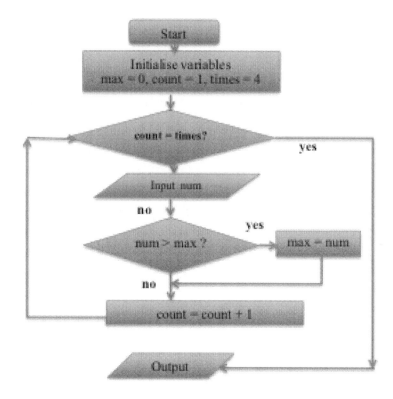

Counting in steps: For loops don't have to increment the counter by 1. You can "count up" (or "down" for that matter) in "jumps" or steps.

Example: Print out the sequence 6, 11, 16, 21, 26
      FOR count **FROM** 6 **TO** 26 **STEP** 5 **DO**
         OUTPUT count
      END FOR

Example: Print out "count down", 10, 9, 8, 7, 6, 5, 4, 3, 2, 1, 0
      FOR count **FROM** 10 **TO** 0 **STEP** -1 **DO**
         OUTPUT count
      END FOR

Python:
For loops in Python are "**iterator**" based loops using the **range()** function.

Example: Print out the first 10 denary digits.
      for count **in range**(10):
         print(count, end=" ")   #end just puts a space instead of a newline
This code outputs (prints): 0 1 2 3 4 5 6 7 8 9

The **range()** function is an "**iterator**" which generates the next number in a sequence. Simply put, it is as if **range(10)** generates the sequence [0, 1, 2, 3, 4, 5, 6, 7, 8, 9]. So in the first iteration of the loop the variable count gets 0, then, in the next iteration count gets 1, then count gets 2. And so on all the way up to **but not including** 10.

If you give the **range()** function three values, say range(6, 27, 5) then the first number is the "starting point", the second number is the "ending point" and the third number is the "step value": **range(start, stop, step).**

Example: Print out the sequence 6, 11, 16, 21, 26
> **for** count **in range**(6, 26, 5):
>> **print**(count, end=" ")

Whoops! This only prints out the sequence: 6 11 16 21
Remember in Python the range() function "counts" up to **but not including** the "stop". If you want to print the sequence 6, 11, 16, 21, 26 then your "stop" needs to be "one more", 27:
> **for** count **in range**(6, 27, 5):

Sometimes it is the computer that "knows" how many times, not you, but it is still known.
For example: myStudents = [5, 7, 5, 9, 8, 6, 5, 6, 5, 3].
The length of the list can be found out which tells us how many students there are. Each student can be accessed using its index in the list. (Remember lists "start" at 0 and so the last element is length - 1. See the section on data structures.)
> **FOR** i **FROM** 0 to length(myList)-1 **DO**
>> num = myList[i]
>> **IF** num > max **THEN**
>>> max = num
>> **END IF**
> **END FOR**
> **OUTPUT** max

This loop will execute exactly the number of times there are students in the list.
Note: The "counter variable" can be called anything. In this case it is called "i". Perhaps "index" would have been a better name? Possibly yes, but "i" and "j" are commonly used variable names for **indexes** to access arrays and lists.

For Each loop:
As you can see from the last example, iterating over ("looping along") an **array** or a **list** of elements is just what for loops do really well. The **for each** loop is even simpler for doing something to elements in a list.
The same example - a list of students: myStudents = [5, 7, 5, 9, 8, 6, 5, 6, 5, 3]:
> **FOR EACH** num **FROM** myStudents **DO**
>> **IF** num > max **THEN**
>>> max = num
>> **END IF**
> **END FOR EACH**
> **OUTPUT** max

Note that the index, or position, of the element in the list is not directly used. This kind of for loop reads as: "FOR each item in the list, one-by-one, DO something." The elements in the array don't have to be numbers!

Example: rainbow = ["red", "orange", "yellow", "green", "blue", "indigo", "violet"]
The problem is to print out all the colours, which have less than 6 letters:

   FOR EACH colour **FROM** rainbow **DO**
     IF LENGTH(colour) < 6 **THEN**
       OUTPUT colour
     END IF
   END FOR EACH

This will print out: red, green, blue.

Note that the **for each loop** can iterate over any **sequence** - not just arrays or lists. A string, for example, is a sequence of characters:
Example: Print out your name with a * between each letter.

   FOR EACH letter **FROM** "Nicholas" **DO**
     PRINT letter, "*"
   END FOR EACH

This will print out: N*i*c*h*o*l*a*s*.

Python: In both of the above cases Python is even simpler. Python just relies on the keyword "**in**":

```
rainbow = ["red", "orange", "yellow", "green", "blue", "indigo", "violet"]
for colour in rainbow:
  if len(colour) < 6:
    print(colour, end=",")
print()

for letter in "Nicholas":
  print(letter, end= "*")
```

Which results in the following output:
   red,green,blue,
   N*i*c*h*o*l*a*s*

Questions on Chapter 3e Loops and Repetitions:

1. Algorithms and programs use loops to control the number of times a particular procedure is used.
Two methods are "**WHILE** condition **DO**" and "**FOR** count **FROM .. TO ... DO**".
(a) Write pseudocode using both these loop methods to input 20 numbers and find the total. At each iteration a number should be input into a variable. Then this number should be used to add to another variable, which keeps a running total.
         (i) **WHILE** condition **DO**   (ii) **FOR** count **FROM .. TO ... DO**
(b) Which of these two loops is most appropriate for this task and explain your reasons.
(**Extension**: Re-write your pseudocode so that your algorithm can calculate and output the average of the numbers input.)

2. Maria uses Internet banking. She uses a 4-digit PIN. (Personal Identification Number). When she logs on to the bank's website, she needs to input the whole PIN.
The following code has been written to check that the PIN is a 4 digit integer:

```
count = 0
INPUT pinCode
num = pinCode
REPEAT
        num = num DIV 10
        count = count + 1
UNTIL num < 1
IF count < 4 THEN
        PRINT "PIN entered is too short"
ELSE
        PRINT "PIN OK"
ENDIF
```

(a) What would be the output message and the value of count if the following PINs were entered?
        i. 6778   ii. 567   iii. 67784

(b) Use your answers in (a) to look for a logical error in the program. You will need to re-write the IF statements at the end of the code to correct this error.

(c) Suggest why the pinCode is first "copied into" the variable num.

(**Extension**: Re-write the entire (corrected) code using a WHILE loop instead of a REPEAT loop.)

3. Write a routine in pseudocode using a **FOR** count **FROM .. TO ... DO** loop, which inputs 100 numbers and outputs how many of the numbers were negative.

4. A motorway warning sign can show a flashing (repeating) message of up to 30 characters.

For example:

ICE ON ROAD DRIVE SLOWLY

Write an algorithm in pseudocode which:

- The user inputs the message and the number of times to print (flash or repeat) the message.
- If the message input is longer than 30 characters
  - A suitable error message should be printed and the code stops.
- You may assume that the warning sign has the following commands that can be used in your code:
  - WipeScreen (cleans the screen of all text)
  - Wait (num of secs) (Example: Wait(10))

You may use any form of pseudocode as long as your meaning is clear. You will not lose any marks for "syntax errors". Use sensible, clear variable names.

Chapter 3f Programming: Data Structures

Points Covered:
Moving on from "simple" variables and their data types such as "integer" or "float", this chapter looks at more complex ways of storing, organising and accessing data. For most, non-trivial, programming problems one of the first and most important decisions will be **"what data structure will I use to hold the data?"**.

	0	1	2	3	4
0	A	N	N	A	
1	S	T	E	V	E
2					
3	C	R	A	I	G
4					

Much of the way the program then works will depend on that choice.

Points Covered:
- Strings
- Arrays
- Python: Lists & Tuples
- 1D and 2D arrays
- Records & Python Dictionaries

Strings: On the face of it a string is a simple data type. It just represents text rather than numbers. Here the **variable** welcome is **assigned** the string value of "Hello":

    welcome = "Hello"

Going a little bit deeper we can say that a string is a **sequence** of **characters**. So, obviously, each character has a position given by its **index**.

Note: Most programming languages will have lots of ways to access and manipulate strings. Much of what follows uses Python code as examples but the principles would be the same in most other programming languages.

String Manipulation: Indexing

```
Hello
0   1   2   3   4
-5  -4  -3  -2  -1
```

Note how strings (like arrays and lists) start with the index 0, counting from left to right. You can also start from the end of the string (index -1) and count backwards.

welcome[0] --> "H"   welcome[3] --> "l" and welcome[-1] --> "o"

Be careful though:

welcome[5] --> IndexError: string index out of range

Length: "How long is a piece of string" may be a silly question but knowing the length of a string is very useful: **len**(welcome) --> 5

But be careful the last character is at index position 4 not 5.

String Manipulation: Slicing

Strings can also be "broken up" into shorter strings by being sliced:

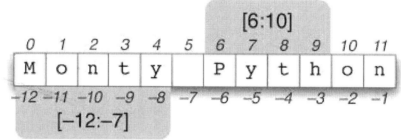

word = "Monty Python"

print (word[6:10]) --> Pyth

This has **sliced** from the character at index 6 up to but **not including** the character at index 10.

You won't be slicing using negative indices very often, but you can if you like:

print (word[-12:-7]) --> Monty

String Manipulation: Concatenating

You can produce **new strings** by concatenating ("sticking together") other strings.

name = 'Charles' + ' ' + 'Darwin'   #Note adding a space " "

print (name) --> Charles Darwin

String Manipulation: Summary

There are many other ways to change strings, all of which you will find useful in your practical programming. Here's a summary of some of the string manipulation functions that come with Python:

method	syntax	result
upper()	word = "parrot".upper()	"PARROT"
lower()	word = "DeaD".lower()	"dead"
capitalize()	word = "dead parrot".capitalize()	"Dead parrot"
title()	word = "dead parrot".title()	"Dead Parrot"
strip()	word = " dead parrot ".strip()	"dead parrot"
isupper()	"DEAD".isupper()	TRUE
isupper()	"dead".isupper()	FALSE
islower()	"Dead".islower()	FALSE
islower()	"dead".islower()	TRUE
slicing [:]	word = "dead parrot" copy = word[:]	a complete copy of the string is made
	word = "dead parrot" copy = word	word & copy now just point to same string

Iterating over strings using a for loop:

As strings are sequences (just like arrays & lists) it is very easy to "loop along a string."

```
        name = 'Darwin'
        for letter in name:          # FOR EACH letter FROM name DO
            print (letter, end= "*")     --> D*a*r*w*i*n
```

This may not seem very useful but the principle of using a FOR loop to iterate over string, arrays or lists is very powerful and you will use it a lot in your practical programming.

Example: Input a message as a string and print out a new string of the message with no vowels:

```
message = input("Type a message please: ")
print("The message with vowels is:", message)
new_message = ""              #Initialise with empty string ""
VOWELS = "aeiou"              #A CONSTANT ... this will not change
#Begin for loop ----------------------------------------------
for letter in message:                  #FOR EACH letter FROM message DO
    #Begin IF THEN -----------------
    if letter.lower() not in VOWELS:
        #concatenates new_message + letter creating a new string
        new_message = new_message + letter
    #END IF ----------------------
#END for loop ------------------------------------------------
print("The message without vowels is:", new_message)
```

Which results in:

```
Type a message please: Love minus zero no limit
The message with vowels is: Love minus zero no limit
The message without vowels is: Lv mns zr n lmt
```

Extension (An advanced topic): Strings are immutable.
In simple terms this means that while you can make "new" strings by manipulating "old" strings you **cannot** actually change a string.

```
name = 'Darwin'
name[0] = 'C'
```

TypeError: 'str' object does not support item assignment
String **immutability** is also illustrated when you assign different variables to the same string.

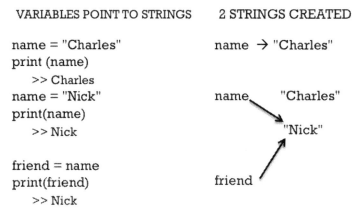

VARIABLES POINT TO STRINGS	2 STRINGS CREATED

name = "Charles"
print (name)
    >> Charles
name = "Nick"
print(name)
    >> Nick
 	
friend = name
print(friend)
    >> Nick
	name → "Charles"
	
	name "Charles"
	
	        "Nick"
	
	friend

Arrays and Lists:

Arrays: "A group of data items of the **same data type** that is stored under **one name** in contiguous (one after another) memory locations."   Note how this definition "fits" strings too as a sequence of "data items" of the same data type ("character").

Problem: Say you want to store the exam results of 20 students and find the average mark. You could create 20 variables:

>   mark1 = 55
>   mark2 = 56
>   mark3 = 80

I suppose it's OK for a few marks but 100 or 2000 marks!!

Solution:

Declare an array (by setting up memory locations) to hold 20 marks of type integer. Note arrays start at "0" not "1":

>   marks: **ARRAY** [0..19] **OF INTEGER**

Assign values by using the name of the array and an **index** to find the correct memory location.

marks[3] = 34

marks: array[0..19] of **integer**

Index	0	1	2	3	4	5	6	7	8	9	10	11	12	13	14	15	16	17	18	19
Value	55	56	80	34	76	89	70	34	55	67	78	69	59	30	67	66	98	67	56	45

marks[3]

Access values by using the name of the array and the **index**:

>   **PRINT**("2nd in the array is: ", marks[1])   --> 56

Manipulate: As we saw in the section on repetitions, **FOR loops** are "made" to work with structured data types like arrays.

>   **FOR** index **FROM** 0 **TO** 19 **DO**
>   total = total + marks[index]
>   **END FOR**
>   averageMark = total / 20

Problem: I want to record the names of my 20 students and be able to print their names in alphabetical order.

Solution:

Declare an array to hold 20 names of type string.

        studNames: **ARRAY**[0..19] **OF STRING**

Assign values using the name of the array and the index:

        studNames[0] = "Nick", studNames[1] = "Sally", studNames[2] = "Dave" .. etc.

Manipulate:

        studNames.**SORT**()

        FOR EACH student **FROM** studNames **DO**

            print student

        END FOR

Python: Lists

Lists can do everything that arrays can and much more!

A list can be thought of as an array that **automatically adjusts its size** as elements are added and removed

Most lists can only hold one type

        scores = [3, 7, 9] or names =["Nick", "Maria", "Sam"]

Python lists can hold different types

        nameNum = ["Nick", 3, "Maria", 7, "Sam", 9]

Lists are **mutable** – They can change!

        inventory = ["pen", "sword","iPhone"]

        inventory[0] = "pistol"   #change item 0   --> ["pistol", "sword","iPhone"]

Arrays are fixed in length. Lists are dynamic. They can get bigger & smaller.

        del inventory[2] # delete item at position 2   --> ["pistol","sword"]

List Methods - Useful functions to use with lists (Python)

Method	Description
append(value)	Adds value to end of a list.
sort()	Sorts the elements, smallest value first.
reverse()	Reverses the order of a list.
count(value)	Returns the number of occurrences of value.
index(value)	Returns the first position number of where value occurs.
insert(i, value)	Inserts value at position i.
pop([i])	Returns value at position i and removes value from the list. Providing the position number i is optional. Without it, the last element in the list is removed and returned.
remove(value)	Removes the first occurrence of value from the list.

Note: Any language that supports lists will have will similar functionality.

Extension: Arrays or Lists?
A Python list is such a versatile data structure that you really won't miss not having arrays. In languages where you have a straight choice which one do you chose?

Arrays are fixed in size at declaration. This can make accessing them very fast as they already have their memory locations allocated. On the other hand if you find your array is not big enough there is no way to make it bigger halfway through a program. So you will probably declare an array to be a little bigger than you really need. This in turn means a small waste of memory for the "cells" that you never use.

Lists are dynamic. They can "expand" and "contract" as you go along. In principle this should make them use memory more efficiently. It certainly makes them easy to use and very flexible. On the other hand this flexibility also means that memory cannot be allocated to a list at the beginning and this could slow access down.

So, in simple terms: An array is probably clearer and more efficient if you know how many elements you are going to deal with and that number is not going to change. If your data is dynamic and unpredictable in nature then perhaps a list is best.

Extension: Python Tuples
Python also supports a kind of "fixed" or "unchangeable list" called a tuple.
>   months = ('Jan', 'Feb', 'Mar', 'Apr', 'May', 'Jun', 'Jul', 'Aug', 'Sep', 'Oct', 'Nov', 'Dec')
Note that the only obvious difference is the use of ( ) rather than [ ].
Data is accessed from tuples in exactly the same way as for lists:
>   months[0] --> 'Jan'   months[1:3] --> 'Feb', 'Mar'
But Tuples are **immutable** – They cannot change:
>   cols = ("red","green","blue")
>   cols[0] = "black"--> TypeError: 'tuple' object does not support item assignment
Tuples' **immutablity** makes them perfect for **constants** since they can't change:
>   yesAnswers = ("Yes", "yes", "y")
This "fixed list" of replies is assigned at the beginning of the program. It is not possible to change it but it is perfect for validation checks such as:
>   **if** response **in** yesAnswers:
>   **print**("Continue")
So, although most of the time Python lists are just what you need, do consider using tuples for constants.

1 dimensional and 2 dimensional arrays

1 Dimensional Arrays: These are the arrays we have seen so far. You just set up the array by declaring its length and data type. The following pseudocode declares an array of 5 elements of type integer. It then iterates over the array filling it with "1s":

>marks : **ARRAY[0..4]OF INTEGER**
>**FOR** i = 0 **TO** 4 **DO**
>>marks[i] = 1
>
>**END FOR**

This results in: [1, 1, 1, 1, 1]

2 Dimensional Arrays: These are used to set up simple tables made up of rows and columns. For example I have the marks of 9 students entered in a table or grid.

>students = [[10, 20, 45], [42, 79, 81], [89, 9, 36]]

In effect this is a "**nested array**". Each element in the array is now an array in itself.
If I just rearrange it slightly, you should see that this is like a table of data.

>students = [[10, 20, 45],
>>[42, 79, 81],
>>[89, 9, 36]]

arr	col[0]	col[1]	col[2]
row[0]	10	20	45
row[1]	42	79	81
row[2]	89	9	36

2D Array Arrangement

Accessing a a 2D array with one index. Remember each element is now an array so:

>students[0]   --> [10, 20, 45]
>students[1]   --> [42, 79, 81]

Accessing a 2D array using two indexes - one for the "row" and one for the "column":
students [row][col]

>students[0][2]   --> 45
>students[1][1]   --> 79

Note: We want a 2D array so all the rows MUST have the same number of elements. You should **not** do this:

>students = [[10, 45], [42, 79, 81], [9]]

Problem: As a war game designer you need to know how many soldiers are at a particular location. Set up a table or "matrix" with 4 rows and 5 columns. Each position or "cell" in the table holds an integer. This will represent the number of soldiers to be found at that position on the board.

Declare (create or set up) the array of 4 rows X 5 columns:

      board: **ARRAY** [0..3][0..4] **OF INTEGER**

Initialise the 2D array with "0". Note the use of **2 "nested" FOR loops** to do this task:

      FOR row = 0 **TO** 3 **DO**

           FOR col = 0 **TO** 4 **DO**

                  board [row] [col] = 0

           END FOR

      END FOR

This results in: [[0,0,0,0,0], [0,0,0,0,0], [0,0, 0,0,0], [0,0,0,0,0]

		Column numbers			
	0	**1**	**2**	**3**	**4**
0	0	0	0	0	0
1	0	0	0	0	0
2	0	0	0	0	0
3	0	0	0	0	0

Row numbers

Assign 15 soldiers to the cell at the 3rd row 2nd column: board[2][1] = 15

		Column numbers			
	0	**1**	**2**	**3**	**4**
0	0	0	0	0	0
1	0	0	0	0	0
2	0	15	0	0	0
3	0	0	0	0	0

Row numbers

Python 1D and 2D Lists:

1 D Lists:

In Python lists there is no real declaration stage so lines like this don't exist:

      marks : array[0..4]**OF INTEGER**

But what if you do **want** to set up a list of a set length and initialise that list?

      marks = [ ]

        for i **in range**(5):

          marks[i] = 1   --> IndexError: list index out of range.

You can't assign to a list element that doesn't exist! You could do this.

      marks.**append**(1)

But it would be nice if we could state the size & contents of a list just like an array. This is where something called "**Comprehensions**" come in.

A comprehension specifies a sequence of values in Python. It is a bit like a compact for loop that generates a list:

      [expression   **for**   variable   **in**   list]

Example1: Initialise a 10-element list with 0
   myList = [0 **for** i **in range**(10)]   --> Results in: [0, 0, 0, 0, 0, 0, 0, 0, 0, 0]
So "i" (index) counts 0, 1, 2 .... 9 and 0 is put in for each element.

Example2: Initialise a 10-element list with 0, 1, ... 9
   myList = [i **for** i **in range**(10)]   --> Results in: [0, 1, 2, 3, 4, 5, 6, 7, 8, 9]

Example3: Initialise a 5-element list with square numbers .. 0, 1, 4, 9, 16
   myList = [i*i **for** i **in range**(5)]   --> Results in: [0, 1, 4, 9, 16,]

2 D Lists:
These kinds of structures (tables or matrices) are, in effect, **nested lists**.
Lists of lists – a nested list:
      dayMonths = [[ ], [ ], [ ], [ ], [ ], [ ]]
      dayMonths = [["Jan", 31], ["Feb", 28], ["Mar", 31], ["April",30]]
Accessing data in nested lists:
      print(dayMonths[1])   --> ["Feb",28]
      print(dayMonths[3])   --> ["April", 30]
      print(dayMonths[3][0])   --> April
      print(dayMonths[3][1])   --> 30
Unpacking nested lists:
      month = dayMonths[1][0]
      print(month)   --> Feb
      days = dayMonths[1][1]
      print(days)   --> 28
Unpacking a nested list in one line:
      month, days = dayMonths[1]
Appending a list to a nested list:
      newMonth = ["May", 30]
      dayMonths.**append**(newMonth)

To "set up" a table or a matrix there is even a kind of "nested comprehension" which does the job in Python:

Example 1: To create a 3 X 3 matrix.
      students = [[0 **for** j **in range**(3)] **for** i **in range**(3)]
The inner comprehension, [0 **for** j **in range**(3)], creates a row:
      [0, 0, 0]
While the outer comprehension, [.... **for** i **in range**(3)], creates a list of rows:
      [[0, 0, 0], [0, 0, 0], [0, 0, 0]]

Example 2: To make a 2D array of say: 6 Rows X 3 Columns
      myTable = [[0 **for** col **in range**(3)] **for** row **in range**(6)]

Example 3: To repeat the array example of a table with 4 rows and 5 columns where each position or "cell" in the table holds a number of soldiers in a board game:

Declare (create or set up) the array of 4 rows X 5 columns:
Array declaration: board: **array** [0..3][0..4] **of integer**
Python comprehension: board = [[0 **for** col **in range**(5)] **for** row **in range**(4)]
This results in: [[0,0,0,0,0], [0,0,0,0,0], [0,0, 0,0,0], [0,0,0,0,0]]

Accessing a particular "cell" or position in the table is just the same as using arrays:
Assign 15 soldiers to the cell at the 3rd row 2nd column: board[2][1] = 15

Column numbers

	0	1	2	3	4
0	0	0	0	0	0
1	0	0	0	0	0
2	0	15	0	0	0
3	0	0	0	0	0

Row numbers

Example 4: Digital Images are really just two-dimensional arrays (See the chapter on Images and Pixels). For example a picture with dimensions of 30 X 20 pixels and a colour depth of 2 bits (3 : Black, 2 : Dark Grey, 1 : Light Grey, 0 : White) and there are 20 rows by 30 columns of numbers!
Array declaration: housePic: **array** [0..19][0..29] **of integer**
Python comprehension: housePic = [[0 **for** col **in range**(30)] **for** row **in range**(20)]
For example row 10 may look like:
    [1,3,2,3,2,3,3,2,3,1,0,0,0,0,0,0,0,3,3,3,3,3,3,3,3,3,3,3,0]

Problem: Make every pixel "one" darker, unless it is already black and then leave it alone:
        for row **in range**(20)
            for col = **in range**(30)
                colourValue = housePic[row][col]
            if (colourValue != 3) #colour value not equal to black or 3
                housePic[row][col] = colourValue + 1
            #end for ....
        #end for ....
Suddenly the whole image, pixel-by-pixel, becomes darker.   Now you know how "PhotoShop" works!!

Records:
As you will see in the section on **databases**, sometimes data is structured in such a way that it resembles a "card" or "record" for each item. For example a record for one book may look like this:

Field	Example	Data Type
Author:	Richard Dawkins	String
Title:	The Magic of Reality	String
Number of Pages:	270	Integer

A record is a collection of fields each of which has its own data type. Like Python lists but unlike "standard" arrays these data types can be different.
- **Arrays**: All the data values have the same type and are processed in the same way
- **Records**: The collection of data values can have different types and can be processed in different ways.

Here is a, simplified, example from the programming language Pascal:

       Books = **Record**
            authorName : String;
            title : String;
            numPages : integer;
       End;

You could then declare a variable to be of this type:

       Var myBook : Books;

Here's the above book being created:

       myBook.authorName = "Richard Dawkins";
       myBook.title = "The Magic of Reality";
       myBook.numPages = 270;

Neither Python nor Java have simple record types. In these languages the logical way to represent records would be **objects** and the **fields** that describe them. Object Orientated Programming is outside the scope of this book but the chapter 6a on **databases** show how structured data is stored and processed.

Python Dictionaries - as a simple alternative to records
Python lists could be used to store records:

       Books = [["Richard Dawkins", "The Magic of Reality", 270],
       ["Catch 22", "Joseph Heller", 500], ["Richard Dawkins", "Selfish Gene", 250] ....]

But it will be tricky accessing data and the structure doesn't really have a way of showing the "uniqueness" of each book. (See chapter 6a and key fields). Python dictionaries, on the other hand, offer a quick, easy to use, solution:

       Books = {"B1" : ["Richard Dawkins", "The Magic of Reality", 270],
       "B2" : ["Catch 22", "Joseph Heller", 500],
       "B3" : ["Richard Dawkins", "Selfish Gene", 250], ... }

Adding a book is easy enough: Books["B4"] = ["Philip Kerr", "Berlin Noir", 300], and processing is pretty straightforward too:

```
#This will print the title of all books with less than 500 pages.
    for book in Books:
        if (Books[book][2 ]<500) :
            print(Books[book][1])
```

Dictionaries are like lists but accessed with a **unique key** instead of an index number.

Example: Store the 4 bases of a DNA molecule with their one letter "code" which can be used to "look up" the full name:

    dnaDict = {"A" : "Adenine", "T" : "Thymine", "G" : "Guanine", "C" : "Cytosine"}

Note the following:
- Dictionaries use { } rather than [ ] brackets;
- Each item in the dictionary is a unique key followed by its value: "A" : "Adenine".
- The unique key is used to "look up" its value - just like looking up the definition of a word in a real dictionary.
    - dnaDict["A"] returns "Adenine"; dnaDict["G"] returns "Guanine"

Here are some other examples of using dictionaries compared to using lists. In each case you can see that using a dictionary is very useful when:
- The data has some kind of unique key that "maps" onto a value;
- You want to quickly "look up" a value using its key.

Example: A telephone contact book:

List	Dictionary
pList = [['Alice', '2341'], ['Beth','9102'], ['Cecil', '3258']]	pDict = {'Alice': '2341', 'Beth': '9102', 'Cecil': '3258'}

```
List
pList = [['Alice', '2341'], ['Beth','9102'],
[ 'Cecil', '3258']]
person = input("Whose number?")
found = False
for i in range(len(pList)):
    if pList[i][0] == person:
        found = True
        index = i
if found:
    phoneNum = pList[index][1]
else:
    print("Not in phone book")
```

```
Dictionary
pDict = {'Alice': '2341', 'Beth': '9102',
'Cecil': '3258}
person = input("Whose number? ")
if person in pDict:
    phoneNum= pDict[person]
else:
    print("Not in phone book")
```

Note how easy it is to check if someone is in the "contact book" or not:
if person **in** pDict:

Example: A teacher's mark book where each student has one grade.

<table>
<tr><td align="center">**List**</td><td align="center">**Dictionary**</td></tr>
</table>

List

```
markBook = [['Alice', 7], ['Beth',6],
[ 'Cecil', 9]]

person = input("Whose mark?")
found = False
for i in range(len(markBook)):
    if markBook[i][0] == person:
        found = True
        index = i
if found:
    mark = markBook[index][1]
else:
    print("Not in mark book")
```

Dictionary

```
markBook = {'Alice': 7, 'Beth': 6, 'Cecil': 9}
person = input("Whose mark? ")
if person in markBook:
    mark= markBook[person]
else:
    print("Not in mark book")
```

Note that in this last example it would be easy to implement each student having a list of grades:

```
markBook = {'Alice': [7,6,7,8,5],  'Beth': [6, 5, 6,7,8] , 'Cecil': [9, 8, 8, 9, 7]}
```

Now to find Alice's 4th mark (index position in list being 3):

```
markBook["Alice"][3]  --> 8
```

Questions on Chapter 3f Data Structures:

Strings: sequences of characters:
1.   (a) What does the following code output?
(Remember sequences start at 0 and " " spaces are characters too!)
>   sent = "Play the song"
>   **print**(sent[0],sent[3],sent[5],sent[6],sent[10],sent[11])
>   (b) A student wants to change the first letter of the string to "F"
>   sent[0] = "F"   Explain why this line is not allowed.

2.   (a) What will you see on the screen after the following lines have been run?
>   outString = "Just" + "Do" + "It!"
>   **print**(outString)
>   (b)What is the technical word for "joining strings together" like this?

 3. Loops – looping over (iterating over) strings ...... For Loops
What will the following code fragments output?
(a)   word = "cool"
>   **FOR EACH** letter **FROM** word **DO**
>   print(letter, end="*")
>   **END FOR EACH**

....

(b)   phrase = "Cool cats out on town"
>   search = "o"
>   sCount = 0
>   **FOR** i **FROM** 0 **TO** (len(phrase)-1 **DO**
>   **IF** word[i] = = search **THEN**
>   sCount = sCount + 1
>   **END IF**
>   **END FOR**
>   **print**(search, "appeared ", sCount, " times.")

....

Arrays: Sequences of data items in contiguous memory locations

1. The program in a vending machine uses an array called Coins to store the value in cents of all the coins that have been entered in the current sale.

After each sale, the array is reset so that all values are 0.

Here is an example of the contents of the array Coins during a sale

Coins

10	100	20	50	0	0	0	0	0	0

In the example above, the value of Coins[0] is 10.

(a) State the value of: Coins[3] and Coins[9]

(b) An algorithm to reset the contents of the array Coins after each sale is show below.

```
index = 0
WHILE index < 10 DO
            Coins[index] = 0
            index = index + 1
END WHILE
```

A better way to "iterate over an array" is to use a FOR loop.

(i) Re-write the above algorithm with a FOR loop.

(ii)Explain why a FOR loop is better suited to this task than a REPEAT loop.

2. The following **pseudocode** fragments are meant to find the average mark of 5 students in a physics exam and compare their average grade to a national average grade.

Firstly the five results are input, in order, into the array: 33, 45, 27, 70, 67

```
results : array [0..4] of integer
FOR index = 0 TO 4 DO
            results[index] = INPUT (nextNum)
END FOR
```

Two results were wrong and are now entered manually:

```
results[1] = 53                  results[4] = 80
```

(a) Copy and fill in the table below to illustrate how the array looks now:

Index	0	1	2	3	4
Contents					

(b)What would be output to the screen with the following code? **print**(results[2])

(c) The remaining code implements the requirements to find the average mark and to compare this to the national average (NATAV).

 i. Copy out the code and complete any missing code shown by ....

 ii. Correct any runtime errors (that is errors that could cause the code to crash when it is run).

#The following lines declare and initialise the variables used:

```
CONST ............        NATAV = 62.5
Var    ............       total = 0.0
Var    float             average = 0.0
Var    ............       betterAv = False
```

#The following lines calculate the total grade of all five students

```
FOR    count  = 1 TO 5 DO
            total = total  + results[.................]
END FOR
average = ................................................
IF average > NATAV THEN
                betterAv = True
    .................
                betterAv = False
ENDIF
```

(d) Explain why the following line of code is not correct and should not be allowed:

```
NATAV = average
```

Python List exercises

1. A list is a data structure that stores a set of elements. Lists are assigned to a name using square brackets.

```
mylist=["apple","oranges","lemon","pear","lime"]
```

apples	oranges	lemon	pear	lime
0	1	2	3	4

- Each element in a list has an index location. The first element of the list is in position zero (0).
- Elements of a list are referenced using their index location (an integer number). List name[index]. For example:
  - myList[4] displays "lime"
- A range of elements can be displayed using [start index: end index]
- Start index is the position to start at. End is the position up to but NOT including End.
  - myList[2:4] displays "lemon", "Pear"

(a) What values do the following list references refer to? (Be careful one is an error!)

     i. mylist[1]
     ii. mylist[1:3]
     iii. myList[5]

(b) What list reference will refer to?

     i. "apple"
     ii. "oranges", "lemon" and "pear"

(c) What does len(myList) return?

2. Python lists can hold different data types. Here is a list holding the name and grades in various subjects for a student called Amy Jones.

studMarks = ['Amy', 'Jones', 'English', 67, 'Maths', 76, 'Computer Science', 96]

(a) Write down the code needed to do the following tasks:

i. The English teacher has entered Amy's mark incorrectly; it should be 72 not 67. Alter this item in the list.

ii. Add the mark for Physics to the end of the list. "Physics", 65

iii. Remove "Maths" and the score 76 from the list.

(b) Write a program to find the average score for the three remaining subjects (English, Computer Science and Physics).

3. Here is a list of strings holding the names of some animals:

animals = ["cat", "dog", "horse", "donkey", "rabbit"]

(a) What does **len**(animals) return?

(b) What does **print**(animals[2:5]) display?

(c) Write the code to add "canary" to the end of the list.

(d) Write a program that will print out the names of the animals that begin with the character 'd'. You should use a simple "FOR EACH" loop.

(Hint: name[0] will return the first letter of a string for comparison.)

1 and 2 dimensional arrays:

1. Here is a simple one-dimensional array:

Index	0	1	2	3	4	5	6	7	8	9
Value		1	2	3	4	5				

Note that some of the cells are empty.

(a) Write down the pseudocode needed to **declare** and then **initialise** the array as shown.

(b) The same data could have been stored in a list instead of an array. Write down one advantage and one disadvantage of using an array to store this kind of data rather than a list.

2. Making and printing a number table. Look carefully at the following pseudocode.

(a) At the places indicated by, for example, (i) .... , write out a suitable comment that briefly explains what that piece of code is doing.

```
myTable: array [ 0..9 ][0..9 ] of integer   (i) .....................................

FOR row = 0 TO 9 DO                          (ii) ....................................
        FOR col = 0 TO 9 DO                        .............................................
                myTable [row] [col ] = 0
        END FOR
END FOR

FOR row = 0 TO 9 DO                          (iii) ....................................
        FOR col = 0 TO 9 DO                        .............................................
                myTable [row] [col ] = (row+1) * (col+1)
        END FOR
END FOR
```

(b) Using squared paper write out what the table looks like now.

3. Look at the table below showing the minimum and maximum temperatures for one week in January in Madrid:

Temperature ºC

Day		Min	Max
	0	**1**	**2**
0	Mon	-5	10
1	Tues	-4	12
2	Wed	-4	12
3	Thurs	-3	13
4	Fri	-4	12
5	Sat	-4	14
6	Sun	-2	15

The data needs to be stored in a structured data type like an **array**. The data type would have to be **string** to include both "Mon" and "-5" in the same array.

(a) Write down a definition for a simple array used in computer programming.

(b) In this case a two-dimensional array will be needed. Using the example of temperature data in Madrid, state what is meant by a **two-dimensional** array.

(c) Write out the pseudocode to **declare** and **initialise** with "X" in all cells the above table (7 rows by 3 columns of **string**) (Name the array "madridTemps")

(d) Write out the **assignment** statements needed to fill in the data for Friday. Note at the moment the data type of the array is **string**. So for numbers assign something like: "12" rather than just 12.

(e) What will the following statement print out? (Assume the table is full of data)
          print(madridTemps[5][1])

Extensions: Once all the data is stored inside the 2D array it needs to be analysed.

(f) Write out the pseudocode to calculate and print out the temperature **range** for each day, where range is given by maximum - minimum temp. For example:

Mon 15

Tues 16 ......

Hints:
- A simple FOR loop for the 7 rows (days of the week) is needed:
  - **FOR** row = 0 **TO** 6 **DO**
- To find, for example, the maximum temperature for that row (day)
  - maxTemp = (**INTEGER**) madridTemps[row][1]
  - Note: We have to "**cast**" a string like "12" to an integer 12.
- To calculate the temperature range is quite easy now:
  - tempRange = (**INTEGER**) maxTemp - minTemp

(g) Write out the pseudocode to calculate and print out the average maximum temperature for the week shown.

Python Programmers:
- First you would need to set up the table using a comprehension.
  - madridTemps = [[0 **for** col **in range**(3)] **for** row **in range**(7)]
- The table will now be 7 rows by 3 columns and would look something like:
  - ["Mon","-5","10"], ["Tues"," -4", "12"], ...]
- A small change: Remember Python can have more than one data type in a list. So it would be possible to iterate over all the rows of data and permanently cast all the "numeric strings" to integers:
  - madridTemps[row][1] = **int**(madridTemps[row][1])

Final note: Data in tables, like spread sheets, are often stored as Comma Separated Values (**CSV**) files. In a more realistic scenario a programmer would open the CSV file and read in all the data into the table (a two-dimensional array or a nested list). For details of this kind of approach see the section on **File-Handling**: Reading & Writing.

Python Dictionaries:

1. The following is a dictionary holding a the details of the weapons a soldier has access to in an adventure game where the key is the name of the weapon and the value is the "damage points" each weapon can inflict.

      arms = {"knife" : 10, "gun" : 30, "bazooka" : 50}

(Hint: You could quickly implement in this in the Python shell to get the answers!)

(a) What do the following evaluate to?

      arms["gun"]
      arms.keys()
      arms.values()
      arms.items()
      "canon" in arms
      arms["canon"]
      arms.get("bazooka")
      arms.get("canon", "Not there!")

(b) How would the <u>whole</u> dictionary look after these lines of code? The dictionary will change after each line.

      arms["bazooka"] = 100
      del arms["knife"]
      arms["machine gun"] = 50

2. This is question is a modified from a previous questions on lists. Here is a dictionary holding the name and grades in various subjects for a class of students. Each key is the student's name and the value is a list of 3 subjects and the grades for each subject.
Only 3 "records" (students) are shown.

      classMarks = {'Amy Jones' : ['English', 67, 'Maths', 76, 'Computer Science', 96],
           'Dave Brown' : ['English', 55, 'Maths', 81, 'Computer Science', 80],
           'Carmen Gomez' : ['English', 59, 'Maths', 86, 'Computer Science', 76], .. }

(a) Write down the code needed to do the following tasks:

    i. The English teacher has entered Amy's mark incorrectly; it should be 72 not 67. Alter Amy's "record" in the dictionary.

    ii. A student called "Ana Alison" joins the class from another set with the following grades: 'English', 85, 'Maths', 75, 'Computer Science', 75. Add her "record" to the dictionary.
(Extension: Write code that first checks that there is not already an "Ana Alison" in the class and only if there is not adds Ana's record to the class dictionary."

(b) Write a program to find the average score for all the students in "Maths".

Chapter 3g Programming: Subprograms - Implementation of Abstraction

In the chapter on **Algorithms & Problem Solving** we discussed the concept of **abstraction**. The main aims of abstraction are:

- **Modularisation**: Break down large, difficult problems into smaller and smaller easy problems or modules
- **Encapsulation**: Each sub-problem or module does one simple job only and "hides" the details of how it does that job.
- **Generalisation**: Carefully structured modules can be programmed so that they can carry out a range of similar tasks rather than just solve one problem.

Subprograms are, perhaps, the "implementation of abstraction."

Points Covered:

- **Subprograms** as Procedures & Functions
  - **Parameters** - passing data into subprograms
  - **Return Values** - getting data out of subprograms
- **Global and Local Variables** - scope
- **Modularisation** - Using subprograms to tackle larger problems

A **Subprogram** is a block of code in a program that performs a specific task. Fundamentally there are two types of subprograms: Procedure and Functions.

- **Procedures** are usually actions and are like commands or instructions to do something.
  - happyBday(person)   --> Sings happy birthday
  - move(numSqaures)   --> Move something on screen
- **Functions** are like asking a question or what's the answer to a calculation and they **return** a value
  - passWordLongEnough(inWord)   --> **returns** a Boolean True or False
  - maxGrade(inList)   --> **returns** an integer - the answer

Procedures:

Let's jump straight in with an example: Here is a block of code (a procedure) that prints "Happy Birthday".

```
PROCEDURE happyBday()
BEGIN
        print("Happy Birthday to you!")
        print("Happy Birthday, dear " + "Nick" + ".")
        print("Happy Birthday to you!")
END PROCEDURE
```

On its own the procedure doesn't do anything. You have to "**call**" it using its name.

```
1. print("Some code before the call to the procedure.")
2. happyBday()
3. print("Some code after the call to the procedure.")
```

Remember usually code is run sequentially line-by-line. So line 1 is run. Then line 2 "**calls**" the procedure happyBday(). The "body" of the procedure (from BEGIN to END) is run line-by-line and then control returns to the main program and line 3 is run.

This is the result:

> Some code before the call to the procedure.
> Happy Birthday to you!
> Happy Birthday, dear Nick.
> Happy Birthday to you!"
> Some code after the call to the procedure

So far this does not seem very useful. After all I could just have written out the code without defining a procedure. Now let's use the power of **abstraction** by **generalising** the procedure so that it can say "Happy Birthday" to anyone. All I need to do is add a **parameter**. Now a **parameter** is a kind of variable that allows the calling code to pass a value to the procedure when it calls it.

> **PROCEDURE** happyBday(person)
> **BEGIN**
> > **print**("Happy Birthday to you!")
> > **print**("Happy Birthday, dear " + person + ".")
> > **print**("Happy Birthday to you!")
> **END PROCEDURE**

"person" is just a variable that can take any value of type string. So now when I "**call**" the procedure I have to give a value for the "person" parameter:

> happyBday("Nick")

In this case "Nick" is the "**argument**" for the call to the procedure. That just means that "Nick" is the **value** that is assigned to the parameter "variable" - person.

```
PROCEDURE happyBday(person)
BEGIN
    print("Happy Birthday to you!")
    print("Happy Birthday, dear " + person + ".")
    print("Happy Birthday to you!")
END PROCEDURE


happyBday("Nick")
```

As the above diagram shows: When the code inside the body of the procedure gets to the parameter "person" it prints the value of that parameter or variable, that is "Nick".

Now I can say "Happy Birthday" to some of my friends in just 4 lines.

> happyBday("Nick")
> happyBday("Dave")
> happyBday("Sally")
> happyBday("Carmen")

Here there are 4 "calls" to the same happyBday procedure each with a different argument or value for the parameter person. Without a procedure I would have had to code 3 lines per person - a total of 12 lines. That's 12 lines where I could have made a mistake. What if I want to make a small change? Say I want to add a line that starts off the greeting with:

> **print**(person + " today is your day!")

With the procedure that is just one line to change and the 4 calls to the procedure are not changed at all. Without a procedure the process would be much more tedious and much more error prone. What if I wanted to say it in Spanish? No problem - just: rename, edit and **reuse** the same procedure:

PROCEDURE happyBdaySpanish(person)
BEGIN
    print("Cumpleaños feliz!")
    print("Cumpleaños querida " + person + ".")
    print("Cumpleaños feliz!")
END PROCEDURE

The call to the procedure would now be:

happyBdaySpanish("Carmen")

The **advantages** of using procedures (and functions) should now be obvious:
- Reduction of duplication of code
- Increase in the clarity of the code
- Reduction of errors and easier to find mistakes (debugging)
- Making changes is easier
- The same code can be adapted and reused.

Functions:

Functions, like procedures, are blocks of code that perform a specific task. The main difference is that they **return** "an answer" to a question or the result of a calculation.

Example: A simple function to tell if an integer is an odd or even number by using "modulo" division. (If a number divided by 2 leaves no remainder then it can't be odd.)

FUNCTION isOdd(inNum)
BEGIN
    IF (inNum **MOD** 2) = 0 **THEN**
        RETURN False
    ELSE
        RETURN True
    END IF
END FUNCTION

The parameter, inNum, is an integer and some code with a call to the function could look like this:

1.   **INPUT** age
2.   **IF** isOdd(age) **THEN**
3.   **print**(age, "is an odd age to be.")
4.   **ELSE**
5.   **print**(age,"is an even kind of age.")
6.   **ENDIF**
7.   **print**("Let's carry on.")

What happens step-by-step is:
- Line1: The user types in 15, which is assigned to the variable age.
- Line2: The condition for the IF statement is a **call** to the function with the value 15 as its **argument**: isOdd(15)
  - Control passes to the function and the value 15 is **passed** to the **parameter** inNum
  - 15 MOD 2 --> 1, so the condition for the IF statement in the function evaluates to False (1 is not equal to 0)
  - The ELSE statement is executed. That is True is **returned**.
- Line2: The IF statement condition is True so go to line 3
- Line3: Output "15 is an odd age to be."
- Line7: Output "Let's carry on."

Functions can call functions: Now we have a function that can answer the question, "Are you odd", we can use it to answer the related question, "Are you even?"

```
FUNCTION isEven(inNum)
BEGIN
        IF isOdd(inNum) THEN
                RETURN False
        ELSE
                RETURN True
        END IF
END FUNCTION
```

Although this is logically pointless it is an instructive example of a function calling a function.

Here's a more complex function that calculates x to the power of y.
For example 2^3 means 2 to the power of 3, which is: 2 X 2 X 2 = 8

```
FUNCTION power(x, y)
BEGIN
        temp = 1
        WHILE y > 0 DO
                temp = temp * x
                y = y - 1
        END WHILE
        RETURN temp
END FUNCTION
```

Calling the procedure is simply something like:
        answer = power(2, 3)
Note that there are 2 integer parameters (x and y) so there needs to be 2 integer arguments when the function is called.

Encapsulation: I am not going to explain how this function works because that nicely illustrates another aspect of **abstraction**: encapsulation. The user who wants to do calculations like 2^3 or 10^4 is not interested in how it works just as long as it does work! The details can and should be **hidden** from the user. Note how "independent" the function is: It does one job only. You **input** the numbers and it **processes** them and **outputs** the answer. Any variables it needs (in this case only one - temp) are created and used within the function. When the function is terminated (with a return statement) these variables are destroyed. There may even be other, perfectly good, ways of implementing the power function but from the user's perspective the function is encapsulated inside a "black box":

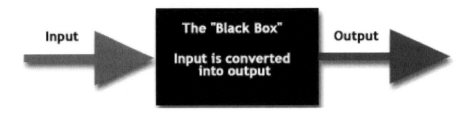

Here's another example showing that: <u>Abstraction, using functions, separates the **how** something is done from **what** it does.</u>
Find the maximum number from a list of numbers.

> **FUNCTION** maxNum(inList)
> **BEGIN**
>> biggest = 1
>> **FOR** eachNum **FROM** inList **DO**
>>> **IF** eachNum **>** biggest **THEN**
>>>> biggest = eachNum
>>> **END IF**
>> **END FOR EACH**
>> **RETURN** biggest
> **END FUNCTION**

Once again the details of how it works are hidden from the user who calls the function. Perhaps the function could have been implemented with a different kind of for loop or even a while loop. The user doesn't care about these implementation details. She just wants to know what she must **input** and what answer will be **output** (returned).

> myList = [23, 45,12,43,53,46,67,2, 567, 15]
> bigNum = maxNum(myList)
> **print**(bigNum)   --> 567

Subprograms in Python:
Python doesn't distinguish, by name at least, between procedures and functions. All subprograms in this context are considered to be functions in Python: Some return a value some do not. They all start with the key word "def" (define function):
Python "procedure":

```
def happyBday(person):
        print("Happy Birthday to you!")
        print("Happy Birthday, dear " + person + ".")
        print("Happy Birthday to you!")
```

Python "function":

```
def isOdd(inNum):
        if (inNum % 2) == 0:
                return False
        else:
                return True
```

Global & Local Variables and their scope:
 Before we move on to look at using abstraction and subprograms to solve larger problems we do need to look at some definitions:
- **Global Variables** are variables defined (declared) outside a subprogram.
- **Local Variables** are variables defined within a subprogram
- **Scope** is a technical term for the parts of the code that have access to a variable.

In the above example of the maxNum() function:

Global Variables: myList and bigNum
Local Variables (local to the function maxNum()): biggest, eachNum

Encapsulation means that the function maxNum() is totally sealed off and independent from the main program.
- The only way to get information into the function is through its **parameter** "inList".
- The only way to get information out is from its **return** value.

The following diagram illustrates these points. Study the diagram and note:
- The main program cannot access the local variable "biggest" which is outside of its scope.
    - The only way it can get the value of "biggest" is when the function **returns** it and that value is assigned to the global variable "bigNum".
- The function cannot (or "should not") access the global variable "myList", which is outside of its scope.
    - The only way the function can access "myList" is by passing it in as an argument for the **parameter** "inList."

Extension & Warning: In most programming languages there are ways around some of these constraints. Python, for example, can use the key word "global" to give functions complete access to any global variable. **This is not a sensible thing to do!** Accessing global variables in this way makes for very confusing code and breaks the spirit and whole point of encapsulation.

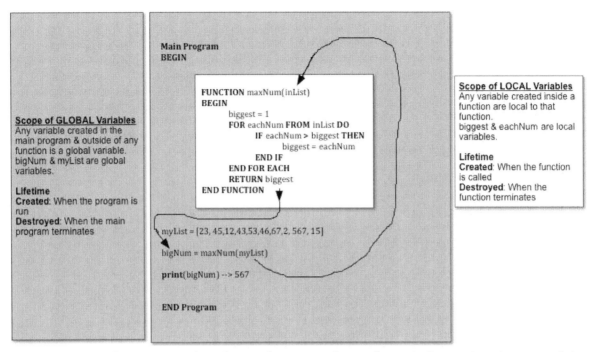

Global & Local Scope: The above diagram shows how information is passed into a function via its parameters and information passes out via its return value.

Question: What happens if I create a local variable inside a function and give it the same name as a global variable created outside of the function? The answer is that it doesn't matter! Encapsulation ensures that the function is a completely independent unit. In the maxNum() function example it would be perfectly legal to use the name "maximumNumber" for both the local variable "biggest" and the global variable "bigNum". We say that the local variable "**shadows**" the global variable. This is important. While you are working on a how a function works you don't want to be distracted by whether your local variables will be affected by global variables - encapsulation again! Perhaps it is a good idea, though, to use different names to make your code clear and easy to read.

Memory, Lifetime & Efficiency: Global variables exist as long as the program is being run. This means they always have some memory allocated to them, even if they are never used. Local variables are only created when the function in which they are declared is called. So over use of "unnecessary" global variables can be inefficient.

Avoid accessing global variables from within procedures: Another example.
Problem: The user is asked to enter their age in years. The program must calculate their age in days and then their age in months.

Bad use of global variables:

```
#Declare and initialise global variables
ageYears = 0,          days = 0,               months = 0

PROCEDURE calcDays()
BEGIN
        days = ageYears * 365
END PROCEDURE

PROCEDURE calcMonths()
BEGIN
        months = ageYears * 12
END PROCEDURE

INPUT ageYears
PRINT("Your age in years is: ",ageYears)
calcDays()
PRINT("Your age in days is: ", days)
calcMonths()
PRINT("Your age in months is: ", months)
```

With an input for "ageYears" of 10 the output "should" look something like:

Your age in years is: 10

Your age in days is: 3650

Your age in months is: 120

Each procedure is "**looking outside of its scope**" and referring to the global variables. This is not a good thing and can and should be avoided.

In some languages this may not even work. In Python, for example, "strange" things would appear to happen. There is no formal declaration of variables in Python.

VAR int days --> does not exist in Python.

But the following line inside the procedure calcDays():

days = ageYears * 365 --> Python creates "days" as a **local variable**.

On the other hand it would "look out" and "see" the **global variable** "ageYears". So the local variable "days" would be set to 3650 but the global variable "days" would remain unchanged. The output, if this code were implemented in Python, would be:

Your age in years is: 10   Your age in days is: 0   Your age in months is: 0

By the way if you tried to directly change a global variable inside a Python function:

days = days + 1 --> UnboundLocalError: local variable 'days' referenced before assignment. This tells you that Python lets a function "look" at global variables but not change them!

There are ways round this: The key word "**global**" would force the procedure calcDays() to use and change the global variable "days".

```
def calcDays():
        global days
        days = ageYears * 365
#end function calc days ....................
```

But why try to "get round" the problem? We should be using **functions**. The functions should be accessing the variable "ageYears" by passing it in as a **parameter**. Any variables the functions need should be created as local variables inside the functions. Global variables can have their values set by the **return** values of the function.

Avoiding accessing global variables by using functions:

```
#Declare and initialise global variables
ageYears = 0,          days = 0,                 months = 0

FUNCTION calcDays(inAge)
BEGIN
        localDays = 0
        localDays = inAge * 365
        RETURN localDays
END FUNCTION

FUNCTION calcMonths(inAge)
BEGIN
        localMonths = 0
        localMonths = inAge * 12
         RETURN localMonths
END FUNCTION

INPUT ageYears
print("Your age in years is: ",ageYears)
days = calcDays(ageYears)
print("Your age in days is: ", days)
months = calcMonths(ageYears)
print("Your age in months is: ", months)
```

This is the "correct" use of functions to **encapsulate** code.

Modularisation: Using subprograms to tackle large problems
Note: I have written this exercise with Python in mind but the principles will be exactly the same for any similar language.

Password Checker Problem: Here are the requirements for the problem:
- **Input**: User inputs a password eg "Nick456"
- **Process**: The program checks that the password is long enough and complex enough
    - Password must be between 6 & 12 characters long (inclusive)
    - Password must contain at least **one** of each of the following:
        - upper (A, K ..), lower(a, k ...) and a digit (3, 6 ..) characters
- **Output**: The program should pass or fail the password. Either way it should print out the result.

Abstraction: To solve problems we need to get an "overview" of the whole problem and not be distracted by the fine detail of the syntax and structure of the hundreds of lines of code.

Modularisation: After looking at the problem I have broken down the main task into smaller sub tasks - functions.

Encapsulation: Each function does one task. In this case each function takes in one parameter (the word that is being checked) and returns True or False depending on whether the check on the word was a success or not. **How** each of the functions works is hidden. We are only interested in **what** they do. So, sorry, what follows is not a final solution to the problem. I have written a comment before each function stating what it should do. I have also written a documentation string (docString): The statement between triple quotes just after the name of each function stating what the function will return.

```
#Password Checker Program
#function to check length is between 6 and 12 characters
def lengthCheck(inWord):
    """Returns True if inWord between 6 and 12 characters, else false"""
#end function lengthCheck ------------------------------

#function to check if word contains upper characters
def checkUpper(inWord):
    """Returns True if in word contains any upper characters, else False. """
#end function checkUpper ------------------------------

#function to check if word contains lower characters
def checkLower(inWord):
    """Returns True if in word contains any lower characters, else False. """
#end function checkLower ------------------------------

#function to check if word contains digit characters
def checkDigit(inWord):
    """Returns True if in word contains any digit characters, else False. """
#end function checkDigit ------------------------------

#function to check word contains upper, lower and digit
#Uses the functions checkUpper(), checkLower() and checkDigit()
def complexCheck(inWord):
    """Returns True if inWord contains upper, lower and digits, else false"""
#end function complexCheck ------------------------------

#function that checks a passWord for length and complexity
#Uses the functions lengthCheck() and ComplexCheck()
def passCheck(inWord):
    """Returns True if both lengthCheck and complexCheck return True, else False"""
#end function passCheck ------------------------------

#BEGIN main program which is where the program actually starts ------------------------
goodPWord = True          #Boolean variable to say if the passWord is good or not
pWord = ""                #Create a variable for the password string
pWord =input("Please enter your password.  ")   #Get a word from the user
 #Calls the passCheck function with pWord as a parameter
goodPWord = passCheck(pWord)
if goodPWord:
        print(pWord, " is a good password.")
else:
        print(pWord, " is not a good password.")
```

Implementation: Now the structure is clear, the actual coding and testing has to be done on each function. Again the very use of encapsulation with functions means that each function can be coded and tested on its own. Indeed, if this were a major problem, there would be a team of programmers. Each programmer would work on one function - Another advantage of abstraction!

Questions on Chapter 3g: Subprograms - Implementation of Abstraction

Procedures and Functions:
1. Copy out the following pseudocode extracts:
a)

       PROCDURE display(message)
       BEGIN
            print(message)
       END PROCEDURE

       display("What a difference a day made.")

b)

       FUNCTION convertMStoKmH(inNum)
       BEGIN
            RETURN inNum * 3.6
       END FUNCTION

       speedinKmH = convertMStoKmH(45)

c)

       FUNCTION askYesNo(inQuestion)
       BEGIN
            response = " "
            WHILE response **NOT IN** ("y", "n") **DO**
                response = **INPUT**(inQuestion)
            END WHILE
            RETURN response
       END FUNCTION

       answer = askYesNo("Get it? Type y or n only please.")

On your copy of the pseudocode make the following annotations – use a pencil!
- Draw a large, long, rectangle around each function or procedure (do not include the function or procedure call)
- Draw an arrow from each **call** to the title or name of the procedure or function
- Use an arrow to, show how the **argument** (in the function or procedure call) "passes to" to the **parameter** in the procedure or function definition.
- If there is a **return** statement show, using an arrow, what is being returned and to where.

d) Use these examples to state the similarities and differences between procedures and functions.

2. Look again at the function used in the text.

```
FUNCTION power(x, y)
BEGIN
        temp = 1
        WHILE y > 0 DO
                temp = temp * x
                y = y - 1
        END WHILE
        RETURN temp
    END FUNCTION
```

(a) What is the result of this **call**?   power(4,3)

(b) This function has two parameters what is the name and data type of each of them:

Parameter 1: .... data type .... Parameter 2: .... data type: ....

(c) Briefly state what this function does (what is its purpose)?

(d) In this context explain the concept of **encapsulation**:

Global and Local Variables

1. Look at this pseudocode extract with a **local variable** that has the same name as a **global variable.**

```
BEGIN main program
        spam = 43


        PROCEDURE silly():
        BEGIN
                spam = 99
                print(spam)
                spam = spam + 1
                print(spam)
        END PROCEDURE


        print(spam)
        silly()
        print(spam)
    END PROGRAM
```

(a) Copy out the code & write these comments next to the appropriate line in the code.

Create a local variable named "spam"   # Create a global variable named "spam":

#Call the silly() function   # Add 1 to the local variable "spam"

(b) Output: There are 4 print statements. Write down what they print, in order, one after the other:

....

2. Look again at the Password Checker Program where only function "stubs" (incomplete code stating what is input and what the function will output) were given.
There were only two global variables used: "goodPWord" and "pWord"
        (a) What were the data types of these two global variables?
        (b) Use these variables as an example to define the term "global variable."
        (c) What is the only way that the function passCheck() can access the global variable "pWord"?
        (d) Explain how, in effect, the function passCheck() assigns a value (True or False) to the global variable "goodPWord".

Modularisation

1. A physics problem: A bullet is fired vertically into the air. The total energy the bullet has at any point can be given by the following formula:
        Total Energy in Joules = Kinetic Energy + Gravitational Potential Energy
        Kinetic Energy = $(mv^2)/2$ Gravitational Potential Energy = mgh
m= mass of bullet in kg, v = velocity in m/s and h = height in meters.
g = acceleration due to gravity = 9.8 m/s^2
Write a program in a programming language of your choice, that does the following:
        Input: bullet mass kg, bullet velocity in m/s & bullet height in meters.
        Process: Uses the above equations to calculate the total energy of the bullet.
        Output: The total energy of the bullet in Joules
For example: Input --> m = 0.02 kg, velocity = 500 m/s, height = 10 m
                  Output --> Total Energy of the bullet is 2501.96 joules

Here is the main part of the program to start you off:

```
#BEGIN main program
#global variables
CONSTANT  float   GRAVITY = 9.8
VAR   float   mass = 0.0
VAR   float   velocity = 0.0
VAR   float   height = 0.0
VAR   float   totalEnergy = 0.0
PRINT("The Energy of a bullet.")
mass = INPUT       "Mass of bullet in kg:  "
velocity = INPUT       "Velocity of bullet in m/s: "
height = INPUT       "Height of bullet in m: "
totalEnergy = calcEnergy(mass, velocity, height, GRAVITY)
PRINT("Total Energy of the bullet is: ",totalEnergy, " Joules.")
```

You must code the following 3 functions:

calcEnergy(mass, velocity, height, GRAVITY) --> as shown in the call above
Which calls, in turn, 2 other functions:
calcKE()
calcGPE()

None of the functions should directly access any of the global variables.

All of the functions should use parameters.

Each function must return the value of its calculation.

(Note: If GRAVITY, which is a constant, was to be used by several functions it just **maybe** a reason to access it as a global variable. On balance I still feel that passing GRAVITY, as a parameter, is "safer" and clearer.)

Chapter 3h Programming: Input and Output

So far in the **Input --> Processing --> Output** model we have focused on programming to solve problems. This is largely about processing data. Your code (software) may be marvellous but outside "in the real world" are humans ("liveware"!!) who are going to use your program. Humans make mistakes when they type in data. Before we process input data it would be wise to check that it is sensible. In larger projects the input data doesn't come in typed on a keyboard but exists as a file that we need to read in.

Points Covered:
- Validation & Exception Handling
- File Handling - Reading & Writing
- Extension: CSV files

Validation

Validation is a software check on input data to make sure that data entered is:
- Reasonable
- Sensible
- Conforms to rules

 After all if the data going in is wrong then, however good the algorithm and the coding, the output results will also be wrong:

> **G.I.G.O. --> Garbage In Garbage Out**
> "On two occasions I have been asked, 'Pray, Mr Babbage, if you put into the machine wrong figures, will the right answers come out?' I am not able rightly to apprehend the kind of confusion of ideas that could provoke such a question."

(**Charles Babbage**, 19th century English mathematician who originated the concept of a programmable computer.)

Note that saying the data is "**valid**" is not the same as saying that the data is "correct".
If you enter that Maria's eyes are blue and they are really green ... this will "pass" any validation check but will still be wrong! While the colour of Maria's eyes is "Madrid" is NOT reasonable, nor sensible and can be stopped by validation checks.

Types of validation checks:

Example: Your friend runs a modelling agency and needs to keep records about her models. Below is a table showing some of the kinds of data needed and some of the types of validation check.

Check	Example
Range	100 < height < 300 cm
Type	Sex – Boolean (M or F)
Length	Address < 100 characters
Lookup	Hair colour: Black, Blonde, Brown, Mixed, None
Presence	Postcode must NOT be blank
Format	Postcode begin with "01"

These "rules" would be given to the programmer and are usually common sense. For example, it may be possible for a model to have a height of 300 cm but any more than that is so unlikely as to be neither logical nor sensible. Nonetheless people using your program may enter, say, 2500 cm by mistake. It is your job as a programmer to try to prevent as many human errors as possible.

Range check: 100 < height < 300 cm
      height = **(INTEGER) INPUT**("What is your height? ")
      IF height > 100 **AND** height < 300 **THEN**
            PRINT(height, " is just fine.")
      ELSE
            PRINT(height, " is not in range 100 to 300 exclusive.")
      END IF
(Note: in Python **if** height **in range**(101,300) is slightly easier.)
This check won't always work. What happens if the height input is the wrong data type? For example: 166.67 (a float) or not even a number "London"??? This will need a "**type check**".

Type Check: height(cm) must be an integer:
This is relatively difficult to program because how can you know in advance what kind of, wrong, type the user is going to input? A simple "solution" might look like this:
height = **(INTEGER) INPUT** ("Enter a height as an integer.")
      IF isAnInteger(height) **THEN**
            PRINT(height, "is an integer.")
      ELSE
            PRINT(height, "is not an integer.")
      END IF
Unfortunately it all depends on the existence of a function like "isAnIntger()". This becomes very language specific. See the section on **Exception Handling** below for how to deal with such problems.

Length check: Surname < 20 characters
>   sName = **(STRING) INPUT** ("What is your surname? ")
>   **IF LENGTH**(sName) < 20 **THEN**
>   **PRINT**("Welcome ",sName)
>   **ELSE**
>   **PRINT**(sName, " is too long!")
>   **END IF**

Look up (list) check: hair colour must be in the list: Black, Blonde, Brown, Mixed, None
HAIRCOLOURS = ("Black", "Blonde", "Brown", "Mixed", "None")
>   **PRINT**("Please tell me your hair colour - You can choose from: ", HAIRCOLOURS)
>   hColour = **(STRING) INPUT**("Hair colour please: ")
>   hColour = hColour.**title**()   --> force string from broWN to Brown
>   **IF** hColour **IN** HAIRCOLOURS **THEN**
>   **PRINT**(hColour, " is a nice colour.")
>   **ELSE**
>   **PRINT**(hColour, " is not a valid choice.")
>   **END IF**

Presence check: Postcode must NOT be blank
>   pCode = **(STRING) INPUT**("Enter postcode. This field cannot be blank! ")
>   pCode = pCode.**strip**()   --> strips white space around string
>   **IF** pCode <> "" **THEN**   --> <> means "not equal" to empty string
>   **PRINT**(pCode, " is a good postcode.")
>   **ELSE**
>   **PRINT**(pCode, " looks 'empty' to me!")
>   **END IF**

Format check: Postcode begins with "01"
>   pCode = **(STRING) INPUT**("Enter postcode. It should begin with '01'. ")
>   firstTwo = pCode[0:2]
>   **IF** firstTwo = "01" **THEN**
>   **PRINT**(pCode, " is good. It begins with: ", firstTwo)
>   **ELSE**
>   **PRINT**(pCode, " is not a valid. It begins with: ", firstTwo, " not '01'.")
>   **END IF**

Extension: Exception Handling
Note that the details here will be specific to Python but the principles will apply to any similar language.
So what can we do when the user enters "London" instead of a number for something like height? In Python all input is initially a string. You can "**cast**" (explicitly convert) the input string into an integer.
>   height = **int**(input("Enter height as an integer."))

So if the user types in "8" then "**int**" will cast or convert "8" to 8.

But what if the user types "London"? Well **int** can't cast the string to an integer. So:

    ValueError: invalid literal for int() with base 10: 'London' --> oh dear!

You could try asking if the string consists of digits using "isdigit()".

```
height = input("integer please.")
if height.isdigit():
        height = int(height)
        print(height, " can be converted to an integer.")
else:
        print(newHeight, " is not an integer.")
```

This code is fine for all positive integers but fails with negatives like "-178" because the first character in the string is "-" which is not a digit! There must be a better and more general way to deal with or "handle" these kinds of problems.

Exceptions: When Python runs into an error that it cannot deal with it "**raises an exception**" indicating that an "exceptional" error has occurred. If nothing is done with the exception, then Python outputs an error message and stops, well "crashes"!

    ValueError: invalid literal for int() with base 10: 'London'

What we need to do is to "catch" the exception and deal with it rather than just let the program crash. We need to **handle the exception**.

The general format for handling exception is:

```
try:
        Commands
except:
        <if there is an exception execute this statement>
else:
        <if there is no exception execute this statement>
```

Example: The user types in "London" for a height in cm.

```
height = input("Height as an integer in cm please: ")
try:
        height = int(height)
except:
        print(height, " is not an integer. 100 will be entered as a default.")
        height = 100
else:
        print(height, " is an integer.  Thank-you")
```

Note: There are many kinds of exceptions. The type of error when "London" cannot be cast to an integer is called a value error. In this case it would be a good idea to be more precise and only "catch" this kind of error:

    except ValueError:

When should you "trap" for exceptions?

Exception handling is an excellent way to "defend" your code from the unpredictable "outside world." So whenever your code is inputting something is a good place to consider putting an exception handler. I will show another example in file handling.

File Handling: Reading and Writing

So far we have only considered storing and accessing data in variables or data structures:

      name = "Nick",   age = 15,   scienceGrades = [67, 78, 80]

This data is often input by the user:

      name = **(STRING) INPUT** ("Name please: ")

And when the program terminates all input data is lost.

- What if you want to save the data in a permanent location "outside" of the program, such as in a text file on a hard disc, so that you can continue to use that data next time the program is run?
- What if the data you need to analyse is stored in an external file, such as a spreadsheet full of the science grades for a class?

We need ways to:

- **Open** a file to **read** data into a program
- **Write** or save data from a program into a file

The following diagram shows a scenario where a user is running a game program and needs to be able to:

- Run the game, changing his location, points etc.
- Save his "game status" to an external file and then quit the game.
- Run the game again but read in his "game status" from the previous game.

Running and Rerunning a Game while saving data in an external file.

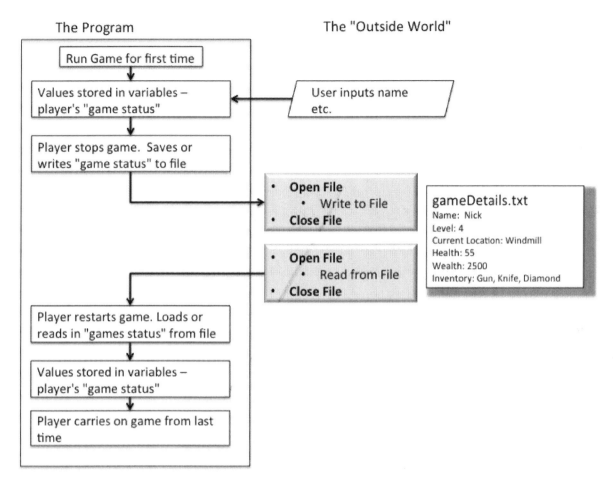

Text files and data structures:

Example Scenario: You want to write a quiz program that asks a number of questions. Your first attempt may be to type in and store the questions & answers in a 2D array or a nested list:

spainQuests = [["Capital?", "Madrid"], ["Longest River?", "Tajo"], ["Highest Mountain?", "Teide"], ["Largest Province?", "Badajoz"] .....]

Once the questions are in a data structure then processing is relatively easy:

```
FUNCTION askQuestions(inList)
BEGIN
FOR EACH question FROM inlist DO
        quest = question[0]
        answer = question[1]
        yourAnswer = INPUT (STRING) (quest)
        IF yourAnswer = answer THEN
                print("correct")
        ELSE
                print("No! The correct answer is: ", answer)
        END IF
END FOR
END FUNCTION
#Call to the askQuestions function:
askQuestions(spainQuests)
```

Generalising the Algorithm: Up to a point this is a good solution but "**hard coding**" the questions into one list is tedious, error-prone and really limits the flexibility of the program. Let's use **abstraction** to **generalise** the code so that it can:

- Read in questions and answers from a text file;
- Store this input data into a nested list;
- And so ask any set of questions

For example the "spainQuests.txt" text file may look something like this:

Capital?
Madrid
Longest River?
Tajo
....

Here's the pseudocode to open any questions file in the above format and to read in each line and store the data as a nested list: [["quest", "answer"], ["quest", "answer] ..].

```
FUNCTION readInDataFromFile(inFile)
BEGIN
        localFile = OPEN(inFile, "READ MODE")
        lines = localFile.READLINES()      #Each line is one string in the list lines
        localFile.CLOSE()                   #Finished with file so close file.
        numLines = LENGTH(lines)
        questList = [ ]                     #Empty list to hold nested questions

        FOR index FROM 0 TO numLines-1 STEP 2 DO
                nextQuest = lines[index]
                nextAnswer = lines[index+1]
                questAnswer = [nextQuest, nextAnswer]
                questList.append(questAnswer)
        END FOR

        RETURN questList
END FUNCTION
#call to the function readInDataFromFile()
myQuestionList = readInDataFromFile("spainQuests.txt")
```

Once you have the questions read in and stored as a nested list, it is very easy to pass that nested list as a parameter to a function such as: askQuestions(myQuestionList).   More importantly, you can now use the same program to read in any question file that is in the same format. You only have to change one line. For example:

        myQuestionList = readInDataFromFile("ukQuests.txt")

The text file "ukQuests.txt" may look something like this:

        Capital?
        London
        Most Popular food?
        Fish and Chips
        ....

Of course the program needs to be able to "find" the text file it has to open. At our level simply putting the file "next" to the program file in the same folder is enough. Finally though, the text files do need to exist!

Handling Exceptions – Unable to open a file

What happens if you try to open a file that does not exist? If the file is essential to the program then why not just quit (exit)?

```
#Python function that tries to open a file and either returns that file or exits.
import sys
def openFile(fileName, mode):
    try:
        theFile = open(fileName, mode)
    except IOError:
        print("Unable to open file ", fileName, " Ending program.")
        input("Press the enter key to exit.")
        sys.exit()
    else:
        return theFile
#end function openFile .............................

#call to function openFile in read mode
myFile = openFile("poems.txt", "r")
```

Read Process and then Write (save):

Here's an algorithm that opens a file; reads in a poem; randomises the lines and then writes (saves) the randomised version to another file.

1. Open the file to read & use READLINES() to store the poem as a list of strings (lines):

```
poemFile = OPEN("zenPython.txt", "READ MODE")
lines = poemFile.READLINES()      #Each line a string element ending in "\n"
poemFile.CLOSE()
PRINT("Here is the original poem as a list:", lines)
PRINT("Here is the original poem line by line:")   #end="" to stop extra line \n
FOR EACH line FROM lines DO
        print(line, end= "")
END FOR
```

The result so far is:

> Here is the original poem as a list:
> ['Beautiful is better than ugly.\n', 'Explicit is better than implicit.\n', 'Simple is better than complex.\n', 'Complex is better than complicated.\n', 'Flat is better than nested.\n', 'Sparse is better than dense.\n', 'Readability counts.\n']
>
> Here is the original poem line by line:
> Beautiful is better than ugly.
> Explicit is better than implicit.
> Simple is better than complex.
> Complex is better than complicated.
> Flat is better than nested.
> Sparse is better than dense.
> Readability counts.

(By the way the poem is by Tim Peters and the advice it contains is excellent!)

2. Iterate through the list of lines, randomly choosing & deleting a line and adding it to a new list:

```
newLines = [ ]                              #Empty list to store randomised poem
WHILE lines <> [ ] DO                       #continue while list not empty
        thisLine = random.choice(lines)         #Choose a line at random
        lines.remove(thisLine)                  #remove this line from the list
        newLines.append(thisLine)               #append this line to newLines
END WHILE
print("Here is the randomised poem: ")
print(newLines)
print("Here is the randomised poem - line by line.")
FOR EACH line FROM newLines DO
        print(eachLine, end="")
END FOR
```

Now the poem looks like this:

```
Here is the randomised poem:
['Complex is better than complicated.\n', 'Simple is better than complex.\n', 'Flat is
better than nested.\n', 'Explicit is better than implicit.\n', 'Sparse is better than
dense.\n', 'Beautiful is better than ugly.\n', 'Readability counts.\n']


Here is the randomised poem - line by line.
Complex is better than complicated.
Simple is better than complex.
Flat is better than nested.
Explicit is better than implicit.
Sparse is better than dense.
Beautiful is better than ugly.
Readability counts.
```

3. Finally save the new poem to another file by using WRITELINES() to write the list of strings to a text file:

```
poemFile = OPEN("zenPythonRand.txt", "WRITE MODE")
poemFile.WRITELINES(newLines)
poemFile.CLOSE()
```

(By the way, in this case, if the file "zenPythonRand.txt" did not exist it would be created.)

Note: Whenever you **open** a file, after you have accessed it, you should **close** the file.

Extension CSV files:

Data often comes in tables from spreadsheets, which can be stored as **C**omma **S**eparated **V**alues (CSV) files:

Spreadsheet of some players and their scores at different levels

Name	Level 1	Level 2	Level 3
Ellie	0	0	10
Kitty	19	17	14
Cris	19	15	16
Ben	20	15	18
Nico	20	3	20

How the data is stored – items separated by commas (CSV)

Ellie,0,0,10

Kitty,19,17,14

Cris,19,15,16

Ben,20,15,18

Nico,20,3,20

The details that follow are specific to Python but will be similar in other languages.

1. Read the file in Python:

```
scoreFile = open("playerScoresCSV.csv", "r")    #open file to "read"
scoreLines = scoreFile.readlines()              #read each line to a list
scoreFile.close()                               #close the file
```

Note: It really doesn't matter if the file is ".csv" or ".txt". The result is the same.
Here is what the list scoreLines looks like:

['Ellie,0,0,10\n', 'Kitty,19,17,14\n', 'Cris,19,15,16\n', 'Ben,20,15,18\n', 'Nico,20,3,20']

Each line of of the file has become ONE element of type string, ending with the newline code "\n".

2. **"Split" the data on the comma and make a nested list:**

```
playerList = [ ]                    #empty list to hold players
for line in scoreLines:             #One line is a string: 'Kitty,19,17,14\n'
    newPlayer = line.split(",")         #Strip off characters at each ","
    playerList.append(newPlayer)        #Add each player to new list
#end of for loop
```

The playerList list is a nested list looks like this:

[['Ellie', '0', '0', '10\n'], ['Kitty', '19', '17', '14\n'], ['Cris', '19', '15', '16\n'], ['Ben', '20', '15', '18\n'], ['Nico', '20', '3', '20']]

Each "outer" element is a list of each player's name and scores: ['Nico', '20', '3', '20']

3. **Tidy up the nested list by converting "number strings" to integers:**

Each score needs to be converted to an integer.

```
for player in playerList:               #player is ['Cris', '19', '15', '16\n']
    for index in range(1,len(player)):  #so index 1, 2, 3
        player[index] = int(player[index])  #cast string to integer
    #end inner for loop
#end outer for loop
```

Now playerList is ready and looks like this:

[['Ellie', 0, 0, 10], ['Kitty', 19, 17, 14], ['Cris', 19, 15, 16], ['Ben', 20, 15, 18], ['Nico', 20, 3, 20]]

Each player is a list with the first element the name (string) and the remaining elements as scores (integers).

Final Extension: Using a CSV reader

As CSV files from programs such as Microsoft's Excel are so common, Python has a special csv "module". This includes a "reader object" that can iterate ("loop") over a CSV file and read each line or record as a list of individual elements. There is no need for the "split on comma" stage:

```
import csv    #Module that deals with csv files
scoreFile = open("playerScoresCSV.csv", "r")     #open file to "read"
rawData = csv.reader(scoreFile)   #reader object is "iterable" (for loops)
playerList = [ ]                  #empty list to hold the records
for line in rawData:              #Each line is a "list of fields"
        playerList.append(line)
#end for loop .....
scoreFile.close()                 #close the file
```

Now playerList looks like this:

[['Ellie', '0', '0', '10'], ['Kitty', '19', '17', '14'], ['Cris', '19', '15', '16'], ['Ben', '20', '15', '18'], ['Nico', '20', '3', '20']]

As before, it will still be necessary to convert the "number strings" to integers. Nonetheless using the "csv reader" is quick and efficient. The Python csv module has many more tools to manipulate CSV data but these are beyond the scope of this book and are left to the reader to research!

Questions on Chapter 3h: Input and Output

Validation
1. Copy out the following paragraph and fill in the blanks with an appropriate word from the list below
Validation is the .... checking of .... data by a computer program. Validation can only check that data is a .... or a ....value. Note: This is not the same as saying the data is .... If you enter that Maria's eyes are blue and they are really green. This will "pass" any .... check but will still be wrong!

correct   input   sensible   validation   sensible   automatic   reasonable

2. A student is working on a program to analyse data about chemical elements. On the left is the original, correct data. On the right a copy of that data entered manually.

	Original	Entered data
Name	Chlorine	Bromine
Symbol	Cl	Cll
Atomic Number	17	17.7
Atomic Mass	35.5	3550.0

In each case there has been a data input error.
(a) State which of these mistakes could have been prevented by **validation**. In each case state, with an example, a suitable type of validation check or rule.
(b) State and explain which mistake could **not** have been stopped by a validation check and explain why.
(c) In this context explain the importance of the acronym, **GIGO** (Garbage In Garbage Out).

File Handling:
1. Andy is writing a program called "Poem Reader". The program requirements are:
- The user is asked for the name of a text file, which is opened and the poem is then stored as a simple array or list, where each line is one "element".
- The program then prints the poem line by line;
- The user can repeat this process as many times as she likes.
Part of the main program is shown here:
```
carryOn = False
carryOn = askToCarryOn("Do you want to carry on?)
WHILE carryOn DO
        fileName = INPUT (STRING) ("Name of poem's text file please: ")
        thePoem = readInPoem(fileName)
        printPoem(thePoem)
        carryOn = askToCarryOn("Do you want to carry on?)
END WHILE
```
For example the following poem (from Monty Python) is held in a text file, "halfBee.txt"

But can a bee be said to be
Or not to be an entire bee
When half the bee is not a bee
Due to some ancient injury?

Here is the poem input and stored as an array or list of lines:

['But can a bee be said to be\n', 'Or not to be an entire bee\n', 'When half the bee is not a bee\n', 'Due to some ancient injury?\n']

Listed below is the pseudocode of the relevant procedure and function. The function "askToCarryOn" simply returns True or False depending on what the user enters and is not shown. There are **two** errors and **two** missing statements (...........................)

What you have to do is:

(a) Copy out the pseudocode but correct the errors and complete the missing statements.

```
FUNCTION readInPoem(inFile)
BEGIN
        localFile = OPEN(inFile, "WRITE MODE")
        lines = localFile.READLINES()
        ...................................................
        RETURN localFile
END FUNCTION


PROCEDURE printPoem(inPoem)
BEGIN
        ...................................................
        print(line, end="")
        END FOR
END PROCEDURE
```

(b) As the code stands it will "crash" if the user types in the name of a text file that does not exist. Write down a suitable "**Exception Handler**" script that will "catch" the exception generated when a file does not exist. In this case the script should print a suitable error message and carry on.

Extension: You may want to implement this program in a language of your choice.

Comma Separated Values (CSV) files - Temperature in Madrid

1. Look at the table on the right showing the minimum and maximum temperatures for one week in January in Madrid:

	Day	Temperature °C Min	Max
	0	1	2
0	Mon	-5	10
1	Tues	-4	12
2	Wed	-4	12
3	Thurs	-3	13
4	Fri	-4	12
5	Sat	-4	14
6	Sun	-2	15

The Problem: The data is stored in a text file as comma separated values looking something like:

Mon, -5, 10,

Tues, -4, 12,

This data needs to be read into a program and stored in a data structure like a 2D array or a nested list.

[['Mon', -5, 10], ['Tues', -4, 12], ['Wed', -4, 12], ...]

The data then needs to be analysed as shown below.

In pseudocode or a programming language of your choice, write down the code for each of the following tasks. Each task should be a **procedure** or **function** so that the start of the main program may look something like:

madridTemps = **makeTableFrom**("madridTempData.txt")

printTempRange(madridTemps)

avMaxTemp = **calcAvMaxTemp**(madridTemps)

Do **not** worry about any validation checks or error handling and so on.

Task 1: **makeTableFrom**(inFile): Open the file to read and store the data in a two-dimensional array or nested list which the function **returns**.

Hints: You can make it easy for yourself by assuming:

(a) There is a CSV reader tool that can iterate over an inputted CSV file and returning each line as a "record" of independent data items.

tempReader = **csv.reader**(inputtedFile)

And then the first line of a for loop would look like this:

FOR EACH line **FROM** tempReader **DO**

OR you will have to show how to "split" on the commas from each line:

["Mon, -5, 10", "Tues, -4, 12", "Wed, -4, 12", ...]

(b) You must decide whether to leave all data as a string or to convert "string numbers" to integers at this point.

Remember arrays can only hold data of one type, so you may have to leave all data as strings. Python lists, on the other hand can have different data types in different "cells".

Task 2: **printTempRange**(inList): To calculate and print out the temperature **range** for each day, where range is given by maximum - minimum temp. Takes in madridTemps nested list as a parameter. For example:

      Mon 15   Tues 16   Wed 16 ....

The day of week is just the first (0) item in the row (day) --> today = day[0]

Task 3: **calcAvMaxTemp**(inList): To calculate and **return** the average maximum temperature for the week shown by passing in the madridTemps nested list as a parameter.

Chapter 3i Programming: Errors and Testing

We all make mistakes - even programmers. This chapter looks at the different kinds of errors or "**bugs**" that can appear in your code and how you can test your code to really make sure that there are no errors. Finally there is a brief look at the tools available to help you "**debug**" code that come with the software you use to write code: the Integrated Development Environment (**IDE**).

Points Covered:
- Errors: Syntax, logic & runtime
- Test Plans & Test Data
- Debugging & IDE

Errors are called "bugs":

In 1946 operators traced an error in the Mark II computer to a moth trapped in a relay, coining the term bug. This bug was carefully removed and taped to the logbook.

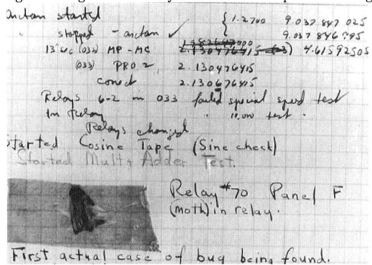

There may be millions of different biological bugs but essentially only **three** computer ones.

1. Syntax Errors "Spelling & Grammar"

Syntax: "A set of rules that defines how program statements must be written in order for the translator to understand them." So if you "break the rules" by say:
- Mistyping (spelling):   "pprint" --> "print"
- Missing key words: WHILE time place DO --> WHILE time AND place DO
- (Open not close brackets .... and so on.

Then that is a syntax error. Syntax Errors are relatively easy to correct. The translator tells you what is wrong & where.

> File "<pyshell#10>", line 1, in <module>
>   paid = **false**
> NameError: name **'false'** is not defined --> It should be "**False**" !!!!

Sometimes the mistake is a little less obvious:

```
print("The Energy of a bullet."
mass = float(input("Mass of bullet in kg: "))
```

The syntax error is highlighted on the variable "mass" but there is no error on that line. Don't worry that very often means the actual error is just above. In this case a missing ")" at the end of the print statement.

2. Logical Errors

An error in the algorithm that means the outcome is not as expected is called a "logical" error.   Sometimes called "semantic errors" because the meaning is not correct.   The program will run but it won't do what it should.

Semantic Errors are the trickiest bugs to fix.

- The bug does not crash the program, and the program appears to work fine.
- However, it is not doing what the programmer intended for the program to do.

For example: You want the variable total to be the **sum** of the values in variables a, b, and c:

```
total = a + b * c
```

The value in total will be wrong! This won't cause the program to crash immediately, but may or may not cause some other code to **crash later on** because of the unexpected value in total.

Another Example: Spot the mistake in this "guess my number" code:

```
answer = 55,        guess = 0
WHILE guess = answer DO
        IF guess < answer THEN
                print("Lower ..")
        ELSE
                print("higher ..")
        END IF
END WHILE
```

Come on it's obvious! Well yes and no. This code could be buried deep in a function inside a program, which is thousands of lines long. There is nothing (syntactically) wrong with it - It just doesn't do what it should do.   (Hint: If guess is less than the answer, shouldn't you prompt the user with "higher"?)

3. Run-Time Errors:

These are errors that occur during the execution or "running" of a program. These can be very difficult to spot because there may be neither syntax nor logical errors in the code. Everything seems fine, **most of the time**.

For example: A biologist is working on the height : mass ratio of mice:

```
ratio = height / mass
```

But while the program was running he entered the mass as 0 and it crashes.

```
ratio = height / mass
```

ZeroDivisionError: division by zero --> Divide by 0 means infinity!

As long as the biologist never input the mass of a mouse to be 0, then the program would run just fine. A simple "IF STATEMENT" would suffice to protect the code:

> **IF** mass > 0 **THEN**
>> ratio = height / mass
>
> **ELSE**
>> print("Error: mass ", mass, " is 0 or less than 0.")
>
> **END IF**

Of course he should have thought about this possibility while he was writing the code. See the chapter on **validation** checks.

An out of range error example - another run-time error: Ana is working on a physics program about the visible spectrum.

> spectrum = ["red", "orange", "yellow", "green", "blue", "indigo", "violet"]
> colourNum = **INPUT (INTEGER)** ("Choose a number 1 to 7: ")
> **PRINT**("The colour you chose was: ", spectrum[colourNum])

There is nothing obviously wrong with the code. Though there does seem to be a **logical error**:

> Choose a number 1 to 7: 1
> The colour you chose was: orange --> This is not the "first" colour.

But much worse is when a user types in 7:

> Choose a number 1 to 7: 7
> **IndexError: list index out of range**

Ana forgot that arrays and lists start at index position 0, so the last element is at index 6.

> spectrum[6]   --> violet

On the other hand, she doesn't want to confuse the user with this problem. The solution is to let the code work out the index and put in a suitable **range validation check**:

> spectrum = ["red", "orange", "yellow", "green", "blue", "indigo", "violet"]
> colourNum = **INPUT (INTEGER)** ("Choose a number 1 to 7: ")
> index = colourNum - 1
> **IF** (index > -1) **AND** (index < 7) **THEN**
>> **PRINT**("The colour you chose was: ", spectrum[index])
>
> **ELSE**
>> **PRINT**("Sorry ", colourNum, " not in range 1 to 7")
>
> **END IF**

Anticipating run-time errors and protecting your code from them is a skill you acquire with experience - **rigorous testing** can discover most of them.

Test Plans & Test Data

A program must be reliable so before you "release" your software on an unsuspecting public you should test your code to "breaking point." Your code should be "**robust**" that is it should not crash - whatever the user throws at it. It is no good just "testing" your code with data that you expect the user to input. You must plan for the unexpected.

For numeric data there are three kinds of **test data:**
- **Normal:**
  - o **Valid** data that is well within the range of what you expect.
- **Boundary**:
  - o "**Extreme**" data at the minimum or maximum of the expected range
- **Erroneous**:
  - o **Invalid** or just plain "wrong" data.

Example: Look again at the initial code for Ana's work on the spectrum:
> spectrum = ["red", "orange", "yellow", "green", "blue", "indigo", "violet"]
> colourNum = **INPUT (INTEGER)** ("Choose a number 1 to 7: ")
> **print**("The colour you chose was: ", spectrum[colourNum])

Here are some examples of the data she should have used to test her program:
> **Normal**
> > 3   --> within the expected range of 1 - 7
>
> **Boundary**:
> > 1 & 7   --> valid but on the "edge" of the expected range
>
> **Erroneous**:
> > -1 & 8 --> invalid because out of range
> > "Ana" --> invalid because of wrong data type - string

Test Plan:

Ana knows what her test data is going to be. A test plan is an excellent method to systematically test a program. Here is a completed test plan for Ana's program:

No	Purpose	Data	Expected result	Actual result	Action needed / comments
1	Normal data in range	3	Output "yellow"	Output "green"	Check index access to lists
2	Boundary (lower)	1	Output "red"	Output "orange"	Check index access to lists
3	Boundary (upper)	7	Output "violet"	Error out of range	Check index access to lists
4	Erroneous out of range	-1	Error out of range	Error out of range	Validation range check required
5	Erroneous out of range	8	Error out of range	Error out of range	Validation range check required
6	Erroneous wrong data type	"Ana"	Error wrong data type	Error wrong data type	Validation type check - exception handler required

Ana would first complete the first 4 columns:

Test number; Test Purpose; Test Data and the Expected result.

Then she would run her code for each of the tests and complete the last two columns:

Actual result and Action needed / comments.

As a result her final code would be something like this:

```
FUNCTION getValidInteger(lower, upper)
BEGIN
        localNum = INPUT("Enter a number between ", lower, " and ", upper,  ": ")
        TRY
                localNum = (INTEGER) (localNum)  #try to cast to integer
        EXCEPT
                PRINT(localNum, " not an integer. 1 will be entered as a default.")
                localNum = 1
        ELSE
                IF localNum NOT IN RANGE(lower, upper+1) THEN #range up to
                        PRINT(localNum, " not in range ",lower, " to ", upper)
                        PRINT("1 will be entered as default.")
                        localNum = 1
                END IF
        END EXCEPTION HANDLER
        RETURN localNum - 1        #changes 1 - 7 to 0-6 for indexing list or array
END FUNCTION


spectrum = ["red", "orange", "yellow", "green", "blue", "indigo", "violet"]
#call function that guarantees to return an index from 0 to 6 inclusive
colourNum = getValidInteger(1, 7)
PRINT("The colour you chose was: ", spectrum[colourNum])
```

And her final, completed, test plan would be something like this:

No	Purpose	Data	Expected result	Actual result	Action needed / comments
1	Normal data in range	3	Output "yellow"	Output "yellow"	Correct!
2	Boundary (lower)	1	Output "red"	Output "red"	Correct!
3	Boundary (upper)	7	Output "violet"	Output "violet"	Correct!
4	Erroneous out of range	-1	Output "-1 not in range 1 to 7"	Output "-1 not in range 1 to 7"	Correct validation range check works
5	Erroneous out of range	8	Output "8 not in range 1 to 7"	Output "8 not in range 1 to 7"	Correct validation range check works
6	Erroneous wrong data type	"Ana"	Output "Ana is not an integer."	Output "Ana is not an integer."	Correct exception handler works

Other types of data such as strings or opening and reading in files will not be as clear as the above example for numeric data. Nonetheless the principle remains the same: **systematically test all code by running it many times with a wide range of test data**.

Beta versions:

Professional programmers will often issue a "pre-release" (or "beta") version of their program to a selected group of users. These "guinea-pigs" will run the program and try to "crash" it and report any unexpected problems. I have even heard of a company that used to let a group of primary students "play" with their software just to see what would happen. Children are very good at ignoring instructions such as "do not hold down the shift key while entering data". If the program "survived" a day at school, without crashing, it was considered "**robust**" or "strong enough" to be released.

An integrated development environment (IDE) is a software application that provides comprehensive facilities to computer programmers for software development. An IDE normally consists of:

- **The compiler or interpreter** to translate high-level code into machine-code;
  - See the chapter on High and Low Level languages.
- **A source code editor**;
  - A "text-editor" where you write your code
- **A debugger**;
  - A tool to help you find mistakes - to debug your code

And various other tools to build and run code.

(Note: The Python "IDE" is actually called "IDLE" after one of the Monty Python team Eric Idle.)

Source code editor:

You can write code in a simple text editor. When you have finished just change the file name from "myCode.txt" to "myCode.py". Now any Python interpreter can run your code. But it is much easier using the editor that comes with the IDE:

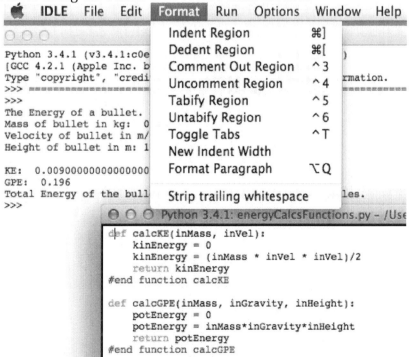

Apart from all the usual text-editing tools there many other commands that are particularly useful for writing code. My two favourites are:
- **Colour coding** key words and data types:
  - Orange for defining a function; blue for the name of the function, green for strings and so on. (None of these may be clear in a grey-scale print out!)
- **Comment Out Region**
  - When I want to work on one bit of code but I don't want another block to run at all, I just comment it out.
  - This is the same as just typing "#" in front of every line but much quicker
  - Then when I have solved the problem I can "put back" the code by using the "Uncomment Region" command.

Debugger:

A program that lets you **step** through your code one line at a time and shows what values are stored in all of the variables. A debugger lets you look at how each line of code affects your program. This can be very helpful to figure out what exactly the program is doing.

Stepping:

Stepping is the process of executing one instruction of the program at a time.   Doing this lets you see what happens after running a single line of code, which can help you figure out where a bug first appears in your programs. The Debug Control window will show you what line is about to be executed when you click the Step button in the Debug Control window. This window will also tell you what line number it is on and show you the instruction itself.

Break Points:

Stepping through the code one line at a time might be too slow. Often you will want the program to run at normal speed until it reaches a certain line. A break point is set on a line when you want the debugger to take control once execution reaches that line. So if you think there is a problem with your code on, say, line 801:
- Set a break point on line 801 and
- When execution reaches that line, the debugger will stop execution.
- Then you can step through a few lines to see what is happening.
- Then you can click Go to let the program execute until it reaches the end (or another break point).

Help I am stuck!

Coding can be a very frustrating experience. You "know" what you mean. You "know" what to do but you keep getting errors. Well at least now you know the different kinds of error that you can make. By rigorously testing your code your program should be nice and robust. You have a range of help and debugging tools in the IDE. Finally **you will get better with practice - You need experience**. Meanwhile here are some simple tips when you just can't find the bug:

- **Go away from the Computer**.
  - Solving the problem is the problem not the coding.
  - Have a walk in the park.
  - Try to explain the problem to a programming friend.
  - Draw a flow chart.
  - If you can't explain it very well maybe you don't really understand the problem.
  - Try some input, processing, output stuff manually - That is work it out your self on a piece of rough paper.
- **Sleep on it**
  - Sometimes the "solution" just comes to you when you weren't actively thinking about it.

Sweet dreams!

Questions on Chapter 3i Errors and Testing:

1. The following pseudocode is supposed to input 10 numbers and then output the maximum number input.

```
1 biggest  = 0
2 count  = 0
3 REPEAT
4        INPUT num
5        IF num > biggest THEN
6                num = biggest
7        END IF
6        count = count + 1
7        OUTPUT biggest
8 UNTIL count < 10
```

There are three **logical errors** in this.

(a) Identify each error by line number, explain what the problem is and write out the correct code.

(b) Use these examples to explain what a **logical error** is.

2. The pseudocode below shows a program that is supposed to add together all the elements of an array to give a total. The total is stored in the variable called total. The program contains a:
- Syntax error
- Run-Time error
- Logical error

The line numbers are not part of the code.

```
1: total  = = 0
2: marks = [15, 10, 45, 20, 67, 41, 56]
3: FOR index FROM 0 TO LENGTH(marks) DO
4:              total = marks[index]
5: END FOR
```

(a)   i. What is a **syntax** error?
        ii. Identify the line number of the syntax error and write out the correct code.

(b)   i. What is a **run-time** error?
        ii. Why might a **run-time** error occur on line 4?

(c)   i. State the line number where the **logical** error occurs and write out the correct code.
        ii. Why are **logical** errors often the most difficult to find?

3. Here are some examples of data that is in some kind of range.

In each case, within reason, decide on an appropriate range and then give an example of data, which is:

I.   **Normal** (within or "inside" the valid range)
II. **Boundary** ("extreme" on the "edge" of the valid range)
III. **Erroneous** (invalid data because it is out of the valid range)

(a) Temperatures (ºC) at which pure water is a liquid.
(b) The age of an African elephant (average lifespan of about 70 - 80 years)
(c) Times for a 100m race in a primary school (World record 9.58 seconds)
(d) Number of characters in a first name.

4. A science lab has a 4-digit security number used to open the door.

If the incorrect code is entered incorrectly three times an alarm signal is sent to the security office.

The following (correct) code is used as a test: 3769

The program displays the following message if the code is accepted:

     DOOR OPEN

Or displays the following message when the code is wrong but has been entered less than 3 times

     WRONG CODE

Or displays the following message when the code has been entered incorrectly 3 times

     ALARM

Assume that only number digits (0, 1 .....9) can be entered at the keypad

Copy & complete the table below with four different test cases. For each test case: identify test data, the reason for the test and the expected outcome:

Test case	Test Data	Reason for test	Expected outcome
1			
2			
3			
4			

Extension: Write an algorithm in pseudocode or a language of your choice to describe this process:

5. An Integrated Development Environment (**IDE**) helps to produce correct code:

(a) Compared to a normal text-editor outline how an IDE's code-editor helps you to write correct code as you type.

(b) Outline how you would use a typical IDE debugging tool to find and correct bugs in code.

Section 4
Data Representation

- **4a Numbers - Analogue and Digital**
- **4b Characters & ASCII**
- **4c Images & Pixels**
- **4d Sounds & Sampling**
- **4e Compression - Lossy & Lossless**
- **4f Encryption**

" The MP3 only has 5 percent of the data present in the original recording. ... The convenience of the digital age has forced people to choose between quality and convenience, but they shouldn't have to make that choice." (Neil Young)

0100

Xujhnfq hfxjx fwjs'y xujhnfq jstzlm yt gwjfp ymj wzqjx. Fqymtzlm uwfhynhfqny3 gjfyx uzwny3.

Chapter 4a Data Representation: Numbers - Bits & Bytes, Binary & Hex:

Analogue and Digital

A computer's Central Processing Unit (**CPU**) consists of millions of electronic units called "flip-flops" that can "flip" between being "ON" (1) or "OFF"(0). That's it. There is no "ghost in the machine". There are no numbers, letters, pictures or sound. Everything that humans need to do has to be represented as a stream of these ONs and OFFs ... 111000111101110111110000001110 ... or **binary digits**. It is for this reason that computers are referred to as **digital** machines. Meanwhile in the "real" world data is very different. For example temperatures can continually change, up and down:

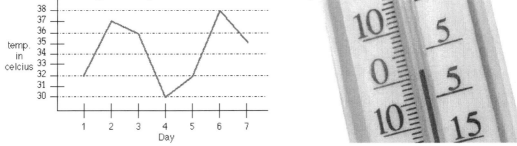

"Real World" data that is **continuously variable** such as temperature, pH, spatial position, voltage and so on is called **analogue data**.

Points Covered:
- Bits & Bytes
- Binary & Denary
- Binary arithmetic: addition, subtraction and multiplication
- Binary Negative Numbers
- Binary - bitwise operations - shifts (arithmetic and logical)
- Extension: Floating point binary numbers
- Hexadecimal

Bits & Bytes

Bits: At the "lowest" hardware level an electronic signal in a computer is either ON or OFF. These two states are represented as the binary digits "1" or "0". So the smallest "unit" of memory that a computer can work with is one **B**inary dig**IT** or **bit**.

Bytes: 8 bits is enough memory to store one character or letter, so is a very useful unit of memory and is called byte.

Nibbles: Half a byte is useful when looking at hexadecimal numbers and is 4 bits long.

Computer Memory:

The diagram below shows 5 bytes of computer memory. (See the section on hardware and memory for more details of how computers store and access data in their memory.)

5 Bytes of computer memory			
Human View		**Computer View**	
Location	Contents	Location	Contents
0	67	00000000	01000011
1	"C"	00000001	01000011
2	"A"	00000010	01000001
3	"T"	00000011	01010100
4	"S"	00000100	01010011

Note that the binary code that represents the integer 67 and the letter "C" are identical. In this sense all data is the same to a computer. It is when a program is run that the computer "distinguishes" between data types and program instructions. Data is accessed or "addressed" by ON/OFF 1/0 binary signals carried on wires (buses). The more of these wires there are, the more memory that can be addressed. For example a 4-bit (4 wires) bus can carry 2^3 or 8 different codes and so can address 8 unique locations.

$\qquad$ 000 $\quad$ 001 $\quad$ 010 $\quad$ 011 $\quad$ 100 $\quad$ 101 $\quad$ 110 $\quad$ 111

(See the section on hardware and the "fetch-decode-execute" cycle.)

Units of Memory:

The diagram below shows the most commonly used units of memory.

Unit	Symbol	Size (bytes)	Size (bytes)
kilobyte	Kb	(K) Thousand 10^3	$2^{10} =$ 1024
megabyte	Mb	(M)Million 10^6	$2^{20} =$ 1,048,576
gigabyte	Gb	Billion 10^9 thousand million	$2^{30} =$ 1,073,741,824
terabyte	Tb	Thousand billion 10^{12}	$2^{40} =$ 1,099,511,627,776

As you can see the memory units "go up" by 10^3 (1000) or in binary 2^{10}. So technically there are 1024 bytes in a kilobyte not 1000. Most of the time that subtlety can be ignored but be careful sometimes examiners expect very precise answers.

For example: How many bytes are in a Megabyte?

$\qquad$ Student answer: 1 Million --> was not accepted!

Answers (acceptable to the examiner): 1024 x 1024, $\quad$ 1024^2, $\qquad$ 1048576, $\qquad$ 2^{20}

Some examples of size:

This sentence: "If is the middle word of life." is 30 characters long (including spaces and the full stop) so occupies 30 bytes of computer memory.

A page of text (2000 characters):	2 Kb
An average book (500 pages):	1 Mb
A high quality digital photo:	12 Mb
A DVD disc with a film:	3 Gb
An external back-up hard drive:	2 Tb

As we use more and more memory to store more and more things we will need even bigger memory units: a Petabyte (PB) 2^{50} bytes or even an Exabyte (EB) 2^{60} bytes!

Binary and Denary:

Perhaps because we have 10 fingers we "count in tens". We use a "**decimal**" or "**denary**" system that has 10 unique digits: 0, 1, 2, 3, 4, 5, 6, 7, 8, and 9. For larger numbers we use "place value" which uses base 10. For example 1000 is 10^3 where 10 is the base.

Thousands	Hundreds	Tens	Ones
1000	100	10	1
10^3	10^2	10^1	10^0
2	3	5	7
2 X 1000 =2000	3 X 100 = 300	5 X 10 = 50	7 X 1 = 7
"Two thousand three hundred and fifty seven"			
		8	4
		8 X 10 = 80	4 X 1 = 4
"Eighty four"			
0	2	0	9
"0" not necessary	2 X 100 =200	0 X 10 = 0	9 X 1 = 9
"Two hundred and nine"			

Computers only have 2 digits: 0 and 1. So they "count" in **Binary or base 2**:

Hundred & twenty eights	Sixty fours	Thirty twos	Sixteens	Eights	Fours	Twos	Ones
128	64	32	16	8	4	2	1
2^7	2^6	2^5	2^4	2^3	2^2	2^1	2^0
	1	0	1	0	1	0	0
	1 X 64 = 64	0 X 32 = 0	1 X 16 = 16	0 X 8 = 0	1 X 4 = 4	0 X 2 =0	0 X 0 =0
64 + 16 + 4 = 84 (Denary)							
1	1	0	1	0	0	0	1
1 X 128 = 128	1 X 64 = 64		1 X 16 = 16				1 X 1 = 1
128 + 64 + 16 + 1 = 209 (Denary)							

Binary to Denary:

To convert binary numbers to denary numbers the easiest way is to write down each binary digit "under" its correct binary place value. Then just add up the value for each binary digit. The example below shows that 1010100_2 (base 2) is 84_{10} (base 10):

128	64	32	16	8	4	2	1
2^7	2^6	2^5	2^4	2^3	2^2	2^1	2^0
	1	0	1	0	1	0	0
	1 X 64 = 64	0 X 32 = 0	1 X 16 = 16	0 X 8 = 0	1 X 4 = 4	0 X 2 =0	0 X 1 =0
64 + 16 + 4 = 84 (Denary)							

Denary to Binary:

To convert denary numbers to binary numbers is a similar process using "place value". The following example shows that 57_{10} (base 10) is 111001_2 (base 2).

- Find the largest column heading that we can subtract from the number.
- Take it away and repeat with the remainder until we get an answer of 0.

57 (largest column is 32) (64 is too big!) so put 1 in the 32 column and 57 – 32 = 25

128	64	32	16	8	4	2	1
2^7	2^6	2^5	2^4	2^3	2^2	2^1	2^0
		1					

25 (largest column is 16) so put 1 in the 16 column and 25 – 16 = 9

128	64	32	16	8	4	2	1
2^7	2^6	2^5	2^4	2^3	2^2	2^1	2^0
		1	1				

9 (largest column is 8) so put 1 in the 8 column and 9 – 8 = 1

128	64	32	16	8	4	2	1
2^7	2^6	2^5	2^4	2^3	2^2	2^1	2^0
		1	1	1			

1 (largest column is 1) so put 1 in the 1 column and 1- 1 = 0 so stop and fill in any zeros

128	64	32	16	8	4	2	1
2^7	2^6	2^5	2^4	2^3	2^2	2^1	2^0
		1	1	1	0	0	1

Check by adding up the columns with 1 and it should give you the number you started with!

128	64	32	16	8	4	2	1
2^7	2^6	2^5	2^4	2^3	2^2	2^1	2^0
		1	1	1	0	0	1
		32 +	16 +	8 +			+ 1 = 57

I have shown each step involved. In practice it is much quicker than it looks and you only need to write out the binary place values once!

Denary to Binary - Alternative method:
If you repeatedly divide a denary number by 2 and note the remainder you will generate its binary equivalent.

- Divide by 2 repeatedly
- Noting the remainder value each time until the answer is 0:

57 / 2 = 28	remainder	1
28 / 2 = 14	remainder	0
14 / 2 = 7	remainder	0
7 / 2 = 3	remainder	1
3 / 2 = 1	remainder	1
1 / 2 = 0	remainder	1

Read the answer up from the last value: **1 1 1 0 0 1**

In general **I don't recommend** this method. It may look quicker but it is prone to mistakes. It is, in reality, an **algorithm** and so can be used to write a denary to binary conversion program.

Binary arithmetic: addition, subtraction, and multiplication
Addition:
Adding binary number is quite straightforward. You just have to remember how you add denary numbers using "carry".
For example, this is how you would do the sum: 5281 + 325

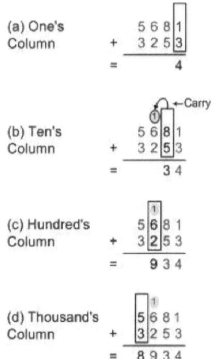

Binary addition is no different:

0 + 0 = **0**

1 + 0 = **1**

1 + 1 = 2 but 2 is 2^1 so the next column or place value: **10**

1 + 1 + 1 = 3 but 2 is 2^1 and 1 "left" in the first place value: **11**

Example: 01010101 (decimal=85) + 01110100 (decimal=116)

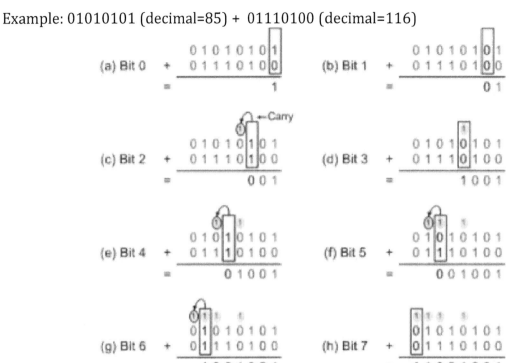

Binary Addition Overflow:

If you add two binary numbers and the result is bigger than 255 (11111111) it will need 9 bits to hold the number. This is called "overflow".

$$\begin{array}{r} 1 \quad 1111 \\ 01011101 \\ +\ 11011011 \\ \hline 1\ 00111000 \end{array}$$

In this case the CPU can handle 8 bits (1 byte). This is its "**word size**". The result of the above addition is now wrong and the CPU "flags" that an overflow error has occurred. It is not just that the result is wrong - Any further calculations based on that result would be wrong. Most CPUs use a much bigger word size than 8 bits. Many PCs have a 64-bit CPU. A 64-bit CPU can handle numbers larger than 2^{64} or 18 quintillion (18,446,744,073,709,551,615 to be precise).

Binary Subtraction:
As long as the result is positive, this is fairly straightforward:

● **Same as denary**
  ■ "borrow one from next column"
  ■ Note that "borrowed digit" is "worth" 2

```
1 0 1        5
  1 1 -      3 -
  1 0        2
```

```
 1 1 1
10101     21
00111      7
01110   = 14
```

Binary Multiplication:
Just use the same method as for denary "long" multiplication:

Same as denary:
1 * 1 = 1
1 * 0 = 0
0 * 1 = 0

Examples
```
  1 1
  1 0 *
1 1 0
```

```
    1 0 1
     1 1 *
    1 0 1
  1 0 1 0
  1 1 1 1
```

Binary Negative Numbers: Sign & Magnitude or Two's complement
Negative numbers are a little bit tricky. Of course when you are programming in a high level language like Python you don't have to worry. The main advice here is "don't panic!" You just need to see that just about any decimal number can be represented in binary. You do not have to do any complex binary arithmetic with these numbers.

Negative numbers In Binary:
Here is 13_{10} as a binary byte: **00001101**
But how could you code **-13$_{10}$**? You can't just stick a " – " in front!

Sign and Magnitude:
Perhaps you can't just stick "-" in front but what about saying that if the "first" (on the left) bit is 1 then the number is negative?
The most significant bit is the 'sign bit': 1 = minus and 0 = plus

2^7	2^6	2^5	2^4	2^3	2^2	2^1	2^0	
1	0	0	0	1	1	0	1	
–	64	32	16	8	4	2	1	
				8	4		1	= –13

So the "1" at the 2^7 position has no value. It just tells us that the whole number is negative.
The rest binary digits represent the size or magnitude of the number.
The largest positive number that can be represented is:
    0111 1111 (i.e. +127)
The largest negative number that can be represented is:
    1111 1111 (i.e. –127)
A couple more examples:

-2^7	2^6	2^5	2^4	2^3	2^2	2^1	2^0	
0	1	0	1	1	0	0	1	
+	64	32	16	8	4	2	1	
	64		16	8			1	= +89

-2^7	2^6	2^5	2^4	2^3	2^2	2^1	2^0	
1	0	0	1	1	0	0	0	
–	64	32	16	8	4	2	1	
			16	8				= -24

Here is an overview of all 1 byte sign and magnitude numbers:

Sign-Magnitude Representation

The problems with sign and magnitude:
Both 1000 0000 and 0000 0000 represent 0, so it "wastes" one binary code.

"Normal" range 2^8 : 0000 0000 = 0   --> 11111111 =   255

"+ or -" range 2^7 : [0]000 0000 = 0   --> 1111111   =   127

Addition doesn't always work!

0	0	0	0	0	1	1	1	=	+7
1	0	0	0	0	1	0	1	=	−5 +
1	0	0	0	1	1	0	0	=	**-12**

Two's complement
In principle this is quite simple: The most significant bit ("on the left") is a minus number:

-2^7	2^6	2^5	2^4	2^3	2^2	2^1	2^0	
1	0	0	0	1	1	0	1	
−128	64	32	16	8	4	2	1	
−128				8	4		1	−128 + 13 = −115

The largest positive number that can be represented is:
  0111 1111 (i.e. +127)
 The largest negative number that can be represented is:
  1000 0000 (i.e. –128)

A couple more examples of two's complement:

-2^7	2^6	2^5	2^4	2^3	2^2	2^1	2^0	
1	1	1	1	1	1	1	1	
–128	64	32	16	8	4	2	1	
–128	64	32	16	8	4	2	1	-128 +127 = - 1

-2^7	2^6	2^5	2^4	2^3	2^2	2^1	2^0	
1	0	1	0	1	0	0	0	
–128	64	32	16	8	4	2	1	
–128		32		8				-128 +40 = –88

Two's complement "solves" the "problems" with sign and magnitude:
There is only one way to represent 0: 00000000
And addition always works:

0	0	0	0	0	1	1	1	=	+7
1	1	1	1	1	0	1	1	=	–5 **+**
0	0	0	0	0	0	1	0	=	**+2**

Binary shifts - Arithmetic and Logical (multiply & divide by 2?)
Arithmetic Shift:
This is **bitwise** operation that shifts all of the bits of a binary number. Every bit is simply moved a given number of bit positions, and the vacant bit-positions are filled in. Arithmetic shifts can be useful as efficient ways of performing multiplication or division of signed integers by powers of two.
(Note: LSB is "Least Significant Bit" and MSB is "Most Significant Bit")

Arithmetic **Left** Shift:

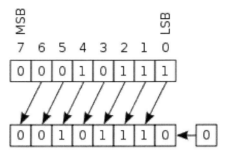

A left logical shift of a binary number by 1. The empty position in the least significant bit is filled with a zero.
Notice how, in effect the number has been **multiplied by two**.

10111_2 (23_{10})   --> 101110_2 (46_{10})

So in general shifting **left** by n bits on a signed or unsigned binary number has the effect of **multiplying** it by 2^n.
This is just the same as multiplying by 10 by shifting decimal digits one "column" along:

34 "shifted" to the left 1   -->   340   --> multiplied by 10 (10^1)
34 "shifted" to the left 2   -->   3400   --> multiplied by 100 (10^2)

Arithmetic **Right** Shift:

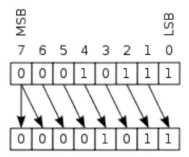

A right arithmetic shift of a binary number by 1. The empty position in the most significant bit is filled with a copy of the original MSB.
Notice how, in effect the number has been **divided by two**.

10111_2 (23_{10})   --> 1011_2 (11_{10})

And also notice how it has been **rounded down**. (The "correct" answer being 11.5)
So in general shifting **right** by n bits on a signed or unsigned binary number has the effect of **dividing** it by 2^n.

This is just the same as dividing by 10 by shifting decimal digits one "column" along:
        340 "shifted" to the right 1 -->   34   --> divided by 10 (10^1)
        340 "shifted" to the right 2 -->   3   --> divided by 100 (10^2) & rounded

Note: When shifting to the right, the leftmost bit (MSB) (usually the sign bit in signed integer representations) is replicated to fill in all the vacant positions. In the above example the MSB was 0 so it doesn't seem to matter but consider this example:
A two's complement number 10000111 is shifted right one place.
        10000111 here the MSB means -127
The rest of the number, 111_2 represents 7_{10} so the whole number is actually - 127 + 7 = - 120
Now when the number is shifted to the right the MSB (sign bit) stays where it is:

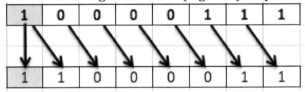

The resulting two's complement number is then:
        -127 plus "the rest" 1000011 --> 67 so -127 + 67 = -60
It works! -120 / 2 = -60

Logical Shift:
This is essentially the same as an arithmetic shift but "vacant positions" are always simply filled with 0s. As we saw in the two's complement example above, this means that a logical shift does not preserve a number's sign bit.

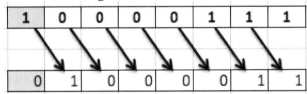

The resulting two's complement number is now:
        0 plus "the rest" 1000011 --> 67 so 0 + 67 = +67
        This is wrong! -120 / 2 is certainly not +67

So if you want to divide a signed (+ or -) binary number by 2 then you should use an arithmetic shift.

On the other hand what if the bits **don't represent a number at all**? A logical shift is often used when the binary digits are treated as a **sequence of bits** rather than as a number. Many electronic devices, from toys to drones and from cars to washing machines, have chips "**embedded**" inside them. The CPU is being specifically used to **control** one kind of device. In these cases each bit may be connected to an input or output device and may, quite literally, mean "ON" or "OFF".

Example: A byte controls the output to 8 LEDs (Light Emitting Diodes):

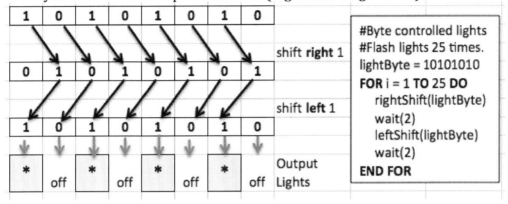

Extension: Floating point or real numbers:

This is a relatively difficult section and should be seen as "extension" work. On the other hand the main point is just to "reassure" you that just about any decimal number can be represented in binary. You would certainly not be expected to carry out complicated calculations with binary floating-point numbers!

The basic idea is the same as denary: Use a "decimal" point that can "float" or move:

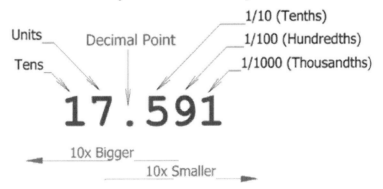

Representing a fraction in binary we can use a "binary point". Here is an example of a "decimal" point number and its close equivalent using a "binary point":

.	1/10	1/100	1/1000	1/10000	
	8	2	3	1	0.8231

.	1/2	1/4	1/8	1/16	1/32	1/64	1/128	
0	1	1	0	1	0	0	0	
	1/2	1/4		1/16				= 13/16

Note that the binary representation evaluates to 13/16 which is 0.8125 is not the same as 0.8231. I would need more binary digits but even then it is sometimes difficult to represent decimal fractions precisely using binary fractions.

For actual floating-point numbers we first need some terminology:

$$15.99 = \boxed{+} \boxed{1\ 5\ 9\ 9} \times 10^{-2}$$

Sign   Mantissa   Exponent

- The **mantissa** is the actual number to represent.
- The **exponent** tells us where to put the decimal point.

With binary numbers it is essentially the same idea.

Here's an example:
A binary number with a mantissa of "0.1111000" and an exponent of "00000011":

Mantissa								Exponent
0	1	1	1	1	0	0	0	0000 0011
0	1	1	1	1	0	0	0	Answer:
	4	2	1	1/2				7½

Exponent is 11_2, which is 3_{10} so move the "binary point" to the right 3 places.
Now each binary digit's "place value" can be seen.

Here's another example.

Mantissa	Exponent	Decimal
0.100 1101	0000 0100	Exponent is 4 so decimal point moves 4 places to the right: 01001.101 = 8 + 1 + ½ + ⅛ = 9⅝

Summary: Possible representation of +ve & -ve floating point numbers.

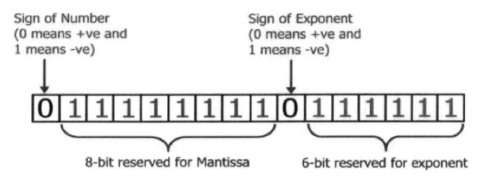

Hexadecimal: Base 16

If binary wasn't enough humans sometimes use base 16. Here's an example: Colours are very often represented as 3 consecutive bytes where each byte represents a numeric value for the "strength" of each colour: **R**ed, **G**reen & **B**lue.

Pure Red:	11111111 00000000 00000000
Pure Green:	00000000 11111111 00000000
Pure Blue	00000000 00000000 11111111
A "Red-orange" colour:	11111111 11001100 00110011

All of these 1s and 0s and very difficult and confusing for humans to read. In the last example I suppose I could convert each byte into a denary number:

Red (255) Green (204) Blue(51)

But, given that sooner or later I will need those binary values, denary is not so easy. What I need is a number system that can show binary bytes in a way that is:

- Easy for humans to "see" and work with.
- Easy to convert to and from binary.

The solution is hexadecimal or "hex":

Hex uses 16 unique digits. The first 9 are the same as denary digits. It then uses **letters as digits** to take it up to a maximum value of 15.

16 Digits: 0, 1, 2, 3, 4, 5, 6, 7, 8, 9, 10, 11, 12, 13, 14, 15

0, 1, 2, 3, 4, 5, 6, 7, 8, 9, A, B, C, D, E, F

HEX is used because it is easy to code one byte as two hex digits. The trick is that a **4-bit nibble** codes directly into one hexadecimal digit:

0000	0001	0010	0011	0100	0101	0110	0111
0	1	2	3	4	5	6	7

1000	1001	1010	1011	1100	1101	1110	1111
8	9	A	B	C	D	E	F

So to change from binary bytes, first cut each byte into 2 nibbles:

Now the " Red / orange" colour: 1111 1111   1100 1100   0011 0011

Can be written in hex as: F   F   C   C   3   3

The hexadecimal number **FFCC33** is **much easier for humans** to read and write and can, when necessary, quickly be converted back into binary. **Computers don't directly use hexadecimal.**

Hexadecimal uses place value just like denary and binary but with base 16.

16^3	16^2	16^1	16^0
4096	**256**	**16**	**1**

But as we will only be using 2 hex digits (0 - 255 or 8 bits) the arithmetic is going to be easy:

Converting Denary Numbers to Hexadecimal and vice-versa:

Just use the place value columns:

Example: Convert 43_{10} to hexadecimal:

16^1	16^0
16	**1**
2	B

11 X 1 =

2 X 16 = 32   11   --> 43

Example: Convert BF in hexadecimal to denary

16^1	16^0
16	**1**
B	F

11 X 16 = 176   15 X 1 = 15   --> 191

Binary to Hex:

The trick is to:

- Cut the binary byte into 2 nibbles;
- Treat each nibble completely separately;
- Convert each nibble into denary (should be quick)
- Convert each denary number into one hex digit (should be very quick)

Example: Convert the binary byte, 01101101 into hexadecimal:

1 Byte is 2 nibbles

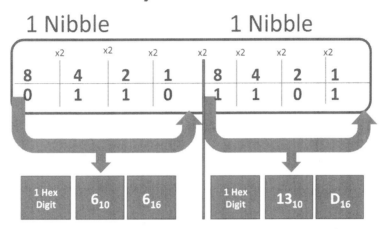

$01101101_2 = 6D_{16}$

Summary:

Here's the binary byte, 11001011, as a denary number, two 4-bit binary nibbles and lastly as a two-digit hexadecimal number.

Binary Denary & Hex 11001011

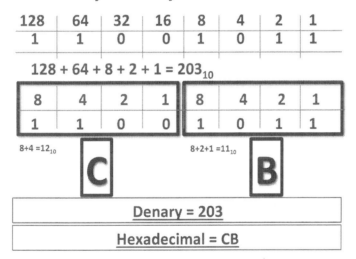

Questions on chapter 4a Numbers - Bits & Bytes, Binary & Hex:

Bits & Bytes:
1. An anemometer is an analogue device that can measure wind speed. Its signal has to pass through an Analogue to Digital Convertor (ADC) before a computer can process it.

(a) Use this example, to describe what **analogue** data means.

(b) Explain why computers cannot process analogue data and how they have to represent all data as binary digits.

2. Basic memory units:

(a) What is a "**bit**"?

(b) How many **bits** are in one **byte**?

(c) How many **bytes** are needed to store <u>one</u> **character** of text data?

(d) How many **bytes** would be needed to store the sentence shown below? (Remember spaces and punctuation count as characters as well!)

There's no success like failure but failure's no success at all.

3. Larger units of memory:

(a) Why isn't a kilobyte 1000 bytes? 1024 seems a strange number. How does it relate to binary?

(b) Use your answer in (a) to explain why the following calculation is not quite correct:

Nick sends a file of size 4096 MB. To convert to GB he simply divides by 1000. After all 1 GB is 1000 MB so 4096 / 1000 = 4.096 GB

4. Big and small units of memory:

(a) Sort the computer memory sizes listed below into **increasing order of size** with the smallest first and the biggest last:

10Mb　　　　**100Kb**　　　　　**5Gb**　　　　**2Tb**　　　　**50Mb**　　　　**500Kb**

(b) What comes after terabytes?

5. Estimate how many digital copies of Tolstoy's Novel "War and Peace" could fit on to a 32 Gb USB pen.

(Assume that an average page of text has about 3000 characters and that "War and Peace" is about 1500 pages long.)

Binary & Denary & Binary Arithmetic
In all calculation work you must show your working. You are not allowed a calculator in the exam!
1. Convert the binary number 10110101 to base 10 (denary).

2. Convert the decimal number 67 to binary (I recommend the "column method").

3. 255 is a significant number in binary. It will come up a lot in other parts of the course. What do you notice about the number 255 in binary?

4. How can you tell, just by looking, that a binary number will be an **odd** denary number?

5. Add the binary numbers 110111 and 10001

6.   (a) Add the bytes (binary numbers) 11010011and 11000101
       (b)Explain what would happen if the answer were stored as an 8-bit (byte) binary number.

7. Do the following binary subtraction: 110 -11

8. What's the problem with the following binary subtraction? 11 -110

9. Do the following binary multiplication: 110 * 11

Extension: Implement the "repeated division by 2" method to convert denary numbers to binary using pseudocode or a language of your own choice:
(**Hint**: Use modulo (%) 2 to get the remainder which will be 1 or 0.
In Python: thisBit = **str**(num % 2)
Note **str** to cast the remainder to a string so we can concatenate to other "bits".)

Binary Negative Numbers
1. Convert the following binary numbers into denary using two different systems to represent negative numbers. In each case the first one has been done for you.
(a) Sign & Magnitude:
       1100 1101   -->   -(64+8+4+1) = -77
       0001 1111
       1000 1010
       0101 1100
       1000 0000
       1111 1111
       0111 1111
(b) Two's Complement:
       1100 1101   -->   -128+64+8+4+1 = 51
       0001 1111
       1000 1010
       0101 1100
       1000 0000
       1111 1111
       0111 1111

Extension: Floating Point Numbers

Copy and complete the following table to convert floating-point binary numbers into mixed number denary fractions. The first one has been done for you:

Mantissa	Exponent	Decimal
0.100 1101	0000 0100	Exponent is 4 so decimal point moves 4 places to the right: 01001.101 = 8 + 1 + ½ + ⅛ = 9⅝
0.001 1111	0000 0011	
1.000 1010	0000 0101	
0.101 1100	0000 0011	
1.000 0000	0000 0010	
1.111 1110	0000 0011	

Binary - bitwise operations - shifts (arithmetic and logical)

1. Here is an 8-bit binary number: 0001 0101

(a) Arithmetical shift left:

    i. Write down the result of applying an **arithmetical** shift **left by 2** to this number.

    ii. By converting both the original and shifted number to denary show that the result of the operation is to **multiply** the original number by 2^2.

(b) Arithmetical shift right:

    i. Write down the result of applying an **arithmetical** shift **right by 2** to this number.

    ii. By converting both the original and shifted number to denary show that the result of the operation is to **divide** the original number by 2^2.

2. Here is an 8-bit binary number using two's complement: 11011001

    (a) Convert this number into denary.

    (b) Carry out an arithmetical shift right by 1.

    (c) Show, by converting the result from (b) into denary, that the original number has been correctly divided by 2 and that the original sign of the number remains unchanged.

    (d) Carry out a logical shift right by 1.

    (e) Show, by converting the result from (d) into denary, that the original number has not been divided by 2.

Hexadecimal

In all calculation work you must show your working. You are not allowed a calculator in the exam!

1. Convert the denary number 106 into Hexadecimal (base 16):

    (a) First convert 106_{10} into a binary number and show your answer as one byte.

    (b) Then cut the byte into two nibbles and convert to two Hexadecimal digits.

2. Convert the denary number 235 into Hexadecimal (base 16):

    (a) First convert 235_{10} into a binary number and show your answer as one byte.

    (b) Now cut the byte into two nibbles and convert to two Hexadecimal digits.

3. What is the principal reason for using hexadecimal notation in computer science?

Extension: Find out how hex used to code colours in HTML (web pages)?
For example what colour is FF 00 FF ?

Chapter 4b Data Representation: Characters & ASCII

Coding letters, words or phrases is nothing new. There are, scratched on the walls of caves, prehistoric symbols that must have meant something to someone. In more recent times, at the battle of Trafalgar, Admiral Nelson signalled to his men: "England expects that every man will do his duty" using flags. Perhaps the first "**digital**" mapping of a code for each letter or character was the **Morse code:**

```
A . —          J . — — —       T —            1 . — — — —
Ä . — . —      K — . —         U . . —        2 . . — — — . .
B — . . .      L . — . .       Ü . . — —       3 . . . — —
C — . — .      M — —           V . . . —       4 . . . . —
D — . .        N — .           W . — —         5 . . . . .
E .            O — — —         X — . . —       6 — . . . .
É . . — . .    Ö — — — .       Y — . — —       7 — — . . .
F . . — .      P . — — .       Z — — . .       8 — — — . .
G — — .        Q — — . —       Ch — — — —      9 — — — — .
H . . . .      R . — .                         0 — — — — —
I . .          S . . .         Understood . . . — .
```

SOS: . . . - - - . . . would be, perhaps, 000 111 000 in binary. Computers use text all the time.

Points Covered:
- How computers represent characters
- Standard codes for character representation such as ASCII

Binary Codes and Representing Characters:
When you type the letter "C" on your keyboard, and the same letter dutifully appears on your screen, the computer must have "received a signal" and interpreted it as the letter "C". But how did the computer "know" that you typed "C"? There must be a wire from the key "C" on the keyboard carrying a signal into the computer. But if it is only one wire then the signal can either be "ON" (1) or "OFF"(0). But that could only represent 2 letters. "Computer when you receive a 1 please put 'A' on the screen and if you receive 0 please write 'B'. With two wires it would be a **bit** (excuse the pun) better: 00 : A, 01 : B, 10 : C and 11 : D.

Problem: How many different characters do we **need** on a keyboard? Here's an estimate for the English language:

Alphabet, upper (A, B ..Z), lower case (a,b ..z)	52
All numeric digits (0-9)	10
Punctuation & other symbols (?, :, %, 'space')	25
Non-printable control codes (newline, para ..)	5
Total	about 100

Well how many wires coming from each key do I need then and what is the relationship between:
- The number of **bits per character** and
- The number of different characters that can be represented?

1 bit = 2^1	= 0, 1	= 2 distinct codes
2 bit = 2^2	= 00, 01,10, 11	= 4 distinct codes
3 bit = 2^3	= 000, 001,010, 011, 100, 101,110, 111	= 8 distinct codes
4 bit = 2^4		= 16 distinct codes
5 bit = 2^5		= 32 distinct codes
6 bit = 2^6		= 64 distinct codes
7 bit = 2^7		**= 128 distinct codes – good!**
8 bit = 2^8		= 256 distinct codes - too many

So the number of different characters that can be represented = 2^n (where n is the number of bits used). It seems also that 7 wires, each carrying 1 bit, will do the job.

Character Set: This a defined list of characters, and their codes, recognised by computer hardware and software. In this sense a character set is a "lookup table" that "converts" a binary code to its corresponding character. And, sure enough, one of the most common character sets, "**ASCII**" uses 7 bits to code for 128 different characters. Actually computers usually used an 8th bit for checking purposes so 8 bits were used per character and **8 bits is a byte**.

ASCII (**A**merican **S**tandard **C**ode for **I**nformation **I**nterchange):
Here's a table showing part of the ASCII set, starting at character 48 (0011 0000) the digit 0 and going up to 122 (0111 1010) the letter "z" and then a few punctuation symbols. Most of the other codes are for "non-printable" characters like (backspace) or strange brackets { } which Java uses all the time!

ASCII Code: Character to Binary

0	0011 0000	O	0100 1111	m	0110 1101
1	0011 0001	P	0101 0000	n	0110 1110
2	0011 0010	Q	0101 0001	o	0110 1111
3	0011 0011	R	0101 0010	p	0111 0000
4	0011 0100	S	0101 0011	q	0111 0001
5	0011 0101	T	0101 0100	r	0111 0010
6	0011 0110	U	0101 0101	s	0111 0011
7	0011 0111	V	0101 0110	t	0111 0100
8	0011 1000	W	0101 0111	u	0111 0101
9	0011 1001	X	0101 1000	v	0111 0110
A	0100 0001	Y	0101 1001	w	0111 0111
B	0100 0010	Z	0101 1010	x	0111 1000
C	0100 0011	a	0110 0001	y	0111 1001
D	0100 0100	b	0110 0010	z	0111 1010
E	0100 0101	c	0110 0011	.	0010 1110
F	0100 0110	d	0110 0100	,	0010 0111
G	0100 0111	e	0110 0101	:	0011 1010
H	0100 1000	f	0110 0110	;	0011 1011
I	0100 1001	g	0110 0111	?	0011 1111
J	0100 1010	h	0110 1000	!	0010 0001
K	0100 1011	I	0110 1001	'	0010 1100
L	0100 1100	j	0110 1010	"	0010 0010
M	0100 1101	k	0110 1011	(	0010 1000
N	0100 1110	l	0110 1100	)	0010 1001
				space	0010 0000

Note:
- The characters are "sequential":
  - A, B, C: 0100 0001 (65), 0100 0010 (66), 0100 0011 (67),
- The character values can be used for alphabetic sorting because:
  - A is less than B
  - B is less than C ...

OK the code did start in America but it is now very "**standard**" and very "**international**". This is very important.   It would be no good if you sent the word "CAT" (010000110100000101010100) by email to **Argentina** only to find that they used a different "code" and your text came out as "ECV". There is still one little problem: What about the Spanish characters ñ, ¿, ! and all those accents in French? As 8-bit computers became more common, the ASCII was **extended** to 256 codes

8 bit = 2^8 = 256 characters

These "extra" codes could represent more non-English characters and strange mathematical symbols. For example: The Russian Cyrillic uses 8 bits. The first 128, codes are the same as the ASCII 7 bit code, and the rest are for these:

—	│	┌	┐	└	┘	├	┤	┬	┴	┼	■	■	█	▌	▐
128	129	130	131	132	133	134	135	136	137	138	139	140	141	142	143
▓	▓	▓	⌐	▪	•	√	≈	≤	≥	nbsp	⌡	°	2	•	÷
144	145	146	147	148	149	150	151	152	153	154	155	156	157	158	159
=	‖	F	ё	╥	╓	╕	╥	╖	╘	╙	╚	╛	╜	╝	╞
160	161	162	163	164	165	166	167	168	169	170	171	172	173	174	175
╟	╠	╡	Ё	╣	╢	╤	╥	╦	╧	╨	╩	╪	╫	╬	©
176	177	178	179	180	181	182	183	184	185	186	187	188	189	190	191
ю	а	б	ц	д	е	ф	г	х	и	й	к	л	м	н	о
192	193	194	195	196	197	198	199	200	201	202	203	204	205	206	207
п	я	р	с	т	у	ж	в	ь	ы	з	ш	э	щ	ч	ъ
208	209	210	211	212	213	214	215	216	217	218	219	220	221	222	223
Ю	А	Б	Ц	Д	Е	Ф	Г	Х	И	Й	К	Л	М	Н	О
224	225	226	227	228	229	230	231	232	233	234	235	236	237	238	239
П	Я	Р	С	Т	У	Ж	В	Ь	Ы	З	Ш	Э	Щ	Ч	Ъ
240	241	242	243	244	245	246	247	248	249	250	251	252	253	254	255

Extension: There are other character sets used that give even more possible codes. **Unicode** for example uses 16 bits. Now that's 2^{16} = 65536 different characters. Now I can really send text around the world - from Japan to Norway from Lesotho to Argentina.

There is even a 32-bit version, which has more than 4 billion codes. These codes can be used for anything from specialist music notation to ancient Egyptian hieroglyphics.
Of course the downside is that each character would then occupy 4 bytes of memory. Most of the time that would be a waste of memory and could even slow the processing down.

Egyptian Hieroglyphs

U+1300A	U+1300B	U+1300C	U+1300D	U+1300E
U+1300F	U+13010	U+13011	U+13012	U+13013
U+13014	U+13015	U+13016	U+13017	U+13018

Questions on chapter 4b Characters and ASCII

1. Character Sets & ASCII

(a) What is the "**Character Set**" of a computer?

(b) How many different codes can be made with **7 bits** (Use a calculator but show your working)?

(c) Explain why the number you calculated in (b) is just about the right number of codes for use with a standard keyboard and the English language. (In other words: Use some examples of the different kinds of character necessary for ordinary everyday use.)

(d) The ASCII code for the character "D" is 68 in denary. Deduce the ASCII for "C" in denary. Use this knowledge about the ASCII code to explain how computers can sort text data alphabetically.

(e) An international company in London employs people from all over the world. They have a database, which stores the names and addresses of all their employees. Suggest a reason why they use a **16-bit character set** for this data rather than 7 bits.

(f) The Unicode system for encoding characters uses up to 32 bits (4 bytes) providing more than 4 billion possible character codes. What is a possible **disadvantage** of using such a character set?

(g) What does "**ASCII**" stand for and explain why it is important to have a "standard" code.

Chapter 4c Data Representation: Images & Pixels

Images, from the simplest cartoon like "clip-art" to the most beautiful, colourful photographs have to be "coded" just like text. Once again the computer only "sees" a data stream of 11001011011000001110110101010101 ...... The question is how does it represent the complexity and colour of an analogue image as digital data?

Points Covered:
- Representation of an image as a series of pixels represented in binary.
- Resolution, Colour depth image size and memory calculations
- Data Structures - arrays and images
- Metadata: Height, width & colour depth
- Extension - Vector Graphics

Pixels and Binary:

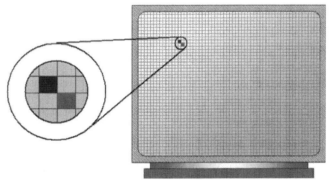

A pixel is short for **Pic**ture **El**ement. It is the smallest element of an image. Pixels are the tiny "dots" that make up an image on a screen. Each pixel is represented by a number of bits.

Resolution - "Sharpness" and number of pixels
Resolution is a measure of the fineness of detail in a bitmap image. It is measured in pixels per inch (**ppi**): The more pixels per inch, the greater the resolution. Sometimes resolution is referred to as "**pixel density**", which is the same thing.

Colour Depth - How many colours?

Each pixel can be assigned a different colour, and each colour must have a unique binary code, which represents that colour. Colour depth is measured by the number of bits per pixel used to code for these different colours.

Problem: Draw a tree and a house with smoke from the chimney:

Attempt 1:

Resolution: 15 X 10 pixels. 5 pixels / inch (5 ppi)

Colour depth: 1 bit per pixel so 2 colours only (1 : Black, 0 : White)

Bit map   Binary representation

	0	1	2	3	4	5	6	7	8	9	10	11	12	13	14
0	0	0	0	0	0	0	0	0	0	0	0	1	0	0	0
1	0	0	0	0	0	0	0	0	0	0	1	0	0	1	0
2	0	0	0	0	0	0	0	0	0	0	0	1	0	0	1
3	0	0	1	0	0	0	0	0	0	0	0	0	1	1	1
4	0	1	1	1	0	0	0	0	0	0	1	1	1	1	1
5	1	1	1	1	1	0	0	0	0	1	1	1	1	1	1
6	0	1	1	1	0	0	0	0	1	1	1	1	1	1	1
7	0	0	1	0	0	0	0	0	1	0	0	1	0	0	1
8	0	0	1	0	0	0	0	0	1	0	0	1	0	0	1
9	0	0	1	0	0	0	0	0	1	1	1	1	0	0	1

Attempt 2: Increase the resolution: Increasing the total number of pixels is not enough. I must increase the "pixel density" - the number of pixels per inch.

Resolution: 30 X 20 pixels. 10 pixels / inch (10 ppi)

Colour depth: 1 bit per pixel so 2 colours only (1 : Black, 0 : White)

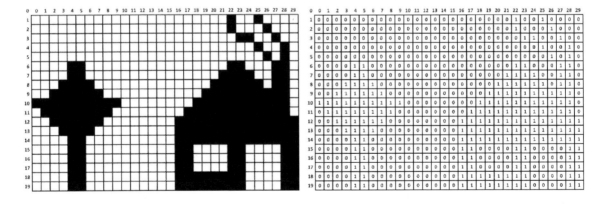

Attempt 3: Increase the resolution & the colour depth
Resolution: 30 X 20 pixels. 10 pixels / inch (10 ppi)
Colour depth: 2 bit per pixel so 4 colours
                              (11 : Black, 10 : Dark Grey, 01 : Light Grey, 00 : White)

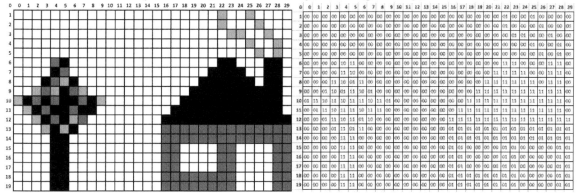

I hope the above examples help to explain the difference between resolution and colour depth. Of course full colour photographs must use much higher resolutions and colour depth.

Resolution

The picture below shows the same image at 72 ppi and 300 ppi. As you can see, when you enlarge the lower-resolution image, you can quickly see the little squares that make up the image. It does, indeed, look "pixelated".

Even when the images are not magnified, it is very clear that the 300-ppi image looks better, "sharper" and has "smoother" edges. But a higher resolution does mean that the image size, in terms of **memory**, is larger. Apart from memory considerations, there are cases where using ever-higher resolution makes no sense. Apple's "retina" display uses 300 ppi. Apple claim, with some justification, that if a mobile phone is held at about 25 cm away the human eye is unable to notice any pixilation:

Colour depth

The relationship between the number of bits used per pixel and the number of different colours than can be represented:

1 bit = 2^1 = 0, 1	= 2 colours
2 bit = 2^2 = 00, 01,10, 11,	= 4 colours
3 bit = 2^3	= 8 colours
4 bit = 2^4	= 16 colours
5 bit = 2^5	= 32 colours
6 bit = 2^6	= 64 colours
7 bit = 2^7	= 128 colours
8 bit = 2^8	= 256 colours
24 bit = 2^{24}	= 16.7 million colours

The number of colours = 2^n (Where "n" is the number of bits used.)

Having hundreds, or even millions, of different colours does, of course, mean that more and more **memory** is needed to store the image.

Choosing the "right" resolution and colour depth, then depends on what you want to do with an image:

- A "clip art", cartoon logo for a pie chart may only have a resolution of 36 ppi and a colour depth of 4 bits. That's fine and it will also occupy very little memory. Besides the image itself may be very small.
- A high quality photograph may be displayed on a full screen, at a resolution of 300 ppi with a colour depth of 24 bits and will occupy several Mb of memory. Editing such an image will require a fairly fast processor.

(See the chapter on **Compression** for issues with large file sizes.)

RGB - Why 24 bits and a use of hexadecimal

The **RGB** (**R**ed **G**reen **B**lue) colour system is an additive colour model where red, green and blue light are added together to make a range of colours. In simple terms:

- 3 bytes --> 1 byte (8 bits) for each colour **Red**, **Green**, and **Blue**.
- Each colour then has a bit depth of 2^8 = 256 different colours (from 0 to 255)
  - So the largest value that each colour can have is 255
- **Red** = 255, **Green** = 255, **Blue** = 255 is "everything on" which is white.
- Yellow would be all Red and Green but no blue: 255, 255, 0
- Now add these three colours together and you have 2^{24} = 16.7 million colours
- But saying the colour I want is 255255000 or 111111111111111100000000 is not easy for humans to read and mistakes can be made.
- Each byte can be represented by two **hexadecimal** digits.
- So yellow becomes: Red = FF, Green = FF, Blue = 00 or just FFFF00
- A mauve-blue colour may be: 6633CC

To "see" all of this in a "grey scale" book is not so easy!! Please go online and do some research on digital images.

Data Structures: Arrays and digital images. (See the chapter on Data Structures)
The data for the pixels in an image could easily be stored in a 2 dimensional array:
Going back to the "House" picture with dimensions of 30 X 20 pixels and a colour depth of 2 bits. Just change the bits to denary (3 : Black, 2 : Dark Grey, 1 : Light Grey, 0 : White) and there are 20 rows by 30 columns of numbers!

      housePic: **array** [0..19][0..29] **of integer**

File Size Calculations:
Both resolution and colour depth affect file size. Let's look at an example of a simple image with colour depth of 2 bits. (Remember that is 2^2 or 4 different colours.)

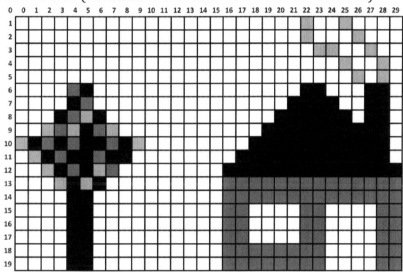

File size (number of bits)   = (number of pixels) X (number of bits used per pixels)
                           = (dimensions)   X (colour depth)
                           = (30 X 20)   X 2
                           = 1200 bits

If you want the answer in bytes, just divide by 8.
File size (bytes)   = (number of bits) / 8
                           = 1200 / 8   = 150 bytes

But what if the dimensions are not given in pixels? Very often the dimensions of a bit map image are given in inches. The above image originally measured 3" X 2" with a resolution of 10 ppi (pixels per inch):
File size (number of bits)
                        = (width X resolution) X (height X resolution) X (colour depth)
                        = (3 X 10) X (2 X 10) X (2)
                        = 30 X 20 X 2
                        = 1200 bits (just like before)

Metadata

In general metadata is "data about the data".

Filename:	townhall.jpg
File size:	2Mb
Dimensions:	3650 X 2430
Resolution:	180 ppi
Bit depth:	24
Color Mode:	RGB

The computer needs this information to display the picture correctly. Computers are not "intelligent". They cannot "know" what the image should look like. Give the wrong size data and the image will be displayed wrongly. For example the "standard" way of stating dimensions is **Width X Height**. What happens if the metadata has it the wrong way round?

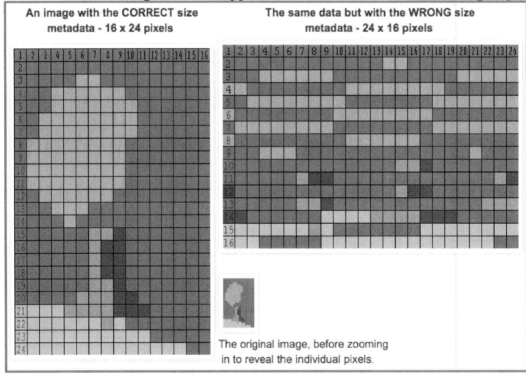

An image with the CORRECT size metadata - 16 x 24 pixels

The same data but with the WRONG size metadata - 24 x 16 pixels

The original image, before zooming in to reveal the individual pixels.

We humans are not so very different! There are no images floating around inside our brains. When natural analogue light hits our retina it is detected by **R**ed **G**reen **B**lue "cones" or light-sensors. These sensors represent this data as electro-chemical signals and send a stream of these signals to our brain where they are interpreted as an image.

Extension: Vector Graphics

Bitmaps are very good at displaying complex colour images like photographs but they are not the only way to represent images in a computer. Vector images store instructions of **how** to draw an image.

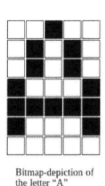

Bitmap-depiction of the letter "A"

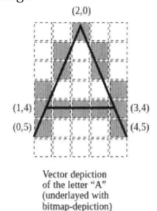

Vector depiction of the letter "A" (underlayed with bitmap-depiction)

Note how in the vector letter "A" the computer stores the information of **how** to draw the letter. Once it has defined the shape in terms of screen coordinates it can then work out what pixels and what colours are needed in order to display the shape on the screen.

All of the instructions are "relative". If you want the shape bigger then all the coordinates will change in proportion. The image will not "pixelate" at high magnifications.

Vector graphics are ideal for drawings with simple shapes that can be mathematically described. Technical diagrams, clipart, architect plans and so on. They also take up a lot less memory than bit-map images.

Questions on Chapter 4c: Data Representation - Images and Pixels

1. Resolution

(a) What is a "**Pixel**"?

(b) Explain what the **resolution** of an image is and how <u>pixels</u> are used to measure resolution.

(b) Explain how the resolution of an image affects the **file size** (amount of memory).

2. Colour Depth

(a) How many different colour codes can be made with **8 bits** (Use a calculator but show your working)?

(b) In **RGB** colour codes, one byte codes for each kind of colour (Red, Green and Blue).

i. How many **bits**, in total, then are used to code for the colour of each pixel?

ii. How many different colour codes does this generate? (Use a calculator but show your working)?

(c) What colour is represented by the following Hexadecimal number? **00FF00**

(d) Explain what the **colour depth** of an image is and how <u>pixels and bits</u> are used to measure colour depth

(e) Explain how the colour depth of an image affects the **file size** (amount of memory).

3. Metadata

(a) Use metadata to fully describe the bitmap image shown below:

0	0	0	0	0	0	0	0	0	0	0	0	0
0	0	0	1	0	0	0	0	0	1	0	0	0
0	0	0	0	1	0	0	0	1	0	0	0	0
0	0	0	1	1	1	1	1	1	1	0	0	0
0	0	1	1	0	1	1	1	0	1	1	0	0
0	1	1	1	1	1	1	1	1	1	1	1	0
0	1	0	1	1	1	1	1	1	1	0	1	0
0	1	0	1	0	0	0	0	0	1	0	1	0
0	0	0	0	1	1	0	1	0	0	0	0	0
0	0	0	0	0	0	0	0	0	0	0	0	0

(b) Explain, <u>with some examples</u>, what image **metadata** is and why the computer needs this data in order to correctly display an image?

4. Memory and file size calculations: An image has the following metadata.
Dimensions 7 inches X 9 inches;
Resolution (pixel density) 300 pixels per inch (ppi);
Colour depth of 8 bits.
Calculate the file size (the amount of memory used to store the file) in bytes.

Chapter 4d Data Representation: Sounds & Sampling

"Natural", **analogue**, sound is the **continuous** vibration of particles. The source can be from the tiny vocal cords in the throat of a nightingale or the explosion of a volcano. Somehow these waves of continual change in pitch and volume need to be converted into a stream of discrete, **digital** ONs and OFFs 1010110110111111.

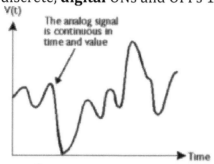
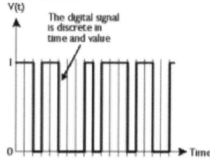

Points Covered:
- How a sound wave can be sampled and stored in a digital form
- Sampling rate - quality & file size
- Sample resolution (bit depth) - quality & file size
- File size - memory calculations

What is a sound wave?

Let's start with a little basic physics to describe a sound wave:

- Air particles vibrate backwards and forwards in the direction the sound is travelling
- **Frequency**
  - Cycles / sec (Hz)
  - How low or high pitched
- **Amplitude**
  - Maximum displacement
  - How loud the sound is

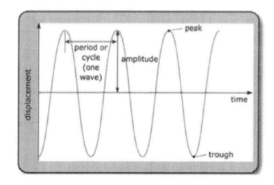

The above diagram shows a very "pure" sound of one "note" of a particular frequency and a fixed volume. "Real" sounds are much more complex. Here's a diagram comparing two very short bursts of sound:

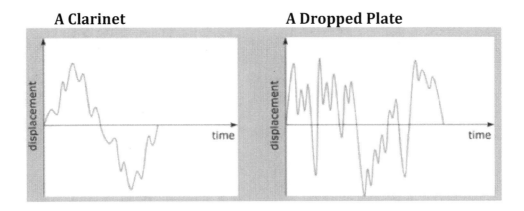

A Clarinet **A Dropped Plate**

Sampling a wave and converting it to binary:
In principle the challenge is much the same as with an image. Here's a table comparing the two processes:

Images	Sound
● Split the image into millions of tiny parts ■ **Pixels** ● Binary code for each pixel	● Split the sound wave into millions of tiny time intervals. ■ **Sampling** ● Sampling rate ■ **Number of times per second we take a sample** ● Binary code each sample

Sampling, then, consists of measuring the **displacement** of a sound wave a fixed number of times every second - the **sampling rate**.

Example: The sound wave below is sampled at a rate of 2 samples / second, that is every half a second. These measured displacements (+9.3, -3.1, -4.1, +8.2, -10.0, +4.0, +4.5) can then be coded into binary.

Original Wave **Sampled Wave**

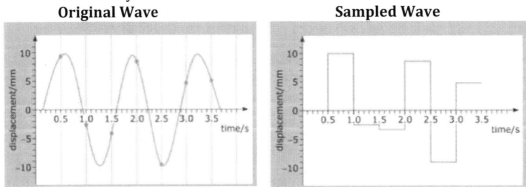

Considering that the object is to make the "digital wave" as close as possible to the "analogue wave", you can see that this sampling rate is not sufficient. Things get a bit better if the sampling rate is increased to 10 samples / second, that is every 0.1 seconds.

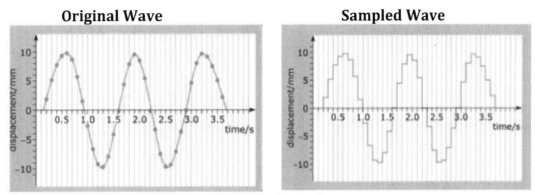

Original Wave   **Sampled Wave**

That's a bit better - the waves now, at least, look similar.

Sample Interval: Note that when you sample at 10 samples / second, the time between each sample is 0.1 seconds. This is called the sample interval and is simply:
Sample interval = 1 / sample rate

Sampling rate - quality and file size:
In general, then, the higher the sampling rate - the more samples there are per second - the "better quality" is the resulting "digital wave." The sampling rate used for CD audio would be in the range of 40 KHz, which is 40,000 times per second. Of course, each sample occupies some computer memory. So high sample rates may mean high quality but they also mean large file sizes.

Sample resolution (bit depth) - quality & file size:
Each sample has to be coded into binary. The samples in the first example above (+9.3, -3.1, -4.1, +8.2, -10.0, +4.0, +4.5) all need to be changed into binary numbers. This is known as "**quantisation**" - the mapping of samples to numbers. As we saw in the chapter on representing numbers in binary, this is a complex process, particularly for "floating-point" numbers. Nonetheless the general principle is that the more bits you use the more precisely you can represent numbers.

Sample Resolution or "Bit Depth":
- Number of bits to store each sample
- More bits means higher precision & better quality but more memory is needed.

Bit Rate:
- Bit Rate = Sampling rate X Bit Depth

Calculations on file size:

Example: Look at the following "metadata" about music digitised on an audio CD:

Metadata:

      Sampling rate: 44 KHz (44 000 times / second)

      Bit depth: 16

      Channels - Stereo: 2

      Song length: 2 minutes 30 seconds

Calculations:

      Bit rate   = Sampling rate X Bit Depth

                   = 44000 X 16 = 704 000 bits / sec

      Stereo (2 channels)

                   = 704000 X 2 = 1408000 or 1.4 M bits / sec

File Size (How much memory needed):

      File size (seconds):

                   = Bit rate X Time in seconds

                   = 1408000 X (2 mins 30 seconds)

                   = 1408000 X 150 seconds = 211200000 bits

    1 byte is 8 bits so file size = 210000000/8 = 26400000 bytes = 26.4 Mb

In Summary: Sound Quality vs. File Size:

- **Sample Interval**
  - Lower the interval, more samples per second so --> Higher quality
- **Sample Resolution**
  - More bits used, more precision so --> Higher quality
- **File size**
  - High quality means high file size

There are algorithms to "**compress**" audio files such that they take up less memory but the quality is still good enough for human hearing. See the chapter on **Data Compression** for more details.

Questions on Chapter 4c: Data Representation - Sounds and Sampling:

1. Sound Waves
Sound is the vibration of particles backwards and forwards in the direction the sound is travelling and can be represented as a sound wave. In a sound wave:
    (a) What is the **frequency** of the wave and how is it measured?
    (b) How do different frequencies affect what **you hear**?
    (c) What is the **amplitude** of the wave and how is it measured?
    (d) How do different amplitudes affect what **you hear**?
    (e) What is the highest frequency that a human can hear?
    (f) Explain, using sound as an example, the difference between **analogue** and **digital** data.

2. Sampling
    (a) Describe how sound waves are "digitised" by sampling. (Use a sketch of a wave to help you explain your answer)
    (b) A sound wave is sampled at a sampling rate of 1000 times / second. What is the **sampling interval** in this case?
    (c) Once a sound wave has been sampled; each sample has an associated number. What does **sample resolution** mean?

3. Sound quality and file size
    (a) State how the **sampling interval** affects:
        i. The **file size** (amount of memory)
        ii. The sound **quality**
    (b) State how the **sample resolution** affects:
        i. The **file size** (amount of memory)
        ii. The sound **quality**

4. Extension: Calculations for digitising sound waves:
    (a) Given the following metadata for CD Audio:
Sampling rate: 50 KHz (50,000 samples per second)
Sample resolution: 8 bits per sample
    i. Calculate the file size of a CD quality sound track that is 5 minutes long.
Give your answer in Bytes and then in Megabytes (Mb) & show your working.
(Hint: Number of bits is = sampling rate X resolution X seconds)

    ii. If the recording used 2 channels (for stereo) what would the file size be now?

    (b) Calculate the bit depth (resolution) of a 10.85 MB, 3 minute, sound track with a sampling rate of 30 kHz).
    i. Round your answer to the nearest whole number of bits / sample
(Hint: resolution = (number of bits) / (sampling rate X seconds)
    ii. If the recording used 2 channels (for stereo) what would the resolution have been?

Chapter 4e Data Representation: Compression - Lossy & Lossless

Data comes in many forms: from text to music from numbers to pictures. Modern computer systems need to store and transmit vast amounts of data. Compressing data means it will occupy less space.

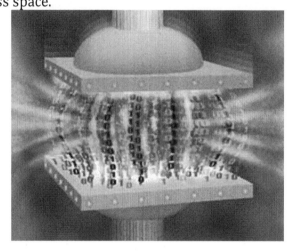

Points Covered:
- Need for data compression - Speed & Memory Storage
- Calculating time to transmit files and storage requirements for files
- Methods of Compressing Data - Lossy & Lossless
- Lossless Compression - Run Length Encoding Algorithm
- Lossy Compression
- Different file types

Why compress data?
The less memory data occupies the faster it can be transmitted from one computer to another.

1. Transmission Time - Speed is important
- Big files will take longer than small files
- Compress files to make them smaller
- Small files take less time to transmit over a network

Calculate time required to transmit a file:
Transmission speeds are measured in bits per second – **bps** (NOT bytes)

Transmission time = (Number of bits) / (Transmission speed in bps)

Example: A file of size 525 KB holds the text of a short novel and is transmitted at a rate of 2 Mbps. How long will the file take to be sent?

Number of bits = (525 X 1000 bytes) X 8 bits = 4 200 000 bits

Transmission speed = 2 X 1000 000 = 2 000 000 bps

Transmission time = 4200000 / 2000000 sec = 2.1 seconds

That's pretty fast but, nonetheless, if the file were half the size it would take half the time!

2. File Size and Memory
The amount of memory a file takes up can be important. And, as obvious as it sounds, small files take up less space.
Example storing music files:
- A Compact disk (CD) stores about 10 songs as CD audio.
- A mobile phone using the same memory stores 120 songs compressed as MP3

Calculate storage requirements for files:
Here are a couple of examples based on the relevant sections on data representation:
A short Book of 250 pages of text:

350 words / page	--> 6 chars / word	--> 350 X 6 chars = 2100 chars/page
250 pages in a book	--> 2100 X 250 = 525000 chars	
1 char is one byte so: 525000 bytes		
525000 bytes	--> 525 KiloBytes	--> 0.525 MegaBytes

A small picture with the following metadata:
    Size (284 X 177) pixels; Resolution 8 bits (256 colours)
    Number of Bits = 284 x 177 X 8 = 402 144 bits
    Bytes = 50268   --> or 50 KiloBytes
But whatever type the files are, the smaller they are the more you can fit in the same memory.

Methods of Compressing Data - Lossy & Lossless
A compression algorithm must, on the one hand, be able to compress the data but there must also be an algorithm that can "decompress" or "restore" the file.

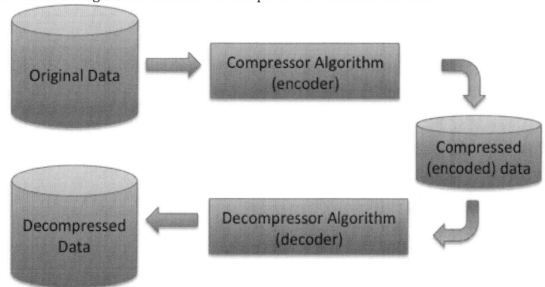

Lossless Data Compression:
- The "Decompressed Data" is identical to the original data.
- No data has been lost.

Lossy Data Compression:
- The "Decompressed Data" is NOT the same as the original.
- Some data has been lost.

Lossless Data Compression:

- Original Data can be **perfectly** reconstructed from the compressed data
- **Essential** for these files:
  - Text Files
  - Program code
- Examples:
  - ZIP file format

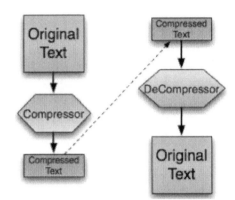

It is no good compressing a huge text file if, after decompressing it, there are words missing and you can't read it! If it was a file with computer programming code, not only could you not read it, it would not work anymore!

Lookup tables:

One kind of lossless compression algorithm for text makes a kind of numbered list or "lookup table" with a number for each word.

Original / Compressed	index > Word

- Original
  - "too wise you are too wise you be I see you are too wise for me"
  - 62 characters so 62 bytes
- Compressed as:
  - 1234123567341289
  - each digit one byte so 16 bytes
  - Some code to count spaces
  - reduced by some 70%

index	Word
1	too
2	wise
3	you
4	are
5	be
6	I
7	see
8	for
9	me

Actual algorithms would be considerably more complex: Perhaps searching for and storing repeating patterns and so on. But the principle remains the same: A text file can be considerably compressed and yet, when it is decompressed, the exact original text can be restored.

Lossless Compression Run Length Encoding (RLE) Algorithm:
RLE algorithms work by looking for repeating patterns (called a "run") and counting how many times they occur (the "length"). They can work on simple text or on basic bitmap images.

Simple Text Example:

Original: CCCCCCCCCTTTTTTTTLLLLL   --> 22 characters   --> 22 bytes
Encoded: 9C8T5L   --> 6 bytes

It's a bit like in the cafeteria when a group of teachers all shout out what they want:
  "coffee coffee coffee .... coffee coffee coffee tea tea .... tea lemonade lemonade .."
The man working behind the bar does not have to write down all the orders. He can simply make a note of: "9 coffees, 8 teas and 5 lemonades".

Simple Bitmap Example:
A house with a bit-depth of 2 (11 : Black, 10 : Dark Grey, 01 : Light Grey, 00 : White)

Bitmap of the house

Raw format

	0	1	2	3	4	5	6	7	8	9	10	11	12	13
0	00	00	00	00	00	00	01	00	00	01	00	00	00	00
1	00	00	00	00	00	00	01	00	00	00	01	00	00	00
2	00	00	00	00	00	00	00	01	01	00	00	01	00	00
3	00	00	00	00	00	00	00	00	00	01	00	00	01	00
4	00	00	00	00	00	00	00	00	00	00	01	00	01	00
5	00	00	00	00	00	00	11	11	00	00	00	11	11	00
6	00	00	00	00	00	11	11	11	11	00	00	11	11	00
7	00	00	00	00	11	11	11	11	11	11	00	11	11	00
8	00	00	00	11	11	11	11	11	11	11	11	11	11	00
9	00	00	11	11	11	11	11	11	11	11	11	11	11	00
10	00	11	11	11	11	11	11	11	11	11	11	11	11	00
11	11	11	11	11	11	11	11	11	11	11	11	11	11	11
12	01	01	01	01	01	01	01	01	01	01	01	01	01	01
13	01	01	01	01	01	01	01	01	01	01	01	01	01	01
14	01	01	00	00	00	00	01	01	00	00	00	00	01	01
15	01	01	00	00	00	00	01	01	00	00	00	00	01	01
16	01	01	00	00	00	00	01	01	00	00	00	00	01	01
17	01	01	01	01	01	01	01	01	00	00	00	00	01	01
18	01	01	01	01	01	01	01	01	00	00	00	00	01	01

There are certainly lots of "repeating patterns" here.

Row	Run Length Encoded
0	6(00) 1(01) 2(00) 1(01) 4(00)
1	7(00) 1(01) 3(00) 1(01) 3(00)
	....
5	6(00) 2(11) 3(00) 2(11) 1(00)
	....
11	14(11)

If the image was using a colour depth of 8 with values between 0 and 255 for the colour of each pixel, then each pixel would represent 1 byte. In this case a "run" of say 100 "dark green" pixels would be 100 bytes. But with RLE that "run" would be encoded as 100("dark green") or only 2 bytes.

Extension: An actual programming algorithm for Run Length Encoding of simple text.

An overview of the problem:

The idea is to replace lengths of repeated letters with a number and the character repeated.

Just work along the string (Iterate with a loop) ...

AAABBBBCADDEE

IF the next letter is the same **THEN** add one to a counter ... and carry on to the next letter.

ELSE the next letter is different to the current letter so add (concatenate) the current letter and the current count to an output string, put the counter back to 1 and carry on to the next letter.

AAABBBBCADDEE
    A = A so count = 1+1
        A = A so count = 2+1
            A <> B so write down "A3" set count = 1
                B = B so count = 1+1 ....

Final Result:

A3B4C1A1D2E2

This could be read as: "There are 3 As, then 4 Bs, then 1 C , then 1A ...."

Now in "formal" pseudocode:
FUNCTION RunLenEncode (STRING inText)
BEGIN FUNCTION

```
        outText = " "                       # empty string ready to hold the answer
        textLength = LENGTH (inText)         #integer length of string
        letCount = 1                         # initialise letter counter to 1
        #start with first letter of the string and loop along letter by letter
        FOR i = 0 TO (textLength-1) DO       #note string index start at 0
                #Compare this letter with next letter on right (note <> is not equal )
                IF (inText[ i ] <> inText[ i + 1 ]  ) OR ( i + 1 = textLength) THEN
                        #different next letter or no next letter as "off the end" of string
                        #so join letter & count (string concatenation) to outText
                        outText = outText + inText[ i ] + (STRING)(letCount)
                        letCount = 1                 # reset letter counter to 1
                ELSE
                        letCount = letCount + 1      #same letter so increment counter
                END IF
        END FOR
        RETURN outText               # "pass out" the encoded text & leave function
END FUNCTION
```

You may want to implement this in a language of your choice!

Lossy Compression:
This is where the data-encoding algorithm does remove some details. The "restored" or decompressed file is not the same as the original. Indeed, you can **never go back** to the original.

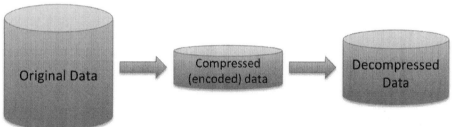

On the face of it lossy compression seems a "bad" thing - you may have reduced the file size but you have lost some detail - so why do it?

Photographs - With large complex images you have no choice.
- Pixel sequences are completely unpredictable - there are no "patterns"
- There will be fewer pixels compared to the "raw" original
- But, if the algorithm is "clever" enough, and the picture is not to be viewed at a high magnification, a human eye won't really notice the difference.

Typical lossy algorithms for Photos:
JPEG (**J**oint **P**hotographic **E**xperts **G**roup)

- Most common format for storing & transmitting photographic images on the world wide web
  - .jpg
- lossy
  - colour depth 24 bits
  - Red (8), Green (8), Blue (8)
  - 16.7 million colours

JPEG typically achieves 20:1 compression with little perceptible loss in image quality. It works by discarding data that the human eye cannot easily see. For example: The human eye is not very good at perceiving slight changes in colour but is quite good with slight changes in light and dark. So JPEG removes any slight changes in colour.

There are other lossy compression algorithms for images:
- **GIF** (**G**raphics **I**nterchange **F**ormat) - colour depth 8 bits
  - Used for small Web logos or even small animations
- **PNG** (**P**ortable **N**etwork **G**raphics) - colour depth 24 bits
  - Largely replacing "GIFs" now but no animations.
- **PDF** (**P**ortable **D**ocument **F**ormat)
  - A PDF file describes all the details of a file needed to display it (text, fonts & graphics)
  - Lossless for text but lossy for images.

Audio - sound waves - With large complex sounds you have no choice.
- Sound samples are completely unpredictable - there are no "patterns"
- There will be a loss of data compared to the "raw" original
- The "trick" is to remove "sound details" so that the human ear will not notice the difference.

An early "MP3" player.

MP3: A very common algorithm for audio files.

The algorithm itself is very complex but it basically works by "playing on" the limitations of a human ear and brain. For example:

- For a start we can only hear frequencies between 20 and 20 KHz, so anything outside of that range can go.
- If two very similar frequencies "arrive" at our ear close together we will really only hear the loud one, so the quieter one can go.
- Perhaps a very loud sound in one track "drowns" out the other tracks, so remove the other tracks at that point

MPEG (**M**oving **P**icture **E**xperts **G**roup)

This is a very common, lossy compression algorithm for video files. (Actually the MP3 algorithm is part of the same group but only works on audio)

As a final note: "Purists" or specialists will still say that they can see or hear the difference. They will need the "**raw**" data and are prepared to "pay the price" in very large file sizes and slow processing and long download times. Indeed the humble analogue vinyl disc and turntable are making a bit of a comeback. People claim that any "digitising" of sound is not "natural" (which I suppose it isn't) and that the "pure" analogue sound from an old-fashioned record is much better. They may be right! High quality "digital" music is, on the other hand, much more "convenient" and if you want the "real" sound then go and listen to a live concert!

Questions on Chapter 4e: Data Representation - File Compression:
1. Files are often compressed before they are sent over the Internet.
    (a) State what is meant by **compression**
    (b) State **one** advantage of compressing files before sending them over the Internet.
Two types of compression are **lossy** and **lossless**.
    (c) Outline the difference between **lossy** and **lossless** compression.
    (d) State which type of compression is most appropriate for each of the following and explain why it is appropriate.
        i. Downloading the source code of a large program
        ii. Downloading a large high quality colour photograph

2. Below is a list of file extensions for common file standards used on the Internet.
    JPG   **PDF**   **MP3**   **MPEG**   **ZIP**
A school allows parents to download different files. For each scenario listed: Choose one of the file formats above and explain your choice.
    (a) A past paper science exam in the correct format to be printed out at home:
    (b) A compressed collection of 100 plain text files of all school information:
    (c) A high-resolution image of the new school auditorium:
    (d) A short video message from the director of the school:
    (e) An audio recording of the school choir:

3. Compress the following stream of characters using Run Length Encoding (**RLE**):
    LLLLLLLOOVVVVVVEEECCCCCSSSSSSSSSSS
Explain why **RLE** is considered as a **lossless** method of compression.

4. The image below has the following metadata:

- **Resolution** 1,024 pixels (a grid of 32 pixels by 32 pixels)
- **Colour depth**: contains 255 different colours (represented by 8 bits)

In all the calculations below show your working.

(a) **Original** (uncompressed) file:

Calculate the numbers of bytes required to store this file.

(b) **Compressed** file:

The image has been encoded using Run Length Encoding (**RLE**).

Each "piece" of data is coded as a colour & a run length:

For example: DarkBlue6, LightGreen20

In binary: 8 bits are used for one of the 256 colours and 5 bits for a run length up to 32, which is a total of 13 bits for each "piece" of data.

The result of the RLE compression is 116 (13 bit) binary codes.

Calculate the numbers of bytes required to store this file.

(c) Show, as a percentage, the memory saved by compression.

Chapter 4f Data Representation: Encryption

So far we have been looking at ways to represent data so that a computer can make "sense" of that data. A computer needs to be "told" what a particular stream of 11111000101010 "means": Is it a number, some text, a program, a picture or a sound? Paradoxically we now need to look at how to make data completely meaningless so no one knows what it contains!

Points Covered:
- The need for data encryption
- The Caesar cipher algorithm
- Extension: Alan Turing and the Enigma machine

Why encrypt data?

Telecommunications are so important in the 21st century yet we scarcely notice. It is only when you lose your mobile phone or the Internet connection "goes down" that you realise just how important communication technology is. Data, from humble SMS messages to huge text files, are being sent from one person to another, millions of times every day.

The problem is that as soon as you send a message, someone else could intercept it and read it. (See Eavesdropping in the chapter on Net Security.) You don't even have to use the Internet: What if you leave a USB pen full of all your personal files on the bus? Anyone could "open" your files and read them. Now, if your files are confidential or secret, you are in big trouble. Password protecting your files, so that only someone with the password can open them, may help but it is not enough.

The solution is to encrypt data using a "key" so that only people you give the "key" to can read your data. An encryption program "garbles" your files into an unreadable mess. Only people with the "key" and the algorithm can "open" and decipher the files.

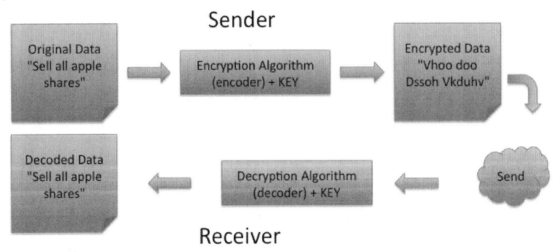

You are still not 100% safe. There are "hackers" out there who will try and "break the code" and read your secret messages. The level of protection you need will depend on who you are and what the data is: Are you a spy for your government working under-cover in a foreign country? Are you a businesswoman in New York sending important instructions to your head-office in London? Or are you just an ordinary teenager saving your English essay onto a USB pen?

The Caesar Cipher

A "cipher" is an algorithm to either encrypt or decrypt a file. Note that, for many people, the word is the same as "code". Yet when we use the "ASCII" character set to "code" binary into characters, it is obviously not a secret code!

The Caesar Cipher is a type of **substitution cipher** in which each letter in the original is replaced by another letter. It works by shifting the alphabet along a known (but secret) number of spaces. Here's a message where the "key" (the number to shift) is 3:

Original (or "plaintext") message: HELLO CAESAR CIPHER
Key: 3 (so shift each letter along 3 and, if at the end, "loop" back to the beginning:

| A | B | C | D | E | F | G | H | I | J | K | L | M | N | O | P | Q | R | S | T | U | V | W | X | Y | Z |

| A | B | C | D | E | F | G | H | I | J | K | L | M | N | O | P | Q | R | S | T | U | V | W | X | Y | Z |

Ciphertext (the encrypted text): KHOOR FDHVDU FLSKHU

The method is named after **Julius Caesar**, who used it in his private correspondence. In modern times it seems a laughably simple cipher. Encryption algorithms used in the 21st century are very complicated indeed. Nonetheless, in Roman times many people were illiterate and perhaps just thought "KHOOR FDHVDU FLSKHU" was written in a foreign language.

   "If he had anything confidential to say, he wrote it in cipher, that is, by so changing the order of the letters of the alphabet, that not a word could be made out."

Suetonius, Life of Augustus

Developing a Caesar cipher: Programming the Caesar cipher is not particularly difficult and is a worthwhile exercise in problem solving.

First version: This will only use capital letters; have no spaces nor punctuation; will only use a positive key and will only encrypt messages – That is convert plain text into coded text.

Structured English:

Store the **LETTERS** of the alphabet – 'ABCDEFGHIJKLMNOPQRSTUVWXYZ'
Store the **length** of the alphabet (i.e. the number of letters)
Input a **key** or "shift" value
Input a **message** as a string
Have an empty string ready to store the **encrypted** message
For each **letter** in the **message**
> Find the numeric **position** of that letter in the alphabet.
> Add to that numeric **position** the **key** value
> If the **position** number is now longer than the length of the alphabet then
> Take away the **length** from the **position** number.
> Use the **position** number to look up the new letter from the alphabet and add that letter to the encrypted string.

Get the next letter in the message
Output the encrypted string.

Pseudocode:

```
LETTERS = 'ABCDEFGHIJKLMNOPQRSTUVWXYZ'          #a constant
lengthAlpha = LENGTH(LETTERS)
key = INPUT (INTEGER)
message = INPUT (STRING)
encrypted = ' '                                 #empty string to hold encrypted
FOR EACH letter FROM message DO
        position = index of letter in LETTERS
        position = position + key               #add key to shift position along
        IF position > lengthAlpha THEN          #check if shift off end of alphabet
                position = position – lengthAlpha
        END IF
        encryption = encryption + LETTERS[position]
END FOR
OUTPUT encryption
```

Python:

```
LETTERS = "ABCDEFGHIJKLMNOPQRSTUVWXYZ"
lengthAlpha = len(LETTERS)
key = int(input("Please enter the key as a small integer: "))
message = input("Type in your short message here:  ")
encrypted = ""
for letter in message:
        #find returns the index of the letter or -1 if not found
        position = LETTERS.find(letter)
        position = position + key
        if position >= lengthAlpha:
                position = position - lengthAlpha
        #end if ..............
        encrypted = encrypted + LETTERS[position]
#end for
print("Your message was: ", message)
print("The encrypted message with a key of ", key, " is: ", encrypted)
```

The above implementation is a very basic version. Here's the result of a simple run:

    Please enter the key as a small integer: 3
    Type in your short message here: ZARA
    Your message was: ZARA
    The encrypted message with a key of 3 is: CDUD

And here's how the Python code deals with letters, which are not in "LETTERS", such as all lower case letters!

    Please enter the key as a small integer: 3
    Type in your short message here: zara
    Your message was: zara
    The encrypted message with a key of 3 is: CCCC

Can you see why the letters in the "encrypted" output are all "C"?

It was explained by the comment just above the line that uses the "find" function:

    "#find returns the index of the letter or -1 if not found"

Ah! So the "position" will always be -1 and -1 + 3 (the key) is 2 or letter C.

I outline some further versions, working towards a full encryption and decryption version in the problems at the end of the chapter.

Extension: **Alan Turing** and the Enigma code:
During the Second World War the Nazis sent top-secret military messages by radio. All of these messages were encrypted using the famous "Enigma" machine. These machines resembled large typewriters:

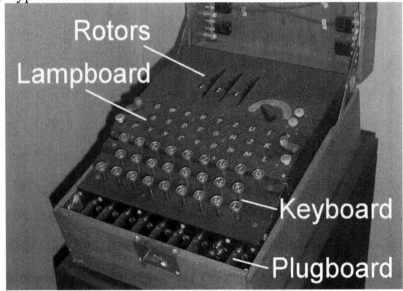

A combination of wiring with the "plug board", and random settings of the rotors, which moved, after every key was typed meant that the Enigma generated a very complex substitution cipher. One estimate puts the number of different settings at 150 million million million different ways! No wonder the Germans thought that their transmitted data was secure.

Meanwhile the British government had assembled a large number of mathematical experts to work as "decoders" and try to "break" messages coded using the Enigma machine. One of the "stars" of this team was a young mathematician called **Alan Turing**. His insight was that only a machine could "break" another machine. He and his team developed a "counter" electro-mechanical machine called the "bombe". Eventually their machine was successful at reading secret messages coded by the Enigma machine.

Turing's contribution to Britain's war effort was tremendous but less well known is his contribution to Computer Science. He formulated the concepts of **algorithms** and **computation** and even **artificial intelligence** long before a working digital computer existed. The annually awarded "**Turing Award**" is generally recognised as the "Nobel Prize of Computing.

Further Extension: You may be interested in discovering more about Alan Turing and the Enigma machine. The film, "The Imitation Game", while not 100% accurate, is a thrilling and moving film. There are many books and websites if you wish to research further into the life of the one of the "fathers" of Computer Science - Alan Turing.

Questions on chapter 4f Encryption:

1. See if you can encrypt and decrypt the following messages, using this alphabet (ABCDEFGHIJKLMNOPQRSTUVWXYZ) and any characters not there are left alone.

(a) Encrypt:

YOU MAY THINK I AM A DREAMER BUT I AM NOT	Key: 1
THINK BEFORE YOU LEAP	Key: -2
FUNCTIONS RETURN PROCEDURES DO	Key: 3

(b) Decrypt:

UQNXKPI VJG RTQDNGO KU VJG RTQDNGO	Key: 2
YZQRPYARGML GQ RM QCC RFC UMMB DMP RFC RPCCQ	Key: -2
NYWX FIGEYWI CSY GER HSIW RSX QIER CSY WLSYPH	Key 4

2. Bob Dylan needs to keep the lyrics to his songs confidential so, when he emails them to his agent, he encrypts them using a Caesar cipher algorithm.

The alphabet with the original and the encrypted message are shown below:

Alphabet	ABCDEFGHIJKLMNOPQRSTUVWXYZ
Original	LOVE MINUS ZERO NO LIMIT
Encrypted	QTAJ RNSZX EJWT ST QNRNY

(a) State the numerical key used to code the message.

Here is part of the algorithm used to encode the original message

```
1     Encrypted = ""
2     FOR letter in Original DO
3         IF (letter in Alphabet) THEN
4             index = Alphabet.find(letter)
5             index = index + key
6             IF index >= lengthAlpha THEN
7                 index = index - lengthAlpha
8             END IF
9             Encrypted = Encrypted + Encrypted [index]
10        ELSE
11            Encrypted = Encrypted + letter
12        END IF
13    NEXT letter
```

(b) Explain the purpose of the condition (letter in Alphabet) in the IF statement in line 3.

(c) State what happens to the letter to be encrypted if this condition evaluates to false.

(d) Explain the purpose of the IF ... THEN .... END IF statements at lines 6,7 & 8.

(e) Explain why the Caesar cipher is, in modern times, not considered very secure.

(f) **Extension**: Outline an algorithm that could be used to "break" the Caesar cipher. That is it could read a decrypted message without knowing what the key was.

3. **Extension**: Look at the algorithm for the Caesar cipher developed in the text.
Either in pseudocode and / or in a language of your choice – Extend the first version as follows:

Version 2: Allow for letters not included in the alphabet constant by checking if that letter is in the alphabet and if it is not just adding the letter, as it is – without "shifting" it, to the encrypted message.

Version 3: Change the input message to all upper case.

Version 4: Extend the "allowed" alphabet by adding lower case letters and digits 0 – 9

Version 5: Copy and make a new version that instead of coding an input message, it decodes (back to plain text) a coded version.

Version 6: Bring together versions 4 & 5 so that the program can either code or decode a message.

Version 7: Functions: Apply **abstraction** by decomposing your code into small subprograms. Each subprogram (procedure or function) will do one specific task:

1. **askStatus**: Checks the user choice and returns only "Decode", "Code" or "Abort"

2. **checkIntKey**: Checks the user only inputs an integer between 1 and 25 for the "key". Returns the integer key or 1 as a default

3. **decodeMess**: Takes in a message string as a parameter and returns the decoded string

4. **encodeMess**: Takes in a message string as a parameter and returns the encoded string

Section 5
Computers Hardware & Software

- **5a Digital Computer Systems:**
- **5b Central Processing Unit**
- **5c Software**

"I think it's fair to say that personal computers have become the most empowering tool we've ever created. They're tools of communication, they're tools of creativity, and they can be shaped by their user." (Bill Gates)

0101

Ivvsvw wlsyph riziv teww wmpirxp2. Yrpiww i1tpmgmxp2 wmpirgih.

Chapter 5a Computers - Hardware & Software: Digital Computer Systems

What is a computer? "An electronic, digital, automatic, programmable, data-processing machine" is a fairly neat definition and each word is defined here:
- **Electronic** – low voltage, solid-state integrated circuits with many transistors
- **Digital** – Uses on / off, 1 / 0 binary signals
- **Automatic** – can run without human intervention
- **Programmable** – follows instructions that are stored as a program
- **Data Processing** - Computers process data to produce information

We should also clearly distinguish between hardware and software:
- **Hardware**: The physical parts of a computer system such as the chip, the keyboard, the screen, the printer and so on.
- **Software**:   The programs or instructions that tell the hardware what to do. Software could include anything from a short piece of code in Python through to the operating system and all the applications that you habitually run such as a Word-Processor or a Web-Browser.

This section of the book looks at computer systems and the hardware and software that make them work.

Points Covered:
- Input Process Output Model
- Input and Output devices
- Extension: Control Actuators & Sensors
- Embedded Systems
- Backing Storage and "The Cloud"

The Input Process Output Model:
In simple but fundamental terms: Computers run programs that take input, process it and output the result. This is the Input Output Process model. The program and any accompanying data can be stored safely on various backing storage devices:

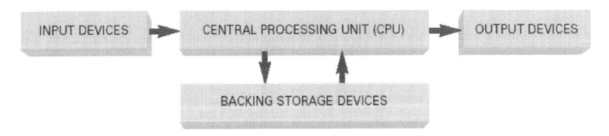

The great scientist John Von Neumann first described this model in 1945. So the basic Input --> Process --> Output structure is sometimes referred to as "**Von Neumann architecture**".

- **Input Devices** are how we get data into a computer, most commonly using a keyboard and a mouse.
- **Processing** is usually carried out by the "brains" of a computer system the Central Processing Unit (CPU). This is where the programs are run or executed.
- **Output Devices** are so that the user can "see" the results of processing usually with a screen or monitor and a printer.
- **Backing Storage Devices** are where data and programs are stored, most commonly magnetic hard discs or solid-state memory. The CPU can "**read**" in any data and "**write**" any changes back to the storage devices.

A slightly more detailed view of computer system is shown below:

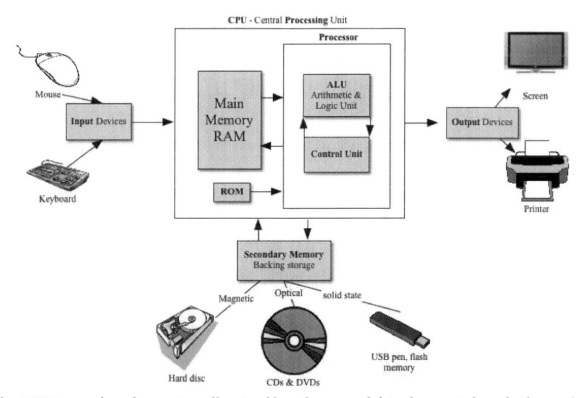

The CPU is worthy of a section all to itself so the rest of this chapter is largely devoted to the "peripherals" - hardware devices which can be connected to the computer but are, in one way or another, external to it.

Input and Output devices

This is not the place to list each and every possible device but here's a brief overview of some of the most important.

Input Devices: All of these devices do, in effect, convert input from the **analogue** "real world" into **digital** signals that the computer can "understand".

The Keyboard

This is still the most commonly used device for "direct" or human input of text into a computer. Each key is a simple switch which, when you press on it, completes a circuit and allows a tiny current to flow. A small "**embedded**" processor detects which key has been pressed, "looks up" that key in its "character map" and sends the appropriate code to the computer. (See the section on data representation: characters and ASCII)

The Mouse

Almost all programs now rely on some kind of "pointing device". By moving your mouse across a surface you are sending the computer x-y coordinates of where the pointer is compared to where it was. A touchpad is really no different. When you finally "click" the computer can work out where on the screen the pointer was when you clicked and carry out the appropriate action.

Touch Screens

Most mobile devices, from tablets to phones manage without a keyboard or a mouse. Now it is the position of your finger on the screen that the computer can use to "know" what you "clicked on".

Microphones

Lastly why not just talk to your computer? The sound wave is converted into a digital signal by careful sampling. (See the section on data representation: sound). Then complex voice-recognition software takes over and will "map" your words to commands. "Computer please show me the latest email from my mother."

Output Devices: As a kind of "opposite" to input devices, these need to convert digital "computer signals" into some kind of analogue form that humans can see or hear.

Screens

From the smallest tablet to the biggest desktop PC we do need to see what we are typing or just sit back and watch a film. The computer has to send a digital signal to each and every one of the perhaps millions of pixels in the display. (See the section on data representation: Images & pixels)

Printers

Modern computers were supposed to lead to the "paperless office" and yet we still print thousands upon thousands of pages of paper - perhaps we shouldn't? Printers vary tremendously in technology and quality but most still put "dots on paper". So the same issues arise for these "dots" as for pixels on a screen.

Loudspeakers

If you can talk to a computer perhaps you should listen to it as well? The "sampled digital wave" stored inside the computer needs to be changed to some kind of continuous vibration that generates an analogue sound wave that we humans can hear.

Extension: Control Actuators & Sensors
Problem: I want a light on in my house day and night. But when it is very dark the light should be bright and when it is very sunny the light should be dimmer or off.

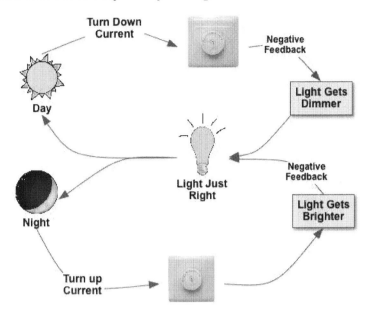

Solution: A dimmer switch! But I don't want to be turning it up and down all the time. There must be a better way!

Computer Control Systems: Automatic Input --> Process --> Output

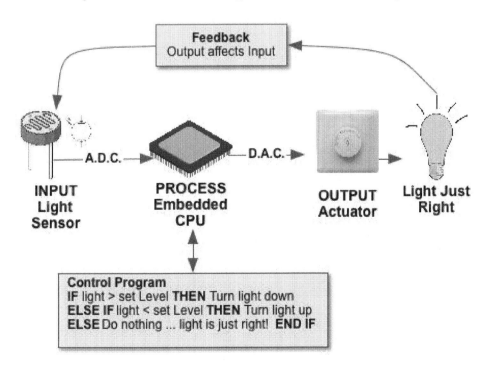

- **INPUT**: A light Sensor
    - Analogue signal - Light varies continuously
    - Analogue to Digital Convertor (ADC)
    - Computer needs digital input
- **PROCESS**: An embedded CPU with a simple control program
    - Result of program sends out digital signals
    - Digital to Analogue Convertor (DAC)
- **OUTPUT**: An **Actuator** - a type of motor that can respond to output from a microprocessor
    - The final output is analogue - Light varies continuously
- **Feedback**: The output affects the input
    - As the lamp gets brighter some of the light may fall on the light sensor
    - The light sensor will "sense" this and the program may respond by dimming the light.
    - In this way the brightness of the light will stay pretty constant
    - Compare this to "homeostasis" in biology. For example the control of the concentration of glucose in your blood.

Greenhouse example: A computer-controlled system is not limited to only one input sensor and one output sensor. Consider a greenhouse where the farmer wants to control the levels of light, heat and water.

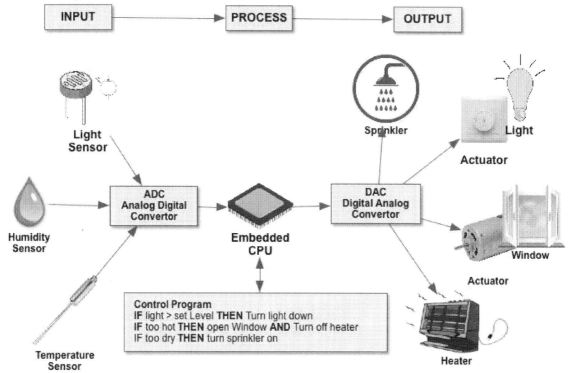

Embedded Systems

Broadly speaking these are any electronic systems that use a computer chip, but not a general-purpose computer. The greenhouse example may well have such a "**dedicated**" chip. "Dedicated" here doesn't mean "hard-working"! It simply means that this device is pre-programmed to do one job only. The programs may well be written in fast, small and efficient "**machine code**" and be permanently "burnt" onto **ROM** (Read Only Memory) chips. These days you can find a "computer chip" in just about anything: From your TV to a cruise missile.

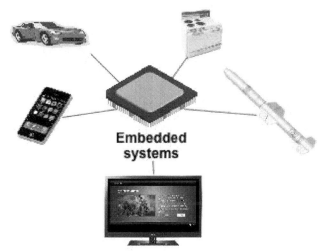

Backing Storage and "the cloud":

The following diagram is an overview of all kinds of computer memory. For the computer to work the program and the data it needs must be rapidly available for the **CPU**. That is why they must be in the CPU's main memory or **RAM**. However this memory is **volatile**. This means that when the computer is powered off all of its memory is erased. Clearly we need somewhere "safe", which is **non-volatile**, to store all the programs and data while the **CPU** is not using them or is turned off.

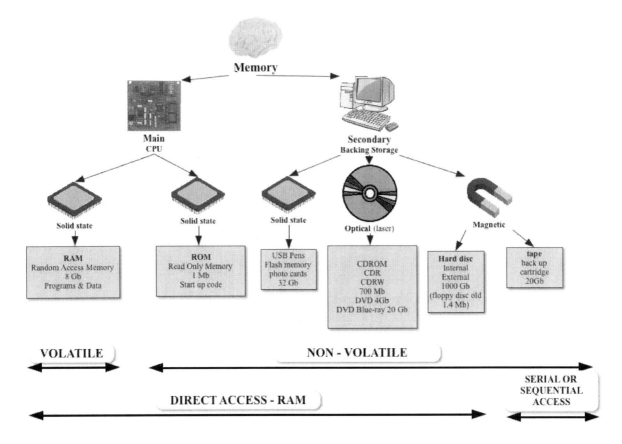

Backing Storage:

It is important to note at the outset that nearly all computer memory is "direct access" or RAM (Random Access Memory). This just means that you can "jump" from one data item to another in any way you like. The only exception is magnetic tape, which stores its data "sequentially" - That is, one item after another, in order.

Example: There are 20 songs recorded on:

> **A tape** - To play the 20th song the tape has to be "wound forward", past the other 19 songs, until the beginning of the 20th song is found. This takes time!
>
> **A Compact Disc (CD)** - You want to hear the 20th song? No problem - It's direct access, you can "jump" straight there.

So tape has very slow access speeds, which is why it is hardly used anymore.

More importantly all the data must be stored in a digital format, that is a "stream" of ONs and OFFs ... 11011011011111101110111110

All backing storage (secondary memory) is, obviously, non-volatile but the data can be stored in different ways on different **media**.

Magnetic:
This is one of the earliest methods to store data - first on tape and then "**hard discs**" coated with some kind of magnetic metal-oxide. Digital data is stored as a sequential series of changes in the direction of magnetism.

     "-> -><-<-<-<->" could be "read" as "1100001"

Hard Disc Drives (**HDD**) have one or more rigid ("hard") discs that spin or rotate at high speeds. IBM first introduced them in 1956. The first IBM drive stored about 3.75 MB and was the size of two domestic fridges! HDDs are now a lot smaller and can store up to about 10 TB (terabytes) of data and are found on most "desktop" computers.

Data is written to and read from a disc as it rotates past devices called read-and-write heads that are positioned to operate very close to the magnetic surface. The read-and-write head can detect or modify the magnetization of the material passing immediately under it.

The recent increase in tablets with limited and expensive "on board" memory has led to a surge in popularity of small, compact, external hard discs capable of storing large amounts of data with a reasonable access speed and a low cost. A 1TB (terabyte) "pocket-sized" disc can be rapidly connected to most devices via a USB cable (which also provides the power) and can store, for example, a huge number of photos or movies.

Optical:
An optical disc stores digital data using a series of "reflect (1)" and "non-reflect (0)" regions. These could be tiny little "pits" on the disc or a series of some kind of dots of a distinctive dye that do, or do not, reflect light. Either way a very narrow beam of **LASER** light is shone at the disc, as it rapidly turns, and a detector "reads" a 1 if light is received or 0 if not.

To store more data on the same sized disc means the "dots" or "pits" have to be closer and closer together. This in turn means that the beam of laser light has to be more and more "focused". Ultimately this means a smaller wavelength of light has to be used. Blue laser has a shorter wavelength than red laser. This explains why a "Blue-Ray" disc can store more data than a standard **DVD** (Digital Versatile Disc).

Optical discs are not as popular as they once were. It is cheaper, more convenient and "faster" to store data on a solid-state USB "pen-drive". Nonetheless the discs themselves are very cheap and the speed of access is fine for playing movies. So if you want to distribute or sell some high-quality digital data (like a high definition film) in a safe, secure and cost-effective way then a DVD is still a good option. Some people still listen to music on CDs (Compact Discs) and claim that, on a good "hi-fi" system, the quality and "richness" of sound is still better than "MP3".

Solid-State:
Essentially this is the same sort of "electronic" memory that the CPU uses in its "main memory" or RAM. "**Flash memory**" (as it is also known) uses millions of tiny electric circuits, a bit like logic gates, to store digital data as a series of "ONs" and "OFFs". Unlike the CPU's memory, flash memory is, of course, **non-volatile**.

This the kind of memory on **flash memory cards** (SD - Secure Digital) used in cameras; **USB "pens"** to carry data and even **Solid State Drives (SSD)** which can be used instead of "traditional" magnetic hard discs. Access speeds may not be as fast as the CPU's main memory but they can certainly rival HDDs (though they do cost a lot more). As there are no "moving-parts" these "memory chips" are very robust and so are ideal for mobile phones, portable computers and tablet PCs. **Hybrid Drives:** Some computers now have small **SSD**s synchronised with large **HDD**s. Frequently used programs and data are stored in the fast access, but expensive, **SSD** while the rest of the software is stored in the slower, but very large **HDD**.

The Cloud:
All around the world there are huge data centres. These, in turn, house huge banks of magnetic hard drives that store amazing amounts of data. Amazon, the online shopping giant, is estimated to have 100,000 servers in each of some 15 data centres. This means they have at least 1.5 million servers spread all over the world! There are many other companies who "host" data. It is estimated that 3% of the world's electric supply goes to keep these data centres active. (See the chapter on Environmental Impact.)

What has all this got to do with you, your computer and storing your data? Well the idea is very simple: You pay a yearly subscription to use some of that data storage space for your own data. Hey if you only want a few gigabytes it may even be free. Otherwise what you pay is based on how much "memory space" you want to use. It's just like renting part of a warehouse to safely store all your household "valuables" that you don't have space for at home, only instead of old books and kids' bicycles what you are storing is digital data. There are a couple of other differences: You have virtually instant access to your stored data 24 hours a day, 365 days a year! You can also access the data, remotely, from almost anywhere in the world, from nearly any kind of computer. How, you guessed, via the **Internet**! You are using "**cloud storage**".

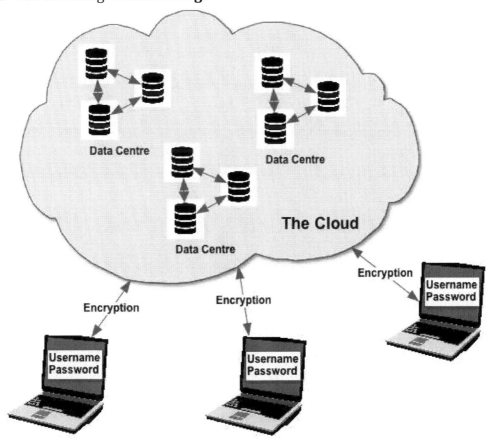

"Cloud Storage" has been around sometime: In 1983 a company called "CompuServe" allowed its customers to store 128 KB on its disk space. Now there are many "hosting" companies offering users almost limitless amounts of cloud storage memory - at a cost of course! Amazon Web Services; Dropbox, Google Drive, Apple's iCloud, Microsoft Azure to name just a few.

Advantages of Cloud Storage:
- Companies need only pay for the storage that they actually use or "consume" each month.
- Companies can end up reducing their energy consumption
- The cloud storage "host" takes over the responsibility of looking after and (ha!) backing up your data
- Employees, or individual users, can access the data from anywhere at anytime
- Different users can have different levels of access so that some data can be "shared": privately, within the company, or even allowing public access.
- Companies are, to some extent, protected from natural disasters: An earthquake at head-office in San Francisco may not affect the data storage centre. After all the data could be backed-up to a number of remote servers at different locations.

Disadvantages of Cloud Storage:
- **Security risks**
  - Cloud storage means many people, not just a few "network managers" at head office have to be able to access the data.
  - Criminals, industrial spies and even governments may attempt to access data that may be critical and at the same time "secret" or at least confidential.
  - **Firewalls** and Virtual Private Networks (**VPN**) are needed to protect data.
  - **Encryption** of data is, as it is uploaded and downloaded, is critical and complex.
- **Legal problems**: "Pirates" may use storage sites to store copyright protected data, like movies, and then provide "public" access to these files. This is illegal. But what if the "remote-server" is sited in a country that does not respect copyright laws?
- A Wide Area Network (**WAN**) is required rather than just a Local Area Network (**LAN**). This can slow down access to the data.
- **Internet**: You will need a fast & reliable Internet connection. If your connection "goes down" you will not be able to access any of your data!

(Note: See the section on networks and the Internet for more about LANs, WANs, VPNs, Firewalls etc.. and the section on Encryption in Data Representation.)

As a final note: Data is valuable! Backing-up and storing that data is important. Every media, from USB pens to external hard drives can be lost or just "fail". So the best advice is to back-up often and in different places. This is just as true for major companies as for humble individual students. You may have your important files (essays, photographs or whatever) stored on your computer's hard drive for fast, secure access - That hard drive is automatically backed-up to an external hard drive. You transfer work to school on a 32Gb USB pen drive. Or, perhaps, all your recent, important stuff is stored in a few folders in the cloud on "Google Drive" or "DropBox".

Questions on chapter 5a Digital Computer Systems:
1. Very briefly, in your own words, explain what a **Computer** is.

2. Maria's "computer system" consists of: a keyboard, desktop computer with a 500 GB hard drive; a touch pad (instead of a mouse); a 1 TB external USB compact hard drive; a 64 GB USB pen drive; a colour ink-jet printer and two external loud-speakers.
Draw a block diagram, with arrows, to show how her system is linked together. Use the basic Input --> Process --> Output and backing storage model. Include arrows to show the data flow between the different components.

3. We use the words software and hardware all the time in computer science.
    (a) Use an example to explain what the word **software** means?
    (b) Use an example to explain what the word **hardware** means?

4. Computer technology can really help people who are blind or "visually impaired".
    (a) Describe a suitable **input device** that can be used by a visually impaired person.
    (b) Describe a suitable **output device** that could be used by a visually impaired person.

5. A school in a cold country would like to grow tropical fruit. They want to use a computer-controlled greenhouse for this purpose.
    (a) **Name** three sensors that they would need to use to measure the soil and growing conditions.
    (b) Explain why an **Analogue to Digital Converter** (ADC) is needed to connect these devices to the microprocessor:
    (c) The microprocessor is connected via a Digital to Analogue Convertor (DAC) to various output **actuators**. Explain how **two actuators** could be used to control the growing conditions. Give clear examples of what the actuators would have to do in different conditions.
    (d) Choose **one** growing condition and describe the computer processing which would be required to maintain that growing condition within a set range.
    i. **Draw a flow diagram** showing carefully the connection between input, processing and output and show an example of feedback.
    ii. Use your diagram to explain how the control system keeps the growing condition within a set range:

6. Embedded chips can be found in most modern washing machines.
    (a) State how embedded chips are similar to but different to the Central Processing Unit (CPU) found inside a "normal" computer.
    (b) All of the programs that the embedded chip runs are permanently "burnt" into its main memory. By outlining how a "normal" computer runs a program explain why programs are permanently stored in a washing machine's chip.
    (c) Outline the role of the embedded chip in the washing machine in terms of Input, Processing and Output.

7. Explain why computers need secondary memory or backing storage.

8. Oxbridge Secondary School year 11 students always have a week's holiday at the end of summer term on the island of Malta. This year Dave and Maria have been asked to take their digital cameras and a portable computer with them to make a movie about the trip. Dave and Maria decide to take a couple of USB memory-sticks with them too.

(a) Choose one of the following terms that best describes a digital camera:
Output Device   Input Device   Secondary Memory

(b) The camera has a small screen on the back and a "self-focusing" lens at the front. Inside the camera is a small, **embedded** chip which includes an analogue to digital convertor (ADC) and a control system to automatically adjust the focus and the amount of light entering through the lens.

i. Explain the terms **analogue** and **digital** in this context.

ii. Explain the term **embedded chip** in this context and outline the function of this chip in terms of input, processing and output.

In Malta, while they are taking photos and video-clips the images are stored on small **SD flash memory** cards inside the cameras. Each evening, back at the hotel, Dave and Maria back-up that day's work on their laptop computer, which has a 256 GB **Solid State Drive**. Maria copies the very best images to one of the **USB memory-sticks**.

(c) State a typical size, in gigabytes, for SD cards in a digital camera.

(d) Briefly outline how digital data is stored in a flash memory card.

(e) Solid State Drives are relatively expensive. State two advantages of using an **SSD** in their laptop computer.

(f) Suggest why Maria bothers to copy some photos to her USB memory-stick and state a suitable size, in gigabytes, for this device.

When they get back home Dave and Maria back up all of their holiday image files to a small external USB **magnetic hard disc drive** (HDD) with a memory capacity of 2 TB.

(g) Outline how digital data is stored on an HDD.

(h) State one advantage of using an HDD as compared to the SSD on their laptop computer.

After a lot of work and a lot of "editing", Dave and Maria finally produce a one-hour movie called "Oxbridge Malta 2016".

Dave wants to "burn" copies of the film onto **DVD-R optical discs** to distribute to parents and students.

(i) Outline how digital data is stored on an "optical disc".

(j) Explain two advantages of distributing the school's film on DVD.

Maria wants to upload the film onto a folder "**in the cloud**" using a company called "DropBox". She will share the movie so that parents and students can download their own copy via the Internet.

(h) Briefly explain what "cloud storage" is.

(i) State two advantages and two disadvantages of distributing their film using "the cloud".

Chapter 5b Computers - Hardware & Software: Central Processing Unit

The Motherboard: Your mother may be the most important person in your life. The computer's motherboard is certainly the most important piece of hardware in a computer. This is the main printed circuit board where all the most important electronic chips are located and connected together. The most important chips are the main memory and the Central Processing Unit (**CPU**) itself.

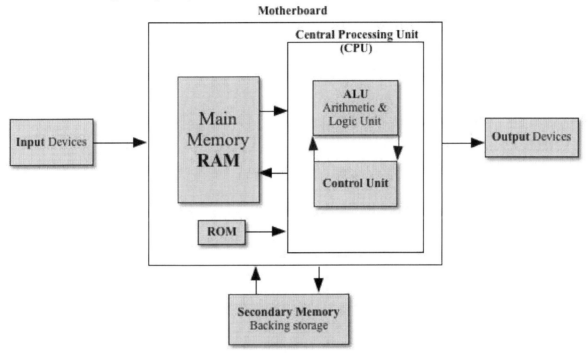

The motherboard will have various connections to other cards and systems such as sound cards, video cards, network cards, access to hard drives and so on. But this chapter focuses on the **main memory** and the **CPU**.

Points Covered:
- Main Memory - RAM, ROM, cache
- CPU - ALU, Registers, Clock, Buses
- CPU - Fetch Decode Execute cycle

Main Memory: This is the "on board", fast, memory that the CPU needs to access rapidly. For this reason these chips are often physically very close to the CPU.

RAM Memory: This is the computer's "**working memory**". It is **where all programs and data that the CPU is using** at any one time are stored. The CPU needs high-speed access to this memory as it "reads" from (accesses) and "writes" (saves) to this memory.

As already explained, almost all of computer memory is "**R**andom **A**ccess **M**emory" or direct access memory. Perhaps a better name for this memory would be: "Working Read Write Memory"? But, for historical reasons, RAM is the name used.

A RAM chip is a complex **integrated circuit** that has to store billions of digital "ON" / "OFF" binary (1, 0) signals. One way of storing these signals is giving each **bit** of data a tiny capacitor, which can either be charged (1) or discharged (0). As the charge slowly "leaks" away the RAM is periodically "refreshed". For this reason RAM chips are often referred to as **Dynamic memory**. Another consequence is that RAM memory is **volatile**: All the stored data will quickly disappear when the power is turned off.

Most computers now have at least 2GB of RAM memory. If you "open" more than one program at once, then they will all have to be stored in RAM. All of the data that these programs use, from text documents to video clips, will also have to be "loaded" into the RAM. So "demanding users" who need to quickly manipulate large files with complex programs, like video editors, will need more RAM. There are limits to the amount of a RAM a CPU can "address" or "access" (see the section on address buses). A "top-end" (expensive!) computer may have up to 32 GB of RAM.

ROM: **R**ead **O**nly **M**emory
As its name suggests this kind of memory can only be "read". That is, the programs and data are stored or "burnt" permanently into its circuits, which means, of course, that the memory is **non-volatile**.

Over the years there have been lots of uses for ROM chips. Games manufactures used to release games on ROM chips for specific machines. Some early computers even stored the operating system on a ROM chip. However these chips were, by definition, difficult if not impossible to "reprogram", change or update. Many **embedded** systems store all programs on ROM chips. After all the programs running in, say, a microwave oven, do not need to change!

In modern computers the main use for a ROM chip is to hold the **start-up code or "boot up" program**. Consider the following paradox: For a computer to do anything it must have access to the operating system. The operating system must be stored in the main or RAM memory. When the computer is turned off the RAM memory is "wiped" clean. When the computer is turned back on again it needs an "instruction" or short program to copy the operating system back into its RAM. But that "instruction" can't be in the RAM because it is volatile and at that point "empty".

So a ROM chip typically has a small amount of memory that holds a short "start-up" program, which does the following: When the computer is powered up various test signals are sent to the BIOS (Basic Input and Output System) checking that devices such as hard drives and RAM chips are present and working. Finally the program "searches for" the operating system (usually on a hard disc drive) and copies the entire operating system to the RAM main memory. The computer is now ready to be used!

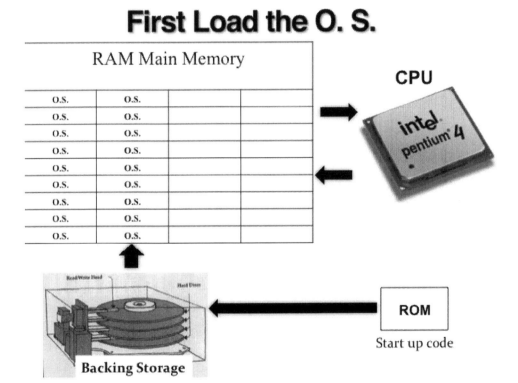

Cache Memory: As processors became faster and faster even the fast access times to RAM main memory were not fast enough. What was needed was a small amount of very fast memory for frequently used instructions and data. These little memory chips are called "cache memory". To make access to this memory even faster cache memory needs to be physically right next to the CPU chip ("level 2") or, indeed, actually part of the CPU chip ("level 1").

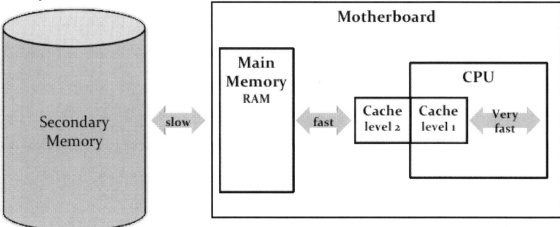

When modern CPUs need to "read" or "write" to RAM they first check in their "on-board" cache memory to see if a copy of that data has been left there from a previous operation. If so the CPU will "read" or "write" directly to the cache memory, which is much faster than accessing main memory.

Cache memory typically stores its digital data in millions of tiny electronic "switches" known as flip-flops. These can "flip on" (1) or "flip off" (0). These circuits, unlike "dynamic" RAM do not need to be constantly "refreshed" so the memory is sometimes referred to as "static" or SRAM. This memory has **very fast** access times but, on the other hand, is very expensive. So a typical system may have 8 GB of RAM but only 4 MB of cache memory. Cache memory, like main memory, is however **volatile** so loses all its contents when the computer is powered off.

CPU - ALU, Registers, Clock, Buses
Now we need to "zoom in" a bit and have a look at what happens to the data and program instructions inside the CPU itself:

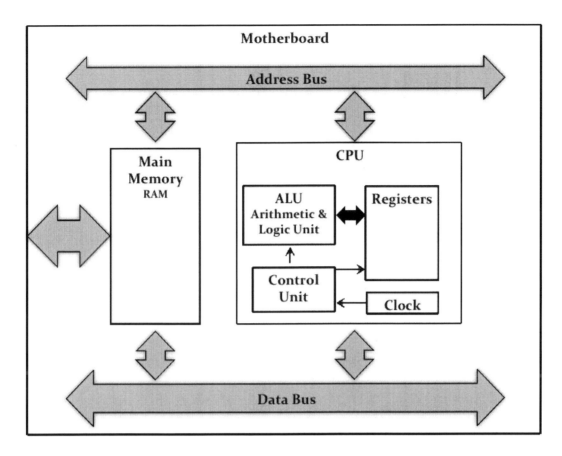

Buses: Are parallel wires that carry data binary signals around a computer. Data or addresses are "loaded" onto a bus and are carried to where they are needed.

Address Bus: Carries the binary address of a location in RAM, which could be storing either data or a program instruction.

Addressable Memory: Every "location" in RAM memory must have a unique address. As usual the address will be in the form of a binary code. Now a "one bit" bus would mean one wire that could carry only 2 different signals, 0 or 1, and so "point to" or "address" only 2 different locations, while a 2-bit bus could carry 2^2 or 4 different codes. The general relationship between the the size of the bus and the amount of memory it can "address" is:

Addressable memory = 2^n where **n** is the number of wires the bus has.

Computers with a 32-bit bus can then address 2^{32} memory locations. Assuming each location can hold one byte of data, that means a maximum of about 4 000 000 000 or 4 GB of RAM memory. Modern computers have as many as 36 address lines, which can address 2^{36} locations or about 64 GB of RAM.

Data Bus: Once the address bus "points to" a location in RAM then the data itself, the value found at that location, travels on the data bus. A "read" or "load" instruction would mean carry the data item from the RAM into one of the CPU registers. While a "write" or "store" instruction would mean the data would travel in the opposite direction, from a register in the CPU and "out" to the RAM. To some extent the "wider" the data bus the more data it can carry at once. A basic minimum would be eight lines to carry one byte in "parallel" along the wires. Faster computers may have 32-bit or even 64-bit data buses.

The Registers:
These are very small amounts of computer memory "inside" the CPU. It is here that the actual instruction and the item of data that the ALU uses are stored and access is very, very fast. Each register will typically be between 16 and 32 bits "wide" and there may be 8 or more different registers. Some of these will be "general purpose" and hold data items that the ALU is using or is about to use. Others have a specific purpose:

- **The accumulator** - holding the latest "running total" of a calculation
- **The Program Counter** - holding the address or "pointing to" where the next instruction is to be found.
- **The Instruction Register** - holding the instruction currently being executed.
- **Address registers** - holding the addresses of data and instructions in RAM memory.
- **Data registers** -holding values from RAM or the results of calculations
- **Status registers** ("flags" often showing a "True" or "False" value)

The Arithmetic and Logic Unit (ALU): This is where the basic mathematical operations are carried out. Usually these operations are very simple: Adding two numbers together and storing the results; Comparing two numbers to see if one is greater than the other or if they are equal and so on.

The Control Unit is responsible for coordinating the movement of data and instructions within the CPU. It sends signals to all other parts of the CPU: "Setting" or turning on one register or another; Adding one to the program counter register so the computer knows where the next instruction in the program is; **decoding the instruction** and so setting the ALU so that it carries out the correct operation and so on.

The Clock: All of the actions of the CPU have to be strictly coordinated and carried out "step-by-step". The clock sends a steady and very regular series of "ticks" which the control unit uses to carefully time its signals. This is the basic "speed" of a computer and is measured in Hz (cycles or "ticks" per second). Modern CPUs operate at speeds of around 3 GHz, which is 3000 000 000 "ticks per second".

CPU - Fetch Decode Execute cycle
Von Neumann's and Turing's insight was that both **the data and the instructions of a program could be stored together in the main memory** of a computer. As each item would be "fetched" from memory sequentially the CPU would "know" whether a particular stream of 1s and 0s was an instruction or some data.

Fetch → Decode → Execute Cycle

* **Fetch** (next) instruction
    * Look up its address in memory.
    * Go to that address and copy instruction into processor
* Processor **Decodes** instruction
    * What is the instruction?
* Processor **Executes** instruction
    * Does it!
* Fetch (next) instruction

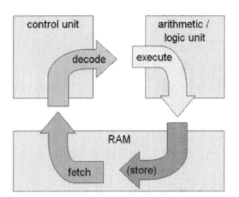

Here's a made-up, but realistic program in "assembly" language showing clearly how instructions and data can "sit side-by-side" in RAM memory:

Address		Data or instruction	Meaning
0	000	LOAD 101, R1	Copy contents of location 101 to Register 1
1	001	LOAD 110, R2	Copy contents of location 110 to Register 2
2	010	ADD R1, R2, ACC	Add registers 1 and 2 & put result in accumulator
3	011	STORE ACC, 111	Store the contents of the accumulator at RAM 111
4	100	STOP	End program
5	101	23	
6	110	15	
7	111	38	

* It looks like a 3-bit address bus is being used giving 2^3 or 8 RAM locations.
* The instructions are held at address locations 0 - 4 while the data is stored in locations 5-7.
* This very simple program just adds two numbers together: 23 + 15 = 38

Following the **Fetch-Decode-Execute** cycle this program would run something like this:

Fetch-Decode-Execute	CPU Registers				
Cycle	PC	Instruction	R1	R2	ACC
Fetch instruction from 000	000	LOAD 101, R1			
Decode LOAD instruction	000	LOAD 101, R1			
Execute copy contents 101 to R1	000	LOAD 101, R1	23		
Fetch instruction from 001	001	LOAD 110, R2	23		
Decode LOAD instruction	001	LOAD 110, R2	23		
Execute copy contents 110 to R2	001	LOAD 110, R2	23	15	
Fetch instruction from 010	010	ADD R1, R2, ACC	23	15	
Decode ADD instruction	010	ADD R1, R2, ACC	23	15	
Execute ACC = R1 + R2	010	ADD R1, R2, ACC	23	15	38
Fetch instruction from 011	011	STORE ACC, 111	23	15	38
Decode STORE instruction	011	STORE ACC, 111	23	15	38
Execute put 38 into RAM 111	011	STORE ACC, 111	23	15	38
Fetch instruction from 100	100	STOP	23	15	38
Decode STOP instruction	100	STOP	23	15	38
Execute STOP end of program	100	STOP	23	15	38

How fast is your computer?

The **system clock speed** does, to some extent, measure how many Fetch-Decode-Execute cycles the CPU can do per second. So, in general a 4 GHz computer is faster than a 3 GHz computer, however the situation is much more complex than that. All of the following will make a computer faster:

- Efficient motherboard architecture (the way the components are connected)
- More and bigger registers in the CPU
- More and faster RAM memory
  - More programs and data can fit into the working memory
  - So fewer accesses to the very slow secondary memory
- Bigger and faster Cache memory
  - Fewer accesses to the slow RAM
- Large (many wires or "wide") data bus
  - 32-bit bus carries 4 bytes at a time while 64-bit carries 8 bytes
- More processors ("cores") in the CPU
  - "Quad Core" should be faster than "Dual Core", if the computer & programs are set up to run "in parallel".
- Fast, dedicated graphics card with embedded processor and memory.
- The CPU is kept cool.

Questions on chapter 5b Central Processing Unit:
1. RAM (Random Access Memory) and **ROM** (Read Only Memory) are types of "Main memory".

(a) What is the **main purpose** of each kind of memory?

(b) **Apart from** what they are used for write down **two differences** and **two similarities** between **RAM** and **ROM**. You should use the following words in your answer:

Volatile   Non-Volatile   Solid state chips   Main memory

(c) Explain how more RAM chips can make a computer run faster.

2. An engineer has the idea of "burning" the entire operating system for a computer onto a large, fast, ROM chip, instead of having it on the computer's HDD. Suggest one advantage and one disadvantage of this approach.

3. Explain what **cache memory** is used for and how it can make the CPU work faster.

4. CPU and Registers

(a) Use the labels below to copy and complete the diagram shown.
Main Memory   Control unit
      Arithmetic and logic unit (ALU)   Registers

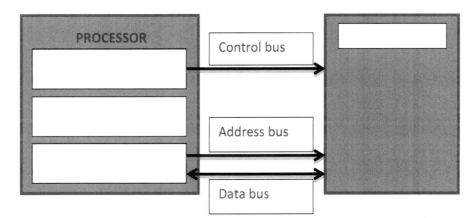

(b) Draw lines to match the parts of the processor with the correct function.

Accumulator register		Sends out signals to other parts of the computer system and fetches, decodes and executes instructions
Control unit		Carries out arithmetic and logic operations
Registers		Individual storage locations which hold an instruction, data or address of a memory location
Arithmetic and logic unit (ALU)		Holds the instruction that is currently being executed by the processor
Program counter register		Holds the accumulated total of results performed in the ALU
Instruction register		Holds the address of the main memory location storing the next instruction

5. Buses

(a) In a computer system what is a bus?

(b) State the function of the **address bus.**

(c) Dave's computer has a 32-bit address bus and 4 GB RAM. He wants to make his computer run faster by doubling his RAM chips to 8 GB. Explain why, in this case, buying more RAM would be a waste of money. (Hint: Use the formula 2^N to calculate the maximum addressable memory where N is the number of wires in the bus.)

(d) Describe how the **size** of the **data bus** affects the speed of a processor

6. Computer Clock:

A CPU's clock runs with a quartz crystal oscillator.

(a) Use the diagram shown to explain the difference between an **analogue** and **digital** signal:

This clock has a "pulse rate" (speed) of 4 GHz.

(b) How many "pulses" ("ticks") does it send out every second?

(c) Explain how the speed of a computer clock is related to the "Fetch-Decode-Execute" cycle and so affects the speed that programs can run.

7. Fetch Decode Execute

(a) Copy out the following text filling in the blanks with the words underneath

Fetches the next .... from memory and .... program counter

Decodes the bit pattern (............) into the instruction to be executed

Executes the instruction and .... the results in memory or registers

     stores   instruction   machine code   increments

(b) A byte of RAM memory contains 00001110 which is a program instruction another memory location contains the same byte which is actually a data value (14). Explain how the CPU when running a Fetch Decode Execute cycle can "distinguish" between an instruction and a data item.

Chapter 5c Computers - Hardware & Software: Software

Software: The programs that actually run on a computer are all examples of software. **System Software** consists of programs that "run" the hardware, chiefly the **operating system** but also smaller programs such as: The "boot" or start-up program (held in the ROM chip); The BIOS (basic input/output system) and some specialist **utility programs**. **Application software** consists of all the programs that the user uses to actually do something. So programs like Word-Processors, Spreadsheets, Databases, Web browsers, games and even compilers and interpreters are all **applications**. The operating system can then be seen as a "bridge" or "**interface**" between the hardware and user applications. It is a little bit like "**abstraction**" in computer programming: The user wants to get on and do some productive work or just play a game. She does not want, nor need, to know how the CPU is accessing the keyboard or saving her game on the hard-drive. These details are "hidden" from her by the operating system.

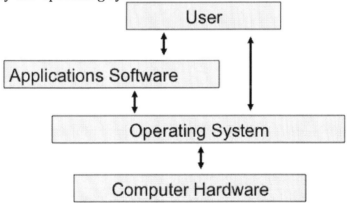

Points Covered:
- The Operating System
- Utility Software
- Models and Simulations

The Operating System: The **OS** is the single most important piece of software on your computer. Without Mac OS X or Windows 8 or Linux or whatever, you could not run any applications. The very first thing your computer does when it powers up is to copy the operating system from the secondary memory into the computer's main memory (RAM). Only then will you see your "home" screen with your "desktop" folders, menu-bars and your latest background, "screen-saver" image.

The main functions of an operating system are:
1. File Management & Storage
2. Input / Output & Peripheral Devices
3. Resource allocation - Memory Management
4. Process Management - Multi-tasking
5. Network Management - Security
6. Human-Computer Interface

1. File Management & Storage

One of the first operating systems for Personal Computers (PCs) to be used on a massive scale was Microsoft's "**MS-DOS**". The acronym DOS stood for **Disk Operating System**, so it is not surprising that much of its work was concerned with writing files to a disk, reading files from a disk and organising files on a disk and so on. More than thirty years later and we still need to store and access files stored on discs.

Saving a file: When you choose the menu command "Save As.." it is the **OS** that "asks you" for a name and a place to save the file. It is the **OS** that is responsible to copy the file from the RAM into an empty place on the hard disk.

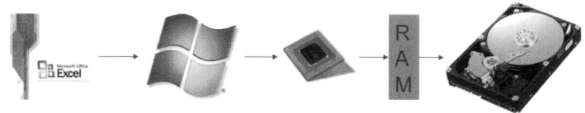

Opening a file: When you double click on a file icon you are asking the **OS** to find that document on the hard drive; load the document into RAM; work out which application created it and, if necessary load that program into the RAM too.

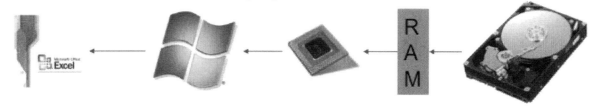

Organising Files: Every time you create a folder and then a folder inside that folder to store your files, it is the **OS** that is carefully "indexing" and "naming" sectors of the hard disk to prepare it to store your files.

2. Input / Output & Peripheral Devices

It is the operating system in RAM that is responsible for monitoring and giving access to the input and output hardware.

3. Resource allocation - Memory Management

The OS has to look after the CPU's main memory (RAM). Apart from the OS itself, it has to copy all the applications and files that the CPU needs at any one time into RAM. It must check that the memory is not full or that newly loaded programs do not "overwrite" programs that are already there.

RAM Main Memory			
O.S.	O.S.	WORD	WORD
O.S.	O.S.	WORD	WORD
O.S.	O.S.	EXCEL	EXCEL
O.S.	O.S.	EXCEL	EXCEL
O.S.	O.S.	letter_mum.doc	cat.jpeg
O.S.	O.S		mum.jpeg
O.S.	O.S		
O.S.	O.S.		
O.S.	O.S.		

4. Process Management - Multitasking

Multitasking is running, or appearing to run, two or more programs at the same time. For example: You could have all of these applications "open" at the same time - A Word Processor, a Spreadsheet a Slideshow Creator and an Internet Browser. On most modern computers it is easy to copy and paste data quickly from one application window to another. The picture shows Mac OS X with various windows open and "running" at the same time.

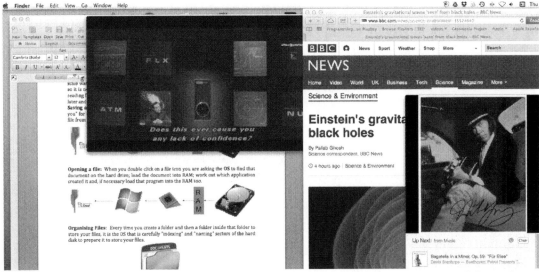

Note: It may appear that two programs are running "at the same time" but this is not possible with only one CPU. Perhaps a CPU with more than one "core" could, in theory, do some "parallel" processing but usually only one program is using the CPU at once. How does the **OS** give us the "feeling" that we are running these programs simultaneously? The **OS** gives each process its own memory space and then switches between each process as necessary. It can give a small amount of time (time slice) for each process to access the CPU. Some processes may have higher priority and so be given more time to access the CPU.

5. Network Management - Security

The **OS** (or Network Operating System), running on a file-server, is responsible for who can access what computer and what they can do when they are logged-on. The **OS** stores the database of usernames and passwords and grants access to valid users.

For more details see the section on networks.

6. Human-Computer Interface

The Human-Computer Interface (HCI) is really just how we communicate with a computer. In the not too distant future it may be as simple as talking to and listening to to the computer - a dialogue. Perhaps one day a chip inside your brain will enable you to exchange thoughts with a computer! Right now it is much more likely that you interact with your computer via a **Graphical User Interface** (GUI).

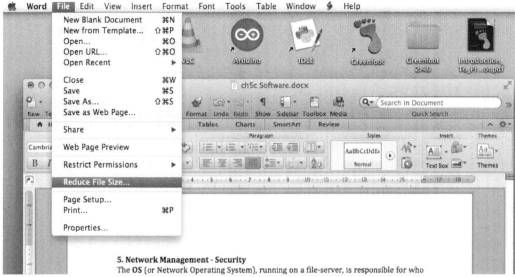

Now your "GUI" is probably a "WIMP" at the same time! WIMP systems:
- **Windows** (Boxes which show a part of the hard disc)
- **Icons** (little pictures that represent options or programs or files)
- **Menu** (drop-down list of options to choose from)
- **Pointer** (arrow controlled by a mouse or track-pad to select an option)

It is, of course, your **OS** that sets all this up for you. There will be some differences between different operating systems and if you are using a touchscreen and so on, but the principles will be the same. Modern GUIs are a wonderful improvement on early OSs like MS-DOS where the HCI was an empty black screen waiting for you to type in a command!

Utility Software:

These are little "extra" programs that carry out routine tasks that assist the **OS**. Some of these programs may well be incorporated within the **OS**.

1. Security

These days no computer is an "island". Whenever you connect to the Internet or simply plug in a USB pen drive, which you borrowed from a friend, you are potentially exposing your computer to a range of "**malware**": Programs specifically designed to damage a computer system. There is, unfortunately, a huge variety of such software. Here we will just focus on two and what can be done about them. (See also the section on Network Security, which refers to such things as "firewalls".)

Automatic Software Updates:

Over time "bugs" are discovered in programs. These may affect the security of your computer as "hackers" may try to exploit a bug to introduce malware into your computer. Sometimes just a small "**patch**" needs to be downloaded to mend the problem. Other times an entire new version of the program is needed. Either way a utility that automatically scans your computer and the Internet for required updates is extremely useful. (See chapter 7d on Net Security)

Keep your security programs up-to-date: A recent estimate from CNN news states that in 2015: "One million new (malware) threats were released each day."   If your security software is months or even years old it will not be able to deal with the most recent "strains" or varieties of infection.

Anti-virus

A computer virus is essentially a piece of code, which is capable of copying itself. This, by itself, would not do much harm, except waste some computer memory. Most viruses, however, are much more malicious than this and are designed to destroy data or corrupt the computer's memory. Your computer can be **infected** whenever and however you connect to another computer: receiving an email; logging on to a web page; downloading a film and so on. Once your computer is infected the virus can rapidly replicate and can then be passed on to other computers. In this sense a computer virus is very similar to biological infectious diseases like the flu-virus.

Anti-virus software "scans" the computer memory for any known viruses. It may check how some of your programs run - looking for telltale signs that they may be infected. Once a virus has been found it can be "isolated" and deleted.

Anti-spyware

Spyware is a program that is designed to secretly gather information about a person or an organisation and send that information on to someone else. The information could be as innocuous as your Internet surfing habits or as confidential as your bank and credit card details. Your computer can be infected in the same way as a virus. Unlike viruses, spyware does not usually self-replicate.

Anti-spyware software is very similar to anti-virus software: Regularly scan the memory, searching for known spyware and monitor programs for "suspicious" behaviour.

2. Disk Organisation

All storage media (disks, memory sticks, cards) must be formatted: There must be a file system so that the OS can store and find files in the memory. Formatting completely erases the memory and then you start filling it up with all your files.

Defragmenting disks

Over time files are broken up and scattered around memory and this slows down access. The solution is to defragment the disk – join up files & delete empty spaces. Here is a disk fragmentation map produced by a utility program called a "defragmenter".

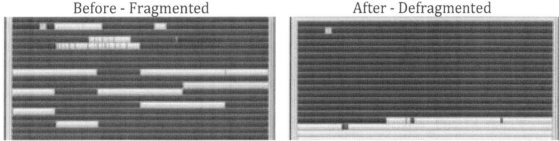

Before - Fragmented   After - Defragmented

Blocks of memory can be cut and pasted together and this, more structured, memory is much more efficient.

Compression

Files, particularly image, sound and video files can take up large amounts of memory. There are various programs that can compress files - see the section on Data compression

Backing-up

As we have already seen in the section on backing-storage, data is very valuable. A backup utility program simply automates the process so that you don't forget to do it. For example: The software will make a backup to a large external hard drive of the entire computer's memory. Then at a set time, like very early in the morning, all recent changes will be backed up.

3. Maintenance

Like any machine that is constantly used, regular - behind the scenes - maintenance is a good idea. There are numerous little utility programs that carry out such tasks as:

- Diagnose problems
    - Monitor CPU usage, memory available etc.
- System clean up
    - Delete files that are no longer used, remove duplicates etc.
- Repairing and Converting Files
    - Attempt to repair files that were incorrectly saved when the CPU crashed;
    - Converting files from one format to another etc.

Models and Simulations: The world is a complex place full of sophisticated systems interacting with each other. Software engineers working with experts in a particular field are able to build computer systems that model the real world.

Example of Abstraction: Doctors want to analyse the feedback mechanisms involved in maintaining blood glucose levels in humans. It is not possible to take into account all of the variables factors from age to diet and from protein structure to genetics. **Abstraction**, as a technique for identifying the most critical processes and ignoring the complexity of other parts of the system, is an essential problem-solving tool. Computer scientists **abstract** from this very complex system the key factors and use these to write a program that models the real, organic system. The doctors can study how the computer model behaves with different glucose concentrations; speed of insulin transport in the blood system etc. and so understand how the real, human system works.

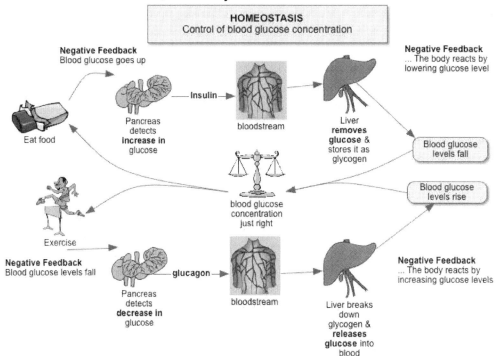

Computer models are used to predict & investigate how a device or process might behave given a certain set of conditions. Potentially almost any system can be modelled in this way: Car Crashes; Earthquakes; Strong winds; buildings & bridges; Aerodynamics of new planes; Economic models of taxes & inflation; Climate change & global warming - to name but a few!

Spreadsheets can model very simple systems. There are many built-in functions and these can be extended with small programs called "macros". Once the spreadsheet is set-up a type of "**What-If**" analysis can be done: What happens to my profits if I increase the price?

Simple Models

- ○ Mathematical
- ○ Economics
- ○ Science

Input, Process & Output

- ○ **Input** – numbers or Variables
- ○ **Process** – formulae & functions or Rules
- ○ **Output** – the answer as numbers, text or graphs

Rules

=B9*Price_per_unit

=IF(D15<=E15,"*****", "")

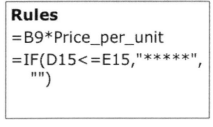

Spreadsheet models are rather limited. They can really only input numbers and output simple graphs and some text.

Programming Languages and specialist packages can model more sophisticated systems. Languages as simple as Logo or Scratch or as complex as Python or Java can all be used to write code that simulates or models real world systems.

Example: **Predator-Prey relationships**, programmed using Object Orientated Programming and implemented in Java. Rabbits and Foxes are programmed as "objects" that can "breed, "eat", "die" and be "eaten".

The following diagram shows the "class-diagram" and some sample output based on the code in the book "Objects First with Java" by Michael Kölling.

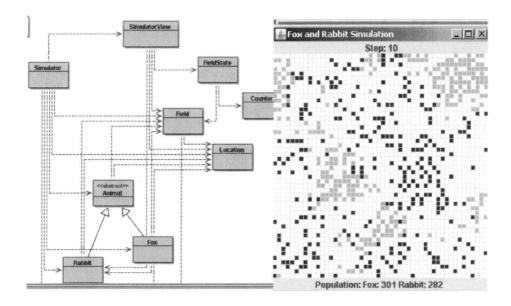

More Complex Simulations

Almost anything can be modelled on a computer: From **flight-simulators** to train pilots to testing how a building "copes" with an earthquake. Computer simulations have become an essential part of **mathematically modelling natural systems** that are far too complex to model in any other way. Here is a picture of a Typhoon simulation using the "Weather Research and Forecasting Model".

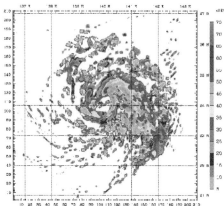

Large and powerful computers are needed to make weather simulations.

- **Input** - Millions of data items of temperature, pressure, humidity etc.
- **Process** - Very complex mathematical models
- **Output** - Animated "real-time" graphics showing weather systems "evolving"

Supercomputers are often needed to simulate these complex systems ranging from molecular modelling and quantum mechanics to nuclear war and global warming. The computers may have over 100,000 processors and be capable of billions of arithmetic operations per second.

Virtual Reality: Computer systems that simulate reality and make you feel like you are in another world, that you interact with, are no longer science fiction. You have to wear very special "head -gear" and strange "tactile" gloves. The program controls everything that you can see, hear or touch. This "immersive" experience is not just a cool way to play video games. Future applications will range from training professionals to work in difficult and dangerous situations to treating patients with phobias (fears & anxieties).

Questions on chapter 5c Software:
1. The Operating System
a) Is an operating system an example of **hardware** or **software**? Explain your answer

b) In what kind of **computer memory** would the operating system be in the following circumstances?

      i. When the computer is turned off.

      ii. When someone is running the computer.

c) One of the tasks of an operating system is to control **peripheral devices**.

      i. State one example of an **input peripheral device** and an **output peripheral device**.

      ii. What is a "**device driver**"?

d) An old operating system was called MS DOS (Disk Operating System), so clearly managing backing storage (usually a hard disk) is a big part of the job of any operating system. Explain what happens in terms of backing storage and RAM (main memory) when a user "opens" a document created by an application like MS Word.

e) **Apart from** controlling peripheral devices and memory allocation, State three other tasks that are carried out by **all** operating systems:

e) Most CPUs can really only run one process at a time. Explain how a **multi-tasking** operating system enables a user to apparently be running more than one program at once.

2. Graphical user interfaces (**GUIs**) are found on many computers.

a) Why do computers need a user interface?

b) State the brand name of 3 different operating systems that use a **GUI**:

c) Give one input device, other than a keyboard, that can be used with a **GUI**:

d) Describe the four features of a Windows Icons Menu Pointer (**WIMP**) GUI

e) Describe two special features of the GUIs of small mobile computing devices such as modern "smart" phones.

3. Utility Software
Maria has a new computer, which runs the latest version of the "Windows" Operating System. She decides to download and install an **anti-virus** utility program.

(a) In general terms what is a utility program?

(b) Briefly outline:

      i. What a virus is;

      ii. How her computer could become "infected" with a virus;

      iii. How her anti-virus utility will help to keep her computer "virus-free".

(c) Explain why it is important that Maria keeps her anti-virus software up-to-date.

(d) Suggest two other utility programs that Maria would be advised to install. In each case briefly explain how they work and how they would make Maria's computer work more efficiently.

Models and Simulations

4. Andrew runs a small shop at school that sells sweets and snacks to students at break time to raise money for cancer research.

(a) Outline how a spreadsheet could be used as a basic "profit-loss" model for Andrew's shop. Include in your answer: the input data required, some simple examples of the calculations needed and what the output "answers" would be.

(b) In this context explain the concept of "what-if analysis".

5. A physics teacher wants to use an Object Orientated Programming language like Python or Java to build a simple simulation of the solar system. Each planet, and the sun, will be an "object". Each object will have a size, mass and velocity. The objects will be programmed to interact using formulas from basic Newtonian Mechanics such as:

Force = mass X acceleration

Force of Gravity between two objects = (G X Mass1 X Mass2) / d^2

Where G is the universal gravitation constant and d is the distance between the objects.

At each "program cycle" each planet will calculate the effect of the force of gravity of each of the other objects in the system. The teacher hopes that this will cause the planets to go into orbit around the sun.

(a) Students can run the simulation and experiment with different numbers and types of planets and moons. In this context explain the concept of **abstraction** in building simulations.

(b) Suggest how this model may differ from the "real" solar system.

6. A supercomputer is used to run a simulation of global warming to help make predictions about how human actions may affect future temperature rises on earth.

(a) What is a supercomputer?

(b) Briefly explain why a supercomputer is necessary to run this sort of simulation.

Extension: Research how modern flight simulators are used to train pilots. Structure your answer in terms of Input devices needed --> Processing involved --> Outputs needed.

In this context explain the terms: feedback and real-time processing.

Section 6
Databases

- **6a Structured Data, Records and Databases**
- **6b Relational Databases**

"Computers are incredibly fast, accurate and stupid. Human beings are incredibly slow, inaccurate and brilliant. Together they are powerful beyond imagination." (Tom Asacker")

0110

Lq wkh idfh ri dpeljxlw1, uhixvh wkh whpswdwlrq wr jxhvv. Wkhuh vkrxog eh rqh— dqg suhihudeo1 rqo1 rqh —reylrxv zd1 wr gr lw.

Chapter 6a Databases: Structured Data, Records and Databases

Humans have been recording data for thousands of years. Stone age people used to record data about such things as livestock and personal goods by carving notches in wood, bone or stone. Such simple tallies were used at least forty thousand years ago - long before formal writing developed. We have moved on a little since then. The American Library of Congress has been described as the world's largest library. It was recently estimated to hold 130 million items including books, photographs and maps. So far it "only" has 5 million digital documents. Meanwhile, Amazon, the world's biggest retail store, maintains records on more than 50 million customers and on the millions of items that it sells. This amount of data needs some structure and a "filing-cabinet" is not good enough!

Points Covered:
- Structured & Unstructured Data
- Records, Keys and Fields
- Computer Databases

Structured & Unstructured Data:

As we saw on the section on programming and data structures, any non-trivial program is likely to use data structures:

Problem: Store student names and grades in Physics, Chemistry & Biology and access, by name, the grades in each subject or answer queries like: "Find all students who scored more than 50 in Biology."

- **Variables - Not really practical**
  - NickPhysics = 50, NickChem = 75, NickBiol = 65
- **Data Structure – Lists or Arrays**
  - Grades=[50, 75, 65] or Students = [[50, 75 , 65], [60, 65, 45], [75, 80, 90]]
- **Data Structure – Python Dictionary**
  - Students = {"Nick" : [50, 75, 65], "Sally" : [60, 65, 45], "Ric" : [75, 80, 90] }

Sample Python code:

```
#Print Chemistry grades
    for student in Students:
            print(student, "Chemistry: ", Students[student][1])
#Print all students with more than 60 in Biology
    for student in Students:
            biolGrade = Students[student][2]
            if  biolGrade > 60 :
                    print(student, "Biology: ", biolGrade)
```

As the data structures get more complex they can begin to follow a regular "record" or "card" like structure. Pascal, an "old" but excellent programming language, even had a "record" data type:

```
Students = record
        fName : String;  (*fields that "describe" each record *)
        phys : integer;
        chem : integer;
        biol : integer;
    end;
```

More modern programming languages "**encapsulate**" the idea of "entities" being described by their "attributes" using **Objects** and fields. Here's some Python code:

```
#Create a student Class to create student objects:
class Student(object):
        #The constructor to initialise a student object
        def _init_(self, fName, phys, chem, biol):
            self.fName = fName
            self.phys = phys
            self.chem = chem
            self.biol = biol
        #end of constructor
    #end of class definition ..........................
    #main ... start by making some student "objects"
    stud1 = Student("Nick",50, 75, 65)
    stud2 = Student("Sally", 60, 65, 45)
    stud3 = Student("Ric", 75, 80, 90)
```

Don't panic you will not be expected to understand object orientated programming at this stage! And besides, even if you could program records to make a kind of database, would you want to? Millions of people need to work with databases in a nice "user friendly" way and they are not programmers. So they buy an "off the shelf" database application! Here's a simple "**data dictionary**" that could be used to describe the data in our example:

Field Name	Data Type	Notes
Student #	Number	Key field -unique
First Name	Text	First Name 20 chars
Physics	Number	Integer 0 - 100
Chemistry	Number	Integer 0 - 100
Biology	Number	Integer 0 - 100

Why structure data? Because it's Easier and Faster to:

- Sort records
- Search & Find records (by using queries)
- Produce reports (based on queries)
- Analyse data
- Keep all the data organised

In general, if the data follows a regular "record like" structure, then it is structured data. Unstructured data is everything else!

Structured Data - Databases	Unstructured Data – Everything else!

• Files – Tables
• Records
• Fields
• Key Fields
• Accessed via SQL
   • Structured Query Language
	• Files on a computer HD – small memory
	   • Word Docs; Spreadsheet files;
	• "Rich" content – large memory
	   • Music files
	   • Video files
	     • Used more & more
	     • Needs more & more memory

Typical database examples would include: Students in a school; Animals in a zoo; Houses for sale; Books in a library; Reservations in a hotel etc.

Records, Fields and Keys: Terms you must know -

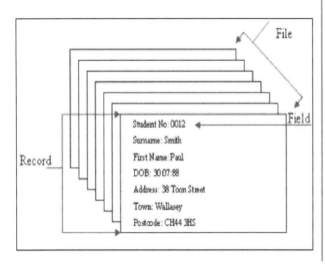

- Data (base) FILE
  - Collection of Related Records
- RECORD
  - Collection of Fields describing one person or thing
- FIELD
  - A single data item in a record
- Primary KEY FIELD

As you can see in the example above of a Student Database:
- **File** - All the students in a school are grouped together into one file.
- **Record** - Each student has one "card" with "fields" which describe him.
- **Field** - This is a single data item such as:
  - First Name: Paul
  - Surname: Smith
  - Date of Birth: 30/07/1998
- **Primary Key Field** - This is the field that **uniquely identifies a record**. Its value cannot be duplicated. For example, there may be many students called Paul Smith but there will only be one with the student number 0012:
  - Student No.: 0012

The importance of the primary key field will be explained in the section on relational databases.

Computer Databases

Databases are so useful and so powerful that there is a big market for data handling software. Microsoft's "Access" and Apple's "FileMaker Pro" are two examples you may have come across. One definition of a computer database is: "**A Persistent, Organised, Store of Data**". Let's look at each part of that definition:
- Store of data
  - Clearly lots of data is being stored in a database
- Organised
  - Data is stored in records
  - Individual items of data have a connection of some sort
- Persistent
  - Non-volatile
  - Stored in secondary memory or backing storage

Modern database software is used to create, maintain and find data in an efficient and quick way.

- **Create**
  - Create Records & fields
  - Enter data
- **Maintain**
  - Kept up to date
  - Insert, delete, update
- **Interrogate**
  - Ask questions - Queries
  - Search or Find information

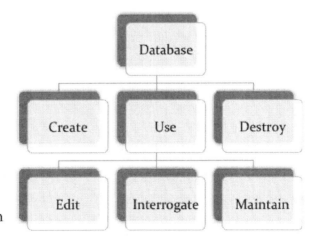

Computerised databases are better than Manual systems, such as card files, because:
- They are fast to interrogate & search
- They occupy tiny storage space compared to shelves and cabinets
- They are easy to Maintain & Modify
- There are fewer errors in data processing
- Data can be accessed by multiple users at the same time
- Data can be output in many ways – reports, graphs etc.

Example: A Hospital in London needs urgent information: A virus has been discovered in the drinking water in a hospital. It can pass from the pregnant mother to a young foetus. The Virus only affects female babies. The baby can be cured with a rare and expensive anti-viral drug. The hospital administrator needs to find the address and parental contact details of all babies that satisfy the following criteria:
- Born in the last year
- Sex - female
- Hospital St. Nicholas

This "search" will take less than a second on a database system!

Here's a picture of a search being carried out on a manual, card, filing system!

In summary then, you use a database when:
- You have large amounts of related information
- Your data has a regular, Record-like Structure
- The database will be used a lot to:
    - Search or Find information
    - Sort information by value or alphabetically
    - Produce complicated reports

Questions on chapter 6a Structured Data, Records & Databases

1. In the following two scenarios each person wants to keep a record of what they have. In each case decide if they should or should not use a database and give two reasons to explain your choice.

(a) Maria has a dog, called "Charles"; A compact disc of "Selena Gomez" and a "Russian doll".

(b) Richard has 500 DVDs of different films. He runs a small company that rents these DVDs.

(c) Use your answers to (a) and (b) to explain the difference between structured and unstructured data.

2. The manager of a car showroom uses a **database** to store data about cars he sells. This is part of the database.

Make	Model	Size of engine	Registration	Price (€)
Opel	Vectra	1.8	VSE 648	19000
Opel	Zafira	2.0	BFK 297	29000
Volkswagen	Golf	1.4	SB A5526	15000
Volkswagen	Polo	1.2	DD B4978	11000
Volkswagen	Jetta	1.6	B G8347	19000
Renault	Megane	1.4	1233 CD 33	17000
Renault	Clio	1.2	6289 XF 54	11000

(a) How many **records** are there in this part of the database?

(b) How many **fields** are there in this part of the database?

(c) The records shown are to be sorted in **descending** order of size of engine. What will be the **registration** of the first record in the database after it has been sorted?

(d) Give the **name of a field** that contains **numeric** data.

(e) Identify the **field type** of the 'model' field.

(f) State which **field** would be the **key field** and explain your choice.

(g) Describe an example where a record would need to be:

      i. Inserted

      ii. Deleted

      ii. Edited

(h) Give three reasons, with an example, why using a computerised database like this is better than a manual (card) filing system.

3. Extension: There has been a huge increase in the amount of data stored in computer systems. In 2007 about half that data was structured and the other half unstructured. In 2015, apart from a huge overall increase in data storage, the ratios are very different: 10% structured and 90% unstructured. Suggest an explanation for this huge rise in the storage requirements of unstructured data. (Hint: Think about file types that are unstructured; require large amounts of memory to store them and we access them more and more often "online".)

Chapter 6b Databases: Relational Databases

Flat Files: So far we have only seen one table holding records about one thing:

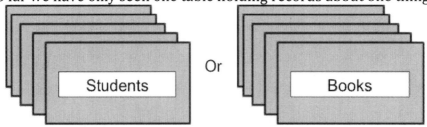

Each file or table has one set of related records and one record describes one person or thing. So, in the Students file each record is one student while, in the Books file, each record is one book. Now we need to see how to link related files together to make a **relational database**.

Points Covered:
- Entity Attribute Relationship
- Relational Database & Foreign Key Fields
- Extension - Queries and SQL

Entity Attribute Relationship:

Problem: Sally is the school librarian. She has to keep track of two very different things: Books and Students. She needs to know who has borrowed which books, when and when they have to return their books. Maria is a computer scientist and she suggests that Sally uses **E.A.R. analysis**: **E**ntities are "things" described by **A**ttributes and joined by **R**elationships. Here is her analysis of Sally's problem:

    1. An Entity is an object or Person or an abstract thing like an appointment or a book loan. Each entity has a **table**, which holds all of the information about one entity:

        Student Table   Books Table   Loan Table

  2. Attributes are **fields**, which describe an entity.

    Student Table
        Student Number - **Primary Key Field**
        First Name
        Surname
        Class
    Books Table
        Book Number - **Primary Key Field**
        Title
        Author
    Loan Table
        Loan Number - **Primary Key Field**
        Start Date
        Return Date
        Student Number - **Foreign Key Field**
        Book Number - **Foreign Key Field**

3. Relationships are links between entities

A Student can borrow more than one book

A Book can be loaned or lent to a student

Relational Databases & Foreign Key Fields

E.A.R. analysis quickly shows that the three tables (entities) are related and should be joined together to make a relational database.

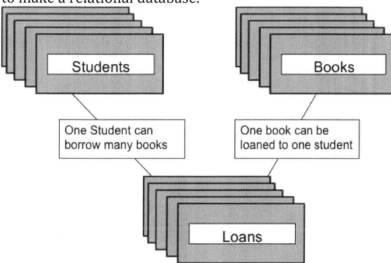

To see why this is better than using flat-file tables consider the following book table, showing who has borrowed which book.

Book Number	Title	Author	Student Num	First Name	Surname	Class
B231	Python Code	Dawson	S007	Sean	Connery	11X
B342	Fairy Tales	Kubica	S444	Ada	Lovelace	11X
B666	Greenfoot	Kolling	S666	Bill	Gates	11Y
B007	Think	Spraul	S666	Bill	Gates	11Y
B451	Animal Farm	Orwell				
B333	War & Peace	Tolstoy				
B423	Ana Karenina	Tolstoy	S007	Sean	Connery	11X
B454	1984	Orwell	S666	Bill	Gates	11Y

We can clearly see that Bill Gates from 11Y has 3 books out, while Ada Lovelace only has one and "Animal Farm" and "War & Peace" are, at the moment, left on the shelf. But there are two major problems:

Duplication: The details of each student are repeated. Bill Gates is repeated 3 times. If he had 10 books out at once his full details would appear 10 times!

Data Inconsistency: If Bill moved class to 11Z we would have to change 3 records.

What if we only changed one of the records? Well then we would have:

Book Number	Title	Author	Student Num	First Name	Surname	Class
B231	Python Code	Dawson	S007	Sean	Connery	11X
B342	Fairy Tales	Kubica	S444	Ada	Lovelace	11X
B666	Greenfoot	Kolling	S666	Bill	Gates	11Z
B007	Think	Spraul	S666	Bill	Gates	11Y
B451	Animal Farm	Orwell				
B333	War & Peace	Tolstoy				
B423	Ana Karenina	Tolstoy	S007	Sean	Connery	11X
B454	1984	Orwell	S666	Bill	Gates	11Y

But this is **inconsistent** or just plain wrong! How can we have one student, Bill Gates, with one unique primary key field, S666, but apparently in two different classes?

You may say that this is unlikely to happen and besides what's wrong with a little duplication? What if there were 20,000 students and 100,000 books? No there must be a better way! We must link the tables together, on their **primary key fields** using, in this case, another table called "Loans".

The diagram below shows how the tables are linked using their primary key fields. When these fields are used in another table they are called **foreign key fields**.

Primary Key Field

Student Number	First Name	Surname	Class
S007	Sean	Connery	11X
S666	Bill	Gates	11Y
S633	Steve	Jobs	11Y
S444	Ada	Lovelace	11X
S457	Charles	Babbage	11Y
S333	Alan	Turing	11X

Primary Key Field

Book Number	Title	Author
B231	Python Code	Dawson
B342	Fairy Tales	Kubica
B666	Greenfoot	Kolling
B007	Think	Spraul
B451	Animal Farm	Orwell
B333	War & Peace	Tolstoy
B423	Ana Karenina	Tolstoy
B454	1984	Orwell

Foreign Key Fields

Loan number	Date Out	S_Num	B_Num
L001	22/05/15	S007	B231
L002	22/05/15	S666	B666
L003	02/06/15	S444	B342
L004	22/06/15	S666	B007
L005	01/07/15	S007	B423
L006	01/07/15	S666	B454

Notice how the 6 loans are now 6 records in the Loan Table. If the system wants to show, for example, "who has which book" in Loan Number L005, it uses the foreign key fields to "look up" S007 as "Sean Connery" and B423 as "Ana Karenina". The full details of S007, his name, class and maybe address, phone number and email address are not duplicated. If Sean Connery changes from class 11X to 11Z then his record in the Student Table is updated and one change is made to one field.

Now the librarian can "**interrogate**" the **R**elational **D**atabase **M**anagement **S**ystem (**RDBMS**) by making complex requests or "**queries**" like:

 "Show me all the students in class 11X who have books out which are overdue, where overdue is defined as due in more than one week ago."

The system responds by printing out a **report** showing every student, and the books that they should return, in class 11X. The "output" doesn't have to be printed, of course: The database system could, just as easily, send emails to all the students involved.

So the advantages of a relational database are:
- Reduces unnecessary **duplication**
- Reduces errors through **inconsistency**
- Enables complex "searches" or **queries** to be made.

Extension - Queries and SQL

As relational databases increased in size and complexity and the resulting "queries" become more sophisticated there developed a need for a special-purpose programming language designed for managing data held in Relational Database Management Systems. The most well known of these languages is called: "**S**tructured **Q**uery **L**anguage" or **SQL**. A full treatment of this language is beyond the scope of this book, so what follows is only a brief outline.

The examples all use data, taken from the Internet, of some houses for sale in California.

Flat file – Queries based on one table

zip	street	city	beds	baths	sq_ft	pool?	price
95820	2561 19TH AVE	SACRAMENTO	3	1	1177	YES	91002
95670	11150 TRINITY RIVER DR Unit 114	RANCHO CORDOVA	2	2	941	YES	94905
95673	7325 10TH ST	RIO LINDA	3	2	1146	NO	98937
95838	645 MORRISON AVE	SACRAMENTO	3	2	909	YES	100309
95842	7340 HAMDEN PL	SACRAMENTO	2	2	1134	YES	110700
95673	6715 6TH ST	RIO LINDA	2	1	844	YES	113263
95621	6236 LONGFORD DR Unit 1	CITRUS HEIGHTS	2	1	795	NO	116250
95833	250 PERALTA AVE	SACRAMENTO	2	1	588	NO	120000
95673	113 LEEWILL AVE	RIO LINDA	3	2	1356	YES	121630
95621	6118 STONEHAND AVE	CITRUS HEIGHTS	3	2	1118	NO	122000
95823	4882 BANDALIN WAY	SACRAMENTO	4	2	1329	NO	122682
95660	7511 OAKVALE CT	NORTH HIGHLANDS	4	2	1240	NO	123000
95834	9 PASTURE CT	SACRAMENTO	3	2	1601	YES	124100
95660	3729 BAINBRIDGE DR	NORTH HIGHLANDS	3	2	901	NO	125000
95843	3828 BLACKFOOT WAY	ANTELOPE	3	2	1088	YES	126640
95758	5201 LAGUNA OAKS DR Unit 140	ELK GROVE	2	2	1039	NO	133000
95660	6768 MEDORA DR	NORTH HIGHLANDS	3	2	1152	NO	134555
95827	3100 EXPLORER DR	SACRAMENTO	3	2	1380	YES	136500
95626	7944 DOMINION WAY	ELVERTA	3	2	1116	YES	138750

An extract from an Estate Agent House sales database in California:

Records – 19 Rows – 19 different houses for sale

Fields – 8 Columns – each field has a specific data type – text, integer, boolean

Key Field – The "zip" or postcode is being used to uniquely identify each record (house)

SELECT: Retrieves selected data that match specific criteria.

SELECT column1 [, column2, ...]
FROM tablename
WHERE condition

Example: "show me the addresses of houses which cost more than $125,000."

SELECT street, city, price **FROM** Houses
WHERE price > 125000
ORDER by price

Results in:

street	city	price
3828 BLACKFOOT WAY	ANTELOPE	126640
5201 LAGUNA OAKS DR Unit 140	ELK GROVE	133000
6768 MEDORA DR	NORTH HIGHLANDS	134555
3100 EXPLORER DR	SACRAMENTO	136500
7944 DOMINION WAY	ELVERTA	138750

Example: "Show me all the details of houses in Rio Linda with a swimming pool, or in Citrus Heights which have 2 bathrooms."

> **SELECT * FROM** Houses
> **WHERE** (city = "RIO LINDA" **AND** pool = "YES")
>> **OR** (city = "CITRUS HEIGHTS" **AND** baths = 2)

Results in:

zip	street	city	beds	baths	sq_ft	pool?	price
95673	6715 6TH ST	RIO LINDA	2	1	844	YES	113263
95673	113 LEEWILL AVE	RIO LINDA	3	2	1356	YES	121630
95621	6118 STONEHAND AVE	CITRUS HEIGHTS	3	2	1118	NO	122000

Now let's see what happens when we link a Clients Table to the Houses Table to make a relational database. As usual the tables are linked via a primary key field.

Relational Databases – Queries from two tables

Client#	Sname	Zip	City	Street	HouseZip
234	Harman	97776	SACRAMENTO	231 MOUNTAIN VIEW	95838
235	Lopex	98888	RIO LINDO	12 LONDON DRIVE	95626
236	Lemon	92222	SACRAMENTO	34 MONKS STREET	95621
237	Bartlet	98765	LOS ANGELES	456 COLONY HIGH	95673
238	Millan	94567	SAN DIEGO	23 MADRID AV	95843

zip	street	city	beds	baths	sq_ft	pool?	price	Buyer#
95820	2561 19TH AVE	SACRAMENTO	3	1	1177	YES	91002	
95670	11150 TRINITY RIVER DR Unit 114	RANCHO CORDOVA	2	2	941	YES	94905	
95673	7325 10TH ST	RIO LINDA	3	2	1146	NO	98937	237
95838	645 MORRISON AVE	SACRAMENTO	3	2	909	YES	100309	234
95842	7340 HAMDEN PL	SACRAMENTO	2	2	1134	YES	110700	
95673	6715 6TH ST	RIO LINDA	2	1	844	YES	113263	
95621	6236 LONGFORD DR Unit 1	CITRUS HEIGHTS	2	1	795	NO	116250	236
95833	250 PERALTA AVE	SACRAMENTO	2	1	588	NO	120000	
95673	113 LEEWILL AVE	RIO LINDA	3	2	1356	YES	121630	
95621	6118 STONEHAND AVE	CITRUS HEIGHTS	3	2	1118	NO	122000	
95823	4882 BANDALIN WAY	SACRAMENTO	4	2	1329	NO	122682	
95660	7511 OAKVALE CT	NORTH HIGHLANDS	4	2	1240	NO	123000	
95834	9 PASTURE CT	SACRAMENTO	3	2	1601	YES	124100	
95660	3729 BAINBRIDGE DR	NORTH HIGHLANDS	3	2	901	NO	125000	
95843	3828 BLACKFOOT WAY	ANTELOPE	3	2	1088	YES	126640	238
95758	5201 LAGUNA OAKS DR Unit 140	ELK GROVE	2	2	1039	NO	133000	
95660	6768 MEDORA DR	NORTH HIGHLANDS	3	2	1152	NO	134555	
95827	3100 EXPLORER DR	SACRAMENTO	3	2	1380	YES	136500	
95626	7944 DOMINION WAY	ELVERTA	3	2	1116	YES	138750	235

Client table:
Key Field
* Client#

Foreign Key Field
* HouseZip

Houses table:
Key Field
* zip

Foreign Key Field
* Buyer#

Example: "Show me the address and price of all the houses that have a potential buyer."
    SELECT Houses.street, Houses.city Houses.price, Clients.Sname,
    FROM Houses, Clients
    WHERE Houses.Buyer# = Clients.Client#

Results in:

street	city	price	Sname
7325 10TH ST	RIO LINDA	98937	Harman
645 MORRISON AVE	SACRAMENTO	100309	Lopex
6236 LONGFORD DR Unit 1	CITRUS HEIGHTS	116250	Lemon
3828 BLACKFOOT WAY	ANTELOPE	126640	Bartlet
7944 DOMINION WAY	ELVERTA	138750	Millan

SQL makes these queries easy to program and automate so that the details of how they work can be "hidden" from user. (Another example of "**abstraction**".) The guy working in the estate agents just wants to "click some buttons", print out or send some letters and get on with the job of selling houses. He does not need nor want to know how the **R**elational **D**atabase **M**anagement **S**ystem works.

Reports– After a query (data has been processed) then the data is presented neatly on a page and ready to print.

Client Number: <u>234</u>   Address: <u>231 Mountain View</u>

<u>Sacramento</u>   <u>97776</u>

Dear <u>Mr. Harman</u>,

All the paper work for the house that you wished to purchase:

654 Morrison Ave, Sacramento, 95838

is now complete.

We await payment, from you bank, for the purchase price of *$100,309* to complete the transaction.

Yours Sincerly

Mr Snapper – Sales

"Snap Them Up Real Estate"

This **report** (letter to a client) is possible becuase the tables, Houses & Clients, were linked together to make a **Relational Database**.
Underlined text → from Client table & Italic grey text→ from Houses table

SQL is not only used for queries. It can also be used to create tables and modify existing tables.

<u>SQL syntax for creating a new table:</u>

    CREATE TABLE tablename
        (column1 data type,
        column2 data type,
        column3 data type);
    CHAR(size):
        Fixed length character string. Fixed size in parenthesis.
    VARCHAR(size):
        Variable-length character string. Max size is specified in parenthesis.
    NUMBER(size):
        Number value with a max number of digits specified in parenthesis
    DATE:
        Date value
    NUMBER(size,d):
        A number with a maximum number of digits of "size" and a maximum number of "d" digits to the right of the decimal

Example: Create a table called "Houses" with the columns (fields) shown below:

zip	street	city	beds	baths	sq__ft	pool?	price
95820	2561 19TH AVE	SACRAMENTO	3	1	1177	YES	91002

CREATE TABLE Houses
    (zip NUMBER(5) PRIMARY KEY,
    street VARCHAR(30),
    city VARCHAR(30),
    beds NUMBER(2),
    baths NUMBER(1),
    sq_ft NUMBER(5),
    pool? BOOLEAN,
    price NUMBER(6));
 Note: This only creates the table. It does not create any rows (records).

Modifying a table that already exists:

Inserting values (adding records or rows) to an existing table:
    INSERT INTO tablename (col1, ... , coln)
    VALUES (val1, ... , valn)
Example: Add the record shown below into the table called "Houses".

zip	street	city	beds	baths	sq__ft	pool?	price
95820	2561 19TH AVE	SACRAMENTO	3	1	1177	YES	91002

INSERT INTO Houses (zip, street, city, beds, baths, sq_ft, pool?, price)
VALUES(95820, "2561 19TH AVE", "SACRAMENTO", 3, 1, 1177, YES, 91002)

Updating (or amending) records or row in an existing table:
    UPDATE tablename
    SET colX = valX [, colY = valY, ...]
    WHERE condition
Example: Change the record shown below so that the street address is "39 ORANGE ROAD" and the city is "SAN DIEGO".

zip	street	city	beds	baths	sq__ft	pool?	price
95820	2561 19TH AVE	SACRAMENTO	3	1	1177	YES	91002

    UPDATE Houses
    SET street = "39 ORANGE ROAD" city = "SAN DIEGO"
    WHERE zip = 95820

Results in:

zip	street	city	beds	baths	sq_ft	pool?	price
95820	39 ORANGE ROAD	SAN DIEGO	3	1	1177	YES	91002

Deleting completely records or rows from an existing table:
>   **DELETE FROM** tablename
>   **WHERE** condition

Example: Delete from the table show below the record with "zip number" 95673:

zip	street	city	beds	baths	sq_ft	pool?	price
95820	2561 19TH AVE	SACRAMENTO	3	1	1177	YES	91002
95670	11150 TRINITY RIVER DR Unit 114	RANCHO CORDOVA	2	2	941	YES	94905
95673	7325 10TH ST	RIO LINDA	3	2	1146	NO	98937
95838	645 MORRISON AVE	SACRAMENTO	3	2	909	YES	100309
95842	7340 HAMDEN PL	SACRAMENTO	2	2	1134	YES	110700

>   **DELETE FROM** Houses
>   **WHERE** zip = 95673;

Example: To delete all the rows (records) but not the table itself:
>   **DELETE * FROM** Houses

Results in:

zip	street	city	beds	baths	sq_ft	pool?	price

Summary: **SQL** is a very useful language for creating, modifying and querying (finding data) from complex databases. SQL can get very advanced but you are not expected to be "fluent" in SQL. Most of the time simple pseudocode and standard logical operators is fine: (Price < $200,000) **AND** (pool? = True)
This is why this has been a brief overview.

Questions on chapter 6b Relational Databases

1. Irene runs a small hotel with 25 bedrooms in Brussels. Many of her clients are Euro MPs and come back to her hotel again and again. She used to use a spreadsheet to make a "flat-file" database to record reservations for each room. Some extracts of some rows (records) is shown below:

Res #	Client #	Client Name	Date In	Date out	Room #	Room Type
R210	C334	Mr Brown	01/01/15	03/01/15	R20	Double
R211	C256	Ms Gomez	02/01/15	03/01/15	R12	Single
R212	C337	Ms Connor	02/01/15	06/01/15	R07	Double
R351	C334	Mr Brown	15/03/15	18/03/15	R20	Double
R352	C777	Ms Neal	15/03/15	16/03/15	R01	Single
R777	C256	Ms Gomez	21/04/15	25/04/15	R05	Single
R778	C790	Ms Hind	22/04/15	26/04/15	R12	Double
R779	C334	Mr Brun	22/04/15	27/04/15	R20	Double

Dave is a friend of Irene's. He is a systems analyst. He wants to help Irene to run her hotel more efficiently.   He says her flat-file system is full of data duplication and data inconsistencies.

(a) Explain, with an example from the file shown above, the terms **data duplication** and **data inconsistency**.

Dave implements a **Relational Database** Management System to help her business.
There are 3 tables (or files) used in the database. Each has a **primary key field** - shown in brackets after the file's name:
1. **Room Table (Room#)** – with one record for every room in the hotel.
2. **Client Table (Client#)** – with one record for every person who has ever stayed in the hotel or made a booking with the hotel.
3. **Reservation Table (Res#)** – this links the Room & Client tables to show who is staying in which room and when.

(b) What is the purpose of a primary key field?

For questions (c) and (d) use data from the flat-file shown above.
(c) Show two "sample" rows for the room table. Think of 3 suitable field names (columns) and show these as "headers" above your two rows.
(d) Show two "sample" rows from the client table. Think of 4 suitable field names (columns) and show these as "headers" above your two rows.

Here is an example of part of a record in the **Reservation** table.

Res #	Start Date	End Date	Room #	Client #	Client Name
R777	21/04/15	25/04/15	R05	C790	Ms Hind

(e) Explain why the fields Room # and Client # are called "**foreign key fields**" in the reservation table.

(f) Show the above relational database by drawing a block diagram linking the three files together. Show clearly how the tables are linked using each table's primary key field.

Room Table

Client Table

Reservation Table

(g) Dave explains to Irene how the new system can generate reports based on "queries". For example: "Show me the names of all the clients who have stayed in room 12 in the last month."
In December Irene wants to send a Christmas card to all her "best" clients. Suggest how the relational database could help her to do this.

(h) Use the context of Irene's hotel to state and explain 3 advantages of using a relational database compared to a "flat-file" database.

Extension SQL:
1. A chess club stores details about its players in a structured database.
When a player plays a game of chess they score -1 for a loss, +1 for a draw and +2 for a win. These points are added to their "running total" score and are used for ranking players in the club.

The relational database consists of the following tables, each having a primary key field:
      Player (PlayerNum, Sname, Fname, RenewalMonth, EmailAddress, TotalScore)
      Game (PlayerNum, GameDate, Venue, Score)
The club wants to send a reminder email to those players whose membership is due for renewal in October.
      (a) Write an **SQL** query to show the Forename (Fname) and Email Address for the players who should be sent emails.
Sally is a member of the chess club (PlayerNum P607) and she won a game of chess at the Town Hall on the 25th of July 2015.
      (b) Write the SQL command to add this data to the database.
As a result of Sally's win her total score will increase by 2 points.
      (c) Write the **SQL** command to add this information to the database.
      (Hint: This is very similar to incrementing a variable in programming.)

Nick is a member of the chess club (PlayerNum P707). He wants to see a list of the date and score of all his games from 01/01/2015 to 01/06/2015.
      (d) Write an SQL query to display this data in order of date.
(Note: In all SQL questions do not worry about precise syntax. Just make sure that you refer to the correct tables and fields and that your meaning is clear.)

Section 7
Networks & Internet

- **7a Networks - Introduction**
- **7b Networks - Data Transmission**
- **7c The Internet**
- **7d Net Security**

"We are still in the very beginnings of the Internet. Let's use it wisely" (Jimmy Wales, Wikipedia)

0111

Pqy ku dgvvgt vjcp pgxgt. Cnvjqwij pgxgt ku qhvgp dgvvgt vjcp tkijv pqy.

Chapter 7a Networks & Internet: Networks Introduction

We live in a very "connected" world. You copy photos from your smart phone on to your lap top computer and upload them to your blog or Facebook page where, potentially, millions of people can see them. At school you log on to a different computer on the school network every day, yet always have access to your "home" drive and all the school printers. This section address questions like: "What is a network?"; "Why bother connecting computers in a network" and "What different kinds of network are there?". (Note: The global "network of networks" is the Internet and has a section all to itself.)

Points Covered:
- Standalone, LAN & WAN, Servers and Peer-to-Peer
- Extension: VPN & PAN
- Topology: Bus, Ring, Star, Mesh & Hybrids
- Media: Wired & Wireless
- Extension: Addressing (MAC addresses)

Standalone, LAN & WAN

A "**standalone**" computer system is simply a computer that is not connected to any other computer. Here's one with an external hard drive and a printer.

Now there's nothing wrong with this system. The PC ("Personal Computer") is full of brilliant applications. The user can word process, calculate on spreadsheets and even program in Python. She can print out her work and back everything up on the hard drive. Now if she password protects access to the computer and never allows anyone else to use her computer or insert USB pens and, above all, never connects to the Internet, then her system will be **very secure and virus-free**.

This is how an early computer classroom may well have developed:

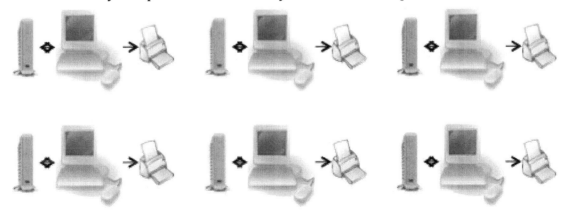

Now we can start to see some problems. There are 6 computers but do we really need 6 printers and 6 back up hard drives? There are lots of students who are using these computers. Do they really have to remember which computer they used last time and always sit at the same computer - after all that is where their work will be saved? By the late 1970s there were more and more PCs and the issue of sharing expensive peripheral devices like printers and backing storage was a real problem. The solution was to connect the PCs together and so make a network.

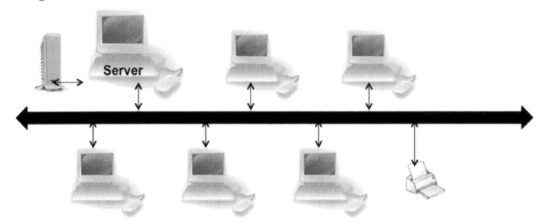

The advantages of networking computers, compared to standalone PCs, are clear: Share, communicate and move:
- **Share** expensive peripheral devices like printers and backing storage;
- **Share** software (data and programs) by storing files and software centrally
- **Communicate** - send emails from one computer to another
- **Move** - Users can log on to any computer because their work is stored centrally

There are, of course, some disadvantages of networks:
- **Expensive**
  - o Cabling and set-up
  - o Maintenance by technicians
- **Reliance** on the network
  - o File server down – can't work.
- **Security** – a big problem!
  - o Passwords, Viruses, Hackers etc.

Local Area Network (LAN):
When the networked computers are within a limited area like a school, office building or a hospital, then it is a Local Area Network.

Client-Server Model
Note in the diagram above that one computer, shown larger and connected directly to a large, external hard drive is often "in charge" of the network. This computer is the **server**, while the other computers are **clients**. A client makes a service request and the server fulfils the request. For example in a school network, the server:

- Runs a Network Operating System
- Controls Access to the network via usernames, passwords and hierarchical levels of access
  - o "Student" users have read-write access to their own, private, "home" drive and read-only access to a "resource" drive, with limited access to some of the printers.
  - o "Teacher" users have read-write access to their own, private, "home" drive and read-write access to the "resource" drive, with access to all school printers
  - o "Administrator" users have virtually complete access and can create or delete users and reset or restrict passwords.
- File Sever - controls access to all files and makes back-up copies.
- Print Server - controls access and queues for all network printers
- Mail Server - enables communications via email between all users.

Peer-to-Peer Model (P2P)

In a small office or domestic situation each computer is of "equal status". There is no dedicated server. Files are stored "locally" in each PC but can be "shared" and opened on any PC. Each file or folder can be assigned a different "status".

- **Read & Write** - anyone can open, look at change these files
- **Read Only** - anyone can open, look at and even save a copy of these files but they cannot change the original.

In effect each node (PC on the network) functions as both a client and a server. Any computer can initiate a request and any, other, PC can respond. A "mesh" topology (see later) could be used to implement a P2P model where every PC is connected directly to every other PC. (Note: Very large P2P networks can be established via the Internet enabling users to share music and video files. This is a complex issue. Here I am only referring to small P2P LANs.)

Wide Area Network (WAN):

When the networked computers extend over a large geographical distance, perhaps across a city or, indeed, between cities, then it is a Wide Area Network. Clearly some sort of telecommunications will be involved. Typically a WAN could be several LANs joined together forming a company **intranet**. That is:

- A private network accessible only by staff working for that company;
- Staff members need to "log on" with a username and a password to gain access.

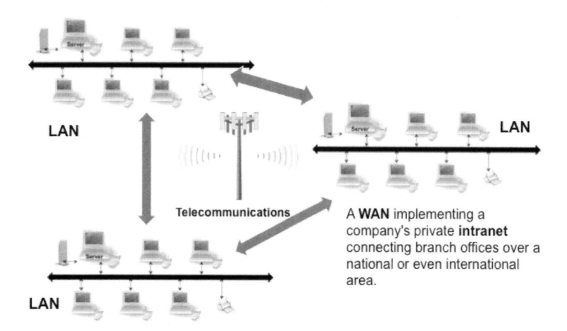

LAN

Telecommunications

LAN

A **WAN** implementing a company's private **intranet** connecting branch offices over a national or even international area.

LAN

Note: Large companies may pay a telecommunications company for a "**leased line**". These "lines", very often **fibre-optic**, permanently connect companies' LANs and are used exclusively by the company who pays for them. Sometimes known as "**data lines**" the data transmission is **fast and secure**, although at a cost!

Extension: Virtual Private Network (VPN)
VPNs enable **remote access to a WAN** from almost anywhere.
Example: A major newspaper has a national WAN linked by high-speed, data lines. The newspaper employs many journalists who could be reporting in from anywhere! The journalists need to access the secure resources of the WAN / LANs – just as if they were sitting in head office and logging on to a workstation. A small office is set up in New York. It is too far away and so too expensive to have a leased line. How can this remote office securely and quickly log on to the LAN in the main office?

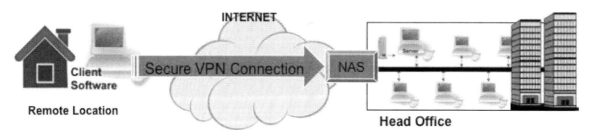

A **VPN** is a private network that uses a public network (usually the Internet) to connect remote users to their private

- **Network Access Server (NAS)**
  - The server that controls remote access to the LAN
  - The NAS will only allow valid users to access the LAN
  - As a minimum it will require a username and password
- **Client Software**
  - Establishes a connection to the VPN via the internet
  - **Encrypts** all data for security

WAN and / or VPN

private Wide Area Network	Virtual Private Network
• Security	• Security
– Very secure, network only used by the company	– Encryption needed as it uses a public network – the internet
• Performance	• Performance
– Fast – bandwidth only used by the company	– Slow - bandwidth shared with other internet users
• Control	• Control
– The company is in complete control of set up and running	– Run by the internet service providor who has other users
• Cost	• Cost
– Expensive and may involve dedicated leased lines.	– Cheap to connect over large distances from anywhere
– Need expensive, qualified, expert, staff to run the network	– Little experitise needed as the VPN is run by the provider

Note: It is not really one or the other. Many intranets will use private WANs for most work but provide access to their intranet for remote, mobile staff using a VPN.

Extension: Personal Area Network (PAN)

Now that so many people have so many different computing devices, each with similar personal data, it makes sense to "link" these devices together. A PAN provides the ability to **"synchronise"** such things as address books, agendas, calendars and so on. If you change a contact on one device, it will change on all of them. Data can be shared between devices as if the PAN was a small P2P network.   The most common implementation has been to use short-range, up to 10m, radio waves (**"Bluetooth"**) to network all devices in an individual person's "workspace." This is a rapidly changing area. When you take a photo on your "iPhone" and you can instantly see it on your "iPad" the data is probably being shared via Apple's **"cloud"** service on the Internet. At home you are probably doing all this using, what amounts to, a wireless personal area network (WPAN).

Topology: Bus, Ring, Star and Mesh
Topology, or network architecture, is the way computers (nodes) are connected (linked) to make a network. There are many ways of doing this - each with its pros and cons.

Bus (Line) Topology:
There is one central line (bus) and data moves back and forth along the line.

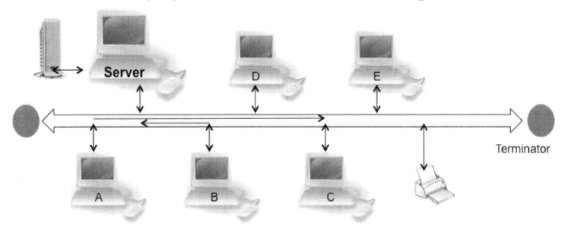

Line topology is a very common set-up. The diagram shows node B trying to send data to the server while, at the same time, node A is trying to send data to node C. These "traffic conflicts" have to be resolved - the nodes involved have to re-send the data when the line is free. Node E is the furthest away and there is a limit to how long the line can be. The terminator stops signals "bouncing back" and causing further "traffic conflicts."

Advantages of Bus
- Cheap – less cables
- Simple to set up
- Simple to add nodes
- Fast enough with few users

Disadvantages
- Slow with many users
  - All data back and forth along bus.
  - Degrades very quickly with large amounts of traffic
- Bus failure is critical

Ring Topology

In this set-up data is sent round the ring in one direction. If node A wants to send data to the server then it has send a "packet" of data all round the ring. Each node, in turn, "inspects" the packet to see if it is for them.

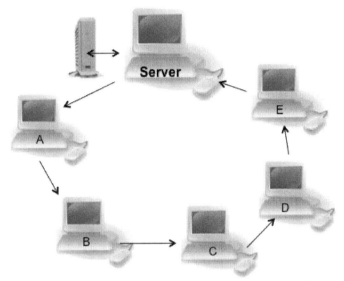

This is actually much quicker than it sounds and there are no "traffic conflicts" in a one-way system. This system works very well connecting a few computers in a small office.

Advantages of a Ring

- Cheap – to set up and expand
- Fast – data in one direction
- Better than bus topology under heavy load

Disadvantages

- Slow with many nodes
- Ring failure is critical
- Adding a node affects the network

Star Topology

Here all the nodes are connected via a central hub or switch. This topology is very common in classrooms and small offices. It is probably what you have at home, where the hub will be a "router" that is also used to connect your little LAN to the Internet.

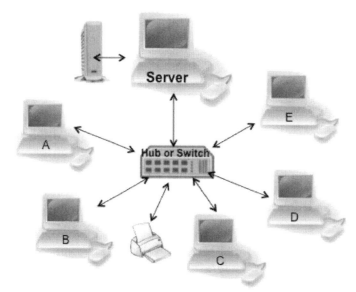

You may think it is more like a bicycle wheel with spokes, rather than a star, but it can be a very efficient little network. If node C wants to send data to the server then the data first goes to the centre. The **hub** then "broadcasts" that data packet to all nodes. The server "recognises" that the data is "addressed" to the server and deals with it. (Note: A data **switch** is a more "sophisticated" piece of hardware. It will actually switch or connect node C to the server. Then, for example, if node E wants to "talk" to node A, the switch will rapidly switch and connect those nodes. Using a switch is, therefore, much more efficient, but at a cost!)

Advantages of a Star

- One station fails doesn't affect others
- Fast data transfer - only involves 3 nodes (counting the hub) and 2 links
- Easy to add / remove nodes

Disadvantages

- Expensive cabling
- HUB failure is critical

Mesh Topology

Here every node, or computer, is connected directly to every other node.

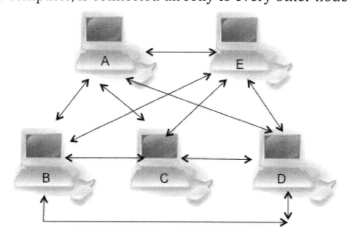

If each computer is equally responsible for sending, receiving and sharing data, then this set-up effectively implements a **peer-to-peer** (P2P) model and no server is required.

Advantages of a Mesh

- A broken node (PC) has no effect on the rest of the network
- Potentially all data can be distributed around the mesh so no server is needed
- Fast: data can be simultaneously transferred between different nodes.

Disadvantages

- Complex and expensive to set up and run
- Large amounts of cable needed (so often used in wireless – Wi-Fi networks)

Because of its complexity a mesh network is not that common. Nonetheless a mesh can be very useful for complex programs and algorithms that require **parallel** or **distributed** processing. In the case of parallel processing each CPU at each node would be given different tasks to carry out simultaneously. In distributed processing each CPU would carry out a specific sub-task of a much larger problem - a kind of **abstraction** by modularisation at work!

Extension: Hybrid Networks

Given that all the different topologies have their pros and cons, a very common solution is to use more than one topology to make a "hybrid" network.

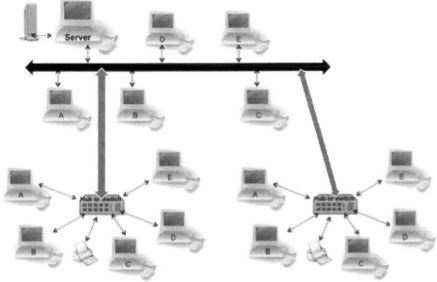

Example: A school could use a **line** topology as a kind of "backbone" running throughout the building and with individual PCs "hooked-on" in offices and classrooms. Meanwhile in an "IT room", there could be many computers configured as a **star** topology but the hub of each star is directly connected to the main line or bus.

Media: Wired & Wireless

Obviously all networks involve connecting computers together, so how the devices are connected is an important issue. Fundamentally there are two ways: wired or wireless.

Wired Connections: Here a "physical" cable or wire is used to connect the computers and carry the data between nodes.

Copper Wire: The simplest of all media is ordinary copper wire. There are usually 8 individual wires, twisted together in 4 pairs - hence the name: "Unshielded Twisted Pair (UTP)".

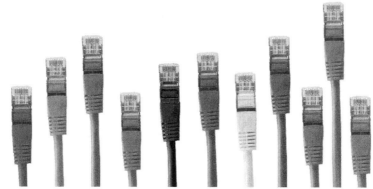

These cables are very often used with the "Ethernet" protocol to connect computers, modems, and routers and so on, so the cables are often referred to as "Ethernet cables".

Advantages with copper wire:
- Cheap & Reliable connections
- Transmission is reasonably fast (up to 10 gigabit per second) and secure.

Disadvantages
- The cables cannot be much longer than 200m
- There can be interference issues with other cables carrying electric current.

Fibre-optic Cable: Pulses of light, amounting to 0/1 digital signals, travelling along a thin glass fibre carry the data. These pulses, when they arrive at their destination, have to be converted into standard, electrical signals. In one cable there may be many separate fibres and each fibre can carry several "channels".

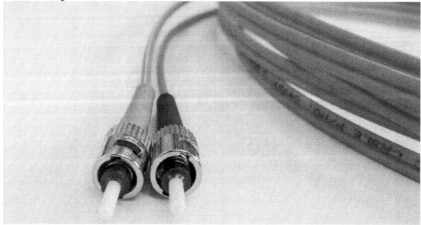

Each glass fibre is very thin, around 10 micrometres, and has a special "cladding" of just the right refractive index so that light stays inside the fibre because of **total internal reflection**. (See your Physics teacher for more details!) Fibre-optic cables have largely replaced copper wire within the telecommunications industry.

Advantages of Fibre-optics:
- Very high data transmission speeds (100 + Gbits/second)
- Large "bandwidth" allowing streaming of video signals
- Light is not affected by electric currents so little or no "interference".

Disadvantages
- Expensive - but the price is going down all the time.
- Relatively fragile and technically difficult to repair breaks.

Wireless Networks

Getting rid of cables altogether is, on the face of it, an excellent idea. Data is carried by broadcast radio signals, which are transmitted and received by all nodes on the network. More often than not a LAN may be a mixture of both wired and wireless connections.

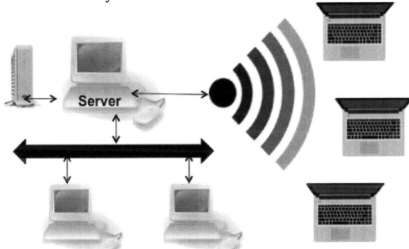

The wired devices enjoy the speed and reliability that comes with cables while the wireless devices have the convenience and mobility that "Wi-Fi" provides.

Note: The generic term for these kinds of networks is **W**ireless **L**ocal **A**rea **N**etwork or **WLAN**. "Wi-Fi" is often used as a synonym for a WLAN but has the specific meaning of a WLAN that follows a particular standard and is a trademark of the Wi-Fi Alliance.

Advantages of WLANs:
- Cheap, easy to set up
- No cables - so devices are entirely mobile

Disadvantages:
- Security issues: Need passwords, can be "hacked" into by intruders
- Interference from other electrical signals
- Short distance only
- Can be slow

Extension: Addressing (MAC addresses)
Every device connected to a LAN has a unique, physical, "address" embedded within the device's Network Interface Card (NIC). This Media Access Control (MAC) address is assigned at manufacture and uniquely identifies every device. This is how LAN data traffic can be directed to the correct device.

It consists of a 48 bit (6 byte) code. This is written, on the card, as 12 Hexadecimal digits to make it easier for humans to read!

Example the MAC address on the above card is:
    00 A0 C9 C7 8D 88
This translates to the binary number of:
    0000 0000 1010 0000 1100 1001 1100 0111 1000 1101 1000 1000
(See the section on data representation hexadecimal and binary to work this out!)

Questions on chapter 7a Networks Introduction

1. Ana starts up a small travel business called "Ana Student Travel". At the start of her business she rents a small office and has 3 computers, a scanner and one laser printer used for administration. A friend recommends that she set-up a small computer network by connecting all of the devices to a central hub.

(a) State and explain three advantages of connecting her computers together in a network rather than having them working independently as "**stand-alone**" computers.

(b) State the name given to the topology, like Ana's network, where all devices are connected together via a **central hub**.

(c) Draw a simple diagram showing how Ana's computers and peripheral devices are connected together.

(d) Ana's initial network implemented the "peer-to-peer" model. State what "**peer-to-peer**" means in this context and explain, how in the present circumstances, it is an appropriate model for Ana to employ.

With time, and a lot of hard work, Ana's business expands and she moves into new and bigger offices. She now has over 25 computers and several printers spread over several offices inside one large building. She has a very large external hard-drive which stores all of the data her administration staff need access to and a second external drive, which is used to back up her company's important data.

She is advised that she should now connect her computers using a **bus topology**, with a single **line** that runs through all of her offices. She also decides to implement the "**server-client**" model. She selects one fast and reliable computer to be the server and to this computer she installs the necessary network operating system and connects her two large external drives directly to this computer.

(e) Draw a simple diagram showing Ana's bus topology network. It is not necessary to show all 25 computers. The computer, which is the server, should be clearly identified as such. The diagram should show at least one printer directly connected to the network.

(f) State and explain one advantage and one disadvantage of a **bus topology** network.

(g) In the context of a "**client-server**" model, explain:
    i. The role of the server;
    ii. How approved office staff access and store the files that they need.

Ana converts one large room in her office building to a "multi-purpose" room with comfortable chairs, tables and a digital projector. Here she installs a kind of "wireless hot spot" which is directly connected to the main bus or line. This establishes a **Wireless Local Area Network (WLAN)** so that staff with lap top computers can log in and access the main office network.

      (h) State and explain one advantage of a WLAN

      (i) State and explain two disadvantages of a WLAN.

Over the years Ana's business expands still further. She sets up a **Local Area Network (LAN)** in each of three different buildings in three different cities. She pays a national telecommunications company for "**leased lines**" to permanently connect these branch offices together to make a **Wide Area Network (WAN)**.

      (j) State the differences between a LAN and a WAN.

      (k) The leased lines used by the telecommunications company are bundles of fibre-optic cables.

            i. Briefly explain how fibre-optic cables carry digital data. (You do not have to explain the physics of light transmission in a cable.)

            ii. State two advantages that fibre-optic cables have over "traditional" copper wire.

            iii. Apart from any advantage in the previous question, state one advantage that fibre-optic cables have compared to broadcast signals using microwaves to connect distant cities.

Chapter 7b Networks & Internet: Networks - Data Transmission

In the previous section we looked at the different topologies and media used to connect computers together in a network. This section focuses more on the actual transfer of data in a network.

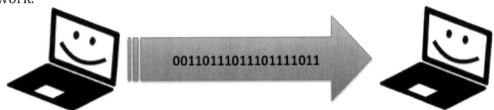

00110111011101111011

Points Covered:

- Network Data Speeds (Mbps, Gbps)
- Addresses, Packets and Layers
- Network Protocols (Ethernet, Wi-Fi, FTP, TCP / IP)
- Extension: Error Detection (check sums)

Network Data Speeds (Mbps, Gbps)

Exactly how data is transferred may be a little bit complicated but, at the end of the day, it is simply a question of sending a stream of binary digits (1110101010110101 ....) from one computer to another. The speed of this data transfer is measured as a **bit rate** or bits per second. (Note: It is bits per second NOT bytes per second). The standard decimal prefixes of k, M and G are used to quantify the large bit rates involved:

1,000 bit/s	rate = **1 kbps**	(one kilobit or one thousand bits per second)
1,000,000 bit/s	rate = **1 Mbps**	(one megabit or one million bits per second)
1,000,000,000 bit/s	rate = **1 Gbps**	(one gigabit or one billion bits per second)

Obviously, all other things being equal, the faster the bit rate, the better.

Calculating time to transmit a file - An Example:

File: A short novel – 600 kilobytes (KB)

- Convert to bits (remember 1 byte is 8 bits):
- 600 KB = 600 X 1024 X 8 = 4915200 bits

Media: Fibre-optic at 500 Mbps

- Convert to bits per second
- 500 Mbps = 500 X 1,000,000 = 500, 000, 000 bps

Time taken = file size (bits) / network speed (bps)

- Time = 4915200 / 500000000 = 0.0098304 seconds

Addresses, Packets and Layers

Example: Consider sending the following Haiku poem to a friend:

"Yesterday it worked.
Today it is not working.
Windows is like that."

Well if you were going to use the traditional post ("snail-mail"), I suppose you would put the text **inside an envelope**. On the front you may write:

For:	Andrew Woods
Address:	Linden Street, Berlin
From:	Carmen Gomez
Address:	Gran Via, Madrid
Contents:	One Haiku Poem

It's really not so very different if you wanted to send the poem from one computer to another on a network.

For:	Computer 21
MAC address:	0 0 A0 C9 C7 8D 88
From:	Computer 15
MAC address:	FC A0 59 C E 34 4 A
Contents:	ASCII text document
Actual Data:	"Yesterday it worked. \nToday it is not working. \nWindows is like that."

(A MAC address is a 48 bit number, written here as 12 Hex digits, which uniquely identifies any computer connected to a Local Area Network.)

Packets: Now let's get just a little more complicated: Suppose the poem is too long to send as one whole poem. I know it is only 3 lines long but just suppose! Well I could divide the poem up into **packets** one line long. Now I am going to have add to each packet:
> **1st of 3**, **2nd of 3** and **3rd of 3**

So if you only receive one packet (labelled as say 2nd of 3) you will know that you should wait for 2 more packets to complete the delivery. But each packet will still need the other information such as the sender's address. (After all if you do only receive one packet out of 3 you are going to need to know who to ask, for the "missing" packets.)

Now the whole, long message that will be sent will look something like this:
> For: 00A0C9C78D88//From FCA059CE344A//1 of 3//ASCII text document//"Yesterday it worked.\n"//For: 00A0C9C78D88//From FCA059CE344A //2 of 3//ASCII text document// "Today it is not working.\n" //For: 00A0C9C78D88//From FCA059CE344A 3 of 3// ASCII text document//"Windows is like that.\n"

Of course it won't "look" like that to the network - It will just a be stream of
> 0101011011010101011110101101011101011100000 ......

Or really just pulses of electrical "on" / "off" signals.

Layers:
What we have actually been doing could be described as "wrapping" the data up in Layers of information needed to send and receive the data. In the Haiku example we have used 3 layers:
1. **Application** - The encoding layer that, in this case, said that the data is ASCII text
2. **Transport** - Cut the data into packets and add packet information such as the 2nd of 3 packets.
3. **Link Address** - Add the MAC addresses of sending and receiving computer.

Here's the same data and "layers" being sent but shown as a table to make it clearer:

3 Link Address Header	2 Transport Header	1 Application	Data
For: 00A0C9C78D88 From: FCA059CE344A	1 of 3	ASCII text	"Yesterday it worked.\n"
For: 00A0C9C78D88 From: FCA059CE344A	2 of 3	ASCII text	"Today it is not working.\n"
For: 00A0C9C78D88 From: FCA059CE344A	3 of 3	ASCII text	"Windows is like that.\n"

Note it does not matter what order the packets arrive at their destination. All the information needed to "reassemble" the poem and display it is included in the layers. For the destination computer it is like receiving a Christmas present - you have to **unwrap** it!

- 3 Link address "wrapper" - Check that the packet is for me.
- 2 Transport "wrapper" - How many packets and what number is this one?
  - o   Wait until you have all the packets.
  - o   Put the packets in order 1st, 2nd, 3rd
- 1 Application "wrapper" - Decode the data as, in this case, ASCII text

Finally the receiver can open their message:

    "Yesterday it worked.

    Today it is not working.

    Windows is like that."

Phew! Well don't worry, it may look a lot of work to you, but computers do this kind of stuff in less than a second. On the other hand the technical reality of sending data on networks can be a lot more complicated:

- There are usually more layers
  - o   For example an Internet Protocol (**IP**) address for devices connected to the Internet.
- There is usually some sort of built in **error checking**
  - o   So it is not only "what packet number is this?" but also "have you been damaged in transit?" If so I am going to have to ask the sender to send me the whole packet again.
- Each network has its own **protocols** for sending and receiving data.

Network Protocols

When diplomats get together for a meeting at the United Nations it helps if they can talk each other's language. Apart from languages there are other "social norms" that a good diplomat should be aware of, such as: hand-shaking, smiling, laughing, bowing or kissing on each cheek and so on. These accepted codes of procedure or behaviour are called **protocols**.

When computers "talk" to each other there have to be similar "rules" governing the exchange or transmission of data between devices. After all, the devices on different networks can be very different, ranging from an Apple Mac PowerBook running Mac OS X to a large desktop computer running MS Windows 8. So a **network protocol is a set of rules that define how devices communicate** and will include definitions of such factors as: Start code, Data Speed, Language, Bits or Bytes, any Error checking and a stop code. There is a range of network protocols available for all the different possible networks and devices:

Ethernet: A family of related protocols rather than a single protocol.
- The most widely used protocol for **LAN**s
- Data transmission speeds of 10 to 100 Mbps
- Up to 1500 bytes per packet
- Very often used with **Star Network** topology

Wi-Fi: A family of related protocols rather than a single protocol
- For communications on a Wireless Local Area Network (**WLAN**) - remember "Wi-Fi" is a trademark.
- All devices transmit and receive on the same radio channel

TCP / IP: Transmission Control Protocol / Internet Protocol
- As the name suggests, the most common protocol for communicating via the Internet
- All devices are "allocated" an **IP address**.
  - This is in addition to their unique, "hardware" or MAC address.
  - The devices are usually connected via a "router" which, in turn, is connected to the Internet.
  - The IP address on a LAN is often "dynamic" which means it can change but at any one time all devices connected to one router will have a unique IP addresses.
  - So each device is uniquely identified.

This means that packets are sent with a **4 level "layered architecture"**. The "extra" layer is for the **IP address**, which consists of four numbers from 0 to 255 separated by full stops.

There will be more on this in the section on the Internet but right now let's just see what happens to the 3 packets that made up our Haiku poem:

4 Link Address Header	3 Network IP Header	2 Transport Header	1 Application	Data
For: 00A0C9C78D88 From: FCA059CE344A	For: 102.231.4.189 From: 98.1.232.99	1 of 3	ASCII text	"Yesterday it worked.\n"
For: 00A0C9C78D88 From: FCA059CE344A	For: 102.231.4.189 From: 98.1.232.99	2 of 3	ASCII text	"Today it is not working.\n"
For: 00A0C9C78D88 From: FCA059CE344A	For: 102.231.4.189 From: 98.1.232.99	3 of 3	ASCII text	"Windows is like that.\n"

FTP: File Transfer Protocol
- Used to transfer files between computers on the Internet using **TCP/IP** protocol
- Uses the **client-server** model architecture
  - One computer, the client, initiates a "conversation" with the server by requesting to download a file from the server or upload a file to the server.
  - The server may, or may not, demand that the user logs on with a username and a password.
  - If all is well, the server opens up a "data channel" and the file transfer can proceed.

Email: An article published in 2015 estimated that almost 2.4 million emails are sent every second! ("email.about.com") No wonder we need special protocols to deal with them.

- Sending Messages:
  - **SMTP** - Simple Mail Transfer Protocol
    - Usually only used for sending messages (leaving POP3 or IMAP) to receive messages.

- Receiving Messages:
  - **POP3** - Post Office Protocol
    - One of the oldest email protocols out there and still very popular
    - **Creates local copies** of emails and deletes the originals from the server.
    - This does mean that the downloaded emails are now tied to the specific computer that was used to access the email.
  - **IMAP** - Internet Message Access Protocol
    - **All the emails are stored on a "remote server"** until a user deletes them.
    - The idea is that you can, access, read and send emails from a range of devices - your smart phone, tablet or desktop computer - and you always see the same mailboxes, folders and so on because they are **"in the cloud"**.
    - You are now "reliant" on the remote server. There may be restrictions on the amount of files you can store there. If the server "goes down" you can't access any of your messages, old or new.
    - You can, of course, always make a local copy of any email or file and then delete the original from the "cloud".

Note: Some protocols, such as HTTP and HTTPS, which are specifically for use on the World Wide Web, will be covered in the section on the Internet.

Extension: The need to Detect and Correct Errors

Errors in Transmission: Whether you are sending a quick note to your friend in another room or downloading a file from your LAN's server, errors can occur as the the data is transmitted.

- Electrical Interference "noise"
  - Anything from electric cables, radio signals to cosmic radiation
  - An "on" can change to an "off"
  - "C" is 0100 0010 if one bit changes
  - 0100 0110 is now "F"
  - CAT was sent and FAT received

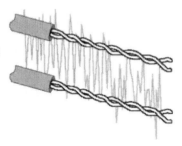

- Media and error rates
  - Radio (wireless) highest – worst
  - Copper wire – high
  - Fiber-optic – very low

Error Detection:

If only the data is sent there is no way of knowing if there has been an error. After all "I love your cuddly FAT" may be correct! How is the receiving computer supposed to know that there has been an error in transmission?   Besides the data could be anything: numbers, music, videos etc. Some kind of "**check bits**" must be added to the data so that any change or error, while the data is transmitted, can be detected by the receiver.

Note that the receiver cannot correct the error! Think about it – the receiver cannot know what the message should have been! All the receiver can do is to send a message back to the sender saying something like: "Error in transmission, please resend data."

Check sums:

The Sender

- Prepares a data packet.
- An algorithm calculates a numerical value based on the number of bits in the packet - The check sum
- This check sum is added to the packet at transmission

The Receiver

- Applies the same algorithm to the data to recalculate the checksum
- If the received and recalculated checksums are not the same then the receiver knows an error has occurred.
- It asks the sender to resend that packet

Questions on chapter 7b Data Transmission

Network Data Speeds:
1. Carla and Marcus each take a digital camera while on holiday.
Carla takes 150 photos and each photo occupies 10 MB on her camera's memory card.
Marcus takes 130 photos and each photo occupies 12 MB on his camera's memory card.

(a). When she gets home home Carla downloads her photos to her computer by directly connecting the camera to her computer with a USB cable. The transmission speed via the cable is 50 Mbps (50 million bits per second). Calculate the time in seconds to download all of her photos to her computer.

(b) Apart from speed of download, suggest another reason why Carla prefers to use a USB cable, rather than using wireless ("Wi-Fi") transfer.

(c) Marcus downloads his photos to his computer using his camera's built in wireless ("Wi-Fi") system. The transmission speed via a radio signal is 10 Mbps (10 million bits per second). Calculate the time in seconds to download all of his photos to his computer.

(d) Marcus knows that wireless transfer can be a little slow. Suggest a reason why he still prefers to use "Wi-Fi"?

2. Sunnyvale Academy has a school intranet, running on a bus (line) topology LAN, where all the connections are with fibre-optic cables. A biology student logs on to the intranet and downloads a 25 MB video file on evolution. The data transmission speed on the school's fibre-optic cables is about 2 Gbps (2 billion bits per second).

(a) Calculate an estimate for the time in seconds it takes for the video file to download.

(b) When all of the biology class of 20 students try to download the video file at the same time they notice that it takes a little longer than when they are on their own.
Suggest and explain a reason why there is a decrease in download time.

(c) Shadowlands College knows that a fibre-optic based LAN can be very fast but still decides to use "Ethernet" copper wire to connect its computers in a network.
Suggest one reason why the college decided not to use fibre-optics:

Packets & Protocols
1. When computers are networked together, what is a network **protocol**?

2. State what the following **protocols** stand for and what they are used for:
   TCP/IP   **FTP**

3. Sally sets up an email system on her computer. She knows she has to use some email protocols. Carmen tells her that she must use the **SMTP** protocol and then she can choose if she wants an email service that uses **IMAP** or **POP3**

(a) What do the following acronyms stand for? **SMTP**   **IMAP**   **POP3**

(b) Why does Sally have to choose **SMTP** for her email system?

(c) Explain to Sally the differences between an **IMAP** and a **POP3** email system.

4. Computers can have a **MAC** address and an **IP** address.
(a) Distinguish between a **MAC** address and an **IP** address by copying and filling in the following information;
MAC address: Number of Bits.................
Example (in Hex) ....
Used to address what? ....
IP address:
Number of Bits.................
Example (as 4 denary numbers) ....
Used to address what? ....

   (b) Explain why a MAC address is permanent but an IP address can be static or dynamic (change).

5. Data is sent on a network broken up into **packets.** Apart from the data itself each packet has to have some other information. Here is an example of a **packet** with 4 parts.
00A0CC5CFF5C // 99ACC00569FF // 3 of 4   //10010111001111001101110 ...... /
(a) Suggest what each components represents (the 4ᵗʰ part has been done for you.)
        Part 1: ....
        Part 2: ....
        Part 3: ....
        Part 4:   The actual data being sent

(b) Suggest one more piece of information, not concerning addresses, which could be added to each packet in order for it to be sent on a Local Area Network.
        (c) Another "layer", with additional information, would have to be added if the data were to be sent on the Internet. What is the additional information required?

Extension: Error Detection
1. Data can be "corrupted" or changed when it is transmitted. Explain one way that data can be "corrupted" during transmission between computers.

2. The following text data is sent as one packet:
 "A fool thinks himself to be wise, but a wise man knows himself to be a fool."
A calculation is done on the bits of data resulting in "45737" which is attached to the packet and both are transmitted to another computer.
        (a) What is the name for the result, 45737, of the calculation on the data?
        (b) Explain what the receiving computer has to do to check if the data has been sent correctly.
        (c) What is the **only** thing the receiving computer can do if it does detect an error?

Chapter 7c Networks & Internet: The Internet

Ask someone, "What is the Internet?" and the answer is usually along the lines of: "That is where I check out the news, watch videos, play online games and do my Internet shopping." Note how the question is not being answered! They are saying what they **do** with the Internet, not **what** it is. A question like, "What is the difference between the **Internet** and the **World Wide Web**?" prompts the bewildered reply of: "What do you mean? They are the same thing aren't they?" This chapter seeks to unravel such confusion and to explain what exactly the Internet is.

Points Covered:
- Architecture IP addressing & Routers
- World Wide Web (WWW) – Servers, URLs & ISP
- HTML & CSS – Importance & Introduction

Architecture IP addressing & Routers
The Internet is an **inter**connection of computer **net**works.
- An international computer network, connecting networks around the world
- A network of networks
- Connected by telecommunications

In essence that's all the Internet is – thousands of computer networks connected together to make a network of networks of networks.

Internet Protocol (IP) Address:
We have already seen that all hardware devices connected in a network have a unique "hardware number" called their **MAC** address, which uniquely identifies that device. Well an **IP address** is a unique number that identifies a computer that is using the **Internet Protocol (IP)** to communicate over a network.

An **IP address** consists of four, one-byte numbers, each ranging from 0 to 255, separated by full stops. For example: 193.127.30.23, or 11000001 01111111 00011110 00010111. That is 32-bits so 2^{32} which is 4,294,967,296 possible addresses. Note: 4 billion different IP address may seem a lot but as the Internet expands we are running out of IP addresses. IPv6 has now been introduced using 128-bit address. This will mean 2^{128} addresses! (That's about 3.4×10^{38}, so it should keep the world going for a bit!)

Architecture – Connecting all the networks with routers

A Router and a LAN: A Router is bit like a hub or switch that can connect computers in a Star-like topology. It can "route" or switch packets of data from computer to computer. It has a **private** IP address for the LAN and it then dynamically allocates unique IP addresses to all computers on the LAN. So, ignoring MAC addresses, the LAN, with IP addresses, looks something like this:

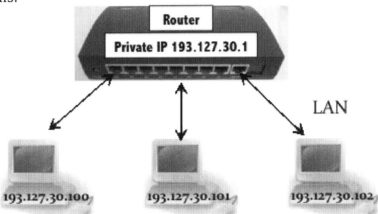

A Router and the Internet: Now let's use the router to connect to the Internet. The router has a second, **public** IP address, which uniquely identifies it on the Internet. It uses that public IP address to connect to a modem (see below) which connects the router, and so the LAN, to the Internet.

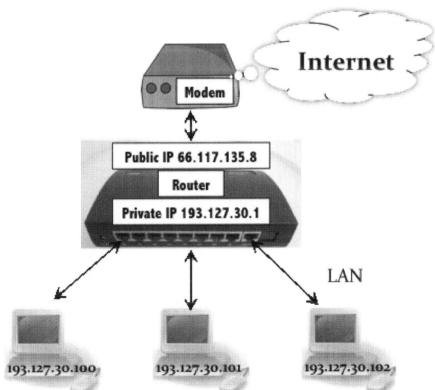

Connecting to the Internet – Modems and a little bit of history:

In the 1970s to connect your computer or LAN to the Internet you used a telephone line and "dialled" a number (dial-up connection)! Telephone lines were all **analogue** – they carried continuously variable electrical signals. So you needed a device that could convert from digital to analogue and vice-versa. This little box of electronics was called a **MODEM** which is short for "Modulator Demodulator", which describes what it did:

- **Modulate** a carrier wave to encode and send digital data which, in effect, "adds" the digital data on top of an analogue telephone signal.
- **Demodulate** the analogue telephone signal which means separating out the digital data from the telephone signal for the computer at the receiving end.

Connecting to the Internet – Now:

Many telephone lines are now "digital" and even use fibre-optic cable. But you still need to "convert" the computer's digital signal to a digital signal that can be carried on the telecommunications system and that device is still called a modem. The modem may be built into a router, or it may even be a tiny, embedded chip inside your smart phone, but it is still there.

Internet Routers and the Internet Backbone:

Essentially the Internet is just lots, and lots, of LANs connected together with routers. **Routers are "packet switches"** – they route (send) packets around the Internet.

- Routers have "routing tables" with all the IP addresses it knows
- When a packet arrives at a router it checks its destination IP address
- If the IP address is in its routing table then it sends the packet to that network
- If the router does not have the IP address then it sends the packet "up" to the next router.

Large and sophisticated routers at **Network Access Points (NAP)** connect many LANs together. Many large networks connected together are called **Network Service Providers (NSP)** providing what is known as the **Internet Backbone** and these are connected to other NSPs and so on and so on...

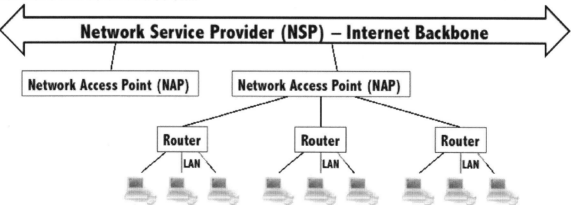

Imagine thousands of the above, all connected together, and you have the Internet. The technology company "CISCO" estimated that by 2020 there would 50 billion "things" connected to the Internet. Mind you, to put everything into perspective and remind ourselves how wonderful humans are: The human brain has about 100 billion neurones and each neurone may be connected to up to 10,000 other neurones giving a million million connections.

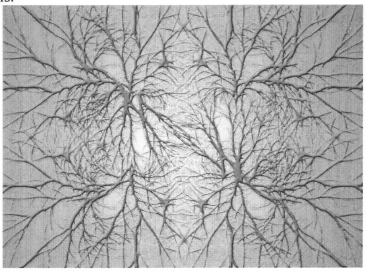

World Wide Web (WWW) –Servers, URLs & ISP

Internet Service Provider:

So you have your Router-Modem with its public IP address and that's all you need to connect to the Internet, right? Not quite - You cannot connect to the Internet without becoming part of it yourself. You need an **Internet Service Provider (ISP)**, like BT, Sky, Virgin, Vodafone, Telefonica, America Online etc., who is permanently connected to the Internet "backbone", that is they have a **point-of-presence (PoP)** with a unique IP address. An Internet point-of-presence is an access point to the Internet. It is a physical location (building) that will have a large number of servers and routers. You connect to your **ISP** via some sort of telecommunications: ADSL telephone line, fibre-optic cable or even a satellite dish.

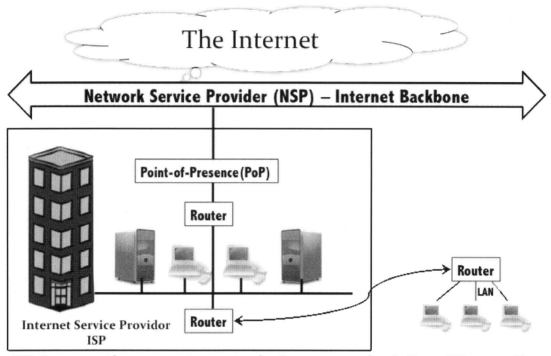

Your **ISP** Company then connects you to the Internet - at last! Your ISP may offer other services such as very high-speed access to the Internet, space on their servers to host your own web sites and so on. The more or better services that you want, the more you pay.

The World Wide Web

Now that you are finally connected to the Internet and are "surfing the web", it is a good time to stress that the Internet is NOT the same thing as the World Wide Web:

Internet	World Wide Web

• An **inter**connected **net**work of networks
 	
• **The Hardware &** Architecture of how networks are connected
 	
• **Protocols** for communication
	• One way to **access** the INFORMATION on the internet
	
	• **Software ("Hyper Text")**
	    • **Browsers** read and display Web Pages with HTML (Hyper Text Mark-up Language)
	    • Data sent with HTTP (Hyper Text Transfer **Protocols**)

So the World Wide Web is just a way of accessing information using the infrastructure of the Internet. The Internet existed before the World Wide Web and even now some services, such as email, instant messaging and File Transfer Protocol (FTP) use the Internet but are not, directly, part of the World Wide Web.

So what is going on when I use my browser to open a web page on the World Wide Web?

- **A web page** is really just a complex document a bit like a Word Processed document with lots of text, tables and pictures. It is most commonly "written" in HyperText Markup Language or **HTML** (see below).
- **A Browser** like Safari, Chrome or Explorer, is just a program that can "read" HTML and so display Web Pages on your computer.
- **A Web Server** is the computer, with large backing storage, which stores the web pages. As it is, obviously, connected to the Internet, it will have a unique **IP address** (see above).
- **Domain names** are just memorable and easy-to-spell addresses for web servers. For example: **185.31.18.81** is the **IP address** for the server for **www.bbc.com**. As 185.31.18.81 is difficult to remember you only have to type in www.bbc.com, or just click on the link, and your browser will send a request to a Domain Name System (**DNS**) server on the Internet.
  - Each **DNS** has a huge database of all domain names and their IP addresses and can quickly direct your browser to connect to the right server.
- **URL:** All of the pages the server stores will have a **URL** (an address), which you type into your browser or just click on a HyperText link that directs your browser to the page you want. For example:
  - **http://www.bbc.com/news/technology**
- will take you straight to the BBC's technology web page.
- **URL** is an acronym for **Uniform Resource Locator** and is an address of a resource, like a web page, on the Internet. A URL has two main components:
  - **Protocol identifier**: That's the "http" bit, which stands for **HyperText Transfer Protocol**, which is the protocol, used by the World Wide Web. **HTTP** defines how messages are formatted and transmitted.
  - **The resource name:** That's the www.bbc.com/news/technology bit.

Here's a typical webpage, showing its URL- "https://www.facebook.com". Notice two small differences with the URL - " http://www.bbc.com/news/technology"
- There is a little picture (icon) of a padlock
- The protocol is not "http" but "https"

HTTPS is an acronym for: **Hyper Text Transfer Protocol Secure**. This is the "secure" version of HTML. It gives you, the user of the website, security because:
- The website and associated web server are "guaranteed" to be **authentic**;
- All communications between a **client and server** are **encrypted**.

This basically means that you can be reasonably sure that you are communicating with the website that you wanted to, rather than an "imposter", and that no one else can read or change any data that you exchange with the website. The HTTPS protocol is used on all types of websites where **security** and **confidentiality** are important:
- Online Banking
- Online Shopping
- Private profiles on social websites etc.

HTML & CSS - Importance & Introduction

HTML is an acronym for **H**pyer**T**ext **M**arkup **L**anguage. Simply put, it defines how web pages are "written" and created. Perhaps I could write a webpage just using a Word Processor like MS Word? After all word processors are pretty sophisticated these days. I could include text, diagrams, tables, graphs, photos and, maybe, even "embed" some video clips. I could even upload my lovely document, via my ISP, to the Internet. The problem is that anyone who tries to "view" my document will need the Word Processing Program that I used to create the program installed on his or her computer. Not only that, I have know way of knowing the size & resolution of the screen, the fonts available, the operating system etc. which will be needed to correctly display my "webpage".

HTML is an international standard. This is very important so that any web-browser, anywhere, can display any web page that uses the HTML standard.

HTML is "coded" using tags that define the page structure. A tag has a beginning and an end. In the following example, the "header" tags, beginning with <h1> and ending with</h1>, will display the text, between the tags, "**Hello**", as a heading - that is it will be the largest text and will stand out from other text.

```
<h1> Hello </h1>
```

Usually the whole web page will begin and end with tags to show that the page was "coded" in HTML. Here's an example:

```
<html>
<head>
  <title>My first web page</title>
</head>
<body>
  <h1>My first web page</h1>
  <h2>What this is</h2>
  <p>A simple page put together using HTML</p>
  <h2>Why this is</h2>
  <p>To learn HTML</p>
</body>
</html>
```

When a web-browser, like Safari or Chrome, "reads" this HTML, they will display it something like this:

My first web page
What this is
A simple page put together using HTML
Why this is
To learn HTML

Of course it can get a lot more complicated than this!

- **HyperText** – Click on a link and "jump" to another page or site
  - <a href="http://www.htmldog.com">HTML Dog</a>
  - This will display the word "Dog"
  - When you click on "Dog" you will be taken to www.htmldog.com
- **Images**
  - <img src="http://www.htmldog.com/badge1.gif" width="120" height="90" alt="HTML Dog">
  - This tells the web browser that there is an image called "badge1.gif" and where that image is.
  - The image will be shown as 120 pixels wide by 90 pixels high

Cascading Style Sheets CSS

Using "Styles" in any document, including Word-Processed documents, enable you to set things like titles (headings), subsections with subheadings, page numbering and so on so that they are the same throughout a very long document. For example you may choose that all subheadings are in font "Times New Roman", in "bold", underlined with a point size of 18. These styles are stored with the document as a "style sheet". If you want to change something - all subheadings should now be in red and not underlined - then you just change the style sheet and automatically every single subheading will change.

Websites, consisting of many webpages, have the same kind of issue. For example all the "pages" of the BBC News Site look very similar: They have that "corporate" style about them. How the pages look - the layout, the background, the text and so on - is all defined in an **HTML style sheet**. If, like the BBC, you have a huge corporate site sub-divided into sections such as News, Entertainment, and Education etc., then there may be a "hierarchy" of style sheets: A "main" style sheet that defines all the pages and then "sub" style sheets defining how a particular section should look and maybe even "sub, sub" style sheets defining how one department's site looks. Such a "hierarchy" of style sheets are known as **Cascading Style Sheets** or **CSS**.

The web browser will "read" the style sheets that are "attached" to a web page, starting with the one "at the top". It will then see if the particular page you are looking at has its own style sheet that "over-rides" any of the instructions in the style sheet "above" it. The browser will do its best, depending on your computer's operating system, to display the pages as the author of the page intended them to look.

Here's an example of a style, written in HTML, as part of a style sheet:

```
h3 {
font: italic normal 1.4em georgia, sans-serif;
letter-spacing: 1px;
margin-bottom: 0;
color: #7D775C; }
```

This style says that all h3 (header text 3) will be:
- **Style** italic
- **Font** "georgia" (or any "sans-serif" font)
- **Letters** spaced with 1 pixel
- **Colour** 7D 77 5C
  - Hex code for Red Green Blue colours

In summary: HTML is used by the browser to display the contents and CSS are used to make the pages look "stylish"!

You can write web pages in HTML using
- Simple text editors (just save the file as "anypage.html") but this is tedious
- Special web page authoring programs like "Dreamweaver" or "iWeb"
  - WYSWYG (what you see is what you get!)
  - These are like "publisher" programs and you layout the page, insert pictures, links etc.
  - The software "translates" all of this automatically into correct HTML.

Professional web page designers clearly need to know their HTML. Of course they will use web page creating software to help them and they are probably pretty good at graphical design and programming too. Nonetheless, most, "ordinary" people, like you and me, most of the time, do not need to be able to "code" in HTML to make great web pages. There is a range of excellent software using templates, "drag and drop", import and embed tools etc. that enables us to create wonderful, interactive web-sites.

One final point; please remember that HTML is NOT a programming language!
- HTML, as a mark-up language, doesn't really "do" anything.
- HTML contains no programming logic.
- It doesn't have statements such as If/Else.
- It can't evaluate expressions or do any maths.
- You can't declare variables and you can't write functions.
- HTML can't take input and produce output.
- Think of it this way: You can't compute the sum of 2 + 2 in HTML
- This is because HTML is **not** a programming language.

There are programming languages that can make web pages respond to user input such as "JavaScript" or even "complete" programming languages like Python or Java.

Questions on chapter 7c The Internet
Architecture IP addressing & Routers:
1. Carmen and her family have 3 computers and a network printer. She wants to connect them all together to make a LAN that can connect to the Internet. She is going to use a combined Router-Modem and Ethernet cables to make a star topology network.

(a) To complete her set-up Carmen needs to pay a subscription to an Internet Service Provider (ISP). Explain why she needs an ISP and what "services" she can expect from her ISP.

(b) Draw a simple, diagram showing how:

i. All the devices connect to the router;

ii. The router connects to the Internet.

(c) Outline the role of the router by explaining:

i. How the router uses its unique, private, IP address to allocate IP addresses to all devices on the LAN.

ii. Why the router needs another, public IP address.

iii. What happens when one computer connects to the Internet and downloads a document to that computer's hard drive?

World Wide Web (WWW) - servers, URLs & ISP.
1. Dave uses his browser to "surf the web". He is a Python programmer and plans a holiday in the beautiful Seychelles Islands.

(a) Explain why the World Wide Web and the Internet are not the same thing.

(b) Every web page has to have a Uniform Resource Locator (URL). Here is an example of a URL from the official Seychelles Islands tourism web page:
http://www.seychelles.travel/
Use this example to explain, in full, what a URL is. Include in your answer an explanation of the acronym "http".

(c) When he is working, Dave downloads programs and code from the official Python website:
https://www.python.org/
Explain why this site uses "https" rather than "http".

HTML - importance of & introduction
1. HTML (Hypertext Markup Language) is the set of markup symbols or codes inserted in a file intended for display on a World Wide Web browser page.

(a) Here is an example of some HTML "code":
<a href="http://www.sallysnacks.com">Sally's Scrumptious Snacks</a>

i. What will this code display on a web page (i.e. what will you actually see)?

ii. What will happen when a user "clicks" on what is displayed?

(b) For an HTML file to display correctly your computer will need to have some special software installed. What is the general name for this kind of software and state one well-known commercial product?

(c) Explain why it is important that HTML is an "international standard."

(d) State two reasons why HTML should not be considered as a programming language.

Chapter 7d Networks & Internet: Network Security

In 1815 it took over 2 days for the news of the defeat of Napoleon at Waterloo to reach London. Today we can see live coverage on the Internet of a conflict anywhere in the world. Crucial research by Gregor Mendel on inherited characteristics, published in 1866, lay "hidden" in an obscure Austrian science journal until it was "rediscovered" 30 years later. Now scientists keep up-to-date via the Internet with live forums and blogs. Major companies use their intranets and WANs to coordinate and run vast transnational businesses.

Net Security is Important: The technological achievements behind these hugely complex data exchange networks are astonishing. We have come to depend on fast and reliable access to the Internet. Yet there is a "darker side" to the Web: Malicious individuals, organised crime rings and, at times, even sovereign states are constantly trying to illegally enter ("hack into") networks to access confidential information or simply hold a company to ransom - "If you don't pay me, then I will destroy your data."

- **Data is valuable** - A company that suddenly lost all its records of clients and transactions would very soon be out of business.
- **Data is Confidential** - Companies, states and even individuals have data that only authorised people should be able to see. The data ranges from private codes to access bank accounts to state defence secrets.

Note: Various security issues have already been covered in other sections:
- 4f - **Encryption** & Data Transmission
- 5a - Digital Computer Systems - The "**Cloud**" and related security risks
- 5c - **Software** - Malware, viruses, updates, Antivirus and Antispyware
- 7c - Web pages and Hyper Text Transfer Protocol Secure (**HTTPS**)

Points Covered:
- **Cyber Attack**
  - 1. Humans & Social Engineering
    - Phishing, pharming and shouldering
  - 2. Data Transmission
    - Email, removable media and eavesdropping
- **Cyber Defence**
  - 1. Identify Vulnerabilities
    - Penetration testing
  - 2. Access Control
    - Physical security, validation & authentication and firewalls
  - 3. Protect Software Systems
    - Best programming practice, versions & patches, audit trail

Cyber Attack

"Cyber Criminals" attack through the two main weaknesses in networks - humans and data transmission.

1. Humans - Social Engineering:

Humans, sometimes disparagingly referred to as "liveware", are: erratic, emotional, naive, trusting, foolish, forgetful and, well, "human". Other, rather nasty, humans use these frailties to break into systems and steal or damage data.

Phishing: You receive an email from your bank:

"Dear Mr John Smith, due to an increase in online crime, we have decided to introduce some new safety features to your online bank account. For your protection and account security please complete the form below and press accept. Thank you for your cooperation. Ms Trust, ABC Bank, Security Management."

As a trusting and cautious person, you fill in the information asked for, including your account number, username, password and Personal Identification Number (PIN). After all the email does come from the bank doesn't it? It does have the bank's Logo. So you click "accept".

You have just been "phished". The letter was not from your bank. Real banks **never** ask you to send them emails with your PIN and login details. A "cyber" criminal is, right now, accessing your bank account and removing all the money she can! Like "fishing", the criminals send out thousands of email letters as "bait". These letters either entice you with special offers - "You have won a special prize" - or alarm you with fears about security.

Prevention: Most people just delete the "phishing" emails - which is a good thing to do. Some people contact their banks directly and / or the police - which is an excellent thing to do. Sadly, some naive, trusting, nervous or old people respond to the emails!

Pharming: This kind of cyber fraud is sometimes called "phishing without a bait". You are working on the Internet. You click on a link or type the URL "https://trustbank.co.uk". Everything looks normal so you login to your account using your normal username and password. Unfortunately the DNS server (which converts your URL into an IP address) has been "hacked". The server re-directs you to a fake website: "https//trustbanke.co.uk". (Can you see the change? There's just one letter added!) Everything looks the same - it is very easy to copy web sites and change the HTML - but you have just sent your username and password to the cyber criminals. They can now access your bank account via the real website.

Prevention: This kind of attack is much more insidious than phishing because it can happen without the victim even being aware of the attack. It is also much more sophisticated: DNS servers are in physically very secure locations and have sophisticated "defence" mechanisms to protect them. It is not, or should not be, easy to "hack" a DNS server! Users just have to be very careful with any "interactive site" that asks for personal information.

Shoulder Surfing: This could be as simple, and effective, as someone looking over your shoulder, while you are typing in your Personal Identification Number (PIN) at a bank "cash point". When your credit card is subsequently stolen, the criminal has instant access to your bank account!

The problem is that we are always being asked to type in and confirm passwords and PINs. You could be sitting in your local, cool, cybercafé, chilling out with some friends. You login to your favourite social website and tap in your password. Is someone watching "over your shoulder"? Don't be paranoid but don't be naive either. Shoulder surfing can be done at a distance with binoculars or tiny portable web cams (placed amongst the flowers just behind you) that film every screen click that you make.

Prevention: It is not just the ignorant and young who can be careless. In a recent survey 80% of IT professionals admitted that it was possible that unauthorised people could have viewed their screens at "critical times". Some bank "cashpoints" do have sophisticated screens that can only be viewed from close up and at a certain angle. When you type in a PIN at a supermarket it is good practice to shield the keypad with one hand while entering the digits with your other hand. Overall though, the main advice must be: "be sensible and be careful!"

2. Data Transmission:

Whenever data leaves one computer and goes into another there are two clear dangers: The data could be "intercepted" on route and / or it could carry a malware infection with it, which will now infect the receiving computer.

Email: We saw the dangers of fraudulent emails with phishing but almost any email could contain malware or a link to a "dodgy" site. Unsolicited email, or "**Spam**", means all those emails, that arrive all the time, asking you to sign up to some cause, advertise special offers, invite you to join a social web-site etc. Most of the time this kind of "junk mail" is just that - junk. Sometimes the mail looks like it comes from a friend and then you open it and read it. Unwittingly you have infected your computer with a virus.

Prevention: Most email companies automatically scan emails for viruses, suspicious addresses and so on. You can change the settings to your email account to block certain names & addresses and to label unknown addresses as "spam". You should report any abusive messages to your ISP and, if necessary to the police. "If in doubt, throw it out". That is, get into the habit of deleting, without opening, all suspicious emails.

Removable Media - Backing Storage: We swop and share data with friends all the time. Perhaps someone has a film that you want to see and lends you his pen drive so that you can copy the film to your computer. If you connect a USB drive, which does not belong to you, to your computer then you could be downloading malware onto your computer.

Prevention: Any USB pen or portable hard drive, with personal and / or confidential information, should, at the very least, be "**password protected**". Many organisations demand that the data be **encrypted** so that only people with the "key" can access the drive.

When any storage device is connected to your computer it should be automatically scanned for malware, particularly viruses. (See the section on utility software.)

Eavesdropping: Long before the world of technology, a neighbour could stand under the eaves of the house next door to listen to the conversation inside. He would then pass on this gossip to his mates in the pub. The modern version of eavesdropping is "listening in" to any private communication on a network. In other words cyber criminals try to intercept messages and conversations in "**real-time**" (as they happen).

Using Internet based "phones" such as "Skype", and built in microphones and web cams have added to the problem. A knowledgeable criminal could "hack" into the **IP addresses** being used and listen to or read the message without either the sender or the receiver being aware. But any connection to a public wireless ("Wi-Fi") network is a potential risk.

Prevention: The software should **encrypt** all conversations, also in real-time. Using conventional phone lines (rather than Internet based software) is more secure. (By the way, illegally accessing these lines is known as "wiretapping"). If you are using a public "Wi-Fi" connection in a coffee shop, stop and think, "Who could be listening in?" Private, password-protected and encrypted "Wi-Fi" is much safer.

Cyber Defence

In a kind of "arms race" with the attackers, computer engineers are constantly trying to defend networks from attack. Their three main weapons are:
1. Identify (and then correct) vulnerabilities in a network;
2. Controlling access to networks;
3. Protecting software by ensuring professional programming standards.

1. Identify Vulnerabilities:

Penetration Testing: An old saying has it that "to catch a thief, you have to find a thief". Perhaps the modern day equivalent is the "**ethical hacker**". This is a computer-networking expert who is employed by a company to "break into" their system. In this way she can identify vulnerabilities and suggest how to "plug the hole."

- White-box - Simulate a malicious **insider** who has some knowledge of the system and basic password access.
- Black-box - Simulate an attack by an **external** hacker

Commercial analysis software tools are also available. In essence, once installed, they "scan" a network looking for "holes" that a cyber attacker could exploit.

2. Access Control:

It may be no good to "lock the door after the horse has bolted", but keeping the "door" secure and controlling exactly who can enter a system and what they can do, when they are in, is clearly a good thing.

Physical Security: This can be as simple as "locking the door". Sensitive hardware, like the LAN's server and racks of backing storage hard disks, should be in a room with very restricted access. Large companies and ISPs will have security guards and cameras monitoring access to their main offices at all times.

Validation and Authentication: There needs to be systems in place to ensure that only authorised personal have access to a network.

Biometric measures (fingerprint, iris-recognition etc.)

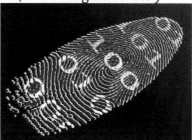

Many systems, including some of the latest smart phones, can "scan" a user's fingerprint or even their iris. If the scan does not match what the system has recorded in its database, then access will be denied.

Passwords and Usernames

To access anything from your smart phone to a workstation at school or an online banking website, you will need a username and password. Most businesses or organisations have **hierarchical levels of access**. This means that different users can do different things when they log on. For example, on a school network: Student - read only; Teacher - read / write; Administrator - read / write & install users, change passwords and so on.

Here are some tips to make up a good, secure password:
- Un-guessable & unforgettable - For example try the city and birthday of a distant relative that only you know - Colchester211. You won't forget it and no one else can guess it.
- Make sure it is complex enough but not too complex. It should have a mixture of uppercase, lowercase and digits. For example: Col211chester.
- Change your password frequently;
- Do not write the password down on a piece of paper!

Email Confirmation: When you first set yourself up as a user on, for example, an online shopping site, the company may send you a confirmation link to the email that you provide. It's not very secure but if it is your email then you will receive the link.

CAPTCHA

Completely Automated Public Turing test to tell Computers and Humans Apart
Their are many malware programs out there that try to automatically gain access by inserting text into online forms. The famous computer scientist Alan Turing (see the section on encryption) devised a simple test to try and distinguish between humans and artificial intelligence. These little widgets just ask you, the human, to make out the strangely appearing text and type in what you can see. The principle being that automatic software can't see nor read the images so if you type it in correctly, then you are not a software program!

Firewalls: In large buildings, like office blocks, hotels and schools, sections of the building can be "sealed off" from other sections by security doors that automatically close in the event of a fire alarm. These "firewalls" work by stopping a fire rapidly spreading from one room or corridor to another area. Network firewalls don't stop fire but they still work by "sealing off" a section of a network from unauthorised access.

Firewalls are often a mixture of hardware and software. All messages entering or leaving a LAN are checked by the firewall. Unauthorised messages are not allowed through. Firewalls are bit like "computerised security guards" who validate the credentials of all visitors to make sure that they are authentic before they allow them to enter a building.

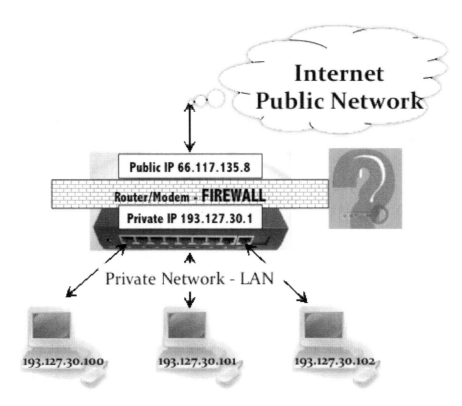

Acceptable Use Policy: Taking into account all the points raised in this chapter it is clear that any company or organisation must have a well planned and up-to-date **policy** governing the security of their network and a clear "**code of conduct**" for all users of that network. These "user policies" could include "rules" like:

- Never write down, nor record, your company LAN password
- Do not use the office intranet for personal business
- Do not download and attempt to install any programs at work
- Never open any "suspicious" email
- Only use company approved "Encrypted Protected" USB drives.
- Always report any LAN "incidents" to the network administrator

3. Protect Software Systems

On the principle that "prevention is better than a cure", it makes sense to consider cyber attacks while you are designing and creating programs, rather than "patching" them after an attack. We have already looked at **validation** checks for input data (see programming section Input and Output). Protecting code from hacking (illegal access) needs to go a little further.

A simple programming example: Asking for a **PIN** (Personal Identification Number), but only allowing for a limited number of errors, is very standard practice. The understanding is that a person who fails to input the correct PIN three times or more may be a "hacker" or even an automatic program that can systematically try all possible codes. The pseudocode for such a "protection system" may look like this:

```
timesAllowed = 3
timesTried = 0
FOR count FROM 1 TO 3 DO
        INPUT (INTEGER) inputNum
        timesTried = timesTried + 1
        IF inputNum = pin THEN
                allowAccess = True
                EXIT loop
        ELSE IF timesTried = timesAllowed THEN
                allowAccess = False
        END IF
END FOR
IF allowAccess THEN
        openSystem()
ELSE
        activateSecurityCheck()
END IF
```

The security check could involve things like: Denying access for a set time; sending an email alert to the correct user and so on.

The above is just a simple example. In the "real world" there would be teams of programmers, each working on different modules or parts of an overall large and complex system. Remember one of the principles of **abstraction** is "Decomposition & Modularisation" - dividing large problems into sub-problems.

Best Programming Practices: Each programmer in every team would be expected to follow the same "coding standards". These would include things like:
- **Commenting** - Always comment your code to explain how it works. You will very soon forget how and why you coded certain parts of a program. Subprograms should be commented to explain what they do, any parameters they are using and if they return a value or not. Remember the comments are not only for you, but also for other members of the team. It is good practice to put the following comments at the head of the code:
    o Name and purpose of the module
    o A brief description of the module
    o Name of the author and the date the code was completed.
- **Naming Conventions** - We covered some of this in the programming section but it is important to stress that all members of the teams must be consistent and use the same conventions.
    o **Variables**: Meaningful names such as dogAge or dog_Age
    o **Procedures**: Names that indicate the action that the procedure is doing like: displayMenu() or moveUp()

- ○ **Functions**: Names that indicate the calculation or the question being asked, such as: calcTotalRevenue() or paidUpMember(), so indicating the kind of return value to be expected.
- **Simple and Readable**: Code should always be clear and simple. It is usually much more important that the code is simple and readable than making it as short as possible. For example the following code extracts do the same thing but the second is much clearer than the first:

  1. **IF** (isAdult **OR** consentGiven) **AND** (isMember **OR** isGuest) **THEN** proceed() **END IF**

  2. ageCheck = (isAdult **OR** consentGiven)
  correctStatus = (isMember **OR** isGuest)
  IF ageCheck **AND** correctStatus **THEN**
      proceed()
  END IF

- **Portability**: Programs designed to work on networks must, more than others, be able to work in different "environments" (operating systems etc.). Code should not have "hard-coded" values for such things as file paths or IP addresses. These values should be passed in as parameters to functions so that they can easily be changed if the program has to run on a completely different server.

Testing: We have already looked at testing in the chapter Errors & Testing in the section on programming. Suffice to say that every module that every team produces should be "tested to breaking point" and so be very robust. In a network context the test plan should include the possibility of "hackers" entering with "malicious intent".

Code Reviews: finally, an expert, perhaps someone who is not part of any team, should review each block of code. She should be looking, not only for bugs and bad practice, but also for any vulnerabilities that could be exploited by a "hacker".

Release, Versions, Updates and Patches:
Finally the program is "released" or "published". If it is "in-house" software then the company just goes ahead and uses it. If it is "public" software it will be either sold as "proprietary software" or made available as "open source software". (See chapter 8c)
- **Beta Version** - This is an early publicly released version where "volunteers" can use the software and test it for bugs, crashes and other errors.
The software is finally ready for "official" release. Version numbering can be complex, but in simple terms the three digits used, A.B.C roughly indicate "Major.Minor.Patch" so:
- Version 1.0.0 - The very first "public" version
- Version 1.0.1 - A tiny update with a "patch" that fixes a bug.
- Version 1.1.1 - A small update with some new features
- Version 2.0.0 - A major and significant update that may include some "backward-incompatible" features. (This may mean that documents created with this version will not work with previous versions.)
- Version 2.1.2 - Some new features and some patches added

A patch is code that fixes a bug or improves a program. After time users report problems or a hacker exploits a weakness in the code. A security patch is supposed to fix these problems. In general the advice is to download and use the latest available version. This is particularly important for security patches. These are released because a possible security breach, or "hack", has been identified, so you should protect your software and computer system by installing the patch. On the other hand, with major version changes, sometimes it pays to "sit back" and wait awhile - "Don't mend what's not broken." Research a little on the Internet and see what users and reviewers are saying about the new release and wait for a small update. With the examples shown above jumping from Version 1.1.1 to Version 2.1.2 is probably "safer" than "rushing ahead" with Version 2.0.

Audit Trails: Whenever someone logs on to a network or a website the system should be able to "keep track" of who they are, what "status" they have, what parts of the system have they tried to access and what they did when they got there. An audit trail is a kind of electronic log of user activity on a network. Some examples:

- A school intranet may want to see when a particular student logged on and what websites he visited.
- In a big company a member of the economics department may have authorisation to enter the wages section but not the medical record section. If such an employee attempts to access an unauthorised section by typing in a password, this improper activity will be recorded in the audit trail.
- An online sales company will record such things as the customer's ID, what they ordered, any payment made and delivery details. The audit trail for this could be used to deal with any inquiry or complaint made by the customer.

Any system designed for any network, from a company's intranet to an online Internet shopping site, should have a built-in audit trail capacity. These "electronic logs" can be used to investigate **cybercrimes**. Sometimes "hackers" can be identified by following the trail they leave in "cyberspace" - anything from activity recorded by their Internet Service Provider (**ISP**) to a profile in a social website or a "conversation" in a "chat room". (See the section on the impacts of technology on society for an overview of privacy and legal implications.)

Questions on chapter 7d Net Security

1. Louise receives the following email:

From: eurootravelonline@gmail.com   To: loolooal@yahoo.com

Dear Louise Alison,

As a regular customer of 'EuroTravelOnLine' (ETOL) we would like to reward you with a special offer. We at ETOL are going to transfer €500 to your bank account to use on your next fantastic Euro Break. To receive this money you just have to answer one simple question and then fill in the details at the bottom of this email. Finally just click on the button marked 'Accept and Send'.

€500 question: 'What is the capital of France?'

Details:

Bank account number: ....   Sort code: ....

Personal Identification Number: ....   Bank Online Password: ....

Accept and Send

Louise is very suspicious of this email, and decides not to press "Accept and Send".

(a) State two reasons why you think Louise is suspicious of the email.

(b) Apart from not pressing "Accept and Send", what else should Louise do?

(c) Assuming the email has come from "cyber criminals", explain what could happen if Louise did complete the information asked for and did click on "Accept and Send".

(d) What is the name for this kind of Internet fraud?

(e) What kind of people are particularly vulnerable to this kind of fraud?

2. Sam Spade works for the company "Trusted Private Detective Agency" (TPDA) based in Los Angeles. Like all the detectives in TPDA, Sam has his own company portable computer. He backs up his most recent cases on a USB "pen drive".

One Saturday evening, Sam takes a break from a surveillance operation, of a criminal forgery gang, in his favourite cyber cafe "Browse & Snack". The cafe is crowded but he manages to find a space at the bar. Sam did not notice that a tall dark stranger had followed him into the cafe and was now standing behind him. He flips open the lid of his laptop and gains immediate access to his computer. He needs to look up some confidential client information so he connects to the Internet using the Cafe's public "Wi-Fi". He types in the URL for his firm's intranet and types in his username - "samspadedec" - and his password - "hullo". He then downloads the files that he needs.

He did not notice a bespectacled redhead working in the corner on her computer. After a few drinks he closes his computer and heads back to the "stake-out" at a house a few blocks away. As Sam heads for the door, the tall dark stranger exchanges a few words with the redhead. He then turns on his heels and follows Sam. Later that night Sam notices that he has lost his USB "pen drive". He shrugs his shoulders and says to himself, "Oh well it was only a back up device and I can buy another one for a few bucks."

The next day Sam sees his boss, "Mobs Malone" and reports the loss of his USB drive. Mobs does not seem too upset and says to Sam, "No worries, you did, of course, protect your drive using the two software techniques stated in the company IT policy, didn't you?" Sam's face went pale and he looked very worried.

In the context of the above scenario, answer the following questions:

(a) State and explain two things wrong with Sam's password and write down your, improved, password.

(b) The redhead working on her computer is actually a professional cyber criminal. Suggest how she:

i. May already have a copy of the files that Sam downloaded while he has in the cafe.

ii. Is now able to log in to the TPDA's intranet whenever she wants to.

(c) Suggest what the "two software techniques" were, that Sam should have used to protect his USB drive.

3. Scientists working at the "Toxic Chemical Research Department" for the Ministry of Defence have secure access to the department's LAN. Every computer on the LAN uses two "biometric measures" for scientists to log on.

(a) Suggest what these "biometric measures" may be.

The LAN is run by a large server supported by a rack of hard drives in a room to itself.

(b) Suggest one simple, physical security method to protect the server.

The LAN is connected to the Internet via a router, which has a built in **firewall**.

(c) Explain the role of the firewall.

The department employs an "**ethical hacker**" to carry out a **penetration test** on the LAN.

(d) Explain what an "ethical hacker" is and the kind of work she would carry out as part of a "penetration test".

4. Here is an extract from a recent news item:

"Websites have been warned they could be exposed to **eavesdroppers**, after researchers discovered a new way to disable their **encryption** protections. The experts said about a third of all computer servers using the **HTTPS** protocol - often represented by a padlock in web browsers - were vulnerable to so-called Drown attacks. They warn that passwords, credit card numbers, emails and sensitive documents could all be stolen as a consequence." (BBC March 2016)

(a) Explain, in the context of the article, the highlighted words:

eavesdroppers   encryption   HTTPS

(b) Explain, with an example, the kind of website that would use the HTTPS protocol.

5. Best programming practice includes such things as: commenting, naming conventions and readability. The following, working, code is a Python function that returns "True" if the text in the parameter has at least one uppercase letter. The programmer has not been following best programming practice:

```python
def doIt(thing):
    y = False
    for x in thing:
        if x.isupper():
            y = True
            break
        #End if ....................
    #End of FOR loop ----------------------------
    return y
#end function doIt -------------------------------
```

Rewrite the code so it better follows best programming practice.

6. Look at this recent news item (BBC March 2016):

"Adobe has issued an emergency patch for its Flash media player that closes loopholes in the widely used software. In its security advisory, Adobe said one of the bugs was being actively exploited in a "limited number of targeted attacks". In total, the patch closes 23 separate security bugs in the Flash player. Attackers abusing the security holes would be able to take over a computer to steal useful data or spy on the machine's owner."

(a) Explain the difference between a new version of software and a software patch.

(b) After reading this news item, what should an individual user of the software do?

7. Here's an extract from an article on the "eWeek" website:

"**Hospital Audits Catch Snoopy Insiders**: It's easy to understand why star-struck hospital personnel can't resist looking up celebrity medical files. But these days even peeking can cost health workers their jobs. In recent years there have been egregious cases where celebrity patient data, perhaps most intimate of all personal information, have been lifted from hospital files and leaked to the tabloid media, presumably with money changing hands. Today, there are laws and regulations banning this kind of snooping. Modern computer systems generate **audit trails** so hospitals can comply with privacy laws. So hospital administrators along with law enforcement agencies and celebrity lawyers can find out who has been peeking at and even stealing patient information."

(a) Explain why some staff at hospitals can, and should, have access to very confidential patient data but others should not have access.

(b) Outline how an **audit trail** could be used to identify a member of staff who may have leaked confidential data to the press.

Section 8
Impacts of Technology on Society

- **8a Environmental Impact of Technology**
- **8b Ethical Impact of Technology**
- **8c Legal Impact of Technology**

"We live in a society absolutely dependent on science and technology and yet we have cleverly arranged things so that almost no one understands science and technology. That's a clear prescription for disaster."
(Carl Sagan)

1000

Jg uif jnqmfnfoubujpo jt ibse up fyqmbjo, ju't b cbe jefb. Jg uif jnqmfnfoubujpo jt fbtz up fyqmbjo, ju nbz cf b hppe jefb.

(Hint: Python: import this)

Chapter 8a Technology and Society: Environmental Impact

One estimate has it that there are more than 1 billion Personal Computers (PCs) in use worldwide. (Forrester Research, 2015). Meanwhile the UK's Independent Newspaper (2014) says, "For the first time ever there are more gadgets in the world than there are people, including a growing number that only communicate with other machines, according to data from digital analysts at GSMA Intelligence. The number of active mobile devices and human beings crossed over somewhere around the 7.19 billion mark." For good, or for bad, Information Technology is the dominant technology on planet Earth right now. Let's look at some of the impacts technology is having on our environment.
Note: All of the fields below are vast and could fill several books. All that can be done here is to highlight some areas to raise awareness, leaving you, the reader, to research particular topics. You will, of course, need a computer and the Internet to do this!

Points Covered:
- **Health**
- **Energy Use**
- **Resources**

Health - The bad news:

Toxic materials are used in the manufacture of technological devices. Hazardous materials used in computers and other electronic devices include cadmium, mercury, lead, arsenic, selenium, PVC plastic and flame-retardants, to name just a few. In 2010 the US disposed of over 2 million tons of computer hardware. Some parts can now be "recycled" but that still leaves a lot of toxic waste to deal with! What the long term effects these poisonous substances will have on the environment is unknown. The indirect effect on our health is a matter of current research, but it certainly won't be a positive effect!

An article in the Huffington post (2014) listed some "sneaky ways technology is messing with your body and mind." Here are a select few, to which I have added some notes:
- **Staring at your phone** all day might wreck your spine. Bending over a screen is not a "natural" position for your back. Young people are developing back problems usually associated with much older age groups.
- **Wi-Fi exposure** may lower men's sperm count.
- **Holding a small transmitter / receiver (mobile phone)** next to your head does have a "biological effect" on your brain. Whether this will lead to long term brain damage, including tumours is a matter of speculation and research.
- **All that messaging** may be giving you "text claw". Bending your thumbs and fingers around your mobile phone and repetitively tapping for hours every day is not good for your muscles and tendons. This is a version of repetitive strain injury or RSI, usually associated with typists who enter data via a keyboard each and every day.
- **Too much screen use** could strain your eyes. Reading lots of books for hours every day is one thing, but staring at an object that gives off light, like a screen, for a long time is very bad for your eyes. Computer programmers are advised to have a rest

from "coding" every 45 minutes. Constant tech-indulgence may be giving you a headache.

- **All that Googling** can cause anxiety. Executives are constantly looking for more and more information, which makes them worry that there is something that they do not know, so they search for more information! Ironically this makes them very unproductive and very stressed.

- **Loneliness and Facebook** browsing are inextricably linked. Having a thousand "virtual" friends is not nearly as good for you psychologically as having one "real" friend. Depression and even suicides have been linked to over-dependence on social websites.
- **You could suffer from withdrawals** (from technology addiction) similar to when a drug addict tries to recover from their addiction to chemicals. Every time you get a "new high score" on a game, or see yet another "YouTube" video your brain releases "pleasure" chemicals. Unfortunately you soon "need" another "hit" so you need something new and even more "exciting". You are now an addict!
- **Too much tech is literally changing your brain**. "We are exposing our brains to an environment and asking them to do things we weren't necessarily evolved to do." Perhaps young people are developing skills at "multi-tasking" but they are also losing the ability to follow through a complex sequence of events by reading a novel or solving a long programming problem, step-by-step.

All of the above could be potentially serious. Many youth groups now plan excursions, camps etc. where there is one rule - no technology allowed. There are even restaurants in Paris that use technology to block technology - "cell jammers" that prevent the use of any mobile phone - "bon appétit!"

Health - The good news:
Without computers most modern, medical research would not be possible.

Human DNA has about 3 billion base pairs, which represents about 20,000 genes. To sequence DNA would have seemed impossible 50 years ago. The **human genome project** began in 1990. Thirteen years and $2.7 billion later and humankind knew for the first time the organic digital code needed to build a human. The hope is now that doctors can find cures for cancers and develop medicines that are "custom-built" for individuals and their particular genome. None of this would have been possible without computers.

Every year seems to herald another advance in medical technology. Here are just a few technologies, either in use now or "coming soon":

- **Magnetic Resonance Imaging (MRI)** uses strong magnetic fields to change the spin of atoms in our bodies. Radio signals detect these tiny changes. MRI computers process this information and construct images of soft tissues inside the body, from the brain to blood vessels.
- **3D printing** has already produced functioning prosthetic hands and regenerated broken bones. Will we one day be able to "print" spare body parts or even organs?
- **Blood nanobots:** Tiny microscopic robots that can do anything from act as white blood cells and fight diseases to helping haemoglobin transport oxygen around your body.
- **Brain implants** that automatically monitor brainwaves could be used in the treatment of Alzheimer's or epilepsy.

I know this is supposed to be the "good news" section but there are ethical issues around the use of technology in medicine. Many argue that the money could be better spent on improving the quality of the environment for all, rather than investing huge amounts of money on possibly curing a few sick people. Nonetheless, the rapid advances in medical technology and the possible health benefits are truly amazing.

Energy Use – The bad news:

As we saw in the section on "the cloud", 3% of the world's electrical energy supply is now used just to power the servers and storage capacity of thousands of "data centres". An article in Time magazine (2013) stated that "Our computers and smartphones might seem clean, but the digital economy uses a tenth of the world's electricity — and that share will only increase, with serious consequences for the economy and the environment." To put this into perspective, that's the same power production of Germany and Japan, combined. "We already use 50% more energy to move bytes than we do to move planes in global aviation."

The same article asked a serious question, "Which uses more electricity: the iPhone in your pocket, or the refrigerator humming in your kitchen?" and gave the surprising answer, "Hard as it might be to believe, the answer is probably the iPhone." The reasons behind this fact depend on: the number of times you need to recharge a phone, how many bytes of data you are downloading (3G, 4G or Wi-Fi) and from where ("the cloud"), the amount of electricity needed to support Wi-Fi LANs and the Internet and so on. The fact that the electricity is produced a long way from your "clean, eco-friendly, cool, coffee shop" just means that most people are blissfully unware of how much energy they are "burning" by constant chatting and web browsing. How is this electricity being produced? Is it by burning fossil fuels or using "renewables" like wind, solar, wave or hydroelectric power? This, of course, is related to resources (see below).

Energy Use – The good news:

Big IT companies are aware of energy efficiency issues – after all they have to pay their electricity bills. "Apple's data centres, for instance, are 100% powered by renewable energy, and is working to increase renewable energy use overall. Google gets 34% of its energy for operations from renewable sources. Smart companies are looking to site power-hungry data centres near reliable sources of renewable energy: large hydro plants, like the ones near the new data centre Facebook recently opened in Sweden, or utility-scale wind farms." (From the same article in Time Magazine)

Then what about technology that can produce cheap and clean electricity? It may sound like "technology coming to the rescue of technology" but it is certainly true that technology is behind the recent huge increase in "alternative" sources of energy. Computer programs analyse data from wind tunnels and simulate building better and more efficient wind turbines. Computer Assisted Design and Manufacture are right behind the construction of generators that can harvest the energy from the tides or waves. Research into anything from nuclear fusion to solar panels would not be possible without computerised technology.

Meanwhile technology is being used to make anything from houses to cars more efficient. Computerised control programs, using sensors and actuators around a house, can cut energy bills by actively and "intelligently" controlling the inside temperature. There are even "carbon neutral" houses, which use techniques as basic as good insulation and as complex as geothermal exchange heaters. These houses are designed and built and are run by computer technology.

Connecting domestic devices to the "**Internet of Things**" is not as far-fetched as it sounds. "**Smart energy** could save £8bn a year, say advisers." (BBC March 2016). "Here's how it would work: At a time of peak demand, an energy firm's computer will contact your smart freezer to ask if power can be switched off for a few minutes to allow your neighbour to use some of the energy to cook dinner. Your well-insulated freezer will stay cold without electricity for a while, so it will agree to power down. On the other hand, at times the grid is awash with energy - at night, or when it's very windy or sunny. In these times of energy plenty, a computer will contact your web-enabled washing machine or dishwasher to ask if they want to turn on to benefit from cheap power."

Electric cars that efficiently and safely drive themselves (and their human passengers) around major cities are already being successfully trialled. These vehicles are designed, built and run by robots - well computer technology with human programmers at least!

Resources:

Fossil fuels: Just a reminder from the energy section above: Technological devices use, globally, huge amounts of electricity. If burning fossil fuels like coal, gas or oil generates that electricity, then, whenever we use technology, we are using up non-renewable energy resources.

As for other resources let's have a quick overview of what goes into the manufacture of a personal computer (PC) or a mobile phone. Here's a list of the main elements used:

Metals (well known):
- copper, aluminium, tin, zinc, nickel, chromium, platinum, iron, gold, silver

Metals (less well known):
- hafnium, neodymium, ruthenium, palladium, rhodium, osmium, iridium, tantalum, niobium

Non-metals:
- silicon, boron, arsenic, phosphorous, carbon, oxygen

Some of these elements have very obvious uses in technology: Copper in wires and circuits to conduct electricity; gold as an excellent conductor that doesn't easily oxidise for "point contacts" and iron oxide to cover the surface of magnetic hard discs. In other cases the uses are rather obscure. For example, neodymium as an alloy, is used to make small, but very powerful magnets for hard disks. It can even be used to make special glass for extremely high-powered lasers used to experiment with nuclear fusion reactions. Arsenic is used to "dope" silicon to change its semi-conducting properties, while hafnium-based compounds are employed to insulate "gates" deep within the latest integrated circuits ("chips").

Some of these elements are very common and others are very rare. Some can be found in deposits all over the world while others are concentrated in one or two countries. Whatever the case, the technology industry is using these elements up at an alarming rate. Supply and demand economics coupled with global politics has produced some wild fluctuations in price in some of these natural resources. For example: China produces most of the world's neodymium. A few years ago the Chinese government imposed "strategic materials controls" on the element, which caused a panic amongst other industrial nations and the price of neodymium and other metals shot up.

No one is suggesting that any of the elements critical to technology are in any danger of "running out" and research scientists are always working to find new, alternative, compounds using different elements. Nonetheless here's a warning from the "Tech Radar" site: "It's been estimated that well over 50 of the 90 naturally occurring elements are used to make the digital age a reality. Many of these are in limited supply and for some there's no known alternative. Given the rate at which irreplaceable resources are being used up, we have to question how much longer we can expect business as usual."

The "three Rs" of Reduce, Reuse and Recycle should apply to technological devices as much as any other.

Unfortunately there is precious little sign of the "first R" - **Reduce**. As was stated at in the introduction to this chapter, there are now more "gadgets" than humans on planet earth. Given that many of the world's poorest have no technological products at all, that must mean that many people have more than one. Do we really need a mobile phone, a tablet, a portable computer and a desktop PC? Certainly the big companies want us to consume as much as possible and that in turn drives the economy of the "information revolution" that we are living in.

As for **reuse**, let's first consider how much we throw away. The website "The World Counts" estimates that we throw away "800 laptops every second" and "an average cell phone user replaces their unit once ever 18 months." As they say, the Electronic Revolution = E-Waste and we have developed a culture of use and throw away. Perhaps we need to change our mind-set and not constantly crave for newer and newer devices? There are some organisations that are trying to refurbish old but fully working devices for distribution, for example, to schools in developing countries. But one wonders how significant this kind of "reuse" really is. Perhaps you could donate your old phone to a friend or a charity? It's got to be better than just throwing it away.

Recycling the expensive resources that went into the making of computers and mobile phones must be a good thing to do. "Cellphones and other electronic devices contain precious metals like gold and silver. The US alone throws away cellphones with $60 million worth of gold & silver yearly." Yet the same website estimates that "only 12.5% of E-Waste is recycled" and "87.5% of our E-Waste are sent to landfills and incinerators."

There are recycle programs and many manufactures are now claiming that their products are "100% recyclable". The website "Do Something" states, "For every 1 million cell phones that are recycled 16,000 kg of copper, 350 kg of silver, 35 kg of gold, and 15 kg of palladium can be recovered." (Figures translated from pounds)

Technology to the rescue of technology (again?): "There is a glimmer of hope though. While each element has unique properties that can be matched by no other, organic chemistry can provide a means of designing molecules with the desired properties. What's more, the synthesis of organic compounds doesn't rely on esoteric and rare elements. Already scientists have produced conducting and semi-conducting polymers and built electronic circuits from nothing more than plastics - although, as yet, they can't match the performance of silicon."

Questions on chapter 8a Environmental Impact

1. Choose one the health and technology issues listed below:
- The use of iPods, mobile phones and other MP3 players to listen to music is damaging the hearing of young people.
- Students in the 21st century have much shorter attention span than students in the 20th century.
- Cyber bullying on social websites is a major cause of stress and depression in young students today.
- Excessive use of mobile phones can damage the growing brain of adolescents.

Write a short report about how serious you think the issue is. Support your argument with factual data from **reliable** websites and make it clear exactly what websites you used.

2. Are you or your friends "addicts to technology"? Compose a simple survey to carry out on children in your school. Write down 10 clear questions with **structured responses**. For example:

> In the following questions please choose a number, between 1 and 5, that best describes your response. Where 1 means: "Yes that describes me very well." and 5 means: "No, that is not like me at all."
>> I use the Internet every night and for at least 2 hours a day in the weekend.
>> I never go anyway without my mobile phone.

You could also try some questions that only give a numeric response. For example:
> "Approximately how many hours a week do you play any kind of computer game?"

When you have your questions ready try and interview at least 20 students and write up your results and conclusions.

Extension: You may want to work as a group on this kind of work. You could choose to try and answer a specific question like, "Is it true that girls use their phones more to chat and text while boys use them to play games?"

3. Choose a major multinational technology company, like Apple, Google, Amazon or Microsoft, and investigate any claims they make regarding using renewable energy to power their data centres. In particular try and find actual examples where these companies use technologies like solar panels, wind turbines, hydroelectric power and so on.

4. Choose one of the "less well known" metals from the list below and research a "case study" of that metal.

> hafnium, neodymium, ruthenium, palladium, rhodium, osmium, iridium, tantalum, niobium

In your "case study" cover the following points:
- Principal uses of the metal in technological devices such as smart phones and computers;
- Occurrence and cost - where in the world it is mined as a natural resource.
- Any notes on waste disposal and toxicity of the element or its compounds.

Chapter 8b Technology and Society: Ethical Impact

Ethical basically means to do with what is right and wrong. It may be possible to plagiarise somebody else's essay by copying and pasting text from the Internet. You may even get a good mark and not be caught. But is it "right" to do it? Should everyone have the "right" to free access to the Internet? Ethics could also be about rules and standards concerning how you work. If you know that somewhere in your programming code there is a bug, is it right to "publish" that code hoping no one will notice? These are questions related to morality rather than the law. Most often there is no right or wrong answer. Citizens on planet earth in the 21st century have to come up with some kind of "moral code" to deal with the many controversial issues raised by the "Information Revolution".

Points Covered:
- **Privacy**
- **Inclusion**
- **Professionalism**

Privacy

In the UK tampering with the "Royal Mail" has always been considered a serious offence. The Postal Services Act 2000 says, "A person commits an offence if, intending to act to a person's detriment and without reasonable excuse, he opens a postal packet which he knows or reasonably suspects has been incorrectly delivered to him." **Most people value their privacy** and do not want other people to open their letters.

Well hardly anyone gets "snail mail" any more, right? What about email, SMS text messages, Internet chats or even "traditional" phone calls? Quite rightly, we do not expect that just anyone can "listen in" to our conversations or read our personal email. For most people "just anyone" includes the government, the police and the security services. (See the section on eavesdropping in Net Security.)

On the other hand, the government, police and the security forces argue that they cannot keep ordinary people safe from international terrorism unless they have access to private data. They say that they cannot wait for a terrorist attack to happen and then act. If the police have some suspicious persons under surveillance, then they need to secretly "eavesdrop" on their private data, even though such people have not actually committed an offence.

This is a very difficult and controversial area where, in democratic nations, there must be a balance between individuals' freedoms and rights and the state's genuine concern for public safety. Many people from all around the world felt, for example, that the US president George Bush did "go too far" against civil liberties when he authorised "spying" on his own citizens, as part of his "war against terror". A report in the Washington Post (December 2005) claims: "President Bush signed a secret order in 2002 authorizing the National Security Agency (NSA) to eavesdrop on U.S. citizens and foreign nationals in the United States, despite previous legal prohibitions against such domestic spying." The article went on to say, "The super-secretive NSA, which has generally been barred from domestic spying except in narrow circumstances involving foreign nationals, has monitored the e-mail, telephone calls and other communications of hundreds, and perhaps thousands, of people under the program." In its defence the NSA said that they, "were worried that vital information could be lost in the time it took to secure a warrant from a special surveillance court."

In a more recent case, February 2016, the FBI ordered the computer giant Apple to "unlock" a terrorist's iPhone. Apple refused to comply saying, "the FBI's court order to access the mobile phone of San Bernardino killer Syed Farook is dangerous, chilling and unprecedented". The interesting thing is that the FBI was not actually asking Apple to break the encryption on the phone, because they can't. Once data on an iPhone is encrypted no one, including Apple, can read that data. The FBI wanted Apple to alter something called a "System Information File" so that their agents could at least "open" the phone and "see what they can see" - perhaps personal contact details, for example. Apple says that introducing a "back door" into the phone wouldn't just make Farook's phone insecure and accessible to the US government - it would make every iPhone inherently weaker. "You can't have a back door that's only for the good guys."

An article in the BBC (March 2016) was headlined as, **"Apple v FBI: US debates a world without privacy"** and asked a very interesting question, **"Is there such a thing as security so good it's a danger to society?"** As I write the above court case is not resolved. As usual in this kind of moral argument it is not easy to say who is right and who is wrong. The government security agency's view is that computer security could create "warrant-proof spaces". That is, even if the police, quite legally and normally, obtain a warrant to "search someone's data", that data just can't be accessed - not by anyone. On the other hand the BBC quotes Californian Congresswoman Zoe Lofgren as saying, "The alternative [to strong encryption] is a world where nothing is private. Once you have holes in encryption, the rule is not a question of if, but when those holes will be exploited and everything you thought was protected will be revealed."

Meanwhile, at around the same time but in the UK, the BBC's politics page has, "The Home Office has tightened up privacy safeguards in proposed new spying laws - but police will get more power to see internet browsing records. The Investigatory Powers Bill will force service providers to store browsing records for 12 months. It will also give legal backing to bulk collection of Internet traffic." Again this is a controversial area and there are, at least, two sides to the story. "Ministers say the new powers are needed to fight terrorism, but Internet firms have questioned their practicality - and civil liberties campaigners say it clears the way for mass surveillance of UK citizens."

Inclusion:

In an ideal world everyone should be "included" in everything or at least given an equal opportunity to be included. In the real, 21st century technological, world it is important that we look at the ethics of "computing for all". Again this is a large and controversial topic. The best that can be done here is to raise a few issues for awareness and further research and discussion.

Rich and Poor:

There was a "digital divide" between people who have access to computer technology and those who do not. The "divide" referred to inequalities between different socioeconomic groups within a country or between developed and developing countries globally. The fact that global mobile phone penetration has now reached over 95% of the world's population is one indicator that the "divide" has been closing over the years. Now the "digital divide" is a relative measure of those who have more and those who have less. There are a lot of issues at play. Poverty, human rights, wealth distribution and so on are social and political issues, which are only indirectly related to computer technology. Nonetheless there is a general feeling that all people in all countries, from whatever social background, should have "reasonable access" to the Internet.

Infrastructure - The provision of "broadband" Internet access, measured as bandwidth per individual (in kbit/s per capita), can be used to generate an index of equal or unequal access.

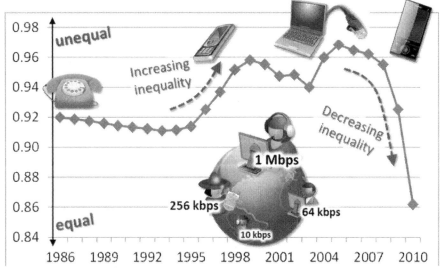

Gini coefficients for telecommunication capacity *(in kbps)* per individual worldwide (incl. inhabitants from 208 countries)

"Technological information inequality as an incessantly moving target: The redistribution of information and communication capacities between 1986 and 2010", Martin Hilbert (2013)

It is interesting to note how new innovations lead to a rapid increase in inequality, which then falls back. Rich countries or people get access to the innovation first which then slowly filters downwards to poorer people. Nonetheless there is still a "divide" with rich people in developed countries having 10 to 100 times "faster" access than poor people in developing countries.

Location: Where can you get access to the Internet? Is it at home, school, a library or an Internet Cafe? Do you live in a large city or in a tiny rural village? Even in developed countries these factors can make a big difference between those who have fast and reliable access and those who do not.

Education and Digital Literacy: Being "connected" is, of course, not the only factor; people need education and training in how to make use of the information available on the Internet. What can young people do with Internet access - play games or learn how to improve their livelihood? Schools have a vital role to play in teaching children how to become "global citizens" in the technologically dominated 21st century.

What can be done? The United Nations has introduced the **W**orld **T**elecommunication and **I**nformation **S**ociety **D**ay. For example, the theme for WTISD 17th May 2016 is "ICT Entrepreneurship for Social Impact." The hope is that young people and professional volunteers from all over the world can help in "unlocking the potential of ICTs for young innovators and entrepreneurs" and that the resulting small businesses could become, "an important source of new jobs, especially for youth, in the current knowledge economy." There are many other initiatives to try and **bridge the "digital divide"**. Both the Gates Foundation and the Carnegie Foundation have started programs to provide libraries, computers and training to poor areas. NGOs like "One Laptop Per Child" are helping to put low cost computers into the hands of children in isolated regions in developing countries. Local community groups and volunteer teachers are setting up "digital clubs" where disadvantaged young people can meet, learn to code and socialise.

Gender - male & female:

Computer science now reaches into just about every field of human endeavour and yet some people still hold the stereotypical view of "geeky" male programmers. Some women even hold the prejudice that computer science is not for them:

"Oh, my gosh, [computer science] isn't for me... I don't dream in code like they do."- Female student at Carnegie Mellon University (Margolis and Fisher 2002)

More recently CNN (May 2015) reported that in large technological companies like Google, Apple and Microsoft, less than 20% of their technical staff are female. To be fair these companies are trying to address the issue:

"Intel has pledged $300 million toward building a more diverse workforce, including tying managers' compensation to their progress in that area. Apple is donating $50 million to the Thurgood Marshall College Fund and the National Center for Women and Information Technology to help swell the pipeline of qualified women and minorities."

Trying to achieve exact gender equality in all professions and walks-of-life is probably futile. Does it really matter that there are more female doctors than males or that most of the workers on an oilrig are male? There are, after all, biological differences between the sexes so it should not be surprising that men and women make different choices. Perhaps the key should be equal opportunities for all so that individuals can make their own choice? This is where schools can play a critical role.

The UK based organisation Computers At School (CAS) advises teachers to, "Take care to counter stereotypes within school (and society in general) that computing is a male-only field," and to, "Highlight the positive contributions of female role models such as Ada Lovelace, Grace Hopper, Jeannette Wing and Dame Wendy Hall."

GCSE Computer Science or Computing is rapidly growing in popularity since its re-introduction a few years ago. Nonetheless figures by the Joint Council for Qualifications (2015) highlight, "The gender gap across the technology subjects remains very pronounced, despite the increase in female students sitting the exams. A total of 24,058 male students took the Computing exam this year compared with 5,678 females."

Universities too still have some way to go in terms of gender equality in numbers: "Fewer women are studying computer science at UK universities than five years ago", (Computer World 2010). Figures from UCAS confirm this; "There were a total of 21,720 places on a computer science course in 2014. Women filled 13% of those places. Across the Atlantic in the US there are similar concerns, "Last year, only 20% of US high school students who took the AP Computer Science test were female." (Education Week 2016)

The "Code.org" website suggests the following 4 ways to recruit girls to computer science classes:
1. Recruit girls with their friends, so they won't be the only girl in the class.
2. Inspire with examples, share how young women are thriving in computer science.
3. Fight stereotypes; highlight women from all walks of life who code.
4. Show how computer science can help in every field - from medicine to law to business.

Computer technology is everywhere, so there is every reason to expect to see an overall gender equality in such an inclusive technology.

Disabled People:
Technology can play a leading role helping overcome any "barriers" that disabled people face in society. Sometimes the technology can be as simple as voice-activated applications on smart phones, which blind people can hear, or video links which, deaf people can see:

A recent article (January 2016) on the BBC News site explains, "Worldwide, around a billion people have a disability, says the World Health Organisation. In Europe and America, this is one in five people. And since they are less likely to be in work, their poverty rate is about twice as high. So technologies that could help disabled people contribute more in the workplace - and improve their quality of life - are surely welcome." Some of the latest developments highlighted in this article are:

- **Eye-Control:** US company LC Technologies has invented a device that enables people to control a computer using just their eyes. A tablet is set up in front of the user, with a small video camera underneath. A near-infrared LED light illuminates the user's eye. The camera then measures the distance between the centre of your pupil and the reflection of LED light on your cornea. This tiny distance shifts as your gaze changes, and this enables a computer to work out exactly where you're looking.

- **Head Control**: A camera tracks the movements of a reflective dot stuck to the user's forehead, and these motions control a computer cursor. Selections are made using a "sip-puff" switch in the mouth, or by dwell time - how long the head stays in a certain position.

- **Smart Glasses**: There are about 39 million blind people in the world, according to the World Health Organisation. But 90% have at least some level of light perception. So Stephen Hicks, a neuroscientist at Oxford University, has developed "smart glasses" that accentuate the contrast between light and dark objects.

Inclusion can and should start at an early age, in the classroom. As CAS states, "Computing can be made accessible to pupils with special educational needs or disabilities (SEND) through the use of assistive technologies, including hardware and software. Examples include adapted mice or keyboards, Braille displays, screen readers and adjusted system settings for dyslexia."

All in all developments in computer technology will certainly continue to help break down the barriers that face many disabled people in being "included" in society.

Professionalism:

Reliability and Systems Failure: Society is more and more dependent on computer systems. Reliability can be more important than how fast a system is or how many features it has. Software bugs can be annoying, but faulty software can also be expensive and destructive. Various estimates have it that software errors cost the U.S. economy $60 billion annually in lost productivity and actual damages. Here are a few famous "bugs" and their consequences:

- **Mariner Bugs Out (1962)**
  - The Mariner 1 rocket headed for Venus diverted from its intended flight path. A programmer missed a single superscript bar. This caused faulty corrections & sent the rocket off course. The result was that Mission Control destroyed the rocket 293 seconds after lift-off. The cost of this programming error was about $18.5 million.

- **World War III... Almost (1983)**
  - The Soviet early warning system falsely indicated that the US had launched five ballistic missiles. Fortunately the Soviet duty officer reported the apparent attack as a false alarm. A bug in the Soviet software failed to filter out false missile detections caused by sunlight reflecting off cloud-tops. The cost could have been the destruction of humanity!

- **Mars Climate Crasher (1998)**
  - After a 286-day journey from Earth, the Mars Climate Orbiter fired its engines to push into orbit around Mars but it fell too far into the planet's atmosphere causing it to crash on Mars. The software that controlled the thrusters used imperial units (pounds of force), rather than metric units (Newtons) as specified by NASA. The cost was about $125 million

These extreme examples simply highlight the fact that being a **professional** programmer is a very responsible position. Of course, the hope is that any code you write will meet any specifications and requirements set and will run without crashing. Nonetheless whether you are working for a major business, a state organisation or a manufacturing company you will be writing code that can have serious consequences.

A Code of Conduct: Here's a quote from Robert Martin author of "The Clean Coder: A Code of Conduct for Professional Programmers" (2010)

> "Programmers are sorely lacking a code of conduct. I compare the software industry to medicine in the dark ages. Anybody could claim to be a "healer". Some did good. Others did bad. There were no standards."

A code of conduct would include such things:

- **Professional Standards** - Everyone doing things in the same way:
  - Standard systems development
  - Standard coding techniques (See the section on Net Security and Best Programming Practices.)
  - Standard Documentation of Programs
- **Considerations** when creating computer systems
  - System requirements
  - Cost & Timescales
  - Health & Safety
  - Ethical Considerations (see above for privacy & inclusion issues)
  - Legal Considerations (see the section the legal impact of technology)
- **Testing** - Programs should be thoroughly tested before they are "released"
  - Test-Driven Development (TDD) takes basic testing further by making coding, testing and (re) designing as a standard way of developing code.

Remember this section is about ethics - There is no right or wrong answer. Different individuals and organisations will behave in different ways. Nonetheless many professional organisations do have formal codes of conduct for their members. For example, here is part of the code of conduct for the "Institution of Analysts and Programmers" (2016)

Following the profession of Analyst/Programmer, members shall:

1. Conduct themselves as professionals at all times.
2. Uphold the dignity and reputation of the profession at all times.
3. Strive to improve professional standards.
4. Strive to advance public appreciation and understanding of computer technology.
5. Not misuse their expertise to mislead or manipulate computer users.
6. Refute false or misleading statements concerning the Profession and its practice.
7. Act with integrity and honesty towards other professionals with whom they may have contact.
8. Not make public statements unless competent to do so.

As a student you are now at the beginning of your career in computer science. One day you will be a professional and the expectation is that you will act in a professional way!

Questions of chapter 8b Ethical Impact of Technology:

1. Most democratic nations have laws that are supposed to protect their citizens' **privacy**. In the UK the **1998 Data Protection Act** allows for access to personal data stored on databases on a "need to know" basis - that is an individual or organisation can access **personal data** about you that they need for their business but no more than that. If the data is considered **sensitive** then the individual concerned must be specifically asked if that data can be accessed. In this context consider the following data:

  A. **Name**: Andrew Roberts
  B. **Address**: 31 The Commons, Smurfville, Devon
  C. **Gender**: Male
  D. **Date of Birth**: 02/07/1970
  E. **Place of Birth**: Smurfville
  F. **Email address:** andyrob@gogomail.com
  G. **Mobile phone number**: 66677889
  H. **Medical Problems**: Diabetic, Allergic to nuts and High Blood pressure
  I. **Bank Details**: Account 77777, ABC Bank, Smurfville
  J. **Bank Balance:** 12,000 pounds
  K. **Ethnic Origen**: Chinese
  L. **Religion**: Catholic
  M. **Trade Union**: Paid up member of National Union of Programmers
  N. **Political Party**: Active member of Anarchists United Front
  O. **Sexual Orientation**: Heterosexual
  P. **Criminal Record**:   Served a probation order for smashing windows in a cafe aged 17

(a) State two data items, which could be considered to be personal but not sensitive.

(b) State two data items, which could be considered to be sensitive.

(c) Mr Roberts signs up for an account with the online shopping giant Amazon. Apart from his name and address, state 3 data items that it would be essential for Amazon to know.

(d) Mr Roberts wants to go on an adventure holiday climbing in the Alps with the firm "Fitness Freaks Climb Peaks". Suggest a data item, which would be:

　　　i. Perfectly reasonable for the travel firm to ask for but, the firm would have to specifically ask for Mr Roberts' permission to include that data item in their database.

　　　ii. Unethical for the firm to ask for - that is, it would be "legal" for the firm to ask for the information, with Mr. Roberts' consent, but it would not be "right" for the firm to ask.

(e) State security agencies, like MI5 and MI6, are completely exempt from the 1998 data protection act. Suggest and explain the circumstances that could lead to MI5 or MI6 holding confidential data about Mr. Roberts.

2. The United Nations has been discussing the following:

"The right to Internet access, also known as the right to broadband, is the view that all people must be able to access the Internet in order to exercise and enjoy their rights to Freedom of expression and opinion and other fundamental human rights, that states have a responsibility to ensure that Internet access is broadly available, and that states may not unreasonably restrict an individual's access to the Internet."

Maria agrees that Internet Access is a " basic human right" for all. Carmen agrees that access to the Internet is very useful but she does not consider it a "basic human right".

Suggest two points in favour of each girl's argument.

3. Here's a quote from a blog by Teresa Ann Taylor:

" Boys Are Better Programmers - As a female programmer, I've gotten a lot of funny reactions over the years. They've ranged from "I've never met a programmer who looks like you before" to "wow, you're a girl, so you must be pretty bad at math - how do you do it?" to "um, so, how did YOU become a programmer?" (to which my response, to a fellow (male) programmer, is: "I dunno, how did YOU become a programmer?"). Of course there are those who play it cool at first, but after a few minutes of conversation there's the inevitable "yeah, I was trying not to say anything, but you're a GIRL CODER??" (A for effort). As much as I wish my gender didn't become the main talking point as soon as I state my profession (despite the amazing set of reactions it elicits), it isn't entirely unjustified. People talk a good game about gender equality and encouraging girls and women in math and sciences, etc, but despite all this there is a very distinct lack of women in the software engineering profession."

Suggest and explain two reasons why you think there are more male programmers than female programmers.

4. Suggest and explain two ways in which a modern smart phone can help overcome barriers to communication for:

    (a) Blind people   (b) Deaf people

5. Here's an extract from a programmer's blog (Richard Banks 2016):

"Just pause for a moment and have a look at some of the epic fails across our industry and then ask yourself again whether we shouldn't think a little more beyond the code we write. How about the 21 dead from a radiation overdose, or the woman killed when an ambulance respirator crashed or insulin pumps that are susceptible to remote attacks. And it's not just software that can directly impact human life either. Think about the regular disclosure of personal information through poor security (too many to cite), regular air travel glitches, entire regions of Canada losing communications, people unsuspectingly racking up massive mobile data charges and a whole lot more. Software runs pretty much everything these days and while some blame lays in the way projects are run, much of what we're seeing in the world these days can be laid at the feet of programmers who acted unprofessionally and forget their prime directive; helping their customers."

Suggest and explain two ways that programmers should act professionally to avoid some of the problems the author highlights

.

Chapter 8c Technology and Society: Legal Impact

The last chapter concerned ethics: "Ethics is knowing the difference between what you have a right to do and what is right to do." In this chapter we are interested in what you can and cannot do and what the law has to say about it. We are living in the "information revolution" where the Internet can be an exciting and transformational technology:

> "The Internet's distinct configuration may have facilitated anonymous threats, copyright infringement, and cyberattacks, but it has also kindled the flame of freedom." (Jonathan Zittrain)

Points Covered:
1. **Intellectual Property - Copyright, Patents and Licensing**
2. **Software - Open Source & Propriety**
3. **Cyber - Security**

1. Intellectual Property

Property means things that belong to you. Suppose Dave the carpenter had just spent 100 hours building a beautiful wooden desk. He would, quite rightly, be very angry if someone stole that desk. No doubt Dave would call the police and they would try to catch the thief. What if Sally the programmer spends 100 hours coding a perfect Python solution to a problem? Does that solution "belong" to her? Well, in a way, yes, the code is a creation of her intellect. It is Sally's "**intellectual property**". Can other people use the code? Do they have to pay Sally to use the code? These are good, simple, questions but we are now in the realm of Intellectual Property Law, lawyers and the legal system.

Intellectual Property Law covers a range of "creations": music, literature, art, discoveries, inventions, movies, photographs and yes, why not, computer programs. Here are some key legal words about "**creator protection**":

- **Patents**
  - Give inventors exclusive rights over use of their **inventions**.
  - Represents some invention that is new and has never been made before. E.g. A new laser-powered hair cutter or a new machine to take the stones out of olives.
  - Protects the **application** of an idea
- **Trademarks**
  - These are legally protected **words or symbols** that represent products or services. E.g. "Coca-Cola" or "Levis".
  - Protects a device that indicates the provider of a product or service.
- **Copyright**
  - Gives "authors" rights over their **originality**
  - E.g. a novel or a computer program
  - Protects the **expression** of an idea

Copyright & Licencing

Because computer programs (software) are not physical things, like books, it is only recently that copyright laws have been established to **protect programmers**. "Computer programs, to the extent that they embody **an author's original creation**, are proper subject matter of copyright." (1974 USA) In the UK, The Copyright, Designs and Patents Act (1988) is pretty much the same and, "requires that the programme is the **author's own intellectual creation**." (Software directive)

So yes, Sally's program can be under copyright and her original work can be protected.
Ah but! It is more complicated than this, which is why there are so many highly paid lawyers employed by software companies. In the UK, copyright protects the "tangible expression" of an idea not the idea behind it. This comes down to: The code that is written is protected but not how the program works or achieves its goals.

But let's assume that Sally's work is copyrightable. She can decide who can use her code, what they can do with it and how much she should be paid. She could:
- **Sell her copyright** and lose all her rights but earn a lot of money;
- **Licence her copyright** so anyone can use her code, for a fee.
- **Give away her copyright** so anyone, anywhere can use her code.

In the UK Sally's copyright will last all her life and for at least 50 years after her death. So her children and maybe even grandchildren could, conceivably, still be receiving "royalty payments" for her code long after Sally's death!

> "I think copyright is moral, proper. I think a creator has the right to control the disposition of his or her works - I actually believe that the financial issue is less important than the integrity of the work, the attribution, that kind of stuff." (Esther Dyson)

A more likely scenario is that Sally is one of a team of software developers working for a big company like Apple Computers and her code is part of a large application. In which case the copyright belongs to the company. **Copyright law is vital in preventing software piracy** - illegal copying, installing and selling software that someone else wrote. Computer programs in general are copyrightable. They could be single applications or huge operating systems.

Infringement of Copyright: Apple accuses the "Lazy Coding Company" of breaking their copyright by copying their Operating System. Lawyers, from both sides, have to fight over details like this:

- How original is the program really?
- How similar is the "copied" code to the original?
- How similar is the structure of the "copied" code compared to the original?
- What happens if someone only copies part of the code?
- What happens if the code is "translated" to another language?
- Did the company, accused of copying, have access to the original code?

Lawyers are expensive and all this takes time. Very often there will be an "out of court settlement."

A real example: Supreme Court declines to hear Oracle v. Google case over software copyright ("The Verge" June 2015)

> "The Supreme Court has declined to hear Oracle v. Google, sending the long-running case back to a lower court where Google will have to argue that it made fair use of Oracle's copyrighted APIs. This has been a closely watched case, as the final decision could have a major impact on software development; a ruling in favor of Oracle, the Electronic Frontier Foundation says, could give certain tech firms "unprecedented and dangerous power" over developers by making it substantially more difficult for upstarts to create new software. That'll be the case unless fair use laws turn out to protect the use of APIs."

As you can see, here are two large technology companies fighting in court over software copyright. The case has been going on for a long, long time. A decision is made (or not), one company appeals to a higher court, which then decides to send the case back to a lower court and so on.

> "The case centers on the code behind Android. Google built Android on top of a modified version of Java, the programming language developed by Sun Microsystems (now owned by Oracle) in the '90s. To help spur the development of apps for its new platform, Google used Java's pre-existing APIs (Application Programming Interfaces), which many programmers were already comfortable using."

So the question revolves around whether or not Google can use pre-existing code to build new applications and if that "old" code was copyrighted and if so who owns the copyright and so on. These are big firms and so big money is involved.

Patents and Licensing

As we saw above a patent is all about protecting the rights of the inventor of a new device or invention. So **patents are about how things work, what they are made of and how to make them.** Now Charles H. Duell, Commissioner, U.S. Office of Patents in 1899, was clearly wrong to state:

> "Everything that can be invented has been invented."

But not "just anything" can be patented. European conventions basically say that for something to be patented it must:

- Be new
- Involve an "inventive step"
- Be capable of industrial application

Mike, the electronics engineer, is a bit of a creative genius. After many years' hard work and lots of failures, he finally invents a hand-held sonic umbrella that creates a force field around him and keeps him dry on a rainy day. So he goes to his local patent office and he applies for his invention to be patented. Mike is asking for **exclusive rights** over his sonic umbrella in exchange for **publishing the details** of his invention.

The patent office has to decide on factors like:

- Is it really new, or is it just a close copy of something else already patented?
- Is it more than just something obvious?
- Is the device useful and does it work?

Assuming Mike's application is accepted then his device receives a patent. That is Mike is granted the "**right of property**" on his invention for the **next 20 years**. During this period no one else can make, sell or even import sonic umbrellas. So now Mike can go ahead and starting making and selling his new invention, right? Well nearly and it depends: Is the sonic umbrella really just an improvement on an older model that is also patented? If so Mike will need approval from the patent holder of the previous version.

The rest of this "scenario" is really about economics. Let's assume that Mike goes ahead and starts a small company manufacturing his umbrellas. All goes well but sales are low because each umbrella is costly to make and so the price is too high. Mike could try and sell shares in his business to raise money (capital) so that he can expand, buy machine tools and so on, so that he can produce more umbrellas at less cost per umbrella and so sell the umbrellas for less. On the other hand Mike could look for a large manufacturing company that could make his umbrellas for him. Like any other property right, Mike could:

- **Sell his patent** to a big company.
  - Clearly he would ask for as much money as possible.
  - Once he has sold his rights - that's it - the invention does not belong to him anymore.
- **License his patent** to a big company.
  - He would negotiate a set fee or a percentage of the sales for every umbrella made using his patent.

- **Give away or just abandon his patent**.
  - o For whatever reason he just decides to give up his rights and let anyone, anywhere, use his patent.

Again a more realistic scenario is that Mike is part of a team of engineers working for a large firm like Sony, in which case the patent would belong to the company. In this case Sony could decide to manufacture the umbrellas themselves or licence other companies to manufacture them, for a fee of course!

Patent law is essential to protect individual inventors and companies from illegal copying. After all it took a lot of time and money to invent the umbrella. It would be very unfair if another company started making their own version of the sonic umbrella, at no development cost, by just copying the ideas published in the original patent.

- Patents are to encourage innovation and the improvement of technology.
- Patents benefit society as a whole since anyone can access, and learn from, the published details of an invention.
- Businesses can check what the competition is doing and come up with their own inventions.
- Once the patent expires it can be freely used by anyone.

Infringement of Patents: Now what happens if a company called "Cheap and Cheerful Copies" starts making and selling sonic umbrellas, which are virtually identical to the ones described in Sony's patent? Well Sony would have to "take them to court". Sony would ask for:

- **Monetary compensation** for past infringement
- **An injunction** that prohibits the alleged "infringer" from continuing to use their patent.

As with copyright law it can swiftly get very complicated:

- Is the device really a copy of Sony's umbrella or perhaps it is just similar and maybe even has its own patent?
- Are the laws governing the patent in the country where the alleged copy is being made the same as the country where the patent was published?
- Are the umbrellas being sold within one country or internationally?
- Are both umbrellas, the "original" and the "copy", actually based on previous patents, which may or may not have "run out"?
  - o After 20 years all patents move into the "**public domain**" and anyone can use them
- Who actually owns the patent or the licence to use the patent? Maybe more than one company has a licence?

Déjà Vu: Lawyers are expensive and all this takes time. Very often there will be an "out of court settlement."

A real example: Ericsson signs patent deal with Apple, shares soar (Reuters December 2015)

" Swedish mobile telecom gear maker Ericsson said it had signed a patent license deal with Apple Inc over technology that helps smartphones and tablets connect to mobile networks, sending its shares up by as much as 8%. The deal ends a year-long dispute with Apple, one of the biggest legal battles in mobile technology and Ericson said it would pave the way for cooperation between the companies on future technologies. Ericsson had said in its filing to a U.S. district court in January that Apple's license to use the technology developed by the Swedish firm had expired, and that two years of negotiations had not led to a new deal. Ericsson on Monday estimated overall revenue from intellectual property rights in 2015 would hit 13 to 14 billion crowns ($1.52-$1.64 billion) up from 9.9 billion in 2014 as a result of the agreement. An Apple spokesman in Europe had no immediate comment, referring to a January statement by the firm where it said it had deep respect for intellectual property and was willing to pay a fair price for rights to patents."

Notice that the patent is over technology that simply "improves" a device - In this case the device helps smartphones to connect to mobile networks. Nonetheless, to get a patent in the first place, the technology would have to be "new" and "non-obvious". Secondly note that the case took over a year to resolve. Finally look at the amount of money Ericson stands to gain – about $1.5 billion – and Apple is "willing to pay a fair price"!

Industrial Secrets: There is no need to seek for a patent. A company may **not want to publish** details of their invention. They may just decide to keep the whole process very, very secret. A lot depends on if the new invention is very easy to "**reverse engineer**". That is, if their competitors can just buy a model and easily take it apart and find out how to build one, then they will! So a patent is a good idea. But if it is very hard to "reverse engineer" a device and the company does not want anyone to know the details of how to make their device, then publishing a patent may be a bad idea. As for keeping secrets, well how good is a company's security? What about industrial spies?

Can you patent software? This is not an easy question and is rather controversial. Copyright is there to protect "particular expressions of an idea not the idea itself." For patent law to apply, the "authors" would have to show "novelty" (newness) and "non obviousness". Ideas or principles, "how things work", can be patented but this is difficult to show in something as "abstract" as computer code, which is usually seen as a "creative work". So the answer is a rather uneasy: "**Copyright is for Software while Patents are for Hardware.**"

2. Software - Open Source & Propriety

We have already seen that software, from the smallest "app" on a smart phone to a hugely complex operating system, can be protected by **copyright**.

Freeware is, obviously enough, software that is free but, less obviously, the user has no access to the **source code**. Way back in the programming section we looked at the difference between compilers and interpreters. Remember that "compiled code" is object code or a kind of machine code. It will run on the computer it was designed to run on but you can't "open it up" and see what the high-level instructions look like. This is not a big-deal. The code is, perhaps, a free game. It doesn't cost anything so sure just download and run it. Do be a little bit careful though, of where it comes from. Is it a simulation of a Physics Experiment from a respected University? Fine then go ahead. Is it a "dodgy game" from a website you have never heard of? Beware it could contain a virus!

Most software, that is not freeware, is copyrighted and, in one way or another, you need to have a "**licence**" to install and run the software. There are two fundamentally different ways to go about **licencing copyrighted software**: "Open Source" or "Propriety"

1. Open Source Software:
- Licenced for use but **No charge for licence**
- Anyone can use it
- Distributed with the source code
  - So anyone can modify it
  - Developers can sell the software they have created but:
    - This software must also be "open source".

Examples of well-known open source software:
- **Linux** - an operating system
- **MySQL** - a database server
- **Apache** - an HTTP website server
- **Firefox** - a web browser
- **Wordpress** - a blog platform
- **BIND** - a DNS server on the Internet
- **Python** - a programming language

It is interesting to note how many of these programs are linked to the Internet. So even if you have never heard of "open source" you have certainly visited a website run by open source code or been directed there by a DNS server that runs open source code. If you have been learning to program in **Python** you have almost certainly downloaded and installed an open source program onto your PC at home.

Office Applications like Word Processors and Spreadsheets: There are open source applications such as FreeOffice and OpenOffice, which you can download and install. These "alternatives" to Microsoft's Office are very popular and of course free! (Note that while "cloud / web based" Google Docs is also free to use, it is not really open source as programmers can't access the source code and collaboratively change the code.)

In its strict sense "open source" just means that you have access to the "high-level" source so, if you are a programmer, you can improve the program, add features or simply fix bits that don't work.   In its broader sense "open source" embraces a more open and collaborative way of working.

> "Open source projects, products, or initiatives are those that embrace and celebrate open exchange, collaborative participation, rapid prototyping, transparency, meritocracy, and community development." (Open Source Website)

This quote may help to answer questions like "How do source code software projects make money?" Well in many cases they don't!

The Python Foundation - An Example:

> "The Python Software Foundation (PSF) is a non-profit corporation that holds the **intellectual property rights** behind the Python programming language. We manage the **open source licensing** for Python version 2.1 and later and own and protect the **trademarks** associated with Python."

Well that's all the legal stuff pretty clear but what is the aim or mission of PSF?

> "The mission of the Python Software Foundation is to promote, protect, and advance the Python programming language, and to support and facilitate the growth of a diverse and international community of Python programmers."

All this must cost money, so who finances Python? "The PSF would not be possible without the generous financial help" of its sponsors. Given that the organisations that sponsor Python include such names as - Bloomberg, Google, Intel, Microsoft and Active State (the founding sponsor) – it is clear that the Python programming language is a serious and important piece of software.

2. Proprietary Software (Closed Source)
- **Sold as a licence**
- Restrictions on use – For example:
    - "Single user licence" – for one person on one computer (though "back-up" copies are usually allowed)
    - "Family licence" – all member of the same family can install the software on all computers used by the family.
    - "Site licence" (1 office or school) - can be installed on all computers in the same building, or campus, where the licence applies
- Users do not have access to source code.
- Strictly Copyright protected – **No Pirates!**
    - Illegal to modify and sell the software
    - Illegal to make multiple copies

Examples of well-known proprietary software:
- **Microsoft Windows** - an operating system

- **Microsoft Office** - A "suite" of applications such as a Word Processor and Spreadsheet.
- **Microsoft Internet Explorer** - a web browser
- **Apple iTunes** - a music and video "player"
- **Adobe Illustrator** - A vector drawing program
- **AutoCAD** - A computer assisted design package for architects and engineers

You may say that some of the above examples are actually free and aren't you supposed to pay for a licence? Well yes and no. Propriety software is copyright protected and licenced to you. The owners of that licence, like Apple, may allow you to download and run a program they own the copyright to, like "iTunes", but not charge you for it. It is still "close-sourced" - you have no access to the source code and you certainly can't make copies and sell them to other people. On the other hand if you buy a computer with MS Windows 10 and MS Office pre-installed that doesn't mean that the software is free. Someone, in this case, the manufacturer of the PC should have paid Microsoft for a licence to install those items of software on the PC. By the way the licence should belong to you now shouldn't it?

Notice then that it is not strictly correct to say, "Yesterday I bought a copy of FileMaker Pro or Adobe Photoshop". What you really bought was a **licence** to use that software from the company who owns the **copyright**.

When you buy a licence you are paying for some very sophisticated software that perhaps took teams of programmers, years to create. You would expect the software to do what it says; does not crash (is robust) and that you will have "free" access to help & support, user manuals and so on. An architect, for example, is going to use "AutoCAD" to produce wonderful designs for buildings. This is part of her business and how she makes money. It seems perfectly reasonable that she should pay an annual licence to use the software.

Software Pirates: In the UK there are government officials who actually visit businesses to make sure that they have the correct "site-licence" to install and run copyrighted software on their computers. If a company breaks copyright law they will be "taken to court" and could have to pay substantial fines. What about "ordinary individuals"? Suppose you have a "legal" version of a computer game running on your computer. If you make a copy of that software and then give it to your friends to install on their computers you are, technically, breaking copyright law. It is the same when you download a copyrighted film to watch at home. You have, in effect, "**pirated**" that film and broken the law. You may argue that, "who is going to know?" and "besides everybody does it". Well there is a difference between what you can do and what you should do. Apart from breaking the law, running pirated software has other risks:
- If it crashes you can hardly ask the software company for any help & support!

- Pirated software and films can have hidden **viruses** installed and are a standard way for "hackers" to carry out a **cyber-attack** on your system.

Summary: Which is "better" open source or proprietary software? As you can probably guess, "it depends", there are pros and cons for both kinds of licenced software:

Open Source	Proprietary
Free	Usually pay for a licence
No direct company support but there is usually a large online community of enthusiastic developers to help	Direct support, online and on demand, available from the company
Can be less stable but excellent open source software, used by millions, exists and is constantly improved.	Stable, robust and upgrades available
Developers can access the source code and program and share improvements or extensions.	No one, except the copyright holder, has access to the source code.
Embodies a 21st Century approach based on collaboration, transparency and sharing rather than the "old-fashioned" reliance on huge monopolistic companies.	Professional or standard business software used by many people and any open source alternatives are just not as good.

3. Cyber - Security

Context: If a criminal broke into your bedroom; sprayed "Kilroy was here!" on your walls and stole all your photos, you'd be pretty angry and upset. Yet there seems to be a public acceptance of, even an admiration for a "cool dude" who "hacks into the net" and thumbs his nose at the "system."

Data is Valuable: As we saw in the section on Net Security, businesses are entirely dependent on storing, using and sharing vast amounts of important and confidential data. Supermarket chains could not operate without access to their private intranets. Hospitals and doctors need access to up to date and very confidential data. Etc.

Information Revolution: Our modern society needs fast and reliable access to a huge range of computer systems: The Internet, Telecommunications, Global Positioning Satellites, Computer controlled dialysis machines etc.

Importance: To "hack" into these systems is at best irresponsible and at worse very damaging. Here's some data from the Symantec security company from 2008, and I doubt if things have improved!
*   A web page was infected every 4.5 seconds;
*   20,000 new samples of "malware" everyday.
*   245 million attacks blocked per month in 2008

Symantec said 90% of attacks target confidential information "Information is the most valuable thing we protect."

So what is a hacker? "A hacker is a person who gains **unauthorized access** to a computer system." That is a rather broad and innocuous sounding definition.
*   Sharp-eyed Sue notices that while her teacher is typing his password into his tablet the characters briefly appear unhidden on the interactive whiteboard. Later on Sue uses the password to log on to the school intranet. Just for fun she changes all her grades to 10.
*   Cool Chris meets some "geeky guys" and they show him how to gain access to pop stars' personal and confidential photos on Facebook.

Both cases seem just a bit of innocent fun, yet Sue and Chris are now both hackers. The fact that "no damage" was done and nothing was "stolen" doesn't matter.

Why do hackers do it? There are many reasons why people become hackers.
*   **Criminal Theft** - To steal large amounts of money, either by direct fraud or holding a "hacked" business to ransom.
*   **Criminal Damage** - Perhaps motivated by revenge or politics, some hackers just want to destroy systems and data and damage a company or organisation.
*   **Protest** - Some hackers sincerely believe that major companies and even governments are too powerful and too secret. They hack into systems to campaign for a freer and more open society.
*   **Fun** - Some hackers just enjoy the challenge of breaking into "secure" systems.

Whatever the motivation hacking is illegal. In the UK "**The Computer Misuse Act 1990**" covers **unauthorised**:

1. Access to computer material
2. Access with intent to commit a further offence, such as fraud, theft or criminal damage
3. Modification, such as adding or modifying a program including viruses.

The act accepts that the "hacker" has to be aware that his access is unauthorised but otherwise simply proving the unauthorised access is enough. As the above are criminal offences anyone found guilty will be liable for a maximum penalty of six months in prison and a £2000 fine. They could also face further charges for any "further offences" as shown above.

Why can hackers do so much more damage than, say forgers in the days when paper files were used?

- Alterations leave no mark
- Huge amounts of data are involved
- Data is transferred via the Internet instantly
- Telecommunications are vulnerable to hackers
- Viruses can spread rapidly

"Poacher Turned Gamekeeper": Some hackers "change their ways" and use their skills as "ethical hackers" (see the chapter on Net Security) or even set up their own technology businesses. Here are a couple of famous examples:

- **Kevin Minick** achieved great notoriety in the 1980s and 90s for a string of hacking offences ending with 5 years in prison. Since 2000 he has earned a living as a security consultant, public speaker and author.
- **Steve Wozniak** was briefly known, in the 1970s, as "Berkeley Blue" after he made a device called a "blue box" that generated telephone-dialling tones to enable free long distance telephone calls. He was more of a "prankster" than a hacker but either way he went on to build the first Apple computer and formed the **Apple Computer Company** with Steve Jobs in 1976.

Questions on chapter 8c Legal Impact:

1. Andy is a bit of a recluse without much contact with the outside world but he is a passionate programmer. He creates, what he thinks, is a very efficient sorting algorithm in Python.

```
def andySearch(key, anyList):
    for index in range(len(anyList)):    #iterate over list with a for loop
        if anyList[index] == key:        #found so
            return index                 #return & exit
    return -99                           #not found so return "dummy value"
```

Andy wants to "protect" his code and only let others use it by paying him a fee. In this context:

(a) Explain the term, "intellectual property".

(b) Andy could try to get his code "copyrighted" or apply for a "patent" to protect his code. Explain which would be the most appropriate in this case.

(c) Suggest why Andy's code would not be accepted for copyright or a patent!

2. Ana writes an entirely new operating system for mobile phones, which is small, fast and very efficient. Copyright law protects her work. A technology company called "Berlin Buzzz" wants to install Anna's operating system on all their new phones. Anna does not want to sell her copyright to "Berlin Buzzz".

(a) Explain how "Berlin Buzzz" could legally use Anna's operating system and how Anna would be paid.

The new phones, and their operating system, are a great success. A London based company, "Unkindest Cut Phones", gives a job to an ex-worker from "Berlin Buzzz". With his help "Unkindest Cut Phones" releases their new phone whose interface is remarkably similar to that of the "Berlin Buzzz" phone. Anna decides to take the London firm to court for breach of copyright.

(b) Suggest two factors the judge would take into account to decide for or against Anna's claim.

(c) Assuming Anna wins her case what could she expect to receive?

(d) A few years later, while driving home to her country mansion in a new Porsche, Anna is killed in a road accident. Explain whether or not "Berlin Buzzz" will still have to pay to use Anna's code.

3. Sofia is a research engineer working for "Clever Clogs Pocket Calculators". She and her team invent a clever modification to existing calculators - Voice activated commands. For example if a user says "decimal two" then the result will be displayed as rounded to 2 decimal places.

(a) Explain why this invention is more likely to be patented rather than copyrighted.

(b) Assuming that the patent application is a success, who will own the patent?

(c) Suggest why the company may not want to patent the invention and just decide to keep the manufacturing process very secret.

4. Michael is showing his friends a great new application on his computer called "3D Theatre Stage Show Maker". Michael shows his friends how easy it is to create a stage design with scenery and how the program reproduces his design in three dimensions. His friends ask him where he got the program and Michael explains that he bought it online for £50 and then downloaded and installed it on his computer.

(a) Now Michael did not actually buy a box with a DVD and he didn't really "buy" the program. When he installed the program, he clicked on a button saying he accepted the "terms and conditions" of the publisher of the software. Explain what exactly Michael did buy?

(b) His friends like the program so much they persuade Michael to burn them a copy each on to a CD-ROM so that they can take the program and install it on to their computers. Explain why Michael may be breaking the law.

(c) Maria says, "Don't worry about giving me a copy Mike. I know a website where I can download any program, including your stage designer thing, for free." Apart from any legal aspect, suggest why Maria should be careful downloading copyright protected software from dubious websites.

(d) Louise says, "Don't bother going to your website Maria. Mike's software is really great and the company that sells it is pretty well known, but it is **'propriety software'**. I know of an **'open source'** program called 'The World is a Stage', which is available to anyone as a free download.

i. State the main differences between "**open source**" and "**proprietary**" software.

ii. Apart from cost, state one advantage of "open source" and one advantage of "proprietary" software.

5. Read this short extract from the CNBC news site (February 2016)

"For more than a week, hackers have shut down the internal computer system at a Hollywood-area hospital for a ransom of 9,000 bitcoin, or almost $3.7 million, according to NBC 4 Los Angeles. The hospital says patient care has not been compromised, though the cyberattack has forced the facility, Hollywood Presbyterian Medical Center, to revert to paper registrations and medical records and send 911 patients to other area hospitals. It's all due to a type of malicious software called ransomware that encrypts sensitive data until it can only be unlocked with a keycode."

(a) What is a "hacker"?

(b) Explain how the hackers are "holding the hospital to ransom"?

CNBC goes on to quote some advice from the cybersecurity firm Tripwire:

"In addition to being wary of email attachments, outside software should have the latest updates and in-house software needs to be screened for loopholes that could be accessed by hackers. At the very least, businesses should back up their data so hard drives"

(c) Explain the importance of the following security measures:

i. "Be wary of email attachments".

ii. "Outside software should have the latest updates"

(d) Explain how backing up the company's data on hard drives could have avoided the hospital from having to, "revert to paper registrations and medical records."

Appendices

Points Covered:
- Solving Large Problems – Controlled Assessment (NEA)
- Flowchart Symbols
- Pseudocode syntax
- Recommended Reading

Solving Large Problems – Controlled Assessment - Non-Exam Assessment (NEA)

If you have read and understood the sections on algorithms and programming and have completed a programming course in a language like Python, Java, C or Pascal, you are now in a position to apply all your skills and knowledge to solve "real" problems. Here I am going to follow the basic structure of an Edexcel "Computer Science Project", which is a good way to work on any small project:

- Stage 1 Analysis   6 marks
- Stage 2 Design   18 marks
- Stage 3 Implementation   24 marks
- Stage 4 Testing, Refining and Evaluation   12 marks

I will try and make the "problem" as realistic as possible but it may be easier than an "exam level" problem. Nonetheless the procedure I will follow is that which is outlined in the specification. I will use, as in the rest of this book, **Python** as the language of implementation.

.... Begin Question ....

Problem Statement: Refraction and Snell's Law

Students carry out a physics experiment to measure the angle of incidence and the angle of refraction as a ray of light passes into a glass block, at various angles of incidence.

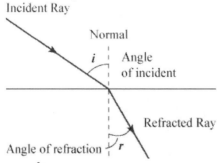

Here is a typical table of their results:

Student	Andy	Carmen	Dave	Anna	Mike	Nick	Rick	Maria
Angle i (deg)	10	20	18	40	140	60	70	80
Angle r (deg)	6	13	30	25	32	35	39	42

These will be available as a simple comma separated values file (csv) looking something like this:

```
Andy, 10, 6
Carmen, 20, 13
Dave, 18, 30
Anna, 40, 25
```

Mike, 140, 32
Nick, 60, 35
Rick, 70, 39
Maria, 80, 42

Each line is one "record" showing: student, angle i & angle r (both in degrees).
If necessary a simple text file (txt) with the same data could also be used.

Program requirements:

Your program must be able to "read in" the student data and calculate the average index of refraction. The calculation needed, for each record, is:

n = Sin(i) / Sin(r)

Where **n** is the refractive index for glass; **i** is the angle of incidence and **r** is the angle of refraction (both in degrees)

Python: For this purpose you will have to import the mathematics module and use the following functions:

import math	
math.radians(x)	#Converts angle x from degrees to radians.
math.sin(x)	#Returns the sine of x radians

Data that is clearly wrong, or "anomalous" as physicists say, must not be used in the calculation. Anomalous Data:

- r > i This is not possible
- i > 90 This is not possible

Records containing such data should be removed. When this happens there should be a suitable output message saying which record is being removed and why.

The program should finally display the calculated average refractive index (n).

All "correct" records of data should be output as a simple text file with one line for each record.

Finally the calculated average index of refraction should be added to this file.

.... End Question ....

Note: There is an explanation and discussion for each stage. The "answer" to each stage or sub-stage is clearly shown between dotted lines and indented.

Stage 1: Analysis:

For this stage, the report should include:

- A short introduction to the problem
- A list of the requirements of the problem that will be programmed
- Decomposition of the problem into sub-problems, including
  - A short description of what each of the sub-problems will do
  - A short explanation of the reasoning behind the decomposition submitted.

An introduction to the problem, in prose, will demonstrate an understanding of abstraction.

.... Begin Answer ....

Data from the results of a student's experiment have to be read into the computer. Each line of student data is, in effect, one record. These records will need to be stored in a structured data type, like a list, so that the problem can be solved.

The problem is to **input** a pair of numbers, **process** these numbers with a calculation and **output** the answer. For example:

Angle i = 40 and angle r = 25 then the refractive index (n) is given by:

$\sin(40) / \sin(25) = 0.643 / 0.423 = 1.520$

It would make sense to add the calculated refractive index to each data record to facilitate further processing.

This is repeated for every "record" or line of data, and the average refractive index is calculated by adding up all of the answers and dividing by how many records there are.

Validation: There is no "user input" required but the data that needs to be read in from the file has to be logical and sensible. The question brief describes two types of "anomalous" data. The refracted angle (r) can never be bigger than the incident angle (i) and the incident angle (i) can never be bigger than 90º - Garbage In Garbage Out (GIGO). In other words, if erroneous data is input to the program, then erroneous results will be output. Records containing such data will need to be deleted. Clearly this should happen before any processing takes place.

Finally the records, perhaps with the extra "field" showing the refractive index, will need to be "written", line-by-line (record-by-record), to a text file. The calculated average refractive index will be read out as a separate line. The text file needs to be saved.

.... End Answer ....

Decomposition: The decomposed list of requirements can be in prose or as a bulleted list, each one clearly identified. Decomposition requires choices to be made, in this case by breaking the given problem down into sub-problems, which will be designed and implemented later. A description, of what each sub-problem will do, is required; it can be in prose or as a bulleted list. An explanation of the reasons why the decomposition submitted is the most appropriate to meet requirements must also be included, in prose.

Data Structure: Now is a good time to think about the **data structure** that will hold the "records". In Python are you to going to use a list, a nested-list or a dictionary? This is a critical decision, which can fundamentally affect the structure of any algorithms.

.... Begin Answer ....

Before I break down the problem into sub-problems, I want to explain my decision about the data structure I will use to hold the "records" of data.

List – 1D array:

dataList = ["Andy", 10, 6, "Carmen", 20, 13 , "Dave", 18, 30, ... "Maria", 80, 42]

If it were an array all the elements would have to be of the same data type, that is "string". A Python list is more flexible and will allow a "mixture" of string and integer data types. So a Python list will work but it does not reflect the "record" structure of the data, where each "line" is one student and their data for that experiment. Secondly it will be "tricky" to access the required data. For example take Carmen's data:

angleI = dataList[4]   angleR = dataList[5]

And Dave's data:

angleI = dataList[7]   angleR = dataList[8]

There is a pattern and it could be done but it is not very clear.

Nested List – 2D array:

dataList = [["Andy", 10, 6], ["Carmen", 20, 13] , ["Dave", 18, 30], ... ["Maria", 80, 42]]

This is looking better: Each element in the list is another, nested, list. This clearly reflects the "tabular" nature of the data. Simple "for loops" can iterate over the list and accessing each data item is relatively clear and simple. For example Carmen's data:

angleI = dataList[1][1]   angleR = dataList[1][2]

And Dave's data:

angleI = dataList[2][1]   angleR = dataList[2][2]

This is the data structure that I have decided to use.

Dictionary:

dataDict = {"Andy" : [10, 6], "Carmen" : [20, 13] , "Dave" : [18, 30], ... "Maria" : [80, 42] }

A dictionary really does reflect the "record" nature of the data. Each student name is a unique "key" and its associated "value" is that student's data. Again simple "for loops" can iterate over the dictionary and accessing each data item is straightforward. For example Carmen's data:

angleI = dataDict["Carmen"][0]   angleR = dataDict["Carmen"][1]

As long as each name is unique, this data structure will work nicely. There is a little work to be done in reading in each record from a csv file and "building" the dictionary but it is not too hard. What dictionaries are particularly good at is rapidly finding a particular record based on the "key" and then, if necessary, editing the associated "value". However there is no requirement in the question brief to search for a particular student's data, nor do we have to update or edit a particular record. For these reasons I have decided not to use a dictionary.

Decomposition – Subprograms

- Read In Data From CSV File into a Nested List.
  - Read in Lines from CSV File and append each line as a list to the main list.
    - The file will have to be opened and a function like "readlines" used to convert the data to a list of lines – each line being one string.
    - The file should then be closed.
  - Convert List to Nested List.
    - Each string is "split" on the "comma" to generate individual data items in each sub list (record).
      - As an alternative I could import the Python csv module to do this step automatically.
  - Convert numerical data items in each record (sub list) to "real" or floating-point number data types.
    - The data could be left as strings and converted, "on-the-fly" when necessary, but it is neater and clearer to convert all the relevant data at one go.
    - Numerical "input" data is all of type integer. Nonetheless the calculations will produce answers with decimal fractions. This is not an issue for Python, which will automatically coerce the result into a float. Nonetheless perhaps some of the input data could be "real" numbers: 75.7º instead of 76º. For these reasons I have decided that all numeric data will be of type "real" (or "float" in Python).
  - Remove Anomalous records from the list
    - As it would be "incorrect" to process "anomalous" data, it makes sense to delete these records before any processing takes place.
    - The project brief requires that there is an appropriate error message output as each record is deleted.
- Calculate Refractive Index for each record and append result to each record.
- Calculate Average Refractive Index from the "new" data in the list.
- Output results
  - Output each updated record showing the calculated refractive index.
  - Output the average refractive index calculated from all the valid records.
- Write List Data to text file
  - A file would have to be opened to write to. Probably easiest to choose a mode that creates a text file if one does not exist and if that file does exist it is overwritten.
    - Write each record to text file.
    - Write the average refractive index to text file.
  - The file would then need to be closed.
- Write Refractive Index to file
  - Open file used to store the list data in mode "append", that is add this data item at the end of the file.
  - Close the file.

Reason for choice of decomposition:
I have carefully chosen each subprogram to **do one job only**. If a subprogram's job can be broken down into further subprograms then it is. The principles of **modularisation** and **decomposition** as part of **abstraction** have been applied.

Any data each subprogram needs from "outside" of the subprogram will be passed in as a **parameter**. Any calculation done by the subprogram that is needed "outside" will be "passed out" as a **return value**. This eliminates the need for access to "global" variables directly and reflects the idea of **encapsulation** in abstraction.

.... End Answer ....

Stage 2: Design:
2.1 Solution Design: The purpose of the design stage is to describe what has to be done when implementing the solution and to suggest an appropriate strategy to test the solution. An **algorithm** or algorithms should be designed that meet **the requirements** of the problem using appropriate conventions (flowchart, pseudo-code, written description). Program code using the chosen language must **not** be included in the design solution.
The algorithm(s) should:
- Show detailed **decomposition into sub-problems** and how they link together (if appropriate)
- Demonstrate clear **abstraction** (for example by including **parameterisation**, links between components)
- Include inputs, processes and outputs
- Use all three basic programming constructs: sequence, selection and iteration.

(**Note**: After implementation the algorithms may have to be modified. That is quite normal. Any such modifications will be shown after the implementation stage.)

.... Begin Answer ....

Algorithmic Steps:

dataList = [ ]   #global "main list" to hold all data, initialised as empty list

avRefractIndex = 0.0   #global variable to hold average refractive index, initialised as 0.0 (a float or real number)

dataList = readInData("studDataFile.csv")
>   #function that reads in data from csv file and returns a nested list.

dataList = calcRefractIndex(dataList)
>   #function that calculates the refractive index for each record, appends the result to each record and returns the modified list

avRefractIndex = calcAverageRefractIndex(dataList)
>   #function that returns the average refractive index using data from data list. Returns the "answer" as a float.

outputList(dataList)
>   #Simple "procedure" that just prints out the updated list in a neat way.

PRINT(avRefractIndex)   #Simple print statement to output the "answer"

writeListDataToFile(dataList, "results.txt")
>   #Simple "procedure" that creates or overwrites the "results.txt" file with the list data

writeIndexToFile(avRefractIndex, "results.txt")
>   #Simple "procedure" to append the "answer" to the text file.

#The actual subprograms (procedures and functions) called in the algorithm.
#Note these would usually appear at the top of the program and the calls beneath.

FUNCTION convertListNested(flatList)
#Parameter a 1 D array or list
#flatList is: ["Andy, 10, 6", "Carmen, 20, 13" , ... "Maria, 80, 42"]
#Returns the flatList of strings to a nested list of elements.
BEGIN
>   localList = [ ] #local variable to hold final list
>   oneLine = [ ] #local variable to hold each line as a list
>   **FOR EACH** result **FROM** flatList **DO**
>   >   oneLine = result.**SPLIT**(",")
>   >   localList.**APPEND**(oneLine)
>
>   **END FOR EACH**
>   #localList is: [["Andy", "10", "6"], ["Carmen", "20", "13"] , ... ["Maria", "80", "42"]]
>   **RETURN** localList

END FUNCTION

.... Insert additional function added during refinement stage ....
FUNCTION convertToFloat(dataItem)
#Exception handler to deal with data that cannot be converted to "real"
#Parameter is any item of data with the expectation that it can be converted to float
# function returns dataItem converted to a float – if possible
# If not possible returns a float 900.0 that is clearly out of range
# The record with this "bad" data will then be removed in removeAnomalousData
BEGIN
   localNum = 900   #local variable for return value
   TRY
     localNum = (**FLOAT**)(dataItem)
   EXCEPT Data type **ERROR**
     PRINT("Could not convert, ",dataItem, " so,",localNum, " is returned.")
   END EXCEPTION HANDLER
   RETURN localNum
END FUNCTION
.... End of additional function added during refinement stage ....

FUNCTION convertNumericaData(nestedList)
#Parameter is a 2 D array or nested list
#nestedList: [["Andy", "10", "6"], ["Carmen", "20", "13"] , ... ["Maria", "80", "42"]]
#calls convertToFloat to deal with data that cannot be converted.
#Returns the local list with all numeric data converted.
BEGIN
      localList = **COPY**(nestedList)   #local variable copy of nestedList parameter
      FOR EACH result **FROM** localList **DO**
          # now calls convertToFloat # result[1] = (FLOAT)result[1]
          # now calls convertToFloat # result[2] = (FLOAT)result[2]
          result[1] = convertToFloat(result[1])
          result[2] = convertToFloat(result[2])
      END FOR EACH
      RETURN localList
END FUNCTION

```
FUNCTION removeAnomalousData(nestedList)
#Parameter a 2 D array or nested list
#nestedList: [ ["Andy", 10, 6], ["Carmen", 20, 13] , ... ["Maria", 80, 42] ]
#Valid records appended to a "good" list which is returned
BEGIN
        goodList = [ ]                    #local variable list to return
        #with for loops, should not delete items while in the loop so ...
        # Append correct or valid records to goodList
        FOR EACH result FROM nestedList DO
                angleI = result[1]
                angleR = result[2]
                #Boundary data check up to but not including 90
                IF angleI NOT IN RANGE(0.1 TO 90.0) THEN
                        PRINT angleI "out of range, so remove this record"
                #Boundary data check up to but not including 90
                ELSE IF angleR NOT IN RANGE(0.1 to 90.0) THEN
                        PRINT angleR "out of range, so remove this record"
                ELSE IF angleR > angleI THEN
                        PRINT angleR " is greater than " angleI "so remove this record"
                ELSE
                        goodList.APPEND(result)
                END IF
        END FOR EACH
        RETURN goodList
END FUNCTION


FUNCTION readInData(anyCSVfile)
#Parameter any simple csv or txt file
#Returns the file converted to a nested list or 2D array
#Calls the following functions to carry out specific tasks
# convertListNested(localList)
# convertNumericalData(localList)
# removeAnomalousData(localList)
BEGIN
        localList = [ ]         #local variable where the data will be stored
        .......... Insert an "Exception Handler" added during refinement stage ................
          TRY
            dataFile = OPEN(anyCSVfile, MODE READ)   #open file in read mode
          EXCEPT File Not Found ERROR
            PRINT("Could not open file, ",anyCSVfile, " so I will quit.")
                EXIT        #no point in continuing so exit program
          ELSE
            PRINT(anyCSVfile, " openened sucessfully.")
          END EXCEPTION HANDLER
        .............. End Insert "Exception Handler" added during refinement stage .........
        localList = dataFile.READLINES()   #each line one long string as element in list
```

dataFile.**CLOSE**()   #good practice to close file after using it

#List is now ["Andy, 10, 6", "Carmen, 20, 13" , ... "Maria, 80, 42"]

localList = convertListNested(localList)

#List is now [["Andy", "10", "6"], ["Carmen", "20", "13"] , ... ["Maria", "80", "42"]]

localList = convertNumericalData(localList)

#List is now [["Andy", 10, 6], ["Carmen", 20, 13] , ... ["Maria", 80, 42]]

localList = removeAnomalousData(localList)

RETURN localList

END FUNCTION

FUNCTION calcRefractIndex(inList)

#Parameter a nested list of experimental data

#Returns that list with refractive index answer appended to each record

#Needs maths functions so need to import module

BEGIN

localList = COPY(inList)   #local variable is a copy of the inList parameter

angleI = 0.0   #local variable for angle of incidence

angleR = 0.0   #local variable for angle of refraction

refIndex = 0.0   #local variable for refractive index

FOR EACH result **FROM** localList **DO**

angleI = result[1]   #may have to convert degrees to radians

angleR = result[2]

refIndex = **SINE**(angleI) / **SINE**(angleR)

result.**APPEND**(refIndex)

END FOR EACH

#List is [["Andy", 10, 6, 1.66], ["Carmen", 20, 13, 1.53] , ... ["Maria", 80, 42, 1.47]]

RETURN localList

END FUNCTION

FUNCTION calcAverageRefractIndex(inList)

#Parameter a nested list of experimental data

#Returns the average refractive index as a "real" or "float" number

BEGIN

refractAverage = 0.0   #local variable float to hold the calculated average

numResults = (**LENGTH**)inList   #local variable for num of results

refractTotal = 0.0   #local variable for total

FOR EACH result **FROM** inList **DO**

refractTotal = refractTotal + result [3]

END FOR EACH

refractAverage = refractTotal / numResults

RETURN refractAverage

END FUNCTION

```
PROCEDURE outputList(inList)
#Parameter a nested list of experimental data
#Prints the list neatly, does not return anything
BEGIN
        PRINT "The final results are: "
        FOR EACH result FROM inList DO
                PRINT result
        END FOR EACH
        PRINT "End of results"
END PROCEDURE
```

```
PROCEDURE writeListDataToFile(inList, anyTextFile)
#Parameters: inList a nested list of data, anyTextFile the name of a txt file.
#Writes data from inList to anyTextFile, does not return anything
BEGIN
        dataFile = OPEN(anyTextFile, MODE WRITE CREATE or OVERWRITE)
        dataFile.WRITELINES(inList)
        dataFile.CLOSE()
END PROCEDURE
```

```
PROCEDURE writeIndexToFile(inNum, anyTextFile)
#Parameters: inNum a value as a float, anyTextFile the name of a txt file.
#Writes inNum to anyTextFile, does not return anything

BEGIN
        dataFile = OPEN(anyTextFile, MODE WRITE APPEND)
        dataFile.WRITELINE(inNum)
        dataFile.CLOSE()
END PROCEDURE
```

.... End of Answer ....

2.2 Test strategy and initial test plan:

Test Strategy:

A test strategy for the solution should be devised based on meeting the requirements of the problem. The test strategy should explain the approaches that the student will use when testing the program. The proposed strategy should be followed when creating an initial test plan; this must be completed before implementation and will be updated before the program is actually tested.

The test strategy should be in prose.

.... Begin Answer ....

Test Strategy:

The only input data is the csv file with the students' results. For the initial test plan the strategy will be to assume that:

- The csv file exists – so there will be no "exception handler" to stop the program if there is no csv file.
- All numeric data exists and can be converted to a float – so there will be no "exception handler" to deal with attempts to convert non-numeric data to "real" or "float" numbers.
- The range for the numeric data (angle i & angle r) will be:
  - 0 < angle < 90
  - That is "boundary" or "extreme" values are, as integers, 1 and 89.
  - As the numbers will be "real" an actual boundary value could be 0.1 or 89.9, for example.
- An "edited" csv file will be created to ensure that there are some records with:
  - Both types of anomalous data (i > r or i > 90)
  - "Out of range" type "erroneous" data
  - "boundary" or "extreme" data

So the test strategy consists of "running" the program with a suitable csv file as test data and seeing how the function "removeAnomalousData(nestedList)" deals with such data.

Later on, as part of the implementation stage and the testing, refining and evaluation stage, there may well appear "exception handlers" and other "refinements" to the algorithm. These "refinements" will be reflected in the final test plan at the end of the project.

.... End Answer ....

Test Plan:

When constructing test data for the **initial test plan**:

- **Normal** data is data that the program will accept – "In the middle of the range."
- **Erroneous** data is inaccurate data that the program will not accept – "Wrong or Invalid" or "Out of range".
- **Boundary** data is typically on the 'edge' of a range of possible values - Technically should be accepted by the program

Not all tests may require data entry.

Test no	Purpose of the test	Test data	Expected result

This test plan will be copied and modified in stage 4.

.... Begin Answer ....

Test no.	Purpose of test	Test data	Expected result
1	Normal data	i = 10, r= 6	n= 1.66 appended to record
2	Normal data	i = 40, r= 25	n= 1.67 appended to record
3	Erroneous data r > i	i = 18, r = 30	Output "30 is greater than 18 so remove this record"
4	Erroneous data, out of range i > 90	i = 140, r = 32	Output "140 out of range, so remove this record"
5	Out of range data	i = -5, r = 40	Output "- 5 out of range, so remove this record"
6	Out of range data	i = 40, r = -6	Output "-6 out of range, so remove this record"
7	Out of range data	i = 40, r = 95	Output "95 out of range, so remove this record"
8	Boundary data	i = 1, r = 0.7	n= 1.43 appended to record
9	Boundary data	i = 89, r = 43	n= 1.47 appended to record

.... End of Answer ....

Stage 3: Implementation

The purpose of this stage is to program the solution to the problem. The sub stages, 3.1 & 3.2 really happen at the same time. As you translate your algorithm from pseudocode into Python you will be applying your knowledge of such things as: selection (if statements), iteration (loops), functions etc. As you go along it is quite normal and very good practice to "refine" (improve) your solution. Perhaps you decide to use a for loop instead of a while loop to make your code more efficient. Maybe you even decide to add a subprogram (function) that you had not thought about before to add "functionality" to your solution. Whenever you make:

- **A small change**, just add a **comment** to your code explaining what you have done.
  - If it was the result of a problem copy and paste a screen shot of how you "debugged" the code. This could be as simple as printing out a result or showing the formal use of any debugging tools.
- **A large change**, then save the code as another version.
  - It is good practice to have 2 or 3 versions of code ending up with the final solution.

- o It could be a good idea to copy and paste a basic working version, clearly labelled as "Version 1 – Basic working version"
  - o Then copy and paste any output, bugs etc.
  - o Then copy and paste you final solution, clearly labelled as "Final Version – Fully working solution."
- **Changes to the algorithm** from the design stage you must:
  - o Record the change and eventually copy and paste it back into the design part of the documentation.
  - o Do not destroy the original design. It is important that you keep both to show how you developed your solution.
  - o Here, for continuity, I will add such changes in this part of the write up.

3.1 Implementing the design

The design algorithm(s), as abstract decomposition, need(s) to be **translated** into Python. This process requires applying an understanding of programming concepts when using this programming language during the implementation.

3.2 Building the solution

The final programmed solution should:
- Address all the **requirements** listed in the analysis stage.
- **Decomposed into subprograms**.
  - o These should clearly reflect the structure of the pseudocode in your algorithm in the design stage.
  - o In Python this means functions but these should be carefully commented to indicate:
    - Their purpose – what they are supposed to do
    - Which ones are "procedures" (that do **not return** a value) and which are "functions" (which **do return** a value).
    - What, if any, **parameters** they expect;
- It should be **functional** – using correct constructs such as: if then else if; while loops etc.
- **Readable** – You may want to add clear "end of loop" or "end of function" comments. These statements are not required in Python but they do help to make the code readable. As Python demands correct indentation to work, that should not be a problem.
  - o Well **commented** – it is not necessary to comment every line, only where there is something that needs some explanation.
    - All functions should be commented to explain: what, if any, parameters they expect; what their purpose is and what, if anything, they return.
  - o Sensible and meaningful **variable names** such as: counter, listOfResults etc.
  - o Sensible and meaningful **function names** such as: calculateRefIndex, checkErrorsInList etc.
- **Validation checks**: simple, clear and commented code that explains how a check that data is logical and sensible works.

(**Note**: formal, recorded testing is carried out in stage 4.)

.... Implementation Begin Answer – Basic working version ....

#Sine Rule - Refractive Index Calculator

#Reads in text or csv file of data like "Andy", 10, 6 where each line is

#name of student, angle of incidence in degrees, angle or refraction in degrees

#calculates refractive index (n = sine (i) / sine (r)) for all valid records

#calculates the average refractive index for all valid records

#Writes results to a text file that is created if necessary.

Version 1 - Basic working version - No exception handling - March 2016

import math #needed for sine and radians functions

def convertListNested(flatList):

  #parameter flatList is: ["Andy, 10, 6", "Carmen, 20, 13" , ... "Maria, 80, 42"]

  #function will split on commas and so produce a nested list

  ##[["Andy", "10", "6"], ["Carmen", "20", "13"] , ... ["Maria", "80", "42"]]

  #this is what the function will return

  localList = []   #local variable to hold data, will be returned

  oneLine = []   #local variable to hold one record of data

  for result **in** flatList:

    oneLine = result.**split**(",")

    localList.**append**(oneLine)

  #end for loop

  return localList

#end convert List Nested function ....

def convertNumericData(nestedList):

  #parameter nestedList: [["Andy","10","6"],["Carmen","20","13"], ... ["Maria","80","42"]]

  #function will convert numeric data to float

  #goodList: ["Andy",10,6],["Carmen",20,13], ... ["Maria",80,42]]

  #local variable, this is the list that the function will return

  localList = nestedList[:] #copy list may have to use deep copy

  for result **in** localList:

    result[1] = float(result[1])

    result[2] = float(result[2])

  #end for loop ......

  return localList

#end convert numeric data function ....

```python
def removeAnomalousData(nestedList):
  #parameter nestedList:[["Andy",10,6],["Carmen",20,13], ... ["Maria",80,42]]
  #function will remove "bad" data for example
  #i or r out of range 0-90 or r > i, which is not possible
  #valid results will be appended to a good list which will be returned

  goodList = [ ]  #local variable for list to return

  #with for loops should not delete items while in the loop so ...
  # append correct or valid records to goodList
  for result in nestedList:
    angleI = result[1]
    angleR = result[2]
    #Boundary data check up to but not including 90
    #note cannot use range(0.1, 90.0) as must be integers
    #for simplicity we will use range(0, 90) which is 0, 1, ..... 89)
    if angleI not in range(0,90):
      print("Error in: ", result)
      print(angleI, " out of range, so remove this record.")
    elif angleR not in range(0, 90):
      print("Error in: ", result)
      print(angleR, " out of range, so remove this record.")
    elif angleR > angleI:
      print("Error in: ", result)
      print(angleR, " is greater than ", angleI, " so remove this record.")
    else:
      goodList.append(result)
    #end if then else ...............
  #end for loop .........................
  print()
  return goodList
#end remove anomalous data function .........................

def readInData(anyCSVfile):
  #parameter anyCSVfile a simple csv or txt file like "Andy", 40, 30 ...
  #opens anyCSVfile and reads in all lines as a list of lines
  #functions called from within this function:
  #   convertListNested(localList)
  #   convertNumericData(localList)
  #   removeAnomalousData(localList)

  localList = [ ]  #local variable where the data will be stored
  dataFile = open(anyCSVfile, mode="r")   #open file in read mode
  localList = dataFile.readlines()
  dataFile.close()
```

```
print("Basic list of strings: ")
print(localList)
print()
#List is now ["Andy,10,6","Carmen,20,13", ... "Maria,80,42"]
localList = convertListNested(localList)
print("Nested list of records: ")
print(localList)
print()
#List is now["Andy","10","6"],["Carmen","20","13"], ... ["Maria","80","42"]]
localList = convertNumericData(localList)
print("Nested list with converted numeric data: ")
print(localList)
print()
#List is now[["Andy",10,6],["Carmen",20,13], ... ["Maria",80,42]]
localList = removeAnomalousData(localList)
print("Nested list with anomalous data records removed: ")
print(localList)
print()

    return localList
#end read in data function .........................................


def calcRefractIndex(inList):
    #parameter inList ["Andy",10,6],["Carmen",20,13], ... ["Maria",80,42]]
    #Needs maths functions radians and sin so import math module
    #iterates over inList calculating refractive index sine(i)/sine(r)
    #returns a new list with refractive index appended to each record

    localList = inList[:]   #local variable copy may need deep copy
    angleI = 0.0    #local varialbe for angle of incidence
    angleR = 0.0    #local variable for angle of refraction
    refIndex = 0.0  #local variable for refractive index

    for result in localList:
        angleI = math.radians(result[1])    #convert degrees to radians
        angleR = math.radians(result[2])
        refIndex = math.sin(angleI) / math.sin(angleR)  #sin(i) / sin(r)
        result.append(refIndex) #add refractive index element at end of result
    #end for loop .............
    #List is [["Andy",10,6,1.66],["Carmen",20,13,1.53],... ["Maria",80,42,1.47]]
    return localList
#end calc refract index function .......................................


def calcAverageRefractIndex(inList):
    #parameter inList [["Andy",10,6,1.66],["Carmen",20,13,1.53],... ["Maria",80,42,1.47]]
    #iterates over inList calculating the average refractive index
```

#returns average refractive index as a float

refractAverage = 0.0   #local variable float to hold the average
numResults = len(inList)   #local variable for num of results
refractTotal = 0.0   #local variable for total
for result **in** inList:
    refractTotal = refractTotal + result[3]
#end for loop ....
refractAverage = refractTotal / numResults

return refractAverage
#end calc average refract index function ....

def outputList(inList):
    #parameter inList [["Andy",10,6,1.66],["Carmen",20,13,1.53],... ["Maria",80,42,1.47]]
    #Simple "procedure" to print inList parameter neatly, so returns nothing

    print("The final results are: ")
    for result **in** inList:
        print(result)
    #end for loop ....
    print("End of results. ")
#end of procedure output list ....

def writeListDataToFile(inList, anyTextFile):
    #parameter inList [["Andy",10,6,1.66],["Carmen",20,13,1.53],... ["Maria",80,42,1.47]]
    #parameter anyTextFile ... simple text file that will be created if it does not exist
    #iterate over inList, convert each line to string and write to anyTextFile
    #In effect a "procedure" as it does not return anything

    dataFile = **open**(anyTextFile, **mode**="w") #create and write or overwrite if file exists
    for result **in** inList:
        dataFile.**write**(**str**(result)+ "\n") #concatenate newline character
    #end for loop ....
    #The following line was not possible as it requires strings
    #This explains why each line is converted to a string and then written to file
    #dataFile.writelines(inList) must use string to write lines

    dataFile.**close**()
#end of procedure write list data to file ....

def writeIndexToFile(inNum, anyTextFile):
    #parameter inList [["Andy",10,6,1.66],["Carmen",20,13,1.53],... ["Maria",80,42,1.47]]
    #paramter inNum is the calculated average refractive index
    #In effect a "procedure" as nothing is returned
    #convert inNum to string and write to anyTextFile .. string appended at end of file

```
dataFile = open(anyTextFile, mode="a")  #open and append data
dataFile.write(str(inNum)+ "\n") #concatenate newline character
dataFile.close()
#end of procedure to write refractive index to text file ................
```

```
#Main program starts here!!!! ................................................
dataList = [ ]   #global variable for main list, initialised as empty
avRefractIndex = 0.0 # global variable hold average, initialised as empty float
```

```
dataList = readInData("studDataFile.csv")
dataList = calcRefractIndex(dataList)
avRefractIndex = calcAverageRefractIndex(dataList)
outputList(dataList)
print("Average refractive index is: ", avRefractIndex)
writeListDataToFile(dataList, "results.txt")
writeIndexToFile(avRefractIndex, "results.txt")
```

```
input("Hit any key to exit.  Thank you.")
```

.... End Answer – Basic working version ....

.... Implementation Begin Answer – Sample output and any errors ....

Note: The print lines that print out the list as it is built up are clearly not necessary in a full version of the problem. Nonetheless they help us to see what exactly is going on at each step.

Basic list of strings:
['Andy,10,6\n', 'Carmen,20,13\n', 'Dave,18,30\n', 'Anna,40,25\n', 'Mike,140,32\n', 'Nick,60,35\n', 'Rick,70,39\n', 'Maria,80,42']

Nested list of records:
[['Andy', '10', '6\n'], ['Carmen', '20', '13\n'], ['Dave', '18', '30\n'], ['Anna', '40', '25\n'], ['Mike', '140', '32\n'], ['Nick', '60', '35\n'], ['Rick', '70', '39\n'], ['Maria', '80', '42']]

Nested list with converted numeric data:
[['Andy', 10.0, 6.0], ['Carmen', 20.0, 13.0], ['Dave', 18.0, 30.0], ['Anna', 40.0, 25.0], ['Mike', 140.0, 32.0], ['Nick', 60.0, 35.0], ['Rick', 70.0, 39.0], ['Maria', 80.0, 42.0]]

Error in: ['Dave', 18.0, 30.0]
30.0 is greater than 18.0 so remove this record.
Error in: ['Mike', 140.0, 32.0]
140.0 out of range, so remove this record.

Nested list with anomalous data records removed:
[['Andy', 10.0, 6.0], ['Carmen', 20.0, 13.0], ['Anna', 40.0, 25.0], ['Nick', 60.0, 35.0], ['Rick', 70.0, 39.0], ['Maria', 80.0, 42.0]]

The final results are:
['Andy', 10.0, 6.0, 1.6612525645028409]
['Carmen', 20.0, 13.0, 1.520420272415569]
['Anna', 40.0, 25.0, 1.5209650596710995]
['Nick', 60.0, 35.0, 1.509869215154447]
['Rick', 70.0, 39.0, 1.493186354915825]
['Maria', 80.0, 42.0, 1.4717720930016023]
End of results.
Average refractive index is: 1.5295775932768974
Hit any key to exit. Thank you.

Errors. Debugging and changes:

Initial attempt to write lines from the final list to a text file:

    dataFile = open(anyTextFile, mode="w") #create and write or overwrite if file exists
    dataFile.writelines(inList)

Resulted in the following error message:
In writeListDataToFile
    dataFile.writelines(inList)
TypeError: must be str, not list

So the program was changed to iterate over the list, and convert each record (list) into a string before writing to the text file:

    for result in inList:
        dataFile.write(str(result)+ "\n") #concatenate newline character

Anomalous Data Range Check:

In the algorithm I wanted to check that the number were in the range of 0 to 90. I decided that the range should be exclusive that is: 0< number < 90. Using a "range" function this would give me: number in **range**(0, 90), but that would include the zero (0). As the numbers would be "real" or "float" I decided on using the range function to check if any of the numbers were "out of range" by: NOT IN RANGE(0.1, 90.0). This did not work:
in removeAnomalousData
    if angleI **not in range**(0.1,90.0):
TypeError: 'float' object cannot be interpreted as an integer

Obviously the range function needs integers so:
    if angleI **not in range**(0,90):
        print("Error in: ", result)
        print(angleI, " out of range, so remove this record.")
While this solution "works", perhaps it is better to not use the range function. So in the final version the code looks like:
    if (angleI < 0) **or** (angleI > 90):

```
    print("Error in: ", result)
    print(angleI, " out of range, so remove this record.")
elif (angleR < 0) or (angleI > 90):
    print("Error in: ", result)
    print(angleR, " out of range, so remove this record.")
elif angleR > angleI:
    print("Error in: ", result)
    print(angleR, " is greater than ", angleI, " so remove this record.")
else:
    goodList.append(result)
```

Too many decimal places:

In general the calculations have too many decimal places.

 Average refractive index is: 1.5295775932768974

Given the accuracy of the experiment, two places should be fine. So in the final solution a simple "round" function was used.

```
    refIndex = math.sin(angleI) / math.sin(angleR)  #sin(i) / sin(r)
    refIndex = round(refIndex, 2)          #round to two decimal places
```

This gives much more reasonable output:

Average refractive index is: 1.53

Exception Handlers and Validation:

The first version dealt quite well with anomalous data values but does nothing in the following situations:

Wrong data type: Values like "x10" or "ten" cannot be converted to numeric values of integer or "real" (float). Attempts to do so will crash the program.

```
  result[1] = float(result[1])
```

ValueError: could not convert string to float: 'x10'

File does not exist: Attempt to open, to read, a file that is not there will crash the program.

```
  dataFile = open(anyCSVfile, mode="r")   #open file in read mode
```

FileNotFoundError: [Errno 2] No such file or directory: 'studDataFileXXX.csv'

What we need to do is to "handle" these exceptions as they arise.

In the case of a data value like "x10", one solution is to "convert" the value to a default "out of range" value, like 900. This record will then be removed by the remove anomalous data function. This will be best implemented as another function.

The file not found error is more serious. There really is no point in continuing to run the program, so a simple error message and then "exit" is what is needed.

The final solution addresses all of the above modifications.

.... End Answer – Sample output and any errors ....

.... Implementation Begin Answer – Final working version ....
#Sine Rule - Refractive Index Calculator
#Reads in text or csv file of data like "Andy", 10, 6 where each line is
#name of student, angle of incidence in degrees, angle or refraction in degrees
#calculates refractive index (n = sine (i) / sine (r)) for all valid records
#calculates the average refractive index for all valid records
#Writes results to a text file that is created if necessary.

Final Working Version with exception handling - March 2016

```python
import math #needed for sine and radians functions
import sys  #needed for exit when file not found

def convertListNested(flatList):
    #parameter flatList is: [ "Andy, 10, 6", "Carmen, 20, 13" , ... "Maria, 80, 42" ]
    #function will split on commas and so produce a nested list
    ##[ ["Andy", "10", "6"], ["Carmen", "20", "13"] , ... ["Maria", "80", "42"] ]
    #this is what the function will return

    localList = [ ]
    oneLine = [ ]
    for result in flatList:
        oneLine = result.split(",")
        localList.append(oneLine)
    #end for loop

    return localList
#end convert List Nested function .........................................

def convertToFloat(dataItem):
    #parameter dataItem expected "45" ie a string that can be converted to a float
    #return, that converted number, or if cannot convert eg "forty" then
    #return a default "out of range" number 900
    localNum = 900.0     #local variable, float, for return value
    try:
        localNum = float(dataItem)
    except ValueError:
        print("Could not convert, ",dataItem, " so,",localNum, " is returned.")
    #end exception handler
    return localNum
#end function convert to float ...............................

def convertNumericData(nestedList):
    #parameter nestedList: [["Andy","10","6"],["Carmen","20","13"], ... ["Maria","80","42"]]
    #function will convert numeric data to float
    #goodList: ["Andy",10,6],["Carmen",20,13], ... ["Maria",80,42]]
```

```
    #this is the list that the function will return
    localList = nestedList[:]   #copy list may have to use deep copy
    for result in localList:
        result[1] = convertToFloat(result[1])
        result[2] = convertToFloat(result[2])
    #end for loop ......

    return localList
#end convert numeric data function ........................

def removeAnomalousData(nestedList):
    #parameter nestedList:[["Andy",10,6],["Carmen",20,13], ... ["Maria",80,42]]
    #function will remove "bad" data for example
    #i or r out of range 0-90 or r > i, which is not possible
    #valid results will be appended to a good list which will be returned
    goodList = [ ]  #local variable for list to return

    #with for loops should not delete items while in the loop so ...
    # append correct or valid records to goodList
    for result in nestedList:
        angleI = result[1]
        angleR = result[2]
        #Boundary data check up to but not including 90
        #note cannot use range(0.1, 90.0) as must be integers
        #for simplicity we will use range(0, 90) which is 0, 1, ..... 89)
        #Modification - not using range function!!
        if (angleI < 0) or (angleI > 90):
            print("Error in: ", result)
            print(angleI, " out of range, so remove this record.")
        elif (angleR < 0) or (angleR > 90):
            print("Error in: ", result)
            print(angleR, " out of range, so remove this record.")
        elif (angleR > angleI):
            print("Error in: ", result)
            print(angleR, " is greater than ", angleI, " so remove this record.")
        else:
            goodList.append(result)
        #end if then else ...............
    #end for loop ........................
    print()
    return goodList
#end remove anomalous data function ..........................

def readInData(anyCSVfile):
    #parameter anyCSVfile a simple csv or txt file like "Andy", 40, 30 ...
    #opens anyCSVfile and reads in all lines as a list of lines
```

```
#functions called from within this function:
#  convertListNested(localList)
#  convertNumericData(localList)
#  removeAnomalousData(localList)
localList = [ ]  #local variable where the data will be stored
try:
    dataFile = open(anyCSVfile, mode="r")  #open file in read mode
except FileNotFoundError:
    print("Could not open file, ",anyCSVfile, " so I will quit.")
    sys.exit()  #no point in continuing so EXIT
else:
    print(anyCSVfile, " opened successfully.")
#end of exception handler ............................
localList = dataFile.readlines()
dataFile.close()
print("Basic list of strings: ")
print(localList)
print()
#List is now ["Andy,10,6","Carmen,20,13", ... "Maria,80,42"]
localList = convertListNested(localList)
print("Nested list of records: ")
print(localList)
print()
#List is now["Andy","10","6"],["Carmen","20","13"], ... ["Maria","80","42"]]
localList = convertNumericData(localList)
print("Nested list with converted numeric data: ")
print(localList)
print()
#List is now[["Andy",10,6],["Carmen",20,13], ... ["Maria",80,42]]
localList = removeAnomalousData(localList)
print("Nested list with anomalous data records removed: ")
print(localList)
print()

    return localList
#end read in data function ......................................

def calcRefractIndex(inList):
    #parameter inList ["Andy",10,6],["Carmen",20,13], ... ["Maria",80,42]]
    #Needs maths functions radians and sin so import math module
    #iterates over inList calculating refractive index sine(i)/sine(r)
    #returns a new list with refractive index appended to each record

    localList = inList[:]   #local variable copy may need deep copy
    angleI = 0.0   #local varialbe for angle of incidence
    angleR = 0.0   #local variable for angle of refraction
```

```
    refIndex = 0.0  #local variable for refractive index
    for result in localList:
        angleI = math.radians(result[1])   #convert degrees to radians
        angleR = math.radians(result[2])
        refIndex = math.sin(angleI) / math.sin(angleR)  #sin(i) / sin(r)
        refIndex = round(refIndex, 2)     #round to two decimal places
        result.append(refIndex) #add refractive index element at end of result
    #end for loop .............
    #List is [["Andy",10,6,1.66],["Carmen",20,13,1.53],... ["Maria",80,42,1.47]]
    return localList
#end calc refract index function ...................................


def calcAverageRefractIndex(inList):
    #parameter inList [["Andy",10,6,1.66],["Carmen",20,13,1.53],... ["Maria",80,42,1.47]]
    #iterates over inList calculating the average refractive index
    #returns average refractive index as a float

    refractAverage = 0.0   #local variable float to hold the average
    numResults = len(inList)   #local variable for num of results
    refractTotal = 0.0     #local variable for total
    for result in inList:
        refractTotal = refractTotal + result[3]
    #end for loop ..........
    refractAverage = refractTotal / numResults
    refractAverage = round(refractAverage, 2)

    return refractAverage
#end calc average refract index function ..............................


def outputList(inList):
    #parameter inList [["Andy",10,6,1.66],["Carmen",20,13,1.53],... ["Maria",80,42,1.47]]
    #Simple function to print inList parameter neatly
    print("The final results are: ")
    for result in inList:
        print(result)
    #end for loop .............
    print("End of results. ")
#end of procedure output list ..........................................


def writeListDataToFile(inList, anyTextFile):
    #parameter inList [["Andy",10,6,1.66],["Carmen",20,13,1.53],... ["Maria",80,42,1.47]]
    #parameter anyTextFile ... simple text file that will be created if it does not exist
    #iterate over inList, convert each line to string and write to anyTextFile
    dataFile = open(anyTextFile, mode="w")  #create and write or overwrite if file exists
    for result in inList:
```

```
        dataFile.write(str(result)+ "\n") #concatenate newline character
    #end for loop .............
    #dataFile.writelines(inList) must use string to write lines
    dataFile.close()
#end of procedure write list data to file ...........................

def writeIndexToFile(inNum, anyTextFile):
    #parameter inList [["Andy",10,6,1.66],["Carmen",20,13,1.53],... ["Maria",80,42,1.47]]
    #paramter inNum is the calculated average refractive index
    #convert inNum to string and write to anyTextFile .. string appended at end of file
    dataFile = open(anyTextFile, mode="a")  #open and append data
    dataFile.write(str(inNum)+ "\n") #concatenate newline character
    dataFile.close()
#end of procedure to write refractive index to text file ................


#Main program starts here!!!! ................................................
dataList = [ ]  #global variable for main list, initialised as empty
avRefractIndex = 0.0 # global variable hold average, initialised as empty float

dataList = readInData("studDataFileTEST.csv")
dataList = calcRefractIndex(dataList)
avRefractIndex = calcAverageRefractIndex(dataList)
outputList(dataList)
print("Average refractive index is: ", avRefractIndex)
writeListDataToFile(dataList, "results.txt")
writeIndexToFile(avRefractIndex, "results.txt")

input("Hit any key to exit.  Thank you.")
```

.... End Answer – Final working version ....

Stage 4: Testing, refining and evaluation

The purpose of this stage is to show that the final program solution has been tested along with any refinements, and the solutions evaluated against the original requirements.

Testing and Refining:

Columns to show the 'Actual result' and 'Action needed/comments' should be added to the initial test plan and completed when each test is run. Any errors should have 'Action Needed/Comments' entries. An attempt should be made to correct and retest all errors.

Test no	Purpose of the test	Test data	Expected result	Actual result	Action needed/comments

.... Begin Answer – Testing and Refining ------------------------------------

Test data (csv file):
Andy,10,6
Carmen,40,25
Dave,x18,30
Anna,40,25
Mike,80,x32
Nick,-5,40
Rick,40,-6
Maria,40,95
Vic,1, 0.7
Sally,89,43
Louise,45,70
Magnus,140,32

Sample output based on the test data:
studDataFileTEST.csv opened successfully.
Basic list of strings:
['Andy,10,6\n', 'Carmen,40,25\n', 'Dave,x18,30\n', 'Anna,40,25\n', 'Mike,80,x32\n', 'Nick,-5,40\n', 'Rick,40,-6\n', 'Maria,40,95\n', 'Vic,1, 0.7\n', 'Sally,89,43\n', 'Louise,45,70\n', Magnus,140,32']

Nested list of records:
[['Andy', '10', '6\n'], ['Carmen', '40', '25\n'], ['Dave', 'x18', '30\n'], ['Anna', '40', '25\n'], ['Mike', '80', 'x32\n'], ['Nick', '-5', '40\n'], ['Rick', '40', '-6\n'], ['Maria', '40', '95\n'], ['Vic', '1', ' 0.7\n'], ['Sally', '89', '43\n'], ['Louise', '45', '70'],['Magnus','140','32']]

Could not convert, x18 so, 900.0 is returned.
Could not convert, x32 so, 900.0 is returned.
Nested list with converted numeric data:
[['Andy', 10.0, 6.0], ['Carmen', 40.0, 25.0], ['Dave', 900.0, 30.0], ['Anna', 40.0, 25.0], ['Mike', 80.0, 900.0], ['Nick', -5.0, 40.0], ['Rick', 40.0, -6.0], ['Maria', 40.0, 95.0], ['Vic', 1.0, 0.7], ['Sally', 89.0, 43.0], ['Louise', 45.0, 70.0], ['Magnus', 140.0, 32.0]]

Error in: ['Dave', 900.0, 30.0]
900.0 out of range, so remove this record.
Error in: ['Mike', 80.0, 900.0]
900.0 out of range, so remove this record.
Error in: ['Nick', -5.0, 40.0]
-5.0 out of range, so remove this record.
Error in: ['Rick', 40.0, -6.0]
-6.0 out of range, so remove this record.
Error in: ['Maria', 40.0, 95.0]
95.0 out of range, so remove this record.
Error in: ['Louise', 45.0, 70.0]
70.0 is greater than 45.0 so remove this record.

Error in: ['Magnus', 140.0, 32.0]
140.0 out of range, so remove this record.

Nested list with anomalous data records removed:
[['Andy', 10.0, 6.0], ['Carmen', 40.0, 25.0], ['Anna', 40.0, 25.0], ['Vic', 1.0, 0.7], ['Sally', 89.0, 43.0]]

The final results are:
['Andy', 10.0, 6.0, 1.66]
['Carmen', 40.0, 25.0, 1.52]
['Anna', 40.0, 25.0, 1.52]
['Vic', 1.0, 0.7, 1.43]
['Sally', 89.0, 43.0, 1.47]
End of results.
Average refractive index is: 1.52
Hit any key to exit. Thank you.

Copy of the text file that "saved" the final data:
['Andy', 10.0, 6.0, 1.66]
['Carmen', 40.0, 25.0, 1.52]
['Anna', 40.0, 25.0, 1.52]
['Vic', 1.0, 0.7, 1.43]
['Sally', 89.0, 43.0, 1.47]
1.52

Final test table:

Test no.	Purpose of test	Test data	Expected result	Actual Result	Action Needed / comments
1	Normal data	i = 10, r= 6	n=1.66 appended to record	As excepted	OK
2	Normal data	i = 40, r= 25	n=1.52 appended to record	As expected	OK
3	Erroneous data r > i	i = 45, r = 70	Output"70 is greater than 45 so remove this record"	Record removed	Anomalous data as in program brief
4	Erroneous data, out of range i > 90	i = 140, r = 32	Output "140 out of range, so remove this record"	Record removed	OK
5	Out of range data	i = -5, r = 40	Output"- 5 out of range, so remove this record"	Record removed	OK

6	Out of range data	i = 40, r = -6	Output"-6 out of range, so remove this record"	Record removed	OK
7	Out of range data	i = 40, r = 95	Output"95 out of range, so remove this record"	Record removed	OK
8	Boundary data	i = 1, r = 0.7	n= 1.43 appended to record	As expected	Unlikely but possible
9	Boundary data	i = 89, r = 43	n= 1.47 appended to record	As expected	Unlikely but possible
10	File does not exist	readInData ("XXX.csv")	Could not open file, XXX.csv so I will quit.	As expected	Exception handler needed
11	Incompatible Data	i = x18, r = 30	Could not convert, x18 so, 900.0 is returned.	As expected & record removed	Exception handler needed
12	Incompatible Data	i = 80, r = x32	Could not convert, x32 so, 900.0 is returned.	As expected & record removed	Exception handler needed

.... End Answer – Testing and Refining ....

Evaluation:

The evaluation should include a thorough and critical evaluation of the program. This should include:

- How successfully the program meets each of the original requirements.
- The reason for adding refinements to the final solution.

.... Begin Answer – Evaluation ....

Evaluation:

How successfully the program meets each of the original requirements:

Original Requirements:

- Your program must be able to "read in" the student data.
    - Opening the file to "read" and using "readlines" to store each line as a separate string item in a list accomplishes this task simply and efficiently.
    - By using functions like "split" and the subprograms, convert to nested list and convert numeric data, a simple 2D array or nested list is created with each "record" represented as a list, which in turn is an element in the "outer" list. This faithfully reflects the tabular nature of the data.
    - I could have imported the Python "module" csv to achieve the same goal. As the task was relatively simple, I decided not to use the csv module.
- Remove anomalous data - Records containing such data should be removed. When this happens there should be a suitable output message saying which record is being removed and why.

- o r > i This is not possible
- o i > 90 This is not possible
- o As the data was neatly stored in a nested list data structure this task was quite straightforward.
- o Simply iterate over the list with a FOR loop and compare the relevant "fields" or "elements" with an IF statement.
- o A suitable message was output and the record removed from the list. (Actually "valid" records were added to a "good" list and the old list was not used anymore.)
- o Although not strictly asked for, my program also removes any "out of range" data where every angle must be between 0 and 90

- Calculate the average index of refraction.
  - o This was a straightforward calculation. Knowing that the result would have decimal places, I decided to make all the numeric data of type "real" or "float". In Python I could have left the "input" data as integers and Python would automatically "coerce" the result to a "float". Nonetheless to allow for input data of type "float" and for neatness sake, it was a good decision to make all the numbers "real".

- The program should finally display the calculated average refractive index (n).
  - o This was correctly displayed.
  - o Note that my program also output the final; "valid" list of records. Although not a requirement, I think this makes the final output of the "answer" clearer.

- All "correct" records of data should be output as a simple text file with one line for each record.
  - o I have included a copy of the text file in the testing and refining section

- Finally the calculated average index of refraction should be added to this file.
  - o I have included a copy of the text file in the testing and refining section and you can see that the last data item is the average refractive index.

Reason for adding refinements to the final solution:
- **Exception Handlers:**
  - o **File does not exist:** As the program is so dependant on data coming in from a file, it makes sense to test that the file actually exists!
    - ▪ I could have gone further here by testing, for example, that the format of the data in the test file was such that a nested list could be created. I did not have time to do this and, besides, it was not a requirement of the task.
  - o **Value errors:** The program entirely depends on valid data being "input". If any of the numeric data values cannot be converted to a "float" then the program would crash. Although not a requirement of the task, it makes sense to carry out such checks. Again I could have gone further, for example, removing any "white space" from around, an otherwise valid, data value.
- **Writing to a text file:**

- o I had to research a little about how the Python "write to file" function works. I thought I could just "write the list" straight to the text file and that was it. It seems that the data must be in string format, hence the modification.
- o There is room for more work here. For example, it would make sense to keep the list format and / or a csv format instead of a simple text file. In that way the data could be "used again". There are ways in Python to do this but it was not a requirement of the task.
- **Decimal Places**:
  - o After a few "runs" of the program it became very clear that large numbers of decimal places for the refractive index were not necessary.
  - o I modified the code to use a simple "round" function so that the "answers" only had 2 decimal places. This was not a requirement but I think it made sense, given the likely accuracy of an experiment like this.
- **Printing out the lists as they built**:
  - o This was not a task requirement. Nonetheless it was very useful for me while working on the code to see what exactly the data structure (list) really looked like at each point. I left this modification in just to show these data structures. Of course, now that the code works, these output lines could be removed.

.... End Answer – Evaluation ....

Summary: It is impossible to predict exactly what the "real" project will look like – after all it is a kind of "exam" and therefore confidential. Nonetheless the key to success, seems to me, to be:
- Decide on the data structure first.
  - o Get the data structure "right" (list, nested list or dictionary) and the solution will follow.
- Dry run the exercise a few times with a paper, a pencil and a calculator.
  - o If you can't do it "manually" it will be very hard to code a solution.
- Follow the steps given.
  - o It is very tempting just to go straight to Python and start coding. This approach will not work for large projects!

Good luck!

Flowchart Symbols:
The table shows the symbols used throughout the book.

Symbol	Name	Function
	START or END	A rounded rectangle represents a start or end of the flow chart
	Arrows	A line that connects objects & shows the direction of processing
	INPUT / OUTPUT	A parallelogram represents input or output. Eg Input age or Print total
	PROCESS	A rectangle represents a process or calculation. Eg. count = count + 1
	DECISION	A diamond shows a "boolean" **decision.** Must have 1 input and 2 outputs. Each output must be labelled "Yes" or "No"

Some exam boards use slight variations to these "standard" symbols. The Edexcel specification, for example, does not have a separate parallelogram for input & output. They just use the rectangle, process box, for both. Personally I prefer distinguishing between a process and input & output. Some authors use other symbols, like a cylinder to illustrate saving to a hard drive. This should not be a problem for you to "read" any flowchart. As for drawing your own flowchart, it should not matter either, as long as your meaning is clear and unambiguous.

Pseudocode Syntax

What follows is a brief overview of the pseudocode used in this book. Pseudocode is a kind of "structured" natural language. It is somewhat between, for example, English and Python. It should be easy to "translate" the pseudocode to any "appropriate" programming language such as Python or Java. The Edexcel specification uses their "own" syntax. However you are not obliged to use this. As always, as long as your "meaning" is clear and unambiguous then you may, within reason, use any "standard" pseudocode, including that used in this book. Nonetheless as Edexcel point out, "Familiarity with the given (their) pseudo-code could increase confidence when interpreting questions."

Type	Pseudocode in this book	Edexcel pseudocode
Data Types	INTEGER REAL (FLOAT) BOOLEAN CHARACTER (STRING)	INTEGER REAL BOOLEAN CHARACTER
Coercion	INTEGER("56") --> 56 OUTPUT "Fred" + (STRING) 18, will display "Fred18"	INTEGER("56") --> 56 SEND "Fred" & 18 TO DISPLAY, will display "Fred18"
Constants	CONSTANT FLOAT PI	CONST REAL PI
Assignment	PI = 3.142, count = 0, count = count + 1 pet = "cat" sum = score + 10 size = LENGTH(word)	SET PI TO 3.142, SET count to 0, SET count TO count + 1 SET pet TO "cat" SET Sum TO Score + 10 SET size TO LENGTH(Word)
Identifiers	dogAge or dog_age	dogAge or dog_age
Comments	#This is an example	#This is an example
Functions	LENGTH([3,4,5,6]) --> 4 LENGTH("Ana") --> 3 RANDOM(5) --> a random number from 0 to 5 inclusive	LENGTH([3,4,5,6]) --> 4 LENGTH("Ana") --> 3 RANDOM(5) --> a random number from 0 to 5 inclusive
Devices	INPUT OUTPUT or PRINT	KEYBOARD (for input) DISPLAY (for output)
Arrays (1D)	Indices start at zero (0) myNums = [3,4,5,6] myNums[2] = 7 --> [3,4,7,6] Initialising an empty array: marks : ARRAY[0..5] OF INTEGER	Indices start at zero (0) SET myNums TO [3,4,5,6] SET myNums[2] TO 7 --> [3,4,7,6] Initialising an empty array: Not specified.
Arrays (2D)	myTable = [[2,3], [5,6],[8,9]] Array[rowIndex] [columnIndex] myTable[1] [0] = 7 --> results in [[2,3], [7,6],[8,9]] Initialising an empty array: myTable : ARRAY[0..2][0..1] OF INTEGER	SET myTable TO [[2,3], [5,6],[8,9]] SET Array[rowIndex, columnIndex] SET myTable[1,0] TO 7 --> results in [[2,3], [7,6],[8,9]] Initialising an empty array: Not specified.

Selection	IF answer = 10 THEN
	   score = score + 1
	END IF
	
	IF answer = "correct" THEN
	  PRINT "Well done"
	ELSE
	  PRINT "Try again"
	END IF
		IF answer = 10 THEN
		   SET score TO score + 1
		END IF
		
		IF answer = "correct" THEN
		  SEND "Well done" TO DISPLAY
		ELSE
		  SEND "Try again" TO DISPLAY
		END IF

Repetition (Iteration)	WHILE flag = 0 DO
	   PRINT 'All well'
	END WHILE
	
	REPEAT
	   go = go + 1
	UNTIL go = 10
	
	FOR 1 TO 100 DO
	   PRINT '*'
	END FOR
	
	FOR Index FROM 1 TO 10 DO
	   PRINT ArrayNumbers[Index]
	END FOR
	
	FOR index FROM 1 TO 500 STEP 25 DO
	   PRINT index
	END FOR
	
	wordsArray = ['The', 'Sky', 'is', 'grey']
	sentence = ""
	FOR EACH word FROM wordsArray DO
	   sentence = sentence + word + ' '
	END FOREACH
		WHILE Flag = 0 DO
		   SEND 'All well' TO DISPLAY
		END WHILE
		
		REPEAT
		   SET Go TO Go + 1
		UNTIL Go = 10
		
		REPEAT 100 TIMES
		   SEND '*' TO DISPLAY
		END REPEAT
		
		FOR Index FROM 1 TO 10 DO
		   SEND ArrayNumbers[Index] TO DISPLAY
		END FOR
		
		FOR Index FROM 1 TO 500 STEP 25 DO
		   SEND Index TO DISPLAY
		END FOR
		
		SET WordsArray TO ['The', 'Sky', 'is', 'grey']
		SET Sentence to ""
		FOR EACH Word FROM WordsArray DO
		   SET Sentence TO Sentence & Word & ' '
		END FOREACH

Input Output	PRINT 'Have a good day.' (STRING) INPUT name (INTEGER) INPUT lengthOfJourney (STRING) INPUT yesNo	SEND 'Have a good day.' TO DISPLAY RECEIVE Name FROM (STRING) KEYBOARD RECEIVE LengthOfJourney FROM (INTEGER) CARD_READER RECEIVE YesNo FROM (CHARACTER) CARD_READER
File Handling	localFile = OPEN("mytext.txt", "READ") lines = localFile.READLINES() localFile.CLOSE() myFile = OPEN("nicText.txt", "WRITE") myFile.WRITELINES(newLines) myFile.CLOSE()	READ MyFile.doc Record Each "READ" statement reads a record from the file. WRITE MyFile.doc Answer1, Answer2, "xyz 01" Each "WRITE" statement writes a record to the file.

Sub-programs	PROCEDURE calculateAverage (mark1, mark2, mark3)
	BEGIN PROCEDURE
	   avg = (mark1 + mark2 + mark3)/3
	END PROCEDURE
	
	FUNCTION avMarks(mark1, mark2, mark3)
	BEGIN FUNCTION
	   total = (mark1 + mark2 + mark3)/3
	   RETURN total
		PROCEDURE CalculateAverage (Mark1, Mark2, Mark3)
		BEGIN PROCEDURE
		   SET Avg to (Mark1 + Mark2 + Mark3)/3
		END PROCEDURE
		
		FUNCTION AvMarks (Mark1, Mark2, Mark3)
		BEGIN FUNCTION
		   SET Total TO (Mark1 + Mark2 + Mark3)/3
		   RETURN Total

	END FUNCTION answer = avMarks(5,7,6) Calls a procedure or a function.	END FUNCTION Answer = avMarks(5, 7, 6) Calls a procedure or a function.

Recommended Reading

You should start learning to program at a young age, but not too young! It is important to start with good languages that can slowly extend a student's ability and keep them motivated. Appropriate languages change with time but here's a reasonable "sliding scale" from "junior" secondary right through to pre-university.

Scratch
Elementary but fun:
- **"Super Scratch Programming Adventure"** Version 2.0 – The LEAD Project – No Starch Press - ISBN-13: 978-1593275310
  - This book shows young programmers how to build some pretty cool games. All of the code is fully explained and the illustrations are excellent.

Beginner to Intermediate:
- **"Learn to Program with Scratch** – A Visual Introduction to Programming with Games, Art, Science and Maths" – Majed Marji – No Starch Press - ISBN-13: 978-1593275433
  - This is a "programmers' approach" to learning Scratch. All basic concepts from variables and data types to loops, procedures and lists are covered. All of the supporting code can be downloaded and the challenges are fun but worthwhile – an excellent book!

(Note: **Logo** is an excellent language choice at this level too. Logo's "turtle graphics" are used a lot in Scratch and there is even a module available for Python.)

Python
Beginner to Intermediate
- **"Invent Your Own Computer Games with Python"** 3rd Edition - Al Sweigart - CreateSpace Independent Publishing Platform - ISBN-13: 978-1503212305
  - Introduces all necessary programming concepts at this level in a fun and interesting way. There's nothing much on reading & writing to files, but it does include basic encryption with the Caesar cipher and even using the pygame module with such things as collision detection. You can download supporting code from the author's website. You can even download an "e-book" version for nothing – An excellent book.
- **"Hacking Secret Ciphers with Python: A beginner's guide to cryptography and computer programming with Python"** - Al Sweigart - CreateSpace Independent Publishing Platform - ISBN-13: 978-1482614374
  - Introduces lots of programming techniques via the engaging method of learning about secret codes and encryption. This could be an excellent source book for a Python Club. All supporting code can be downloaded from the author's website. You can even download an "e-book" version for nothing – An excellent book.
- **"Python Programming for the Absolute Beginner"** – Michael Dawson – Course Technology PTR - ISBN-13: 978-1435455009
  - As the title suggests, can be used with no previous programming experience. The first seven chapters covers everything needed at this level – from simple

"if statements" and logic right up to complex functions, data structures and reading and writing to files. Meanwhile, if you do want to move on to object orientated programming with Python, then this book gives an excellent introduction. The challenges at the end of each chapter are good, and you can download all the supporting code from the author's website – an excellent book.

Intermediate

- **"Practical Programming: An Introduction to Computer Science Using Python 3 (Pragmatic Programmers)"** - Jennifer Campbell - Pragmatic Bookshelf - ISBN-13: 978-1937785451
  - o Every aspect of Python required at this level is extensively covered with lots and lots of practical examples based on useful tasks - an excellent book.

Java
Intermediate

- **"Introduction to Programming with Greenfoot: Object-Oriented Programming in Java with Games and Simulations"** – Michael Kölling - Pearson - ISBN-13: 978-0134054292
  - o Introduces the basic concepts behind object-orientated programming using the wonderful programming environment that is Greenfoot. Although no previous programming knowledge is needed, it would help, as the learning curve would otherwise be quite steep. Excellent for pre-university courses or youth clubs.

Advanced

- **"Objects First with Java: A Practical Introduction Using BlueJ"** - Michael Kölling - Pearson - ISBN-13: 978-0132492669
  - o As the title says, you start off, virtually on page 1, using objects. The book is brilliantly written and develops your skills on a kind of "spiral" - always a bit higher but constantly revisiting previous material until you are confident. The first half of the book could be used for pre-university level, the rest takes you further.

Programming Techniques
Intermediate

- **"Computational Fairy Tales"** – Jeremy Kubica - CreateSpace Independent Publishing Platform - ISBN-13: 978-1477550298
- **"Best Practices of Spell Design"** – Jeremy Kubica - CreateSpace Independent Publishing Platform - ISBN-13: 978-1481921916
  - o These two charming books illustrate quite high-level computer science concepts by telling fairy stories full of castles, dragons and wizards - Wonderfully enough, it works! The first part of the first book could be used at schools but the rest, paradoxically enough, goes a bit far. Nonetheless the explanations of concepts as diverse as binary search trees and defensive programming, are at once entertaining and very instructive - highly recommended.

Advanced

- **"Think Like a Programmer: An Introduction to Creative Problem Solving"** - V. Anton Spraul - No Starch Press - ISBN-13: 978-1593274245
  - "The real challenge of programming isn't learning a language's syntax—it's learning to creatively solve problems so you can build something great." The first few chapters are excellent at prompting you to think about solving problems. After then the topics do get quite advanced and the implementation language is C++.

Others:

Intermediate

- **"Code: The Hidden Language of Computer Hardware and Software"** – Charles Petzold - Microsoft Press - ISBN-13: 978-0735611313
  - This book takes you on a "back to basics" journey. Starting with on and off, proceeding to binary logic and flip-flops and ending with microprocessors and high and low level languages. You can program at a high level without even knowing what a transistor is but it helps - Future digital engineers will enjoy this excellent book.

General Interest

- **"Alan Turing: The Enigma: The Book That Inspired the Film The Imitation Game"** - Andrew Hodges - Vintage - ISBN-13: 978-1784700089
  - A very thorough biography of Alan Turing, which may inspire future generations of computer scientists.
- **"How The Mind Works"** - Steven Pinker - Penguin - ISBN-13: 978-0141980782
  - This is, quite literally, a thought provoking book. As computer scientists become more and more interested in Artificial Intelligence (AI) it is worthwhile to study how human intelligence evolved. One of the main themes of the book is "the computational theory of the mind" - An excellent read!

Printed in Great Britain
by Amazon